W9-CMA-528

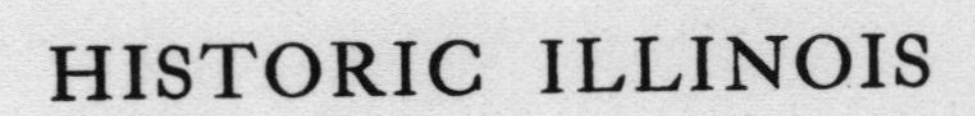

HISTORIC ILLINOIS

TONTY'S STRONGHOLD

STARVED ROCK ON THE ILLINOIS RIVER

HISTORIC ILLINOIS

4

THE ROMANCE OF THE EARLIER DAYS

BY

RANDALL PARRISH

AUTHOR OF
"WHEN WILDERNESS WAS KING," "MY LADY OF THE NORTH,"
AND "A SWORD OF THE OLD FRONTIER"

WITH MAP AND FIFTY ILLUSTRATIONS

SECOND EDITION

CHICAGO
A. C. McCLURG & CO.
1906

Published Nov. 15, 1905
Second Edition,
January 30, 1906

The Lakeside Press
R. R. DONNELLEY & SONS COMPANY
CHICAGO

TO THE
MEMORY OF MY FATHER

RUFUS PARKER PARRISH

GENTLEMAN, PATRIOT,
AND PIONEER

INTRODUCTORY

THE intention of this book is not scholastic, nor has any special effort been made along lines of original research, the single purpose being to render Illinois history of interest to the many who seldom discover it to be so. The writer believes that historical occurrences, properly presented, should prove more enticing than even the most fascinating fiction, because those men and women thus depicted were actual living entities.

In the preparation of this volume no particular originality is claimed, other than the mode of arrangement chosen for the subject-matter, and an earnest effort to give vividness to the narrative. Like all compilations, it is the production, not of one mind, but of a multitude. Every known writer on Illinois history has been consulted in the endeavor to attain accuracy, yet it has not been considered expedient to clog the pages with continual notes of reference. Wherever the language, or direct thought, of any former writer has been utilized, the endeavor has been made to give full acknowledgment in the text.

The rare charm of European travel, as well as of journeying in our own Eastern States, is largely enhanced by the constantly recurring scenes of picturesque, historic interest. Comparatively few realize that no State of the Union surpasses Illinois in the romantic incidents of early days. These are full of color, action, and adventure, for above these peaceful plains and woods once waved the flags of four contending nations, while men of the white race and the red strove continually for mastery. Here came priest and soldier, honest settler and fleeing outlaw, noble and peasant, *coureur de bois*, and Canadian *voyageur*, each bearing his part in the great struggle of two centuries. The continual conflict with savagery, the conspiracy of Pontiac, the Wars of the Revolution and of 1812, all had their fields of battle on Illinois soil; and there is scarcely a county without its romantic legends, its interesting traditions of the past.

The hope of impressing some few of these happenings upon the minds of the many to whom historic narrative has heretofore proven dull and unprofitable, has been the main purpose of author and publisher in the volume here presented.

RANDALL PARRISH.

CHICAGO, Sept. 1, 1905.

NOTE OF ACKNOWLEDGMENT

THE following authorities have been freely consulted, and occasionally quoted, in the preparation of this work, to each of whom it is desired to give full credit: "Illinois Historical Collections," Vol. I, and "Historical Transactions" for 1900–1903, especially those articles by Dr. Snyder, Mr. John F. Steward, Mrs. Matthew J. Scott, and Joseph Wallace; Spears and Clark's "Mississippi Valley"; Dr. Thwaites's "How George Rogers Clark Won the Northwest," and "France in America"; Stevens's "Black Hawk"; Davidson and Stuvé's "History of Illinois"; Moses's "History of Illinois"; Edwards's, Blanchard's, Ford's, and Reynolds's Histories; Reynolds's "Story of My Own Times"; Parkman's "La Salle and the Discovery of the Great West"; Howe's "The Great West"; Roosevelt's "Winning of the West"; Mason's "Chapters from Illinois History"; Gould's "Fifty Years on the Mississippi"; McMaster's "Upper Mississippi"; Margry's "*Découvertes*"; Thwaites's "Hennepin's 'New Discovery'"; Thwaites's "Jesuit Relations"; Thwaites's "The Great River"; as well as the numerous and valuable county histories, which give many interesting details otherwise overlooked by the more general writer.

R. P.

CONTENTS

ILLUSTRATIONS

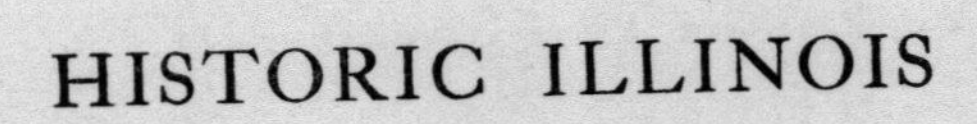

HISTORIC ILLINOIS

HISTORIC ILLINOIS

THE ROMANCE OF THE EARLY DAYS

CHAPTER I

SOME MONUMENTS OF LOST RACES

THE recorded history of Illinois began in 1673 with the canoe voyage of a Jesuit missionary and a Canadian explorer, and their companions. Yet there is a far earlier story, still only partially disclosed, which reaches back into the dim, mysterious past. Scattered widely from east to west and from north to south all over this America, remain relics of dead and gone populations, exhibiting a culture and advance in civilization very difficult to associate with the Indian as first known to white explorers. To-day, archæologists and antiquarians differ widely as to the origin of these strange works of human hands, nor are they even agreed with regard to the race of the long-vanished builders.

The earliest Europeans discovered here roving tribes of savages, possessing no written languages, no fixed habitations, no knowledge, other than merest traditions, of origin or ancestry. Yet, scattered over hills and valleys, and beside lakes and rivers, where these vagrants hunted, were discovered strange mounds, fortifications, altars, town sites, and vast cemeteries, regarding which the Indians possessed not so much as a vague legend. Who these people were, whose centre of population was evidently the Mississippi valley, no living man can say with certainty. They have been named Mound-builders, because of those monuments of earth which tell of their previous existence, but whether they were but a higher development of the red Indian race, an exodus from the semi-civilization of Central America, or an entirely different type now totally vanished, remains to be revealed. Apparently, so utterly have they disappeared within the enshrouding mist of that recordless past, their identity can never be completely established.

From the comparatively few discoveries already made, it seems highly probable that this people were not as greatly advanced in civilization as the earlier investigators imagined. This belief tends rather to the conclusion that they were more likely of the red race, and not so vastly different from the Creeks, Natchez, and other more southern nations of Indians encountered first by De Soto and later by La Salle. Like these latter, they were also worshippers of the sun. The mounds, and other prehistoric earthworks, revealed by the investigators, were doubtless signal stations, military defences, tombs of the dead, remains of destroyed towns, or elevations erected for purposes of worship and sacrifice. The builders had certainly made no very marked advance toward higher civilization; the ruins thus far disclosed being far behind those discovered in Central America, and but a grade beyond others undoubtedly of early Indian origin. Evidently, these people had emerged from dense savagery, but, at the best, had attained scarcely higher than the middle status of barbarism. Their religion was still the grossest superstition, and cruel with sacrifice; they possessed little, if any, knowledge of metals, never having learned their fusibility, a discovery which is always one of the marked steps of human advancement. They utilized copper as a malleable stone, beating it into shape with harder substances. In domestic and industrial arts they had attained to rather a higher degree of proficiency; especially is this evidenced in the making of pottery, and the weaving of cloth from vegetable fibres. Nothing distinctive appertaining to these people has survived, excepting that certain objects, manufactured from poles and canes, have been found buried in mounds; nearly all of their handiwork has long since passed into oblivion. Yet, little by little, some important facts relative to their lives have been learned, — literally dug out of the earth. Their arts of subsistence had progressed as far as the use of salt — which was not true of the first Indians known to Europeans — and the cultivation of corn. This would seem to imply that they were no longer entirely nomadic, but possessed semi-permanent settlements. Their only known domesticated animal was the dog, and that probably a tamed wolf. The burdens and drudgery of domestic labor fell to the lot of the women, the chief pursuit of the males being war and the chase. In stature, features, and cranial development they did not greatly differ from the well-known Indian type. The hue of their skins is not known, and no normal specimen of their hair has been preserved. The portraits transmitted to us on pottery picture features approximating those of the Indian, with coarse, straight hair.

The culture of these Mound-builders was undoubtedly a slow growth from lower savagery, and it is probable that their antiquity is not as great as the earlier investigators supposed. The commencement of mound-building in the Mississippi valley can hardly be dated farther back than six centuries ago, nor did it entirely come to an end until after the discovery of this country by the Europeans. De Soto, very likely, on the lower Mississippi, came into direct contact with the surviving remnant of this same people, still practising all the arts, customs, and superstitions of their ancestors.

There is, however, some considerable evidence to be found, that a yet more advanced race than even these Indian builders of mounds once inhabited the great valley. The copper mines of the Lake Superior region were extensively worked in an age far antedating all Indian tradition. At the Illinois Salines, fragments of pottery have been found from four to five feet in diameter, dug from thirty feet beneath the surface. Accumulating facts would seem to prove beyond question that this earliest people of whom we can gain any positive trace were not of the modern Indian mould. They were short and stout, possessing low foreheads and high cheek-bones, with remarkably large eyes and broad chins. Remains of their art even bespeak a different race. Silver, iron, and copper implements have been unearthed, exhibiting superior skill in their construction. The manufacture of earthenware was one of their most advanced arts; vessels made of calcareous breccia have already been discovered, said to be equal in quality to any now made in Italy. Mirrors, constructed of mica brought from the Carolinas, are frequent, some large and even elegant in design.

Casting aside all theory as to the nature and race of these differing peoples, let us note some still existing evidences of their former occupancy of the Illinois country. Those which seem directly connected with the Mound-builders are quite numerous and important. In form, design, dimensions, and tantalizing interest, their manufactured products are unsurpassed elsewhere. It is evident that their favorite haunts in those old days were along the principal streams and lakes. The shores of Lake Michigan, the bluffs of the Mississippi, the Ohio, Wabash, Kaskaskia, and Sangamon, are even now teeming with vestiges of their villages, altars, and graves. Along the valley of Rock River, extending as far south as Kishwaukee, in Winnebago County, there are most curious earthworks, apparently intended to represent figures of men, birds, quadrupeds, reptiles, with others not so clearly defined. Some of these were formed on a gigantic scale, being more than four hundred feet in length. In the city of Rockford is the famous "Turtle

Mound," described as "a hundred and fifty feet long by fifty feet in width behind its front legs; and resembles an alligator with its head cut off more than it does a turtle." No human remains having been found in any of these upheavals of earth, as thus far explored, it is now believed they represented tribal totems, possibly signifying the extreme boundary of some old race. The place where the turtle's head, in the Rockford mound, should naturally be may once, as suggested by Dr. Snyder, have been occupied as a council-house or an altar. Such emblematic mounds as these are to be found only in Wisconsin, and along the upper Rock River in Illinois, with the exception of two or three in Ohio, and two in Georgia.

Near Mendon, in Adams County, Wisconsin, is a most peculiar mound of this character, worthy of mention here, it being in the form of a gigantic serpent, or rather a series of small mounds so connected as to suggest this figure. In Illinois, from Peoria down the banks of the Illinois River, and thence farther down the eastern shore of the broader Mississippi, lies a region unsurpassed anywhere in antiquarian interest. Here these vanished peoples evidently dwelt in vast numbers during many years, carried on their varied industries, and interred their dead. Throughout its entire extent this district is fairly strewn with relics of that dim, forgotten past, and doubtless contains, as yet locked securely in its earthen heart, evidences of many different races occupying it through indefinite periods of time. It will prove a rich treasure-house for the patient, scientific investigator. At some far-away date — how long ago no man can tell — a colony of the "stone-grave people," probably journeying from the valley of the Cumberland, came into Illinois and settled near the junction of the Ohio and Mississippi Rivers. From this point they gradually spread northward until they reached the present county of Monroe, where they evidently made an extended residence, but finally crossed the Mississippi and settled in Eastern Missouri. They left behind them a plain and unmistakable trail by their peculiar manner of burying their dead. This was in stone cists, or graves lined and covered with thin rough flagstones. Usually the bodies are found resting in their last sleep alone, but occasionally several were buried together, all enclosed within a mound of earth. Such graves have been discovered as far north as the Sangamon River, but are most numerous throughout the extreme southern portion of the State. In the main, this peculiar form of sepulchre is identical with that discovered in the ancient cemetery near Nashville, Tennessee, and this tribe, emigrating to Illinois in that far-away age, was undoubtedly a branch of the same ancient stock. Plates of thin, hammered copper, with strangely masked human figures impressed upon them, have been found in these Southern Illinois graves, greatly resembling similar discoveries in the famous Etowah mound of Georgia. So exactly do these resemble the early art of Central America, and that of the Aztec dynasty in Mexico, as to make it probable these "stone-grave people" were at least in direct communication with that ancient semi-civilization far to the southward. An impressed copper plate, bearing the well-executed design of an eagle, was discovered in a mound near Peoria, far in artistic advance of the best efforts of the Indian mound-builders.

A singular monument of this latter race is found in the lead region, situated at the summit of a ridge, near the east bank of Sinsinawa Creek. It has the appearance of a huge animal, the head, ears, nose, legs, and tail, as well as the general outlines, being as perfectly conceived as if made by men versed in modern art. The ridge on which it has been upbuilt tops an open prairie, and stands three hundred feet wide, one hundred feet in height, and rounded off at the top by a thick deposit of clay. Centrally, along the line of the summit, is an embankment, three feet high, forming the outline of a quadruped measuring two hundred and fifty feet from tip of the nose to end of the tail, and having, at the centre, a width of body of eighteen feet. The head was thirty-five feet long, the ears ten, legs sixty, and tail seventy-five. The curvature of the limbs was natural to an animal lying upon its side. In general, the figure resembles the now extinct quadruped known to science as the megatherium. Many scientists believe this animal actually lived in and roamed over the Illinois plains when these ancient Mound-builders first entered the valley of the Mississippi, and that this outline was later drawn from memory. As a curious coincidence, it may be stated that bones of some similar gigantic creatures have been exhumed on this same stream, not more than three miles distant.

In the upper portion of the American Bottom, nearly opposite the city of St. Louis, and some fifty miles above the stone-grave cemeteries of Monroe County, was the settlement of yet another distinct branch of pre-Columbian people. These are known to moderns as the "Temple" Mound-builders. Their chief work in the Illinois country is the famous Cahokia mound, probably the largest in the United States. It is situated six miles and a half northeast of St. Louis, is ninety-seven feet in height, with a base seven hundred feet in length by five hundred feet in width, covering more than six acres, and comprising in its solid contents 1,076,000 cubic yards of earth, the greater portion of which was taken from the bluffs three miles distant. This gigantic monument of a vanished race is commonly known as the "Monks' Mound," from the monks of La Trappe having settled on and about it. In shape it is an irregular oblong, extending north and south, with its shorter sides east and west. Its top contains about three and a fourth acres, while nearly half-way down the sides is a terrace, extending the entire width of the mound, and sufficiently broad to afford sites for several spacious buildings. The present irregularity in outline is doubtless due to the washing of heavy rains, thus changing materially the original design. A Mr. Hill, who once lived upon it, while making excavation near the northwest extremity uncovered human bones and white pottery in considerable quantities. The bones, which instantly crumbled to dust on exposure to the air, appeared larger than ordinary, while the teeth were double in front as well as behind.

Nor does this huge mound stand alone. It is seemingly the king of many others of similar construction but less magnitude, and the entire section must at one time have been densely populated, if merely by the workmen employed on this gigantic task of mound-building. Close at hand, sixty-one smaller mounds have been counted, ranging in size from fifty to four hundred feet in diameter, and from fifteen to sixty feet in height. Wherever one journeys in this region, such mounds appear. Fifteen miles east of this spot, on the border of a high open prairie in St. Clair County, rises a most beautiful and symmetrical mound, known locally as the "Emerald Mound." It is a truncated pyramid with square base, each side two hundred and twenty-five feet in length, forty feet in elevation, while its level top, exactly corresponding in form with its base, is one hundred and fifty feet square. Its lines and angles have been well preserved, and are yet sharply defined and regular. Only a few yards distant, to the northeast, is a smaller circular mound, having a flat top, while eight hundred feet from its west angle is a long ridge, undoubtedly of artificial construction, and possibly sepulchral.

Near the base of the Emerald Mound there have been found sixteen large flint spades, polished by long use. Near the present business centre of East St. Louis, a number of these were also unearthed, together with several flint hoes, most neatly finished. These, with other relics dug from the earth, such as artistic pottery, fine polished stone implements, shell beads, tortoise shells, parts of the lower jaws of deer with incisor teeth intact, and some objects exquisitely plated with thin sheets of copper, attest the advance in culture of these Cahokia Mound-builders, as well as their industrial progress. In their system of earthworks there is a marked similarity to those of Eastern Arkansas, Mississippi, and Georgia, and in all probability they were a branch of the same people. Where, and how, they disposed of their dead has not yet been ascertained.

The entire valley of the Illinois River from Starved Rock to the Mississippi was, unknown ages ago, the home of a still different race from any yet enumerated. Their style of mound-building and their method of disposing of their dead connect them plainly with the well-known Mound-builders of the East. Here are to be found numerous examples of the "altar" mounds, usually elevated above the low alluvial bottom land bordering the stream. Here are also uncovered vast quantities of "platform" pipes, together with finely wrought implements of war and chase, with ornaments of copper. In this same neighborhood have been unearthed a vast number of relics, evidently propitiatory offerings to some deity. Dr. J. F. Snyder, whose valuable contributions to the State Historical Society have yielded me much data, describes the discovery of immense deposits of dark-colored, or black, flint disks, from three to eight inches in diameter, under conditions leaving no doubt as to their sacrificial intent. Buried in the river bank at Beardstown he found fifteen hundred well-finished disks of black hornstone closely laid together, which were uncovered a few feet below the surface. A deposit of thirty-five hundred similar flints was found four miles above, on the opposite side of the river. Two very large mounds standing side by side, in Brown County, were opened. One produced 6,199 of these oval disks, and the other 5,316 complete lance-shaped instruments from three to eight inches in length. A noteworthy point regarding this find is, such black flint is nowhere discovered *in situ* in Illinois, but occurs in Southeastern Indiana and some portions of Kentucky. These thousands of buried flints must have been transported, either overland or by means of water-ways, to their present burial-spots with immense toil and sacrifice.

Every evidence is present that the Mound-builders maintained a very widely extended system of barter with distant races. "In these mounds along the Illinois," writes Snyder, "are to be found marine shells from the Gulf of Mexico; copper from Lake Superior; catlinite from the pipestone ledges of Minnesota; obsidian from New Mexico or the Rocky Mountains; mica from North Carolina; and hematite and galena from Southeast Missouri or the upper Mississippi." The age of these "altar" mounds remains a problem unsolved, but beyond doubt the builders had not yet become skilled in the ceramic art, one of the earliest usually mastered by aborigines. The few pottery vessels found are coarse, rude, and without noticeable artistic decoration. The human skeletons discovered in these earth-banks exhibit anatomical characteristics of a very low order. Their crania were similar to those of the lower American Indian type, but with a wide variation of facial angle. They possessed low, narrow, and retreating foreheads, having a general appearance that was ape-like and hideous, yet these people developed into exceedingly skilful artisans.

Early white settlers were surprised to discover—especially in Gallatin County—evidences of salt-production in very ancient times. All about the saline springs in the southern portion of the State were found fragments of huge, shallow, earthenware vessels, with fire-scarred stones and camp-refuse, indicating that the early method of obtaining salt was by evaporation. Near by were extensive cemeteries, the bodies of the dead lying in stone-lined graves, thus apparently identifying them clearly with the stone-cist people of the American Bottom. This ancient use of salt would seem

INDIAN MOUNDS NEAR CAHOKIA

TRACES OF THE MOUND-BUILDERS

to separate this race widely from the known Indian tribes subsequently occupying this territory, as the liking for salt was with the early Indians an acquired taste. The Pottawattomies, and indeed all the tribes north and west of Lake Michigan, when first visited by French explorers, are reported to have regarded salt with great disgust, believing it a poison. This was also true regarding the nomads of the western plains and Rocky Mountain region as late as the Fremont expedition. Yet, in far more ancient times — hundreds of years, it may be, before the first white man floated down *La Belle Riviere*— these salt-makers were laboring to supply a vast population, which has forever vanished.

In this brief review, we have not touched the existing evidences of a yet more ancient people, a people dating so far back that the mind fails to comprehend the vast distance of time intervening. This Illinois country has still much to offer to antiquarian and archæologist which may some day proclaim it as one of the earliest-settled portions of the earth's surface. Comparatively little investigation has been made, but that little points to an antiquity of population before which the mind halts aghast. In the glacial drift underlying Chicago, flint implements of the true Palæolithic age have already been found. "This would imply," writes Snyder, "the presence of man on that spot as long ago as the Glacial or Interglacial epochs. Much more remains to be explored throughout the State, with every probability of important discoveries. Ancient moraines, and other glacial deposits, are predominant features of our surface geology, and hold many a secret locked from sight, yet to be revealed to the scientific investigator. Primitive man, it is now generally conceded, had already attained to the Neolithic stage of stone art at the period of his first arrival here. It remains to be discovered, through diligent research of the clay and gravel beds of Illinois, new and clearer conceptions of these earliest inhabitants. Possibly, evidences may be unearthed which will carry the primitive American back to that immensely distant period of the Quaternary deposits." As it is, time can scarcely be reckoned in considering the ages in which human life has found existence along the rivers of the State. Again and again has this land been trodden by different races, cities have risen and fallen, and great peoples have vanished utterly, leaving behind them no record of existence, except their voiceless graves.

CHAPTER II

OLD INDIAN VILLAGES AND BATTLE-FIELDS—TRIBAL BOUNDARIES

WHEN the first white man, floating down the bosom of the majestic Mississippi, finally landed and placed adventurous foot upon the soil of Illinois, this was entirely the country of the Indian. In its virgin wilderness beauty, it would be difficult to imagine a more magnificent domain. Nature had done her part, and had been most prodigal with her bounties. No dark and brooding forest shrouded the landscape, as was the case farther eastward; no forbidding mountain-masses frowningly denied easy access. Here the green and brown prairies smiled cheerfully back to the sun, beautified by countless wild flowers, with scattered groves dotting their wide expanse, and everywhere diversified by sparkling water-courses. Outwardly, it was as the Garden of Eden, a vast park designed by the one Great Architect, and beautified by His genius. A magnificent river swept majestically along its western boundary, while one scarcely less important divided it in twain.

Yet, fair as was the prospect from the summit of any hill-top, it was the rough beauty of untamed wilderness. Nothing disturbed the dead monotony of hill and dale, plain and woodland, excepting a few scattered and dirty villages with their savage inmates. The unbroken prairies were browsed over by countless herds of buffalo, while in the dark coverts of the woods bears lurked in search of prey, and the timid deer skulked, affrighted by the slightest sound. From village to village ran snake-like trails, along which the solitary hunter stole like a shadow, or some fierce party of bedecked warriors passed swiftly in search of their enemies. It was indeed a scene of nature, untouched as yet by the artificial restraints of civilization, wild, lonely, savagely beautiful, but in no sense was it anywhere a scene of prosperity or peace.

Want and suffering were constant visitants in these black wigwams — improvidence ever stalking a grim skeleton through months of cruel Winter, — while death and torture haunted each mile of the dim trails. It was everywhere war, cruel, devastating, cowardly, — war in which men, women, and children perished like flies beneath the war-club and the tomahawk. What races may have dominated these plains and valleys — whence they came, whither they passed away — in those lost centuries, is to-day beyond conjecture. But we know enough to write with calm certainty that whatever may have been the names of the tribes and peoples holding this fair hunting-ground, they accomplished it through force of arms, and were, each in turn, compelled to yield it up unto a stronger. There was no cessation in the struggle; it had been centuries long, and would continue while savagery held mastership. When the first white explorer came, drifting along those inviting water-ways from the north and east, he discovered here people of the Algonquin race. "They were of a great family of savages," comments Parkman, "at one time occupying nearly all of the United States between the thirty-fifth and sixtieth parallels of latitude, and the sixtieth and one hundred and fifth meridians of longitude. Those were Algonquins whom Cartier found on the banks of the St. Lawrence, whom the English discovered hunting and fishing along the Atlantic coast from Maine to the Carolinas." And they were men of this same lineage who first greeted the Jesuit Marquette upon the banks of this far-off Mississippi. How they originally came here we may never know with certainty, nor what other people they dispossessed in order to gain these hunting-grounds. Yet, there they were in that year of earliest white discovery, 1673, squeezed in between the encroaching Sioux upon the west, and the raiding Iroquois upon the east, barely holding their own in the unequal struggle, their day of exile already near at hand.

To Marquette these first Indians with whom he met, near the mouth of the Des Moines River, spoke of themselves as the "Illini." Literally interpreted, this simply meant that they were men, the term being used to distinguish themselves from their rapacious enemies, the Iroquois, whom they were accustomed to designate as beasts. Yet from that hour this particular confederation of Algonquin tribes has been known in both French and English records as the Illinois. They had long been, and were still, a powerful people, the five tribes composing the confederation being the Tamaroas, Michigamies, Kaskaskias, Cahokias, and Peorias. These tribes, thus loosely banded together in an Indian alliance for purposes of defence, claimed and yet held for their special hunting-grounds all that country bounded on the east by the ridge dividing the waters flowing into the Illinois from those flowing into the Wabash, between the head waters of Saline Creek, and extending as far north as the debatable ground between them and their nearest encroaching neighbors, the Sacs and Foxes, Winnebagoes, and Kickapoos. In other words, their territory may roughly be said to have extended from a line drawn directly southward from the junction of the Des Plaines River with the Illinois to a point on the Ohio about where Golconda now stands, extending westward to the banks of the Mississippi, and northwestward as far as Rock River. Their favorite and most populous villages were situated upon the Illinois, the Des Plaines, and the lower Kankakee. Marquette describes their principal town as being situated upon the bank of the Illinois River, seven miles below the present city of Ottawa. It was then called Kaskaskia, and contained seventy-four lodges. In 1679, six years later, according to the reports of Hennepin, it had four hundred and sixty lodges, with a total population of from six to eight thousand. These lodges extended along the river for fully a mile, and the Indians cultivated the adjacent meadows, raising crops of pumpkins, beans, and Indian corn. Father Rasles mentions ten or twelve other smaller villages, scattered throughout their territory. The exact position of very few of these can be traced, although it is known that in 1680 there were Illinois villages five miles below the site of Peoria, and others very nearly where the city of Beardstown now stands. In 1697 there was one in the immediate neighborhood of Spring Bay, and a very old Indian village, probably of this same people, stood slightly south of the present town of Toulon, in Stark County. If these latter were the Illinois, then this spot must have marked the extreme limit of their permanent residence, for Henry and Bureau Counties were, even at this time, hunted over by bands of Kickapoo warriors.

The remaining portions of the State were at this date occupied by the following Indian tribes: East of the central dividing ridge, or water-shed, were three branches of the Miami confederation, the Weamiamies having their hunting-grounds in Cook and Lake Counties, the Miamis proper, the country lying closely along the Indiana state line north of Danville, and the Piankishaws the country extending from that point south to the Ohio. This latter tribe was the only one of the three to retain possession for any length of time, the others being early forced eastward by the encroachments of other tribes from the north. The Kickapoos were in the extreme northwest, their southern limit being Rock River. Just across the Wisconsin line, in the country adjacent to the great lake, were scattered the Pottawattomies, who were slowly but resistlessly pressing southward.

It is hard to conceive of a more pathetic story than that revealed in the fate of the Illinois. Less than a year after La Salle first visited them, the Iroquois made a sudden raid into their territory, captured and burned their principal town near Ottawa, and drove the confederated tribes down the river as far as the Mississippi. Here the Tamaroas were overtaken by their merciless pursuers, a large number of warriors killed, and seven hundred of their women and children taken prisoners. Many of these were burned at the stake, or cruelly tortured, until, their fierce passions satiated, the invading savages finally returned eastward, bearing with them into slavery those who remained alive. With this withdrawal of the enemy the survivors of the scattered and disheartened Illinois tribes began slowly drifting back to the neighborhood of their old home, and, uniting together, partially rebuilt their destroyed town. In 1682, when La Salle collected his Indian colony about Fort St. Louis (Starved Rock), the Illinois furnished twelve hundred of the total of thirty-eight hundred warriors thus banded together in defence under French protection.

Their safety, which then seemed assured, was, however, but short-lived. La Salle's purposes of exploration, his lack of available men for suitable garrisons, and the jealousies in Canada which tied his hands, resulted in the necessity of his finally leaving these Indians to their fate. Nor was it long in coming. The savage Iroquois, busied with war in their own territory, did not return in force to complete their bloody work on the Illinois prairies, but other enemies were numerous, aggressive, and scarcely less cruel. The Sacs and Foxes from west of the Mississippi, the Kickapoos from beyond Rock River, and the Pottawattomies from Southern Wisconsin, all alike eager to gain possession of these superb hunting-grounds, swarmed down in merciless raids upon the dispirited remnant of the Illinois. Some resistance was attempted, and the Foxes were defeated in two severe battles at Starved Rock and near the Peoria Lake, losing more than a hundred warriors. But the Illinois tribesmen were not the fighters they had once been, and little by little they abandoned the country. Peoria, Cahokia, and Kaskaskia became centres for the tribes bearing these names. The Tamaroas amalgamated themselves with the Kaskaskias, while the Michigamies located near Fort Chartres. By the year 1736 these were nearly all gathered in the immediate vicinity of the little French settlements on the Mississippi, and numbered in warriors as follows: Michigamies, 250; Kaskaskias, 100; Peorias, 50; Cahokias and Tamaroas, 200, — making a total of 600 fighting men. Considering that only fifty-seven years before this same people numbered twelve thousand souls, with large prosperous villages and a hunting-ground covering fully two-thirds of the State, the suffering and barbarity of those early times can be somewhat comprehended.

Nor were their misfortunes as yet at an end. In common with all other western tribes, they became involved in the conspiracy of Pontiac, but apparently were unwilling to take active part in the field. When that great chief visited them in 1764 to make his final appeal, their zeal did not meet his desires, and he told them that if they hesitated longer he "would consume their tribes as fire consumes the dry grass on the prairies." After Pontiac's final defeat, he fled for refuge to Illinois, and was killed by an Indian at Cahokia. This act was laid to that tribe, — whether rightfully or wrongfully has never been established, — and greatly angered the Indian nations who for so long had been loyal to the great chieftain. They swarmed down from the north and the east, eager to avenge his death, and almost annihilated the tribes of the Illinois. Tradition states that a band of these fugitives, seeking to escape the general slaughter, finally took refuge on the summit of that high rock which had been the site of Fort St. Louis. There they were besieged by an overwhelming force of Pottawattomies, which the great strength of this natural fortress enabled them easily to keep at bay. But hunger and thirst united to defeat them, when the savage

ILLINOIS RIVER VALLEY NEAR PEORIA

THE SCENE OF MANY INDIAN CONFLICTS

foe could not. Their small quantity of provisions quickly failed, and their supply of water was stopped by the enemy severing the cords attached to the vessels with which they elevated it from the river below. Thus surrounded by relentless avengers, they took one last lingering look at their beautiful hunting-grounds, spread out like a panorama along the gently rolling river beneath them, and then with true Indian fortitude laid themselves down, and expired without a sigh or a tear. Their tragic fate has given to this lofty citadel the name of Starved Rock; many years afterward their bones were seen whitening on its summit. The Tamaroas, while not entirely exterminated, lost their identity as a separate tribe, in a fierce battle with the Shawnees fought near the eastern limits of Randolph County; and at the conclusion of this avenging war the entire confederation of the Illinois had been reduced to two tribes, the Kaskaskias and Peorias. Together they could muster but a hundred and fifty warriors. In the year 1850, when the remnant was removed from its old home to the Indian Territory, only eighty-four of the race were found.

Let us turn again to the map, and note those changes which less than a hundred years of savage, relentless war had wrought in this Indian-haunted land. It is 1765; the wasted remnant of the once powerful Illinois confederacy are now huddled, fear-stricken, and broken of spirit, about the French settlements on the Mississippi, occupying as a hunting-ground the present counties of Madison, St. Clair, Monroe, and Randolph. The Piankishaws have meanwhile spread their boundaries slightly toward the west, having obtained control of the Mississippi, south of the Randolph County line, but the warlike Shawnees, pouring in from the east, have won from them a considerable strip along the Wabash and Ohio, probably most of White, Hamilton, Gallatin, Pope, Saline, and Massac Counties. Farther north, even a greater change is noticeable. The northern Miamis have been driven westward beyond the State limits by an inroad of Pottawattomies from Wisconsin. These latter have swept entirely around the head of the great lake, and have spread out across the prairies as far south as the Kankakee. Pressed forward by the invading Sacs and Foxes, the Kickapoos have crossed Rock River and taken possession of the deserted lands of the Illinois, ranging throughout the entire central portion of the State. Close behind them the Sacs and Foxes have pushed their way, until they now control all that country lying west and north of the Illinois River.

As late as 1812 these same Indian tribes divided the State between them, but the boundaries of their possessions had changed. The Piankishaws had been pressed eastward, merely retaining a small section along the upper waters of the Wabash. The Pottawattomies had driven the Kickapoos yet farther south, taking to themselves the central portion of the State, and compelling the Sacs and Foxes to retire north of Rock River. Here these latter were somewhat closely hemmed in by an entering wedge of Winnebagoes from Wisconsin. The Kickapoo hunting-grounds were nearly as extensive as before, but had been changed to the southwestern counties of the State. A brief sketch of these tribes so intimately connected with the early history of Illinois will be found full of interest, and of the unspeakable pathos of Indian life.

More than all the others combined, the Kickapoos served to retard the advance of white settlement. From the earliest days, their bitter hatred of the encroaching race was implacable, and they were ever a powerful and fierce tribe. Their historical records run back to the first occupation of the St. Lawrence valley by the French. Champlain found them along the shores of Lake Huron. From that early day they proved an untractable people, never forming any lasting alliance with either the French or the English. They reached Rock River from the north about the same time as the first white explorers of Illinois, and from that date remained prominent in all the savage warfare incident to early colonization, roaming at different periods over nearly every county within the present limits of the State. They were more civilized, industrious, energetic, and cleanly than their neighbors, but equally cruel, treacherous, and unforgiving. They were always among the first to commence war, the last to submit and enter into treaties. They were in the field against Generals Harmar, St. Clair, and Wayne, and were leaders in all the bloody charges at Tippecanoe. For many years they harassed the exposed settlements, and were long the terror of the Illinois frontier. When finally removed from the limits of the State, they yet retained their old animosity against Americans, retiring to Texas, then a province of Mexico, rather than remain on United States territory. It is impossible to estimate the number of warriors composing this tribe in the days of their power, but it is evident from the country controlled by them, as well as the number and importance of their villages, that they must have formed a large fighting force. Their principal towns were located on Kickapoo Creek, and at Elkhart Grove.

The Piankishaws, while never making any great impress on early Illinois history, yet occupied for some years much of its territory. They held membership in the Miami confederation, and hunted over that country lying to the westward of the Wabash, as far as the dividing ridge, and at one time attained to the Mississippi. They were more largely represented in La Salle's colony at Fort St. Louis than any other one tribe, and later took active part in the conspiracy of Pontiac. Within the knowledge of white men, they held place on Illinois soil for two hundred years. Like the other original Illinois tribes, they were constantly harassed by the raiding Iroquois, and finally were crushed between the invading Kickapoos and Shawnees, and thus forced across the State boundaries. They were but seldom mentioned in the early records as being connected with raids on the white settlers. When removed to Indian Territory in 1850, their pitiful remnant numbered but one hundred and seven persons.

The Mascoutins were a tribe holding close relationship to the Illinois confederation, and are believed to have occupied some portion of the State for brief intervals. Marquette met them in 1673, near the portage of the Fox and Wisconsin Rivers; and Marest states that in 1712 they had settlements on the Wabash, and later ranged over the prairies between there and the Illinois River. They became associated, and finally absorbed, with both the Foxes and the Kickapoos, whom they resembled in deceit and treachery. Charlevoix states that they, with the Kickapoos and Foxes as confederates, formed a plot against the French, but before it could be consummated were surprised by a band of Ottawas and Pottawattomies, with the result that one hundred and fifty of them were destroyed. After the surrender of the French possessions to the English, Colonel Croghan was sent to conciliate the western tribes. Having descended the Ohio to a point a little below Shawneetown, the Mascoutins, together with some Kickapoos, attacked and made him and his men prisoners. Under the name of Meadow Indians, they were mentioned by General Clark, whom they endeavored to surprise by treachery in 1778.

The Sacs and Foxes, except in raiding parties, were probably never south of the Illinois River, nor did they for any considerable length of time exercise control over the country lying between that river and the Rock. But throughout the entire northwestern portion of the State they enter largely into its early history, while during the Black Hawk War their fame became national. While originally composing two separate tribes, they had, by long residence together and intermarriage, become practically one people. Both tribes came from the St. Lawrence, in the neighborhood of Quebec and Montreal, the Foxes being the earliest to emigrate, making a new home for themselves on the banks of that river in Wisconsin which has ever since borne their name. A bloody and disastrous war with the Iroquois soon induced the Sacs to join them, when, for mutual protection against the surrounding savages, they united as one nation. Moving steadily southward, they finally gained foothold in northwestern Illinois by driving out the Sauteurs, a branch of the Chippewas, who then held possession. It is said that in the course of this migration they also had a severe battle with the Mascoutins, nearly opposite the mouth of the Iowa River, in which the latter were not only defeated but almost exterminated. Having thus conquered the country, they established their chief village near the mouth of Rock River, occupying a high bluff overlooking the present town of Milan, now known as Black Hawk's Watch Tower. They also had several smaller villages on the west side of the Mississippi. They were almost constantly at war, both offensive and defensive, with the Sioux, Pawnees, Osages, and Kickapoos, nor in any of these fierce and savage conflicts were they found deficient in courage. In the struggle of 1812 they took active part upon the British side and rendered good service, defeating and driving back every American expedition despatched into their country. Later, in the Black Hawk War, although defeated and literally cut to pieces by overwhelming numbers, their old reputation as hard fighters was abundantly sustained. In the year 1805 their numbers were given as follows: Sacs, 2,850, of whom 700 were warriors; Foxes, 1,750, of whom 400 were warriors. In 1825 the total number in the two tribes was reported at 4,600. When finally transferred to Indian Territory, they numbered only 1,600. These tribes possessed one very peculiar custom, unnoted anywhere else in Indian life. Each male child at birth was marked with either black or white paint, the mother being extremely careful to apply the two colors alternately, so that each family, and the entire nation, might be thus divided into two nearly equal classes, the blacks and the whites. The object of these distinctive marks, which were retained through life, was to keep alive a constant spirit of emulation in the tribe. In their games, hunts, and public ceremonies, the blacks were always the competitors of the whites, while in war each party was ambitious to take more scalps than the other.

The Pottawattomies were for a long period a power in the Illinois country. They originally fought their way in along the shore of Lake Michigan, and then, battling constantly, drove back the struggling Kickapoos beyond the Sangamon, and forced the fierce Sacs and Foxes to retire behind the Rock, while they promptly annexed all the hunting-grounds lying between. On the earlier French maps the principal village of this people was situated at the mouth of the St. Joseph River, in Michigan. Here for more than half a century Jesuit priests labored with them, but apparently to little avail. During Pontiac's War, disguising their object under a mask of friendship, they attacked the small English garrison stationed there, and killed all but three men. In Illinois, some years later, they were the principal participants in the massacre at Fort Dearborn, one of the most atrocious acts of treachery in the annals of the Northwest. Portions of both the Chippewa and Ottawa tribes were closely associated with them during their career in Illinois. The Sauteurs, of the Chippewa branch, at an early date dwelt along the eastern bank of the Mississippi, having villages at Rock Island and Quincy. Driven out by the Sacs and Foxes, they crossed the river, and built a new town on the present site of Davenport. The Pottawattomies were among the most energetic and powerful of the Indian tribes of the Northwest, and fought with savage ferocity in all the wars along the border. At Detroit, Mackinaw, and other British posts, in Pontiac's time, they were without rivals in the work of carnage and death. They were the last native tribe to take their departure from Illinois, lingering about Chicago until 1835. In 1850, in the Indian Territory, they numbered 1,500, many of them prosperous, and all seemingly more ambitious than Indians of other stock.

Two other tribes require consideration in this connection. For some years a fragment of the Shawnee nation dwelt in the southeastern portion of the State, their principal village being Shawneetown, in Gallatin County, on the Ohio River. They were a bold, roving, adventurous people, who had fought their way eastward from the Atlantic coast. Constantly in broils, their stay in Illinois was a bloody one. During the French and Indian War, they obtained arms from the French, and overran the frontiers of Pennsylvania and Virginia. So atrocious had been their conduct, that when the war was over they supposed themselves excluded from the general amnesty, and prepared to murder their prisoners and fight to the death. Just before the coming of Clark, they exterminated the Tamaroas and moved eastward out of the State. They fought battles with the Kickapoos and the Piankishaws in order to hold their territory. The Winnebagoes were another tribe who gained a foothold in Illinois, pushing down in wedge-like form from Wisconsin between the Sacs and Foxes and Pottawattomies, occupying the county which now bears their name and some territory adjacent to it upon the east. They took part, although in a small way, in the harassing of early American settlements, even assailing a steamboat on the Mississippi as late as 1827. It is supposed that they had formerly lived in Illinois, their traditions stating that their ancestors had built a fort there, which some authorities connect with the archæological remains of an ancient work found on Rock River.

This, in brief, is the Indian record of Illinois since the coming of white men. Similar scenes of savage war and desolation, of exterminated tribes and decimated nations, undoubtedly extend back for hundreds of years previous.

For many centuries Illinois had been a battle-ground, a bone of contention among the red men. Hardly a foot of its territory but has witnessed scenes of savage atrocity before which the civilized mind shrinks in horror. From the coming of the first Frenchman, it yet continued a place of struggle for nearly three hundred years, until the Indian was finally banished beyond its borders. Red against red, red against white, and white against white battled almost unceasingly, until scarcely a county but has its memory, scarcely a spot remains without its associations of war. The prairies have drunk of human blood, and the streams have run red with sacrifice.

CHAPTER III

THE FIRST EXPLORERS

WHO was the first white man to set foot upon the soil of Illinois will probably remain forever unknown. It may have been some wandering *coureur de bois*, some adventurous fur trader, scarcely more civilized than those savages among whom he dwelt, and whose life finally went out unmissed in the dark forests, or upon the desolate prairies. It may have been La Salle, during that mysterious year which has disappeared from his history, when rumor says he crossed from the shores of the great lake to the banks of the Des Plaines. Whoever it may have been, the world was no wiser for his discoveries, and hence the honor of first explorer cannot justly be accorded him.

Stand near the head of the little island breasting the downward sweep of the vast Mississippi, and look about you. It lies opposite where the present dividing line between Illinois and Wisconsin touches the eastern river bank. It is the 18th of June, 1673. This is the heart of the wilderness. Hundreds of miles to the northeast, a little stockade of logs shelters a Jesuit priest or two, while, east of that point, scattered here and there amid the surrounding desolation, are others similar, the merest isolated sentinels of French occupancy, stretching a thin line of communication through thousands of leagues of Indian-haunted forests to the far-off St. Lawrence. Everywhere is the brooding silence, everywhere absence of human activity. The trees bordering the streams are filled with birds; the rice-swamps are vocal; out on the open prairies range the buffalo and the deer. Down in some valley hides an Indian village, dark, forbidding, ever fearful of the bursting upon it of cruel, savage foes. Dim trails wind sinuously from point to point for guidance to the hunter or the war party, but for league on league in every direction of the compass expands that same unvexed vista of silent plain and mysterious forest.

Nothing moves along the glistening surface of the great river. In solitary grandeur it pours its mighty flood through the wilderness, as it has done for unknown centuries. Past forest and grove and prairie its murmuring waters run, by thickets and marshes and silent islands, rippling gently over broad sand-bars, and swirling back at the dark trees high above on some bold bluff. It is the monarch of all this mysterious land—the unnamed ruler upon whose bosom no white man's keel has ever made impress. But the hour has now dawned for the unlocking of the great secret, and around that distant curve steal silently two birch canoes, their adventurous prows turned southward, their occupants of the white race. Mark them as they sweep swiftly past, the explorers' anxious eyes upon the unknown shores, their ears listening intently for any strange sound which may warn of danger. They are the first of their blood to pass this way in all the centuries. Hundreds of leagues from nearest companionship, fronting the unknown, the savage Indian on every side, the solemn wilderness a weight upon them, they yet press sternly forward, feeling their uncertain passage mile by mile deeper into the desolation.

In the first of these canoes are three men. At the paddles two Canadian *voyageurs*, swarthy of face, roughened to every hardship of this far frontier, their heads wound about with gay-colored kerchiefs, their wide-collared shirts flung open to the waist. But up within the bow, his eye scanning every object, is a man of another type — strong of build, dark of eye and beard, alert, with intelligent face and energetic gesture. It is Louis Joliet, the son of a Quebec blacksmith, himself a fur trader, and the man especially selected by Talon and

STATUE OF MARQUETTE

MARQUETTE, MICHIGAN

Frontenac to unlock the secrets of this great, mysterious river of the west, the wonders of which have been borne to French ears from the lips of wandering Sioux. Behind, urged on by three other paddling *engagés*, the counterparts of those commanded by Joliet, sweeps the second canoe; but he who sits within, unoccupied, his eyes searching the waters or uplifted in prayer toward the blue sky, has little in common with that aggressive fur trader so sternly pointing the way. He is a man of thirty-six years, smooth-shaven, delicate of frame, his face thin and care-worn from excessive vigils, his eyes deeply sunken, his form enveloped in a shapeless black robe, frayed and rusty from long travel. At his girdle hangs a crucifix, and his white hands finger the rosary about his throat, his lips moving in continual supplication. It is Père Jacques Marquette, of the Society of the Jesuits, for five years past missionary to the Upper Lakes. To look at him is to read his traits of character beyond mistake. He is a religious enthusiast, a true successor to those other priestly martyrs of the frontier—Jogues, Garnier, and Brébeuf. For Christ and the Virgin he burns to dare and to suffer, to discover new lands and to conquer new realms. His one ever-present thought now, as these boats sweep swiftly downward, is the salvation of souls; Joliet may scan those banks with apprehension, but Marquette longs for sight of savages, that he may deliver to them the message of his religion.

We know not when, nor where, these strange companions first placed foot upon the soil of Illinois. Somewhere along that upper river they made their earliest bivouac, drew up the inverted canoes upon the bank, built their flickering fire, talked together over the meal of bison flesh and their evening pipes, to finally slumber beneath the watchful stars. All around them nature was most beautifully arrayed, the country stretching away on either hand like a vast park, diversified by dark groves, flower-strewn prairies, and streams of silvery water. But it seemed deserted of inhabitants — it was a solitude, unrelieved by faintest trace of man's presence. Knowing not what dangers might lurk below, they advanced only during the day, making camp with each twilight to cook their evening meal, then anchoring their canoes well out in the wide stream while they slept. For some ten days they thus slowly advanced southward, without gaining a glimpse of a human being, their souls oppressed by the intense loneliness of their surroundings and the silent majesty of that mighty river on which they journeyed, when, on the twenty-fifth, they discovered the unmistakable footprints of men in the mud of the western bank. Landing, probably, close to the mouth of the river Des Moines, they found a deeply indented path leading directly across the surrounding prairie. Determined to learn something of their whereabouts and surroundings, Joliet and Marquette, leaving their canoes in charge of their *engagés*, set forth alone on their dangerous mission of discovery, the one anxious for guidance on the further journey, the other eager to find savages to whom he might preach.

The day was beautifully clear, and for some two leagues they walked, scarcely exchanging a word, following that narrow trail across the open prairie and through dark forest, their hearts filled with apprehension, until they suddenly came upon an Indian village along the river bank, and could distinguish two others crowning a hill still farther away. With anxious hearts they continued to advance, finally coming within sound of the voices of the unsuspecting savages. Then they stood boldly forth in the open prairie and shouted aloud to attract attention. Instantly all was confusion in the near-by village. The inmates swarmed forth from the huts, while four old men, a little later, stalked gravely out to meet them. Their earliest greeting proved friendly, and to Marquette's inquiry in the Algonquin tongue they made answer that they were "Illini," and offered to their visitors the calumet of peace. All the remainder of that day and night the two adventurers passed in these villages, being continually feasted by the tribe, and receiving much valuable information relative to the surrounding tribes of Indians. Marquette preached to them in the Algonquin dialect, of which he was master, and the principal chief, in return, presented them with a young slave, which they felt obliged to accept. In the morning, six hundred savages, gay in their barbaric adornment, escorted them in safety back to their canoes, and lined the river bank as they departed.

Once again they were left without guidance and alone, drifting down the vast, solemn river unexplored by white men, past unknown shores, and constantly facing mysterious perils. They thus glided by the mouth of the Illinois, gaining a fleeting glimpse up the quiet, silvery stream, and noting its peaceful current, while a little later their adventurous canoes swept silently beneath the shadow of those strange rocks guarding the eastern bank, which had been chiselled into such oddly sculptured forms by wind and wave. On ancient French maps attempting to depict these regions, these were later marked as "The Ruined Castles." Only a short distance below this point, just above where the city of Alton now stands, they swept swiftly around a sharp curve in the shore-line, and, as Parkman says, were "suddenly reminded that the Devil was still lord paramount of this wilderness." On the flat face of a high rocky bluff were painted in red, black, and green a pair of hideous monsters, such as could only be conceived within the brain of savages—each "as large as a calf, with horns like a deer, red eyes, a beard like a tiger, and a frightful expression of countenance. The face is something like that of a man, the body covered with scales, and the tail so long it passes entirely around the body, over the head, and between the legs, ending like that of a fish." This is the description given by the horrified

Jesuit, but his later drawing of the two monsters has unfortunately been lost. That such paintings were there, there can be no doubt, although as early as 1699, when St. Cosme saw them, they were already almost completely effaced. Douay and Joutel also mention them, although then the colors had doubtless greatly faded, the former thinking them not at all terrifying. The rock upon which they were painted has of late years been partially quarried away, but is still of considerable size, and impressive when viewed from the river below.

These earliest voyagers had scarcely recovered from their shock at this sight, when they were suddenly plunged into a real peril. A perfect torrent of yellowish mud gushed furiously forth into the quiet blue of the Mississippi, threatening to overwhelm their frail canoes, and compelling them to skirt the eastern shore closely for safety. It bore down in its tumultuous course huge masses of driftwood, including entire uprooted trees, its invading current sweeping directly across the broad stream, on which they had travelled so long in security. This was the mouth of the Missouri, where that turbulent and muddy river, descending through a vast desert of prairie, poured its swollen floods into the keeping of its more gentle sister, discoloring its waters. "I never," writes Marquette, "saw anything more terrific." Yet they escaped all injury, and held bravely on their course southward, finding the current of the river ever more troublesome and swift from this uniting of the two streams. With wondering eyes, yet unseeing of the marvellous future, these daring explorers, tossing in their frail bark canoes, swept past the site of the coming city of St. Louis, as well as the spot where Kaskaskia was to stand, and yet later, marvelling still at every new discovery, discerned on their left the mouth of that stream already visited by La Salle and to which the Iroquois had given the name Ohio, "river of beauty."

Day following day, the intrepid little party pressed steadily southward. The river broadened almost into an inland sea, the marshy shores became buried beneath dense masses of cane, so as to hide their outlines, the sun glowed through the hazy air with stifling heat, while myriads of mosquitoes afforded them little peace either by night or day. They floated slowly with the current, crouching beneath the grateful shade of small sails hoisted to aid their progress, their wearied eyes eagerly marking each peculiarity of the passage. Occasionally they met with Indians of different tribes, some of whom threatened to attack, but kind words won safe passage, and the zealous Jesuit found means to preach to them, in hopes of saving some. Just below the mouth of the Arkansas, the travellers, at their night-camp, held council together regarding what further course to pursue. They determined they had already proceeded far enough southward, for they had discovered the one important fact underlying their early purpose of exploration: the Mississippi — which they called the Colbert — beyond doubt discharged its mighty waters into the Gulf of Mexico. Fearful of the Spaniards, whom they believed had control of that lower country, they finally resolved on an immediate return to Canada, with a report of their discoveries for the French authorities.

They began their upward voyage the 17th of July. It was a hard task, in which all took incessant part. In the stifling heat of that southern midsummer, pressing steadily against the fierce sweep of the mighty current, "toiling all day under the parching sun, and sleeping at night in the exalations of the unwholesome shore," they won their slow and painful passage northward. Exhausted by the strain, his naturally delicate health weakened by continual exposure, Marquette suffered an attack of severe dysentery. Unable to assist in the labor, he could only lie helpless in the bottom of the narrow canoe, praying fervently to the Virgin for strength, while day after day, week following week, his companions battled with the current. It was in this stress they finally attained the mouth of the river Illinois, and, following the advice of a friendly Indian, entered its peaceful waters. Here the sweep of the current proved far gentler, the waters about them more placid, while on either side, amid dark forests and sunny prairies, were seen vast herds of buffalo and deer. They were now in the very heart of Illinois as it appeared in all the virgin beauty of the wilderness in Summer-time. The prairies were abloom with rarest coloring, the wide valley, stretching on either side back to the far-away bluffs, was green with waving grasses, the silvery waters about them reflected back the overarching blue of the cloudless sky. It was as if these weary, toil-worn voyagers wandered through some forgotten corner of Paradise. And the good father wrote gratefully, "We have seen nothing more beautiful."

Well up the river, probably at the Peoria village beside the strait, they discovered their first natives, and finally made halt at a spot which, later, became well known in the story of the West. This was upon the western bank, where the meadows now lie between the present village of Utica and the river, about seven miles below the city of Ottawa. Here was the principal village of the Illinois Indians, called by them Kaskaskia — a name later applied to another locality on the Mississippi, at the mouth of a river bearing a similar name. The town consisted at that time of seventy-four lodges. Each of the lodges contained several families, and they were spread out for a considerable distance both up and down the river bank. Here the explorers were received with the utmost kindness, but any long delay was impossible, in spite of Marquette's zealous desire to convert the savages. Guides were procured, and amid earnest promises from the Jesuit of an early return, the little band again turned their battered prows up stream toward distant civilization. One chief with several younger warriors accompanied them. Following the Illinois and the Des Plaines Rivers, they made portage to

MEETING OF MARQUETTE AND JOLIET WITH THE "ILLINI"

DEATH OF MARQUETTE

the Chicago, thus reaching Lake Michigan, then known as the Lake of the Illinois. Saying farewell on the lovely prairie where Chicago stands, and following the western shore-line of the lake, they finally attained to Green Bay the latter part of September, having been absent four months, and having travelled a distance of more than twenty-five hundred miles in their frail canoes.

Great as was this achievement, its sequel was the loss of a most valuable life. Joliet, after lingering at Sainte Marie to write his report and prepare a map, departed eastward to tell his story to Frontenac. Just before reaching Montreal, his canoe was overturned in the foaming waters of the Sault St. Louis, his papers were lost, and two of his men and an Indian boy were drowned, he himself remaining unconscious for hours. Nevertheless, he was received with joy, a *Te Deum* was chanted in the Cathedral, and he was later given the island of Anticosti as a reward for his toil. But Marquette remained all that Winter and the Summer following, seriously sick with his malady in that dismal station at Green Bay, the mission of St. François Xavier. His one prayer during all these months was, that he be given strength to return with his message of salvation to the waiting Illinois. At last, when Autumn came, he received orders from his Superior, and departed on his desperate trip, although far from well. He left Green Bay the twenty-fifth of October, 1674. Two *engagés* — Pierre Porteret, and Jacques — were his sole white companions. Some Pottawattomies and a few Illinois Indians, whom they met on the way, completed the party, there being ten canoes in all.

They followed the east shore of Green Bay, and at the head of Sturgeon Cove made portage to Lake Michigan. It was already November, one of the most stormy months on these inland seas, yet it was not in Marquette to hesitate before physical danger. He was ever in the hands of God. They were more than a month feeling their slow way southward along the desolate and storm-lashed shore until they arrived at the mouth of the Chicago River. Snow and chilly wind buffeted them continually. It was a deserted, dreary spot, wrapped in all the sombreness of Winter. With infinite labor they pushed their frail canoes through the ice already coating the narrow stream for about two leagues. Here Marquette suffered from a severe hemorrhage, and the party were reluctantly compelled to make camp on the frozen earth of the river bank. To press on farther with so sick a man was manifestly impossible. A slight distance up what is now known as the South Branch, in the midst of a dreary desolation of snow-clad plain, the two *engagés* built a rude hut, realizing that they must remain there through the Winter.

For Marquette, who felt that he must now be fast approaching his end, the time passed in spiritual exercises, and prayers that he might be spared to continue his work. The others hunted with success, killing buffalo, deer, and turkeys. Cold as the weather soon became, the dreary plains sheeted with snow, with ice forming half a foot thick on the streams, game was easily procured. A camp of Illinois Indians was within two days' journey of them, and in kindness these savages brought them some corn meal. Eighteen leagues away to the northward, two adventurous French traders were passing the Winter. One was the noted *coureur de bois*, Pierre Moreau, better known as La Taupine, his companion being called the Surgeon. They also visited Marquette, bringing supplies, and aiding him in every way possible in such a wilderness.

By the last of March (as he firmly believed, in direct response to prayer) the Jesuit was able to resume his toilsome journey. On the thirtieth the little company left their miserable hut, which already had been invaded by a sudden rise of the river, and bore their light canoes, through mud and water knee-deep, across the portage leading to the Des Plaines. Amid the ceaseless rains of Spring they swept down the surging current, past leafless woods and prairies half under water, until they attained the broader stream of the Illinois, down which they made rapid progress toward the old Indian town on the Utica meadows. Here Marquette was received, as he reported, "like an angel from heaven," and, instantly forgetting all his physical weakness and suffering, with Jesuit enthusiasm he passed from wigwam to wigwam, telling his story, as Parkman says, "of God and the Virgin, Paradise and Hell, angels and demons." Then he summoned the crowds to a grand council, that he might instruct them in the mysteries of faith.

That gathering must have formed one of the most remarkable scenes in all Western history. It was held on those great meadows stretching between the river bank and the present village of Utica, in La Salle County. Imagine it, if you can — the sweeping plains, beginning to show green beneath the Spring sun, the distant ridge of darker hills obscuring the horizon, the narrow fringe of trees along the course of the stream, the silvery sparkle of the wide river. And then that assemblage in the centre of this wilderness picture — Marquette in his frayed and rusty gown, his pale face exhibiting his illness, his eyes burning with fever, his slender frame trembling from weakness and enthusiasm. Before him, in a vast ring, were seated five hundred chiefs and old men; behind them stood fifteen hundred youths and warriors, while farther back still were grouped all the women and children of that great village. Where in all history is there another such a sight? And Marquette did his duty as he understood it. Upholding before them four large pictures of the Virgin, he addressed them on the mysteries and duties of Christianity, exhorting them to save their priceless souls while there was yet time. As a dying man to dying men he made fervent appeal. And they met him kindly, beseeching him to remain in their village and tell them more. But the Jesuit knew his life was fast passing away; that some other missionary of the Cross must carry on this mighty work he had begun; that he must instantly return north to send to them a brother of his Order. He had claimed the land for God, naming his mission the Immaculate Conception; he had sown the seed; it was his purpose now to discover the reaper.

It was a few days after the celebration of Easter that he departed, a large concourse of Indians voyaging with him in their canoes, and showing him a new route by way of the Kankakee. At St. Joseph he left them, embarking in a frail canoe, accompanied only by his two white companions. They set out to reach Michillimackinac, and shaped their course along the eastern shore, seeking thus a more peaceful passage. All about them was the fresh beauty of the Springtime, yet as the faithful Pierre and Jacques paddled their boat past the desolate shores, the dying Jesuit lay helpless in the canoe, his sight already dimmed, his small strength rapidly waning. On the nineteenth of May he conceived that his hour of departure was indeed at hand, and as they discovered the opening of a little river in the shore-line, requested his companions to paddle in toward the bank. Hastily the two sorrowing servants erected a shelter of bark on some rising ground near the southern bank of the stream, and bore the fast dying priest there. He gave solemn directions regarding his burial, asked forgiveness for all the trouble he had ever given them, administered the solemn sacrament of penitence, and "thanked God that he was permitted to die in the wilderness, a missionary of the faith and a member of the Jesuit brotherhood."

That night he bade them sleep all they could, pledging himself to call them in time of need. Three hours later they heard his faint voice calling, and found him dying. He expired, breathing the name of Mary, his dim eyes fastened on a crucifix held before him. The two sorrowing Frenchmen dug a shallow grave in the sand beside the hut, and having buried his emaciated body, and raised a wooden cross over it, hastened northward with their sad news. In the following Spring a party of Kiskakon Indians carried his bones to St. Ignace, where they were again buried with solemn ceremony beneath the floor of the little mission chapel of Michillimackinac. So, in the savage heart of that wilderness where he had labored so long, and not for earthly reward, passed away this discoverer of the Illinois country, this truly heroic soldier of the Cross, Père Jacques Marquette, in his thirty-ninth year. An unfinished letter, describing his last visit to the Illinois, was lately found at the College of Ste. Marie, at Montreal. Particularly interesting does it become with the knowledge that it was doubtless largely written while he was lying sick in that desolate hut within the present limits of Chicago.

CHAPTER IV

LA SALLE AND HIS VOYAGEURS IN THE ILLINOIS COUNTRY

AMONG all those French names connected with earliest Illinois history the one which looms largest is that of Réné-Robert Cavelier, Sieur de la Salle. Whether or not, as some ably contend, he was the first European to visit the head of the great lake, and to attain the Mississippi at its junction with the Ohio, even penetrating to the juncture of the Des Plaines and the Illinois Rivers, it remains certain that no other in his century had so much to do with the destinies of this vast inland empire of wilderness. As early as 1678 he describes this land with all the accuracy of an eye-witness. In now dealing with his life-work, we must pass but lightly over its wider scope of operation, contenting ourselves with somewhat careful tracing of that narrower portion directly appertaining to this country of the Illinois.

Born in 1643, at Rouen, France, the son of a wealthy merchant, becoming an earnest Catholic, educated under the guidance of the Jesuits, he came, at the age of twenty-three, to Canada, to seek his fortune in that new land. From his first landing in 1666, his imagination had been kindled by those vast leagues of untravelled wilderness stretching westward beyond the uttermost French frontier, and in 1669 he cast aside all restraints of property and civilization to devote his entire future life to exploration and the extension of French dominion. His is a story, sad and heroic, of constant struggle, not only against the inhospitable wilderness, the dangers innumerable of unknown forest and prairie, lake and river, but the continual conspiracy of enemies in

Canada, jealous of his hard-earned success. A weaker man would have fallen early beneath the ever-increasing burden, but La Salle battled on grimly to the end, a brave, pathetic figure, and has written his name indelibly across the heroic annals of the West.

It was in October, 1679, that, so far as can be positively ascertained, La Salle first set foot on Illinois soil. The spot was somewhere along the Lake Michigan shore, within the limits of the present county of Lake. Let us note what brought him there. After combating obstacles seemingly unsurmountable, involving the necessity of a personal trip across the sea to the French court, and amid labor that appears incredible, this iron man of energy had finally, on the Niagara River, constructed a small vessel of forty-five tons, which was christened the "Griffin," besides gathering together the necessary crew for the boat, as well as a considerable company to assist him in land exploration. His purpose was clear, his ideal truly a great one. Had he been permitted to carry it out, and loyally supported in his plans by the Canadian authorities, it would doubtless have changed our entire Western history. It was, in brief, this — the establishment of a complete chain of French forts, extending from Lake Ontario to the distant mouth of the Mississippi, thus holding firmly and for ever all this vast inland empire beneath the sway of the *fleur de lis*. Frontenac had already been established, Niagara begun, Detroit was destined soon to follow, and now this intrepid leader plunged out into the farther wilderness to seek a suitable site along the Illinois. In August, 1679, the voyagers set sail, their little vessel the first, other than frail canoes, to navigate the waters of the great lakes. At Green Bay the "Griffin" was sent back eastward, under her captain, with a load of furs, being ordered to return as early as possible. Then La Salle, with his few chosen companions, embarked in canoes, and started southward for the mouth of the St. Joseph.

His was a motley company of fourteen men, crowded within the narrow confines of four canoes deeply laden with tools, merchandise, and arms. Of these, ten were Canadian *voyageurs*, one a Mohegan Indian hunter; the others, priests of the gray robe, the Récollet friars, Louis Hennepin, Gabriel de la Ribourde, and Zenobe Membré. The weather proved exceedingly stormy, the lake rough; savages disturbed them in their night-camps along the shore, and their progress was slow and full of constant peril. For several days they were unable to proceed at all. It was thus they reached the limits of Illinois, and their first night upon the soil proved a memorable one. A heavy east wind lashed the waters into madness, and toward the close of day fairly hurled their frail cockle-shells upon the beach. No sooner were they safely ashore than they discovered undoubted evidence of Indian presence. A guard was set, but during the night, while the careless sentinel screened himself from the floods of cold rain, a party of Outagamies crept close upon them under cover of the bank, from whence they scanned the sleepers for some time unobserved. Challenged at last, they came reluctantly forward, pretending friendship, but in the early dawn numerous thefts were discovered. There was but one thing to do, and La Salle did it. Seizing upon a young warrior as hostage, he marched boldly forth to the chief and demanded return of all the goods taken, threatening otherwise to immediately kill his prisoner. The Indians, confident of their strength, prepared to fight. It was a moment of intense strain. Three Flemish friars and eleven Frenchmen, guns in hand, stood desperately at bay before one hundred and twenty yelling savages. Yet neither party ventured to commence the attack, and finally substantial justice was achieved by means of a parley, and the restoration of most of the articles stolen.

Once free from this trouble, La Salle pushed resolutely on, passing beyond the mouth of the Chicago, and skirted the desolate sand-dunes until he at last attained the entrance to the St. Joseph River. Here he expected to be joined by another party of twenty men, under command of his lieutenant, Henri de Tonty, who had been ordered to proceed down the eastern shore from Michillimackinac. The company waited twenty days before the latter made appearance, busying themselves meanwhile by the erection of a rude log fort. Considerable more time was wasted waiting for the arrival of several of Tonty's men, who had become lost in the wilderness, and still more in daily expectation of the return of the missing "Griffin." No sail gladdened the eye of the discouraged commander along that desolate expanse of inland sea. Somewhere, tossed on the stormy waves of upper Michigan, his little vessel of adventure had met her fate, leaving the wayfarers utterly alone amid those leagues of wilderness. Of this La Salle could not then know, but he dared delay his advance into the interior no longer. Already ice was forming on the streams, and would soon block the passage.

December 3, the party, numbering twenty-nine Frenchmen and the Indian Le Loup, reëmbarked in eight canoes, poling these with great labor through the floating ice of the St. Joseph as far as the present city of South Bend, Indiana. Here, after La Salle had been lost in the woods all of one bitter Winter night, they finally discovered the dim Indian portage leading across to the Kankakee, some three miles distant. It ran across a desolate snow-drifted plain, along a marshy path, past deserted Indian lodges. On the way, La Salle's life was attempted by a mutinous follower. Finally, they came to a dark, lazy current, across which a tall man might easily step, and which ran twisting like a snake among the rushes. Here they set their light canoes afloat, and for a considerable distance toilfully worked their way down the narrow, turgid stream through a confusing labyrinth of swamp, on every hand a wilderness of morass and rushes. As they thus crept into what is now Illinois territory, the scene about them began rapidly to change. Ranges of higher and densely wooded hills appeared close beside the bank, while as they mounted these rocky bluffs, the eye looked out afar over a vast sea of rolling prairie, with distant glimpses at herds of grazing buffalo and deer. With anxious eyes for ever scanning the banks on either side, they turned the prows of their canoes into the Illinois River, floated slowly past the present beautiful site of the city of Ottawa, pointing out to each other Buffalo Rock, which rose majestically upon their right. A short distance below, the river was divided by several islands, and stately woods guarded the shores with green. Here they paused, gazing with awe at a majestic and peculiar cliff, crowned with vast forest trees, which, rising sheer from the south bank, overhung the current where they rested. Sweeping beneath these gloomy shadows, suddenly just before them, in front of where Utica now stands, appeared a vast assemblage of Indian lodges covering the entire northern shore (Hennepin tells us numbering 460), each fitted to shelter several families. But they were silent and deserted of inhabitants, a lonely sight enough in the heart of such drear desolation. The tribes were absent on their Winter hunt, and that Jesuit missionary whom Marquette had sent had retired to Wisconsin.

Borrowing thirty minots of corn from out a hidden store found in the earth, La Salle again embarked his men, and the voyage was resumed. On New Year's day they landed to hear mass and wish each other a happy year, and four days later the prows of their venturesome canoes entered that wider expanse of water now known as Peoria Lake, making their way along the northern shore-line and through the straits until they reached the present site of the city of Peoria, where they established night-camp, seeing nothing to alarm them but some distant spirals of smoke. The next morning at nine o'clock, having attained that point where the waters again narrowed into a river, they discovered eighty Illinois wigwams, some appearing on opposite sides

STATUE OF LA SALLE

LINCOLN PARK, CHICAGO

the stream. Not knowing what to expect, La Salle instantly prepared for war. Ordering his startled men to throw aside their paddles and take up their guns, the little flotilla swept swiftly down on the current toward the surprised savages, who stood awaiting them, arms in hand. On touching land, La Salle instantly leaped ashore, Tonty on his left, his armed Frenchmen pressing close behind him. This act of audacity won; two chiefs approached their visitors, bearing the peace-pipe, and the council which followed resulted in pledges of mutual friendship. But the trouble was not yet over — the savages strenuously objected to his plans, as they were presently outlined to them; they desired no French fort erected in their country, nor did they wish the white men to proceed any farther south on their proposed exploration of the Mississippi; moreover, they considered the Canadian French as allies of the Iroquois, who were their most cruel enemies. For several days of council, peace and war balanced on almost even scales, but at last La Salle won, by pledging himself to defend their village against all Iroquois raiders. Yet hardly had this result been accomplished when the sorely harassed leader was compelled to face serious mutiny among his own followers. In the darkness of night, frightened by wild Indian stories, six men, among them his two best carpenters, deserted into the woods, doubtless intending to join those vagabond hunters who, even at that early day, were beginning to appear in Indian villages. Others of his little company sought to poison him, hoping thus to escape from iron discipline, while back from distant Canada news drifted across the weary leagues of forest that scheming enemies were eagerly seeking to overthrow his cherished plans and counteract his influence with those in authority.

Feeling his absolute helplessness while thus remaining exposed within the Indian camp, La Salle now began the erection of a small fort. The exact site selected yet remains uncertain, but it was probably situated on the eastern side of the river, about two hundred yards from the bank as then existing, and a short distance below the outlet of the lower lake. From Hennepin's description, it stood upon a low hill or slight eminence, having a deep ravine on either side, with lower ground, inundated at high water, lying directly in front. A ditch was excavated across the rear, running between the two ravines, thus leaving the hill nearly square in form. An embankment of earth was thrown up along each side, the declivities being sloped sharply down to the lower ground beneath. These were further guarded against Indian assault by *chevaux-de-frise*, while a palisade of logs, some twenty-five feet high, but unstrengthened by bastions, was firmly planted around the whole. Within this primitive enclosure the men were lodged in small huts built at the angles to somewhat strengthen them; La Salle and Tonty shared together tents near the centre; another similar structure was erected for the use of the three friars; while the blacksmith had a special shed for the shelter of his forge, and there was a magazine. Such was Fort Crèvecœur — Broken Heart — the first fort ever built in the Illinois country, and the fourth in that long chain projected to extend from Montreal to the Gulf of Mexico.

Not for one moment did this frontier leader permit any idleness to sap the spirits of his men. No sooner was the fort completed, than they were immediately employed at the construction of a vessel of forty tons with which to explore the lower Mississippi. Seeking to inspire the others with some of his personal enthusiasm, La Salle worked beside them with his own hands, cutting the heavy logs into planks with a whip-saw. By the first of February their task was half accomplished. A little later he despatched an expedition of three men — the priest Hennepin, with two *voyageurs*, Michel Accau and Le Picard du Gay — to explore the Mississippi from the mouth of the Illinois northward. They never again returned to the Illinois country, being captured by the Sioux in what is now Minnesota, and finally taken to Canada by their French rescuers, where the friar wrote a deeply interesting, but hardly veracious, account of their many adventures and discoveries. Hennepin, hesitating to undertake so hazardous a trip, was finally persuaded into it by the advice of his brother friars.

Two days after these men had disappeared from the little fort, floating down the gleaming river into the mystery below, La Salle also departed. Despairing of the safety of the "Griffin" and the coming of necessary supplies, with five men — the Mohegan, Hunault, La Violette, Collin, and D'Autray — as his companions, he started back across the broad intervening wilderness in desperate effort to procure another outfit in far-away Canada. He left Crèvecœur under command of Tonty, who had remaining with him there "three honest men and twelve plotting knaves" with whom to maintain French ascendency in the Illinois. The story of that terrible trip eastward cannot be retold here in any detail. The Winter had been unusually severe, the streams were yet ice-bound, sufficiently strong to withstand the advance of their canoes while not thick enough to upbear the weight of a man. Unable to desert the canoes by means of which La Salle intended to send back corn, knee-deep in half-melted snow they dragged their boats through the dreary woods for more than fifteen miles, until they finally discovered a current sufficiently rapid to keep the stream clear. Launched again, they were constantly blocked in their passage upward by masses of wedged ice, compelling continual portage. Cold rain fell in torrents, while the temperature remained so low as to freeze their clothing stiff upon them. So severe was one blinding snowstorm as to involve a three days' halt. Ten days of severe exertion and terrible privation were spent in travelling the distance from Peoria Lake to Buffalo Rock,—a distance we now pass over by rail in less than three hours.

In the course of their advance, the Indian chief Chachagouessiou was met with and a council held, at which, the savage presenting them with a boat-load of corn, two of the Frenchmen were sent back to Crèvecœur in charge of it. The others, with the single canoe, left them, pressed on up the river through the thickening ice until, at last, they could proceed in that way no longer. Hiding their boat on what has since been named Treat's Island, just above the junction of the Du Page and Illinois, they started out afoot. Bearing their load of supplies, they plunged through a great marsh until they came out on the banks of the Little Calumet River. Here with great difficulty a raft was constructed, but it lacked buoyancy, and they crossed, standing deep in the icy water. A similar experience met them at the Grand Calumet Lake, but at last the strugglers came forth upon the sand of the shore. At Fort Miami, two Frenchmen — La Chapelle and Le Blanc — were found, and what little news they possessed was bad; the "Griffin" had made no appearance in these waters, and rumors had reached them of trouble for La Salle in Canada. Ordering these men to report to Tonty at Crèvecœur, the intrepid leader, with the others, plunged into the forests of Southern Michigan, and defying storm, hunger, and threatened Indian attack, made straight for the Detroit. In all this heroic struggle La Salle led the way, breaking the drifted path for the others to follow. That he was, at this time, a man of marvellous physical power was plainly evidenced by the fact that he finally reached the fort on Niagara River in good condition, although four of his men had been compelled to halt by the way, and the fifth was left to recruit his strength at Niagara, while the commander alone pressed steadily forward upon his imperative mission. He reached Fort Frontenac April 21.

Here the worst possible news met him. The "Griffin" had never returned; the fate of both vessel and crew was a mystery not yet solved; a consignment of goods, worth twenty-two thousand livres, sent him from France, had been lost by shipwreck; while two *coureurs de bois* overtook him with a letter from Tonty, back in the Illinois wilderness, saying that all the garrison, excepting four or five men, had mutinied, destroyed the fort with its stores, and fled.

Such a condition of affairs, such utter failure of long-cherished plans, would have crushed most men. La Salle's real greatness and true majesty of character are abundantly revealed by the noble manner in which he met these terrible reverses. He acted at once. By August, surmounting every obstacle of means, every opposition of enemies, he had succeeded in enlisting twenty-five new men with La Forest as lieutenant, obtained another outfit, and started immediately back to the relief of Tonty, whose faithfulness to duty now remained his chief's sole abiding hope for the future.

Leaving La Forest at Michillimackinac to follow him as rapidly as possible with the others, and the store of supplies, La Salle chose a few picked men, and pushed swiftly forward.[1] He selected the old, familiar route, leading up the St. Joseph and down the Kankakee, until that stream united with the broader Illinois. The time was the last of November, 1680. At last his eager, speeding canoes rounded the last obstructing point of land in their long journey, and his anxious eyes again looked forth on that plain where Utica now stands. So changed was the once familiar scene, the first glimpse must have struck him like a blow. Those meadows which he had left little more than six months previous fairly swarming with life, and thickly crowded by Indian dwellings, were now a waste of desolation, a charnel-house of death, strewn with ashes, and whitened by human skulls. The lodges had been burned, and on their blackened poles severed heads impaled. The field before him was fairly strewn with torn

[1] Those chosen included D'Autray, the Surgeon, You, Tamisier, Baron, Hunault, Noël Blanc, and the Indian La Loup.

and mangled corpses. No one needed to tell La Salle the cause — he recognized instantly the fiendish handiwork of the revengeful Iroquois. The blow which had so long threatened had at last fallen; the peaceful Illinois tribes had been smitten as by a flaming breath.

Stunned and horrified, but one thought held him firmly, *What had become of Tonty and his faithful men?* He searched the ghastly corpses, turning them over one by one, but all were alike Indian. Evening came before this horrid task could be completed; then night darkened, and the solemn stars brooded over that savage waste. Crouched about their camp-fire, in the midst of the ghastly dead, La Salle and his seven remaining companions kept dreadful vigil through a lonely night of surpassing horror. Wolves howled and fought above their prey, while the dense shadows might easily serve to conceal the skulking down upon them of those same ruthless savages who could scarcely be far distant. By dawn, the leader, dauntless still in his one stern purpose, had reached final decision — defying every danger, he would continue search for his lost comrades. Near the river bank, in the early light, he discovered six posts daubed red, while drawn rudely on each was the figure of a man with bandaged eyes. Believing these to represent six French prisoners yet alive in the hands of the Iroquois, La Salle turned his canoes down the river in relentless pursuit.

So desperate was this venture, that, in hope of preserving some lives, he again divided his little band. Three, the Surgeon, Tamisier, and Baron, he hid on an island, with minute instructions for their safety. The baggage was hastily concealed in a cleft of the bluff, and then with four men — the Mohegan Indian, D'Autray, Hunault, and You — he set forth undaunted on his perilous adventure in a single canoe. Each man was armed with two guns, a pistol, and a sword. All alike realized that if once discovered by the prowling Iroquois, ever pitiless enemies of the French, their certain fate would be death by torture. Yet none hesitated; with bated breath they swept past the silent, deserted shores, witnessing everywhere fresh evidences of savage cruelty. They passed camp after camp, lying deserted and desolate, while just across the river, opposite each former dwelling-place of the Illinois, was now the more recent camping-spot of pursuing Iroquois. The facts were plain to be read: that as the one had hastily retreated in canoes, the other, without boats, had as rapidly followed. Near the site of Crèvecœur they discovered merely the naked keel of the vessel which had been so long building, the iron nails and spikes all drawn. On one of the planks had been written, probably by one of the deserting knaves, "*Nous sommes tous sauvages.*" The silence of death reigned everywhere; earth and river, wood and plain, all about them, were like a vast graveyard. Here and there along the banks were discerned hideous blackened figures bound upright against stakes, but examination proved they were all the bodies of women and children. Evidently the warriors had fled in panic, leaving these weaker ones to their doom.

The Frenchmen sought everywhere, tramping through scenes too horrible for description, yet nowhere was there slightest news of Tonty. At last they attained the Mississippi, and pausing only long enough to leave a message there for the missing, posted in a conspicuous place — a painted board nailed to a tree,— the despairing commander again turned the prow of his speeding canoe up the desolated Illinois. Night and day they toiled at the paddles, taking turns at the labor, and in the incredible space of four days were back once more at the great Indian village, having in that time covered a distance of two hundred and fifty miles. Night after night during their upward travel the heavens above them glowed resplendent with the "Great Comet of 1680." Parkman calls attention to the fact, that while in New England hamlets, even at cultured Versailles, it was looked upon with superstitious awe, here in this far wilderness, with death in form of horror on every side, La Salle coolly noted it down as a mere scientific curiosity. Could any single act better characterize the true greatness of the man?

To remain amid the ruins of that destroyed and reeking village for the return of the victorious Iroquois would have been suicidal; so, gathering all his men once more together, La Salle, heart-sick and despairing, reluctantly began the ascent of the river. They departed December 28, and on January 6, 1681, reached the juncture of the Des Plaines and Kankakee. A slight distance up the former stream stood a rude log hut, and within its walls was found the first slight evidence that Tonty might have passed that way. It consisted of a block of wood which had recently been cut with a saw. This small discovery kindled new hopes, and leaving D'Autray and the Surgeon here to guard stores, the others pushed on with lighter hearts, making their slow way directly overland toward the fort on the St. Joseph, where La Forest and his men must by this time be waiting their appearance. It was a most terrible midwinter trip. Snow fell constantly in blinding storms, but too soft for snow-shoes. They could only plunge desperately through it, La Salle ever struggling in the lead, beating a path for the others. Frequently he was buried to the waist, but there was no halting, and at last Fort Miami was attained. Here they found La Forest, but he had received no tidings of the lost Tonty. The brooding wilderness yet hid the secret of his fate from the distressed commander.

But, whether in safety or danger, there was no rest possible for La Salle. Instantly his mind began planning anew for the future. He must relieve the guard on the Des Plaines; he would explore the Mississippi; he would colonize those harassed Indian tribes of the Algonquin family about some strong French fort in the heart of the Illinois country, in mutual protection against further inroads by the Iroquois.

With him, to think was to act, and as it chanced, his material was even then at hand. The Puritans of Massachusetts had fought out King Philip's War, and a band of Abenakis had fled for refuge to this very region. They promised to follow him, and he also received a similar pledge from the Miamis. This arrangement, however, was scarcely completed when La Salle was obliged to journey again to the St. Lawrence "to appease his creditors" and "collect his scattered resources." How he did it is a mystery to his best biographers; yet, in spite of two years of disaster in these western wilds, in spite of debts bearing interest at forty per cent, in spite of a hundred scheming, revengeful enemies, he once more obtained the necessary means for a new voyage. Meanwhile the encouraging news had filtered through the distance to him that Tonty and Membré were safely arrived at Michillimackinac, where they anxiously awaited his coming.

They were all together again on the St. Joseph in December, ready for fresh adventure. Determined first to explore the Mississippi, so as to more thoroughly outline his plans for the future, La Salle chose eighteen New England Indians to accompany his party of twenty-three Frenchmen. As many of these insisted upon taking their women along, the entire company, when finally embarked, numbered fifty-four. The frozen river rendered the Kankakee route impossible, and Tonty and Membré led the way with six canoes across the lake to the mouth of the Chicago River. La Salle, with the remainder, followed a few days later. New Year's day was passed on the site of Chicago. It was the middle of Winter, and all the smaller streams were solid with ice. They constructed rude sleds, strapped their canoes upon them, and, in a straggling procession, dragged them wearily along the shining surface league after league, until they finally discovered open water below Lake Peoria. Here they embarked, and on the 6th of February, 1682, found their way into the majestic Mississippi.

Upon the details of this trip, extending so far beyond Illinois territory, it is not necessary to dwell. Sufficient to say, it extended to the mouth of the Mississippi, where the entire country was formally laid claim to in the name of France, in the month of April, 1682. The claim was the entire valley of the Mississippi, a magnificent domain. As a well-known historian has said: "From the oil-spring in Allegheny County, New York, to the dividing of the waters of Two Ocean Creek in Wyoming; from the Wisconsin lakes, where the wild goose nested and the Sioux ranged, to the tide-kissed marshes of the Gulf of Mexico, Louis the XIV now reigned supreme by virtue of the work of Réné-Robert Cavelier, Sieur de la Salle." Fortunately for American civilization, no other Frenchman his equal ever found way into these wilds to complete that gigantic task he had so well outlined and begun. Of those Frenchmen accompanying him upon this desperate venture, the names known may well be preserved: Membré, Hunault, La Violette, Crèval, Père Zenobe, Récollet missionary, Henri de Tonty, François de Boisrondet, Gabriel Barbier, Jean Bourdon, Sieur D'Autray, Jacques Cauchois, Pierre You, Gilles Meucret, Jean Michel, Surgeon; Jean Mas, Jean Dulignon, Nicholas de la Salle, and Pierre Prudhomme.

Few words are necessary to tell the remainder of this strange life-story. In July, La Salle was back again on the Illinois, and upon the summit of Starved Rock built a fort, which was called St. Louis. It was the sixth in his proposed chain. Here he gathered his colony of Indians — Miamis, Shawnees, Abenakis, Mohegans, and Illinois, nearly fourteen thousand all told — and here he granted land to his followers, as he probably had the legal right to do.

But, back in Canada, his numerous enemies were not idle. A new Governor — La Barre — had succeeded his old friend Frontenac, and was opposing La Salle's schemes with all the power of his high office. Finally, in desperation, the latter

LA SALLE TAKING POSSESSION OF THE MISSISSIPPI

FROM PAINTING BY CHARLOTTE WEBER

left his colony to the command of Tonty, and proceeded direct to France, hoping thus to better his fortunes.

To his surprise he found himself famous. He was presented to the King, who listened to him, and was persuaded. Four ships were fitted out for the purpose of making a permanent settlement near the mouth of the Mississippi. The ambition of La Salle—the one man who stands conspicuous in the New France of his day—seemed at last realized. Yet the fates had in his hour of triumph tangled the lines of his life. By mistake, the fleet, poorly outfitted and manned, passed beyond the Mississippi, and landed at Matagorda Bay, on the coast of Texas. Here the ill-starred colony languished for two years, at which time they were almost exhausted by disease and death. La Salle decided to push his way to the Illinois country in search for assistance. Accompanied by a few companions, he started on this desperate journey, but in the depths of that wilderness, somewhere on the banks of the Trinity River, was assassinated by one of his own cowardly men. Seven of his party succeeded in reaching the Illinois, but of the hapless colony left behind all perished. The date of La Salle's death was March 19, 1687, when he was but forty-three years of age.

Thus perished one of the most remarkable explorers whose names live in history. "Never," writes Parkman, "under the impenetrable mail of paladin or crusader, beat a heart of more intrepid mettle. America owes him an enduring memory." Illinois especially should for ever do honor to his name. Whoever reads the marvellous story of his twenty years' toil must confess his greatness, and the power of that ideal which held him firm. His life and death constitute the one supreme tragedy of the Mississippi valley.

CHAPTER V

THE FASCINATING STORY OF TONTY

AGAINST the dim and barren background of that seventeenth century struggle amid the Illinois wilderness, one figure stands forth conspicuous like a hero of romance. Clad in burnished breastplate and glittering headpiece, his hand hard-gripped upon sword-hilt, faithful, loyal, and devoid of fear, soldier, gentleman, and faithful friend, few indeed are the characters in frontier history more attractive than Henri de Tonty.

It was while in Europe in 1678 that La Salle was first brought in contact with this young soldier, who from that hour was destined to prove his closest friend, his most trusted associate in daily peril. An Italian by birth, Tonty had been an officer of the French army, a *protégé* of the Prince de Conti, and had lost one of his hands by the premature explosion of a grenade during the wars in Sicily. His father, who had been Governor of Gaeta, was also a financier of note, having devised the form of insurance now known as Tontine. A man yet young in years, of apparently delicate physique, possessing an agreeable presence, easily making and retaining friendships, La Salle again and again in his letters speaks of "his honorable character," "his amiable disposition," "his capability for doing things." In place of the lost member he wore a hand of iron, usually covered with a glove. This he was more than once compelled to use to good purpose when Indians became too unruly to be handled by mere words. La Potherie records that not knowing the secret of such severe blows the savages soon regarded him as a "medicine" of the first order.

Plunging into the backwoods almost as soon as he reached Canada, the remainder of Tonty's life was intimately connected with the American frontier, and particularly associated with the country of the Illinois. His earlier services, under La Salle, have already been mentioned. It is upon March 2, 1680, that day when the great leader left him in command at Fort Crèvecœur, that he first stands forth separate and distinct in history. One can but wonder at his thoughts as he stood there on the frozen shore at the foot of Peoria Lake in that far-off lonely day, and watched La Salle's canoe fade away into the distance. He was yet hardly a frontiersman, for he had been scarcely more than a year upon the border; he was young, ambitious, trained to strict obedience in European military camps, yet now he was left entirely alone to command this uttermost post of France, with league on league of wilderness stretching about on every side, unknown, mysterious. Just above the little fort, on the opposite river bank, the great village of Illinois Indians swarmed with suspicious savages, while here within the log walls of Crèvecœur mutiny was already being shown openly before him. It was a situation desperate with peril, despairing in loneliness.

He had with him only fifteen men with which to defend his position — smiths, ship-carpenters, housewrights, and soldiers, besides his servant, L' Espérance, and the two Récollet friars, Membré and Ribourde. Most of these were already openly dissatisfied, while to make matters worse, La Salle had unluckily met during his eastward journey on the St. Joseph River two men — La Chapelle and Leblanc — whom he immediately hurried forward to join Tonty. They arrived six weeks later, bearing a tale of woe and disaster. The "Griffin" had been lost at sea, and La Salle ruined beyond recovery. This story they poured with many additions into the willing ears of the already mutinous garrison at Crèvecœur, and the response was sudden and disastrous. Tonty, accompanied by a few men, departed to examine and fortify Starved Rock, according to orders left him by La Salle. No sooner had they disappeared from sight than those left behind destroyed the fort, stole powder, lead, furs, provisions, and everything else portable, and deserted into the wilderness leaving no trace behind. Among them all, only two remained faithful to their absent leader, the young Sieur de Boisrondet, scarcely more than a boy, and the servant L'Espérance. These two, escaping from the mutineers, hastened with the news to Tonty, who instantly despatched four messengers by two different routes to inform La Salle of this new disaster which had befallen him. This left with Tonty, in addition to the two above mentioned, only Renault, and the two Récollet priests, who were then in the Indian camp. With these he took up his abode in the great village of the Illinois, in the midst of eight thousand Indians. The Spring and Summer passed slowly, while they thus waited anxiously for the return of La Salle. By adroitness and firmness, Tonty managed to disarm the suspicion of the Illinois, but in the meanwhile, all unknown to both white and Indian, a storm was gathering in the East which would soon drench these prairies with the blood of its victims. This was an outpouring of the ferocious Iroquois, who had crushed the Hurons, the Eries, with others along the great lakes, and now turned their hungry eyes toward the Illinois in search after new victims. Five hundred warriors, moving with the celerity of demons, swept across the wide waste of forest and prairie toward their intended prey. All was idle repose and peace in the great town on the banks of the Illinois. Suddenly, like a clap of thunder from a clear sky, came news of the fierce invaders. A wandering Indian hunter brought the earliest warning of danger to the Illinois village, and instantly all was in the wild confusion of fear. Women snatched their children and fled screaming; warriors rushed about, nerving themselves for the coming battle, or clustered around Tonty and his little band of Frenchmen, openly accusing them of conspiracy with the ferocious invaders. That entire night the camp presented a hellish spectacle, in the midst of which the helpless Frenchmen remained in constant deadly peril at the hands of those affrighted, half-crazed warriors. Huge bonfires cast their red glare for miles around, while frenzied savages circled about them in the war-dance. At dawn the scouts came in, closely followed in their retreat by the advancing Iroquois. These scouts had perceived among the ranks of the enemy a chief arrayed in French costume, and reported that it was La Salle. Instantly the aroused Illinois, now convinced of treachery, rushed impetuously upon Tonty, brandishing their gleaming weapons, and shrieking madly for revenge. In order to save himself he promised that both he and his men should go forth to battle with them against the enemy.

In the early dawn they crossed the river in their canoes, and spread out to block the path of the Iroquois, now swarming forth in dense columns of warriors from the fringe of woods skirting the Vermilion. Guns began to crackle along the whole line of combat, which soon became fiercely engaged. Tonty, noting that the Illinois were largely outnumbered, and certain to be defeated, determined, at the risk of his own life, to go forward and attempt mediation. It was a daring venture, but alone promised hope for the Illinois. Dismissing the three men who voluntarily started with him, throwing away his arms, and exposed to a heavy fire, he advanced alone, holding out a wampum belt as a sign of peace. A hundred yards was thus passed, and he came, miraculously unhurt, into the very midst of that frenzied band, who were wild with rage and thirsting for his blood. For an awful instant, deceived probably by his dark complexion and half-savage dress, they supposed him an Indian, and one savage made a vicious stab at his heart. The blade struck a rib and was turned aside, even as the chief discovered his real character, and interposed to protect him from violence. Led aside, but already faint from loss of blood, Tonty boldly advanced the claim that the Illinois Indians were under French protection, and that, by the terms of the treaty existing between that nation and the Iroquois, they should not be molested, or made war upon. As he spoke a warrior snatched his hat, and held it aloft upon his gun. The distant Illinois seeing it, and believing that he had been killed, instantly renewed their fire, and the enraged warriors about him nearly broke from all control. Back and forth among themselves they debated in their anger how to dispose of their helpless victim, even lifting his hair for the scalping knife, while he was again seriously wounded.

At last he succeeded in curbing them by the stern declaration that the Illinois tribes were twelve hundred strong, and that sixty Frenchmen were present to assist them. This statement was at least partially believed, and they finally despatched him back to his friends, in pretence of a truce. The older warriors commanded the firing to cease and then Tonty, dizzy from loss of blood, which was trickling from three wounds, was sent staggering back across the open plain, bearing his word of hopefulness to the Illinois. Encouraged by this message of peace the outnumbered tribes recrossed the river to their village, but were closely followed by their suspicious enemies as far as the bank. Nor did the latter make any long delay even there. Under the pretence of hunting, band after band of painted Iroquois warriors swam the intervening stream, and soon hung in threatening clouds about the doomed town, their shrill cries evidencing their fiendish determination at conquest. Becoming more and more alarmed by this evidence of ill-faith on the part of their treacherous enemies, the Illinois hastily decided on flight. Setting fire to their lodges, they sprang into their waiting canoes and hurried down the river to rejoin their women and children, who had been despatched before, leaving Tonty and his little handful of helpless Frenchmen utterly alone amid the smoking ruins, to meet the inflowing horde of baffled Iroquois.

Immediately their fate hung suspended in the balance. The victorious savages constantly vacillated between mad courage and pusillanimous fear, one day preparing to despatch Tonty to the retreating tribes with another message of peace, the next threatening him with death and torture for having deceived them regarding the number of warriors among the Illinois. Out of all this turmoil and threatening, one fact at last became plainly evident — the Iroquois chiefs feared arousing the displeasure of Count Frontenac, and desired to get rid of these French witnesses before going further with their bloody work. To this end a council was finally called, and Tonty was offered six packages of beaver skins if he would leave the country. The young Italian soldier kicked their present away with scorn, haughtily demanding in turn that they leave the Illinois tribes alone, and return in peace to their own country. His stern words of rebuke led to his expulsion from the council, and the following day the enraged chiefs drove all the whites forth from the camp.

Tonty had by this time done all possible to avert disaster. Repeatedly, at the risk of his life, and the lives of his men, he had interfered in behalf of the retreating Illinois. To remain longer amid such danger, was clearly useless. Realizing this, the little party of whites, six in number, set out in one wretched bark canoe furnished them, and departed up the river. Scarcely were they out of sight of the rejoicing Iroquois when their boat began leaking so badly they were obliged to hastily land for the purpose of repairing it. While the others were thus working, Father Ribourde strolled away, breviary in hand, across the meadows for a few moments' silent meditation and prayer. When evening came he had not returned. Tonty, alarmed at his long absence, accompanied by one man went in search. They found no sign of the aged priest, but discovered the fresh tracks of a band of prowling Indians. Still hoping anxiously for the best, they fired guns to guide him back to the camp if still alive. Later a huge fire was built upon the bank for this same purpose, the cautious little band crossing the river and crouching low in the shadows, so they could watch unseen from the other shore. At midnight the dark, indistinct figure of a man hovered around the distant blaze, then many more joined him, but the friar was not among them. It was later learned these composed a prowling band of Kickapoos, who had accidentally met, and wantonly murdered the inoffensive old man, then in his sixty-fifth year, bearing his scalp in boasting triumph to their village. Somewhere on the Illinois River between the Fox and the Des Plaines the aged missionary had laid down his life in martyrdom.

Convinced that Ribourde must be dead, Tonty and his men, giving up further search, proceeded up the river. Their craft again became disabled, and was finally abandoned, the party pressing forward on foot toward Lake Michigan. Their scant provisions became exhausted, and for days together they were compelled to exist on roots and acorns. Tonty fell sick with fever, while Boisrondet became lost for two days, and as they pushed on northward along the desolate west shore, the cold grew more intense while the means of subsistence decreased. All would have perished in the black forests, had they not discovered a few ears of corn and some frozen squashes near a deserted Indian village. Helped thus, they managed to stagger blindly forward, and by the close of November reached the camp of the Pottawattomies near Green Bay, where they were received with kindness.

Meanwhile, relieved of their hindering presence, horrible deeds had been wrought in the Illinois country by the fiendish Iroquois. Tearing open the graves near the great village, and terribly mutilating the dead bodies, which were

HENRI DE TONTY

FROM BAS-RELIEF IN MARQUETTE BUILDING, CHICAGO

left scattered everywhere across the prairie as prey for wolves, these savage demons, yet unsatiated in their ferocity, started down the river in pursuit of the retreating tribes. Day after day the two — the pursued and the pursuers — pressed southward, the one on water, the other on land, an equal distance being maintained between them. Finally the Iroquois won by treachery an opportunity for the striking of a deadly blow. They pretended a desire merely to drive the Illinois from the country, not to destroy them. Deceived by this statement the allied tribes separated, some going farther down the Mississippi, others crossing to its western bank. The Tamaroas, apparently more credulous than the others, remained encamped near the mouth of the Illinois. Suddenly the Iroquois swept down upon them; the men fled in dismay, while women and children, to the number of seven hundred, fell into those bloody, clutching hands. That which followed is, in its details, too horrible for record. Tortures, butcheries, burnings, such as only the terrible Iroquois could perpetrate, were common scenes up and down the banks of the Illinois. Some evidences of their horrid work remained when, two weeks later, La Salle passed along that way in his fruitless search after Tonty, but in the meantime the murderers had fled, bearing away with them as slaves all those captives who had been preserved from the torture. Slowly, as returning courage crept back into their chilled hearts, the Illinois came creeping again into their desolated country, even reëstablishing themselves in their old village, along those meadows which now front Utica.

Undismayed by all the peril and suffering through which he had already been called upon to pass, Tonty, the moment sufficient strength returned to his body, sought communication with La Salle, and an opportunity to plunge once more into the depths and dangers of the wilderness. This young European soldier already felt the strange spell of the woods upon him, the spirit of adventure calling him back to peril and hardship. By the end of May, 1681, these two comrades met once again behind the log palisades at Michillimackinac, told each to the other their disheartening tales of disaster, and then sternly set to work to plan anew. Paddling their frail canoes a thousand miles eastward, they held audience with Frontenac, straightened out, as best they could, the tangled threads of La Salle's finances in Quebec and Montreal, and then again turned westward, their heroic faces set grimly toward the haunted wilderness. The Summer had already waned when they attained the shores of Huron on the return passage, and week after week their laden canoes crept slowly forward along the lonely banks, by desolate ranks of bristling firs; lake and forest, forest and lake, a dreary scene, haunted ever by memories of horror. At last the wearied prows found rest on the gravelled shore at the mouth of the St. Joseph, and La Salle and Tonty stood once more together on the edge of that vast country they had set their hearts upon winning for France.

The season was already far advanced, the sullen December air nipping with the chill of Winter, but neither leader nor lieutenant hesitated before exposure or trial. Accompanied by Father Membré, and a small party of followers crowded into six frail canoes, Tonty departed a few days in advance of the main body. The great lake was swept by fierce storms, but skirting the sand-dunes of what is now Indiana, they succeeded in reaching the mouth of the Chicago River. Dragging their boats on rudely improvised sleds, along the frozen water-courses, often wading deep in snow that swirled about them in clouds, the struggling advance finally attained to open water below Peoria. Here they were joined by the others. The great village of the Illinois was discovered deserted, the tribes being absent on their Winter's hunt, and the prows of the venturesome canoes were pointed southward in exploration of the lower waters, as yet almost unknown. It was a dismal, dreary picture of desolation amid which they floated, the wide prairies wrapped in a mantle of obscuring snow, the tall trees lining the banks sheeted with frost, the river full of running ice. February 6, 1682, they swept forth from the mouth of the Illinois into the broader Mississippi, but were here compelled to camp for a week waiting until the ice should open sufficiently to permit farther passage. All this time no sign of human life was apparent anywhere. A deserted village of the Tamaroas was passed just north of the juncture of the Ohio, but the first Indians met in all this immense stretch of wilderness were Chickasaws far down amid the dreary rice swamps.

Constantly, as they thus drifted downward into the unknown, frequently wrapped in a dense curtain of mist, the savage war drums would boom ominously from the banks, and it was Tonty—fearless for adventure—who went boldly ashore to make friends with the natives. Thus feeling their uncertain way, three hundred miles below the mouth of the Arkansas they approached the great village of the Taensas. Tonty and Membré set out daringly through the swamp and visited it after a two hours' toilsome journey. Never before had they seen so pretentious an Indian town. It consisted, by his description, of large, square dwellings, built of sunbaked mud mixed with straw, arched over by dome-shaped roofs of cane, all placed in regular order about an open area. The following morning, when again on the wide river, Tonty gave chase to a wooden canoe filled with Indians. He had nearly come up to it, when more than a hundred savages made their appearance on the shore, close at hand, their bows bent ready for battle. La Salle ordered Tonty to come back. The Italian obeyed, and crossing the river, the entire party went into camp on the opposite shore. Immediately the intrepid Tonty volunteered to cross alone to negotiate peace with this unknown tribe. Desperate as the mission seemed from the war-like motions of the savages, the calm audacity of this one-armed soldier carried the day, and soon all were seated about a camp-fire smoking the peace-pipe together. These were the Natchez, a tribe destined to play an important part in the Indian history of the Southwest, and by many believed to have been the last remnant of the ancient Mound-builders. They were sun worshippers, and their towns and customs were found most interesting and peculiar.

On the sixth of April the river divided into three broad channels, the boat containing La Salle followed that trending toward the west, D'Autray the more eastern, while Tonty took the middle passage. A little later all floated forth upon the blue waters of the Gulf.

After claiming for France the wide territory drained by the great river they had traversed so long, the hardy adventurers turned the battered prows of their canoes once more up stream, their task accomplished. It was a hard struggle pushing steadily against that stiff current, but mile by mile they made it. La Salle, taken sick, lay helpless for some time at the mouth of the Arkansas, but Tonty was hurried forward to far-away Michillimackinac, from whence he was to send word of their important discoveries to Canada, and then return to the Illinois. There he was directed to build a fort, and draw together the nucleus for an Algonquin Indian colony, thus carrying out the plan long formed in the mind of La Salle for a permanent establishment.

Of that lonely trip up the long stretch of water-ways — the Mississippi, the Illinois, the Des Plaines, the Chicago, and the great lake — little record remains. Those weeks of continuous toil and hardship amid the dreary wilderness were but the common things of this frontier life, and not worthy of being mentioned. He was accompanied by Brossard, Cauchois, Maso, and a Saco Indian. Like all else in his life, the work given him was thoroughly accomplished. By September he had reached Michillimackinac; two months later he was again back upon the Illinois, and in December had actually commenced the building of Fort

St. Louis. The point selected was the summit of that great natural curiosity now known as "Starved Rock," on the opposite side of the river a few miles below Ottawa. Rising directly from the water, a sheer wall of stone for one hundred and twenty-five feet jutting far out over the wide stream, its western brow reared high above the tops of great forest trees below, its eastern side impregnable because of a wide, deep gorge, no more perfect natural fortification could have been found. The cliff was accessible only from the rear, where, with extreme difficulty, a man might succeed in climbing up along a steep and narrow passage. Here, laboring all Winter, now joined by La Salle, Tonty built his entrenchments — cut away the forest surmounting the rocky summit, erected store-houses, and log-huts in which to quarter his men, and finally dragged timber up the difficult pathway, from the plain below, encircling all with a log palisade. While he was thus at work La Salle held council here and there with the scattered Indian tribes throughout that country, gathering them together in one vast confederation of Algonquins on the site of the old-time town of the Illinois. Fearful still of the threatening Iroquois, they gathered about this rock castle, in Parkman's words, "like timorous peasantry of the Middle Ages," seeking the protection of French power.

Almost at once three hundred cabins were reared on the plain below, and as Spring advanced toward Summer Tonty — who was most of the time virtually in command of this fortress — must have gazed upon a strange and marvellous scene, as he looked off from those log ramparts. The beautiful valley of the Illinois would lie before him like a map, bounded in the dim distance by the far-away bluffs. The river spread directly beneath, a silvery stream, diversified by numerous green-clad islands, and sentinelled by forest trees, until finally disappearing in the far-off haze of the horizon. Across, amid that sea of prairie stretching back from the bank of the stream, were the clustered Indian lodges, in groups of villages, where squaws labored, warriors lounged idly in the sun, and naked children played in the shadows. Everywhere, as far as the eye could wander, arose the smoke of tepees. Here were Illinois, Shawnees, Abenakis, Miamis, Mohegans, as motley a collection of aborigines as were ever gathered in peaceful intercourse, at one time reaching the surprising total of twenty thousand souls.

Here, until the Autumn of 1683, La Salle and Tonty remained, with their little guard of Frenchmen, amid that vast surrounding concourse of savages. Then La Salle departed on his final trip to France, and Tonty was left there alone, and in supreme command of the Illinois country — its first governor. Nor was he ever again privileged to look upon the loved face of his great chief. There on that isolated rock of St. Louis, patient, courageous, manful to the last, he did his full duty, and, excepting the short time when De Baugy ruled, held his solitary post for six years, the uttermost sentinel of French power in all that wild Western wilderness. The details of that lonely occupancy, its constant vigils, its dealing with timorous Algonquins and revengeful Iroquois, its exploration of unknown country, its struggles with mutinous Frenchmen, the treachery within, the cruel savagery without, have never been told in written story. But the hours of loneliness and despair, the long waiting for word from the absent La Salle, the sturdy performance of duty unrewarded, stamp this one-armed Italian soldier, stern, kindly, and capable, as a true hero of chivalry.

But meanwhile Le Barre, urged to action by the fur traders of Mackinac, and other jealous interests much nearer at home, had not been idle. Two officers, bearing special orders against La Salle's projects, were despatched westward, Sieur de La Durantaye, of the regiment of Carignan-Salières, to Mackinac, and the Chevalier de Baugy, of the King's Dragoons, to Fort St. Louis. Peremptory orders were sent to La Salle commanding him to report in person without delay to the governor at Montreal. Somewhere between the Fox and the Kankakee Rivers De Baugy and La Salle met, exchanged messages and parted, the former continuing his journey to Fort St. Louis, where Tonty, acting under the instructions of his chief, gave him soldierly greeting. All that Winter the two lived together, not altogether in harmony, while the one commanded for the Canadian governor, the other for La Salle. In March the Iroquois swept suddenly down upon them, and these two, mustering their few Frenchmen and Indian allies, fought side by side, while for six days the ferocious savages assailed the Rock in hopeless attempt at dislodging its defenders. On the twenty-first of May, Durantaye, accompanied by Father Allouez, and a party of sixty Frenchmen, reached the fort. They came ostensibly for the purpose of relieving the garrison, but brought with them orders to Tonty to yield up the command entirely to De Baugy. Loyal to the instructions left him by La Salle, he obeyed the distasteful order, and, almost alone, departed in his solitary canoe for that far-off Canada which he had not seen for six years. One can almost picture the sad scene of that departure; the few faithful ones, with Boisrondet in their midst, gathering by the shore to say farewell, while above, peering down from the palisades, the others rejoiced over their apparent victory.

But this was not destined to be for long. La Salle had found the ear of the king, and his lieutenant, La Forest, bore back with him to Canada from France a communication to La Barre which made that governor's ears tingle, and caused him to rescind his action hastily and restore Tonty to his command in the Illinois. Late in June, 1684, bearing the order with him, the Italian entered the fort gate and handed a copy to De Baugy. The same day the dragoon, accompanied by his followers, departed for Mackinac, leaving Tonty in loneliness and complete control. Of what he accomplished at St. Louis, following this date, we know but little. He was ever a man of action, not of words. We catch glimpses of him here and there throughout the Illinois country, exercising his power and influence among the tribes, and pushing out along new lines of discovery and trade. Once he was at Mackinac, seeking news of La Salle, and while there rejoiced to learn that La Barre was no longer governor, but had been succeeded by the Marquis de Denonville. Once, he journeyed eastward, accompanied by all the Frenchmen he dared withdraw from the fort, and numerous Indian allies, to take gallant part in battle against the Iroquois, being companion on that campaign with Durantaye, Du Lhut, and La Forest. On his return he brought back with him a number of French families, together with wives, sisters, and sweethearts of the garrison, to make the wilderness life more endurable.

Again he made that long journey to Michillimackinac, his heart anxious to learn something of what had become of La Salle. While there he heard that a trader who had touched at Mackinac Island bore with him a letter from De Denonville, praising his work in the Illinois country, and requesting an audience at Montreal. But at the same time rumors reached him also that his chief had met with disaster in the South, of his landing on the coast of Louisiana, and the subsequent loss of his ships. This decided Tonty. For him to learn of La Salle's predicament was to act at once. Immediately he turned his canoes down Lake Michigan with the determination of forming a company at Fort St. Louis for an expedition of rescue to the Gulf. It was late Fall, and his voyage a stormy one. Ice formed so heavily that the canoes had to be abandoned, and for three hundred miles the little party toiled along the shore-line on foot, thus finally reaching the newly constructed fort at Chicago where Durantaye was then in command. A brief stop here, and Tonty pushed on to St. Louis, where he at once matured his plans for the relief of La Salle.

La Forest, leaving Frontenac to the charge of his lieutenant, came west hastily to assume command of St. Louis, with its little garrison of thirty-one white men, during Tonty's absence. The latter took with him twenty-five Frenchmen and eleven Indians. Pushing their way through the ice to the Mississippi, they swept down that mighty stream clear to its mouth, meeting with no unusual adventure on the way. There they found merely "a solitude, a voiceless desolation of river, marsh, and sea." East and west the anxious searchers explored that dreary coast for thirty leagues, but all in vain. The loved commander for whom they sought so faithfully, eager to assist him in his adversity, was even then aimlessly wandering on the distant plains of Texas. Disheartened and baffled at this failure of his search, Tonty turned his prows once again toward his fortified rock castle on the Illinois. There was his duty; there he must remain until word came from his chief.

Who can picture the intense anxiety with which he waited the coming to him of news from out that vast wilderness, the hours he hung above those rude palisades staring down the silent river, the patience of his long vigil, his heart ever troubled by the unknown fate of his absent friend? Here at last, in September, 1687, ragged, disheartened, half-crazed with the sufferings of their long journey, straggled in the miserable remnant of La Salle's last expedition — the two Caveliers, uncle and nephew, Douay, De Marle, and Teissier. Tonty, at the time of their arrival, being absent, engaged in a campaign against the distant Iroquois, they repaid all the courtesies of his lieutenant, Bellefontaine, with a lie, stating that La Salle yet remained alive and well on the lower river. To Tonty, on his final return, this base falsehood was again repeated, and Cavelier even had the meanness to draw upon him for four thousand livres in furs in La Salle's name.

The miserable fugitives departed eastward in March,

1688, supplied with everything the fort could furnish, but Henri de Tonty, remaining on his isolated rock of St. Louis, did not learn the truth of the cowardly assassination of his chief until late September, when he was visited by Couture, and two Indians from the Arkansas. His action was immediate and intensely characteristic of the man. He might yet save the remnant of the despairing colony, and hunt down the cowardly murderers. For him decision ever spelt action. By December he had left Fort St. Louis, travelling in a single wooden canoe, accompanied only by five Frenchmen, a Shawnee warrior, and two Indian slaves. By the twenty-eighth of March he was on Red River, marching alone into hostile Indian villages boldly demanding the murderers of his chief. With only two men remaining faithful to his service he pushed recklessly on into the far interior, facing deadly peril at every step of the way, the frightened fugitives fleeing before him, and seeking safety among distant tribes. At last every trace of their presence suddenly disappeared, and he was led to believe, through crafty Indian lies, that those he sought so persistently had already perished in the wilderness.

Laden with bitter disappointment, the three avengers finally turned reluctantly back. They found the country they must traverse flooded by a sudden rise in the streams. As Parkman describes it, "Sometimes they waded to the knees, sometimes to the neck, sometimes pushed their slow way on rafts. They slept on logs placed side by side to lift them above the mud and water, and fought their way with hatchets through inundated cane fields." From hunger they were forced to eat their dogs. "I never in my life," writes Tonty, "suffered so much." When one recalls that this Italian was never a robust man, and that he possessed only one hand, the desperation of his position becomes more apparent. They reached the Mississippi on the eleventh of July, the Arkansas villages on the thirty-first. Here Tonty was stricken down by an attack of fever, and it was not until September that he again attained the fort upon the Illinois.

Of what followed in his life we know but little. In 1699 he still commanded on that rock of St. Louis. In 1702, by royal order, he was bidden to reside on the Mississippi, and the Illinois establishment was abandoned. During that same year he joined D'Iberville in lower Louisiana, and was despatched by that officer from Mobile to influence the Chickasaws. From that moment he disappears from history, not even his death having been made matter of record.[1] We only know that somewhere in the midst of that vast wilderness, for the regeneration of which he had fought and suffered, doubtless passed away this gallant comrade, this loyal friend, this incomparable knight of the frontier, this soldier and gentleman.

[1] There is an Indian legend that, white-haired and feeble with age, accompanied by a single faithful Indian companion, in 1718 he returned to St. Louis to die.

CHAPTER VI

THE FOOTPRINTS OF THE FRIARS

IN the very advance of exploration and settlement, long the foremost figures on the far French frontier, were the priests of the black robe and of the gray. Heroic beyond words, pathetic beyond expression, is the simple story of their labors, hardships, and defeats. Nor is it possible to say that the greater meed of honor lies with either the Jesuit or the Récollet Order. Both alike, in their chosen missionaries, exhibited devotion, patience, and heroism to the highest possible degree, and although the records of the former are far the more complete and easily accessible, yet their more modest brethren did, within somewhat narrower limits, equally notable work throughout this Illinois wilderness. Marquette, Allouez, Gravier, and Mermet wore the black robe; Hennepin, Membré, Ribourde, and Zenobe wore the gray. Yet final political conditions in Canada favored the Jesuits, and they consequently became more numerous and influential throughout the early settlements.

With the single exception of Father Senat, who, accompanying D'Artaguette's ill-fated expedition to the south, was burned to death at the stake by the Chickasaws, the self-sacrificing priests of the Illinois were not destined to suffer martyrdom through torture. Few Indian races were ever so merciless as the Iroquois, and none other, save under great provocation, chose unarmed priests for their victims. Yet, if constant suffering, hardships innumerable, patience, and a life of rigorous self-denial, with death at last in the drear wilderness, be an open door to true martyrdom, then many an almost unknown priest of the Illinois should have his name written high on that roll of honor beside Jogues, Brébeuf, Daniel, Bressani, and Lallemant. Oftentimes in that wilderness it required greater heroism to live than to die. Certain it is that these pioneers of Christ, upheld by the zeal of faith, penetrated every nook and corner of this great wilderness country, zealously seeking the salvation of souls. They encountered danger and suffering in every possible form; the perils of nature, the inhumanity of savages. Some were drowned, some starved to death, some, losing their way, perished alone in the dread desolation. Yet none hesitated before the call of duty, and wherever a soldier of the Cross fell, another came forward to walk unhesitatingly in his footsteps. That the years have proven all this to have been comparatively useless labor, and that neither Jesuit nor Récollet has left permanent impress on the inhabitants of the Illinois country — either red or white — in no way detracts from the heroism of the effort, the magnificent courage, patience, and fortitude of these wandering missionaries. Whatever the mistakes of their officers, or the misdirection of their zeal, these soldiers in the ranks, wearing their coarse robes of black and gray, did their complete duty, and deserve the applause of the world, the "Well done" of God.

Among them all, Marquette, a Jesuit, and Hennepin, a Récollet, stand forth conspicuous for the peculiar services performed. The former, as companion of Joliet, was first to explore the great water-ways, and earliest to preach the Gospel to Illinois Indians. Already stricken by disease when he stood before that great concourse on the Utica meadows, it was not given unto Marquette to carry forward to completion the work of his heart, but he had laid the foundation upon which another brother of his Order was to build. Nor was that brother long forthcoming; but it is to be regretted that we know so little of what occurred at old Kaskaskia between the departure of Marquette and the coming of La Salle. Those six years are all but recordless. Yet this we know. It was in May, 1675, that Marquette died on the dreary Michigan shore, and it was in October, 1676, that the veteran missionary of Lake Superior, Father Claude Allouez, left De Père, accompanied by two boatmen, to take up the waiting labors on the far-away Illinois. We have glimpses of his desperate voyage down the storm-racked shores of Michigan, of suffering and hardships during the months of that dreary Winter — just such little vistas as these missionaries sometimes give of their hard life toil, as though they felt it weakness to complain. It was Spring before the struggling three reached the mouth of the Chicago, and met there members of the Illinois tribe, and it was April 27 when their eyes first beheld the great Indian village where Marquette had preached. At that time it contained three hundred and fifty-one cabins, yet it is almost impossible to discover how long Father Allouez remained there in his first ministry, probably until the coming of La Salle, toward whom he ever held great enmity. Once during his stay the town suffered an attack by the Iroquois, which was repulsed. Beyond this but little fragments remain regarding the life of Allouez, although he was for some years in the Illinois country, ever a strenuous worker. We catch a glimpse of him lying sick at Fort St. Louis in the Fall of 1687, and he died on the Miami River two years later.

Hennepin, Membré, and Ribourde were the priests who accompanied La Salle; they were of the Récollet Order, and the gray robe held ascendency in the Illinois country so long as that commandant exercised control at Fort St. Louis. Of these three, Ribourde, already an old man for such adventures, met death by the tomahawk in the hands of wandering Kickapoos; Membré served long and faithfully, accompanying La Salle to the Gulf on his last expedition, and proving his zeal and devotion in many ways. Undoubtedly the leading friar of his Order to serve in the Illinois country, he met his tragic death in Texas soon after the murder of his great leader. It was Hennepin's good fortune to receive a special mission of exploration which has written his name more deeply on history than any of the others. From Fort Crèvecœur, on the last day of February, 1680, he was despatched down the Illinois in a canoe, accompanied by two *voyageurs* — Michel Accau, who was the real leader of the party, and Le Picard du Gay. Their purpose, under La Salle's instructions, was the careful exploration of the upper Mississippi. The work thus assigned them was accomplished with fair success, but unfortunately for Hennepin's reputation for truthfulness, the various accounts he afterwards published of his adventures and achievements, were in much so palpably false, as to leave even his truths long discredited. The facts seem to be that the little party proceeded up the Mississippi, hunting a wide variety of game on their way, until the eleventh or twelfth of April, when they landed to repair their canoe. Suddenly a fleet of Sioux boats, manned with warriors, swept down the river, and made them prisoners. Suffering great hardships, they were taken north, passing Lake Pepin, and finally reaching the Indian villages in the vicinity of Mille Lac, Wisconsin. Here Hennepin spent the Spring and Summer in hunting, practising as a physician among the savages, and studying the Sioux language. The three men were finally rescued from their wearisome captivity by the opportune arrival of the famous *coureur de bois*, Daniel Greysolon du Lhut, with four companions on a fur-trading expedition. The next Winter was spent in the huts of friendly Jesuit missionaries at Green Bay, after which Hennepin made his way to France, never again to appear in the Illinois country.

Membré, while on his first visit to the Illinois country, made a journey to the Miamis on the river St. Joseph, and was also in a village of the Kaskaskias, probably somewhere on the Kankakee. He had, however, little success in converting the savages, although he baptized several, including the famous chief, Chassagonache. The latter was later reported as dying under the hands of the medicine men of his tribe, utterly forgetful of the good missionary. These early laborers were greatly distressed by a lack of wine for the celebration of the mass, but this was later relieved by the abundance of wild grapes discovered along the river bottom. A league distant from the great Indian village of the Illinois a cabin was transformed into a chapel, where such savages as could be interested were instructed in the mysteries. After the missionaries had been driven from the country by the Iroquois, some of the dusky converts saved the chalice and sacerdotal vestments left in this chapel in the haste of retreat and brought them with reverent care to the distant mission at Green Bay, where Hennepin found them on his arrival there. When Membré finally departed on his mission to France for La Salle, never again to return to the Illinois, he sorrowfully summed up his labors in these words: "I cannot say that my little efforts produced fruit. With regard to these nations perhaps some one by a secret effort of grace has profited; this God only knows. All we have done has been to see the state of these nations, and to open the way to the Gospel, and the missionaries; having baptized only two infants whom I saw at the point of death, and who in fact died in our presence."

The work accomplished by the few friars of St. Francis coming to this wilderness amounted then to little by their own confession, although they may be safely said to have been in complete ascendency during all the time of La Salle's command of the Illinois. At Fort Crèvecœur the Indian mission was carried on until the Iroquois came, and later, Membré remained for several years at Fort St. Louis, acting as chaplain to the garrison, and missionary among the surrounding tribes. Fathers Douay and Le Clerc also saw service in the Illinois country, and it is highly probable that others of the gray robe were there likewise to assist in this labor, although their names have not been preserved. Some evidence exists to show that the Récollets never wholly abandoned the country until the English obtained possession. As late as 1768 the Jesuit Meurin writes about removing the bodies of two priests from Fort Chartres to Prairie du Rocher. These were Fathers Gagnon and Collet, priests of St. Anne of New Chartres, the latter a Récollet.

The "Mission of the Immaculate Conception," which was the name given by Marquette to the Jesuit station at Kaskaskia on the Illinois, languished sadly during all of La Salle's commandership, but on April 27, 1677, Father Allouez returned from his self-imposed exile, and again began active missionary work among the gathered tribes of Illinois Indians. Father James Gravier joined him there in 1690, and early became the leading spirit of the mission, although for three years their combined labor exhibited only very inadequate results. A little later than the date above given, Fathers Marest, Mermet, and Pinet came also to work in the Illinois country. Pinet was stationed near the present site of Chicago, where a mission had been established as early as 1698, but it is impossible to locate the earliest mission work of the others. They were probably at small stations now utterly forgotten. Father Rale was also in the Illinois country from 1692 to 1694, and Father Julien Binneteau was, at least, travelling upon this field as early as 1699, going west as far as the Mississippi River, but whether merely as a traveller, or in an endeavor to preach to the heathen, is not recorded.

It is to be regretted that even in the Jesuit Relations no complete and connected account of the work done by these priests is to be found, nor even a satisfactory list of those actually engaged in Illinois service. At best we obtain but tantalizing glimpses here and there of the labor being attempted in the heart of this vast wilderness. After a short and unexplained absence from his post Father Jacques Gravier returned to labor with the Illinois tribes in April, 1693. He was delighted to discover them in much better frame of mind for ministry, and for the first time the work appeared to prosper, and to promise definite results. He built and dedicated a new chapel at the little French trading stockade near the Peoria straits, which was soon crowded with Indians anxious to hear him preach; but in the meantime he became involved in an unfortunate quarrel with the chiefs, who apparently took little interest in his labor. In spite of much opposition and threatening he married Ako, a French fur trader, to the daughter of the chief of the Kaskaskias. So great grew the interest in his work that the chapel had to be enlarged. From April to November he reports the baptism of two hundred and six persons. In September, 1700, Gravier undertook the long canoe voyage down the Mississippi to the lower French forts. While on this trying journey down the Illinois he discovered that the Kaskaskias were about to emigrate beyond the Mississippi from their overpowering fear of the Iroquois. Marest was then the priest stationed at this particular village. The two Jesuits, uniting their efforts, endeavored to induce the Indians to remain where they were, but, finding this impossible, accompanied them in their migration down the two rivers until a landing was finally effected within the present limits of Randolph County, and the second town of Kaskaskia established. After a short delay here, Gravier proceeded on his voyage down the river. The exact date of this settlement is unknown, but it was probably in 1698 or 1699. Returning later to the Illinois country, Gravier became missionary to the Peorias. Trouble occurring among them, he was shot at with arrows, and so badly injured that he nearly lost his life. Marest, learning of his condition, made a hasty overland journey to his assistance from Kaskaskia, but the stricken priest had to be taken down the river as far

A "LONG–ROBE" OF THE WILDERNESS

SHOWING THE DRESS OF THE EARLY MISSIONARIES

as Mobile in order to reach a surgeon. He died in Louisiana, April, 1708.

Somewhere about 1700 Father Francis Pinet established the missions at Cahokia and Tamaroa, for the tribes bearing these names. The point selected was about sixty miles north of the Kaskaskia site and almost opposite the present St. Louis. A small French fur-trading post had previously been built there, and may have been even then occupied. The following year, however, this mission was transferred from the control of the Jesuits, and given over to local priests sent out from the Seminary at Quebec. Father Burger was the first of these to have charge here. He died some years after, and Marest, forgetting in that hour all jealousy between the priestly orders, walked from Kaskaskia to conduct the funeral service. These Seminary priests began coming into the country as early as the Fall of 1698, and were at first warmly welcomed and cordially entertained by the few Jesuits then on the field. Later we find in letters much bitter complaint regarding their encroaching labors and officiousness. Toward the last, however, the work seems to have naturally divided itself, the Seminary priests confining themselves almost entirely to the care of the French settlers in the small villages, and leaving the scattered Indian missions entirely to the Jesuits.

By 1702 Pinet was stationed at Kaskaskia, engaged almost exclusively in Indian work. His labors were highly successful, the small log chapel being unable to hold those desiring to listen to his earnest words. Associated with him at this time was Father Binneteau, who later lost his life while accompanying the Kaskaskias on one of their Summer hunts into the interior. Exhausted by the severe travel and exposure, he fell sick and passed away. It was but shortly after that Father Pinet also died, and then Marest came down to Kaskaskia and took up the work. In August, 1702, Father Jean Mermet accompanied Juchereau's expedition to establish a French trading-fort somewhere near the mouth of the Ohio. The point selected was close beside the present site of the city of Metropolis, and here the *voyageurs* laid the first foundations of what later became Fort Massac, by building a log stockade, while the priest established a mission near by which he called the Assumption. Mermet remained here preaching with success for three or four years, the southern Indians coming in their bark canoes down the Cumberland and Tennessee Rivers to hear him repeat the Gospel story. In 1706 we discover Mermet back once more in Kaskaskia, assisting Marest, his mission of the Assumption having been broken up through Indian trouble, and the hasty dispersal of the fur traders.

Mermet was, in many respects, the most noteworthy of the many Jesuit priests laboring in the Illinois country. It is said of him:

"The gentle virtues and fervid eloquence of Mermet made him the soul of the mission at Kaskaskia. At early dawn his pupils came to church, dressed neatly and modestly, each in a deer-skin, or robe sewn together from several skins. After receiving lessons, they chanted canticles; mass was then said in presence of all the Christians, the French and the converts — the women on one side and the men on the other. From prayers and instructions the missionaries proceeded to visit the sick and administer medicine, and their skill as physicians did more than all the rest to win confidence. In the afternoon the catechism was taught in the presence of the young and old, when everyone, without distinction of rank or age, answered the questions of the missionary. At evening all would assemble at the chapel for instruction, for prayer, and to chant the hymns of the Church. On Sunday and festivals, even after vespers, a homily was pronounced; at the close of the day parties would meet in houses to recite the chaplets in alternate choirs, and sing psalms till late at night. Saturday and Sunday were the days appointed for confession and communion, and every convert confessed once in a fortnight. The success of this mission was such that marriages of the French immigrants were sometimes solemnized with the daughters of the Illinois according to the rites of the Catholic Church."

By 1712 the French population had increased to considerable proportions, most largely concentrated at Kaskaskia, although a few other smaller towns were established in the immediate neighborhood. Mermet, full of the spirit of martyrdom, nearly lost his life ministering to sick Mascoutins during an epidemic, but his lack of strength prevented him accompanying the Indians on their annual hunt, and Marest took his place. In 1711 the latter journeyed across the country to visit the Peorias, who had been left without a missionary since their treacherous attack on Father Gravier. Finding them now in much better spirit Father de Ville was despatched there to take up the work the following year. Marest died in Kaskaskia in 1714, and two years later his life-long friend and companion, Father Mermet, likewise passed away. Both were reinterred in the Kaskaskia church by Father Le Boullenger in 1727. A complete list of the missionaries laboring in this Illinois country during the period of French rule is impossible to obtain. Among the Jesuits we know that Father Kereben died here in 1728, Largilier in 1714, and Guymoneau in 1736. Father Senat had been in the Illinois work about eighteen months when he accompanied D'Artaguette on his disastrous expedition to Mississippi, only to perish at the stake. Father D'Outrelean was reported as badly wounded by Indians firing on his canoe while on his way down the river from Illinois about 1730. In 1750 Father Vivier, then residing at Cahokia, writes that over six hundred Indians had been baptized, but that French brandy, introduced by *voyageurs*, was ruining the work of the mission. At this time De Guyenne was associated with him at Cahokia, Watrin being stationed at Kaskaskia, and Meurin at Peoria. Five years later five priests are reported in the neighborhood, with two lay helpers, the fifth priest being Julian de Verney. Xavier de Guyenne, *curé* at Fort Chartres, was Father Superior. He died in 1762, after thirty-six years of active service in the wilderness.

Early in 1763 trouble came to the Jesuits in France, and they were expelled the country. Their persecution followed all over the world wherever France held sway, and in September of that same year the long expected order arrived in this distant Illinois country to expel the priests and confiscate their property. However the Order may have failed in the salvation of savages, they had proven most successful in the accumulation of worldly stores. In Kaskaskia alone they possessed a church, a chapel, and a Jesuits' house, the latter valued at forty thousand piasters, and all built of stone. Their plantation consisted of two hundred and forty arpents of land, and was well stocked with cattle. They also owned and operated a brewery. All this property was promptly seized by the French commandant, while the Jesuit priests, with the single exception of Father Meurin, were driven from the country. The latter, then an extremely old man, broken down by hard frontier service, was permitted to remain, but it is not probable he continued to exercise his office. His death occured at Prairie du Rocher in 1777.

So all these efforts of one hundred years of sacrifice, toil, and exile came to naught. Nothing material remains to-day, in all this Illinois country, to recall these early labors of Jesuit and Récollet. The great silent wilderness amid whose solitudes and desolation they wandered in religious zeal has become the abiding-place of civilization, the vast prairies are smiling farms, the savage-haunted streams are highways of commerce, but the black robe and the gray have alike vanished like a forgotten dream. Yet, surely, even while we trace the mistakes of administration which resulted in such waste of effort and of lives, we can give full honor to the magnificent sacrifice, the supreme heroism, of those men who sunk their all in unrewarded toil in the heart of the black wilderness. With all her later names of honor, Illinois can not afford to ignore Marquette, Gravier, Marest, and Mermet, those humble soldiers of the Cross who died in her service.

Nor can any mere arrangement of names and dates justly tell their story. Thousands of leagues in the wilderness, oftentimes in advance of all their race, dwelling amid the squalor of Indian camps, travelling hundreds of miles on foot, parched in Summer, frozen in Winter, hungry, footsore, discouraged, facing death almost every day, their sole companions savages, their home the silent wood or desolate prairie, these priests struggled on, upheld by their faith, inspired by a reward beyond this world. Of their suffering and hardships they wrote little; in all their reports there is scarcely a line of complaint regarding physical hardships. Hunger and cold, exposure and danger, were merely incidents of their service — they went wherever they were sent; they did their work in silent patience, whether the end was destined to be life or death. These men, in their frayed robes, aided by their *donnés*, or oftentimes native companions, explored the water-ways of the Illinois, pressing their frail canoes up narrow streams. On foot, and frequently alone, they toiled over the Indian trails, bearing with them scarcely more than breviary and rosary, their one consuming desire the salvation of souls.

Little mission stations sprang up here and there throughout the wilderness. To-day the very locations of most of these are unknown, yet there was scarcely a stream of any importance that had not been the labor spot of a "long robe" — mere dots in the surrounding savagery, like those established at Chicago, Peoria, and at the mouth of the Des Moines. We cannot even tell the names of the men who toiled in them, how they lived, or where they died. Yet it is safe to say there was little difference in the stations. There would be a log chapel, with a few houses nestled close. If intended for permanency, a general storehouse and workshop would be added, the whole fenced about with log palisades, thus forming a rude stockaded fort, surrounded by clearings and cultivated fields. In their outside work, such as building and cultivating, the priests usually had others to assist them. Occasionally the savages could be induced to work, but generally a few lay brethren were attached to all stations of importance. These were men accustomed to manual labor and frontier life, able either to guide canoes or handle tools or weapons as need arose. In the earlier years of missionary effort, in Canada, and along the upper lakes, these were commonly volunteers, inspired by devotion to the cause, and serving without pay, and were then known as *donnés*, or "given men." But later, and, indeed, during nearly all the period covered by the Illinois missions, hired men, called *engagés*, were employed. These did all the manual labor about the stations, and accompanied the fathers as canoemen on their journeys, besides acting as the intermediaries between the priests and Indians in a rather profitable fur trade, whereby the missions greatly prospered.

It is easy now to criticise these Jesuit enthusiasts, and to point out the causes of their failures. But the truth and justification is they were ever battling for their own existence. At the time when Marquette first explored the Illinois country, the religious exaltation of the earlier Canadian missions had already seriously declined. The marvellous *esprit de corps* of the Jesuits, that total extinction of self, which has distinguished their work throughout the world, remained as strong as ever in this wilderness, but the same grand enthusiasm was not behind it. Canada had advanced from a mere church mission; it had become a state colony, and the civil power was constantly pressing the religious farther into the background. In their Western mission fields the representatives of the Church naturally desired to rule supreme; they dreaded the fur traders, not only because they interfered with their spiritual labor, and perverted their religious teachings, but because their brandy corrupted the converts. La Salle, behind his purposes of exploration, as Parkman points out, was a fur trader; even more, "he aimed at occupation, fortification, settlement." In every step he took he was directly in their way, and as a consequence they were compelled to fight him with every weapon in their power.

On his part he sought to counteract their efforts by supplanting them with Récollets, and in this he received the support of Count Frontenac. In his letters to France the latter is continually asking for more friars of this order. "Not," as Parkman says, "because he had any peculiar fondness for ecclesiastics of any kind, regular or secular, white, black, or gray; but he wanted the Récollets to oppose to the Jesuits. He had no fear of these mendicant disciples of St. Francis." And La Salle wanted them, and for precisely the same reason. So it was that during all the earlier stage of French occupancy in the Illinois it was a continual struggle between the two Orders for supremacy. While La Salle remained in control, the gray robes ruled the wilderness; but the moment the great commander departed, the superior discipline of the Jesuits prevailed, and at once their priests were everywhere, influencing alike savages and Frenchmen, and building their isolated chapels throughout the wilderness. So for a hundred years they toiled, suffered, and died, and to-day there remains scarcely a memory of their self-sacrificing labor.

CHAPTER VII

OLD WATER-WAYS AND THEIR VOYAGEURS

WHILE English colonists were scarcely venturing beyond view of the Atlantic surges, their utmost advance extending merely a few miles inland, the daring French *voyageurs* were breasting the stormy waters of the vast interior lakes, and even bartering for furs amid the black lodges of the far Dacotahs. While Eliot, the famous Puritan missionary, was laboring among the Massachusetts Indians within a few days' ride of Boston, priests of the black robe and of the gray robe were building their rude log chapels on the bleak shores of far-away Superior, and exploring that vast river which cleaves the continent in twain. Yet this difference was not so much one of boldness and energy as of opportunity. The French advance westward was expedited by natural advantages, the most marked being the superb system of water-ways constantly inviting them to the interior.

From the mouth of the St. Lawrence, westward to the far plains of the Red River and the Missouri, extends an almost uninterrupted chain of water communication, which the French were quick to explore, and utilize for both commercial and spiritual purposes. The Canadian *voyageur*, the *engagé* of fur trader or of mission, early became an expert canoesman, and soon developed into the finest river boatman of the world. Actuated by love of gain or by spiritual enthusiasm, they pressed their adventurous passage up and down the swirling currents of unnamed streams, seeking convenient portages, and thus ever attaining greater distance into the mysterious Western wilderness. The broad Ottawa, flowing through the grim Canadian forest, brought them within easy reach of Huron, and a little later their venturesome prows were skirting the rocky shores of the vast inland lakes, and exploring those rivers flowing into them from out the farther West. To push up against these streams was merely a question of time, so that while New England yet largely remained unexplored, the *fleur de lis* floated over all the central portion of the continent, and the French tongue was spoken in Indian lodges from Superior to the Gulf.

They were largely rough, uneducated men who wrought these historic changes,— swarthy of face, small and wiry of body, half savage in manner and dress, meeting every hardship with a smile, and beguiling the weary miles of tiresome travel with merry song and quip. Plunged for years at a time into the dreary depths of wilderness, surrounded by constant danger, accustomed to death and privation, to incredible toil and protracted isolation, for ever fronting the unknown and mysterious, they developed a reckless daring in their calling which can but awaken admiration. Little higher in grade than the naked savages with whom they so freely consorted, and among whom they often married, they yet lived and died Frenchmen, loyal to the traditions of their race, and ever responsive to any demand upon their patriotism.

Among these appeared leaders of a vastly different type. Some were ambitious fur traders, with financial influence at Montreal, and authority in the lodges — men shrewd, often unscrupulous, willing to risk much for gain. Soldiers and explorers rode the waters also, seeking new power for France, bold, adventurous men, clad in the light mail of their century, laughing at all peril, fighting to win new domain for their King, or at least a word of praise from his lips. And hither came also the Jesuit and Récollet priests, barefooted and emaciated, their purpose the salvation of the heathen, yielding up life gladly if only they might thus attain to martyrdom or rescue a soul from the fires of perdition. These were the three classes who led the advance into the wilderness, their helpers those half-savage *voyageurs* who wielded paddles and bore rifles at their order, their open doorway the innumerable water-courses ever inviting them onward. The story of their adventures, hardships, dangers, and exploits is as fascinating as romance, and from among them names have been written on the page of history — Marquette, Joliet, Du Lhut, La Salle, Tonty — never to be blotted out.

Long before land trails crossed the Illinois prairies the great natural highways of both Indian and white communication lay along the navigable streams. The discovered relics of lost races are unearthed in the river bottoms; the more ancient Indian villages were upon the banks of streams; the earliest white settlements crept slowly in beside the water-ways. The first Frenchmen came into the Illinois country by means of canoes, and for many a year comparatively little was definitely known regarding the land of the interior, away from the principal water-courses. These were the mainly marked features upon all the earlier French maps of the region, for along them flowed the fast increasing commerce in furs to far-away Montreal. The mission houses, the *voyageurs*' camps, the traders' stockades, the forts of palisaded logs, the little isolated French villages dotting the wide wilderness, were all located beside navigable streams, or along the shores of lakes. Ever it was the gleaming water-way — inviting the boat in Summer, the sled in Winter — that pointed the easier path through thousands of leagues of wooded desolation, to the semi-civilization of Lower Canada.

These open gateways leading into the Illinois country were both numerous and inviting. The great Lake of Michigan touched it upon the northeast, with portage of scarcely a mile leading to the southerly flow of the Des

Plaines, and that across an almost level prairie. When the *voyageur* had once dipped the sharp prow of his canoe in those silvery waters, no obstacle of land lay between him and the blue surge of the Mexican Gulf. Before him stretched, unvexed, almost unruffled, a thousand leagues of magnificent water-way, ever tending southward. As early as 1673 Marquette passed over this route, northward bound, with his fur-trading companion and four *engagés*, in birch-bark canoes, and ever after it was in constant use by the French. Along the entire western line rolled the vast Mississippi, with many a side-stream leading into it from the east, nearly all having their sources within easy portage of the great lakes. Of these the Wisconsin, by portage from the Fox, was early found the most convenient, and remained long an extensively used highway from Green Bay westward. Rock River was also utilized to some extent by the fur traders, but was never esteemed a popular route for the longer journey, although the Fox was thus considerably used. Far to the south the Ohio — *La Belle Rivière* of the French — bore many a brave burden along its gleaming waters, while adventurous prows pushed up the Wabash, the Kaskaskia, and numerous contributory streams. During the latter portion of the French military occupancy, the Ohio-Wabash route, with its easy portage to the Maumee, became quite a favorite for the transportation of troops destined for service along the English border, and in still later times this same Ohio proved a favorite gateway for inflowing American settlers from Virginia and the South. But during all the period of earliest exploration, the regime of the fur trader, and the one hundred and seventy years of French control, the most popular water route eastward to Canada followed the course of the Illinois. Its gentle current, and its total freedom from rapids, together with the easy portages to lake or to other streams, made it an ideal highway for boat travel, whether attained by way of the Des Plaines or the Kankakee.

It is somewhat peculiar in this connection to note that, while Marquette and Joliet on their return toward civilization in 1673 were guided by friendly Indians up the Des Plaines to the Chicago, and thence to the open lake but two miles away, six years later La Salle chose the longer, harder route leading into the Illinois country via the St. Joseph and the Kankakee. He had met Joliet since the return of the latter, and doubtless had learned their route from his own lips. He even passed down along the western shore of the great lake in a season of incessant storm, and possibly camped at the very mouth of the Chicago, yet amid intense hardships pressed on in his frail overloaded canoes entirely around the head of the lake to where he had appointed a rendezvous with Tonty on the river St. Joseph. Later the Des Plaines route became a favorite with both these hardy explorers, but their first entrance into the Illinois country was made by means of the narrow, swampy, reed-bordered Kankakee, along which for many miles the *voyageurs* scarcely found space in which to wield their paddles.

The mouth of the Chicago River was from earliest times an important spot, the natural gateway leading into the Illinois country, the key to the entire water-way system of the State. There are evidences that it was so recognized, not only by the Indians, but also by those unknown races occupying this territory in ages gone. The earlier white explorers were quick to perceive its many advantages. The Indians gathered there in large numbers at certain seasons of the year, engaged in fishing and barter, although it is hardly probable any permanent village was established. The French early built a hut there in which to rest on their frequent journeys — or possibly merely utilized the remains of that one erected by Marquette's *engagés* on the South Branch — and at times kept here a permanent establishment. La Salle, according to Mason, had a stockade here, with two men as garrison, as early as 1683, while a few years later the

ROCK RIVER, FROM BLACK HAWK'S WATCH TOWER

Jesuits built a palisaded station just west of the forks of the stream. There is an Indian rumor that La Salle's fort stood not far from the later site of Fort Dearborn. Tonty says M. de la Durantaye commanded there in 1685.

It is interesting to note the changes in nomenclature regarding the various Illinois water-ways. Few streams now bear the names originally bestowed, or those of record upon the earlier French maps. Lake Michigan is "Lac Mitchiganong, ou des Illinois"; Marquette called the Mississippi, "Rivière de la Conception"; the Missouri, the "Pekitanoui"; and the Ohio, the "Ouabouskiaou." He leaves the Wisconsin and the Illinois nameless. Another Jesuit map calls the Mississippi "Rivuiere Colbert," which is the name retained in Joliet's map as presented to Frontenac. In this latter, the Des Plaines is called "Rivière Divine." In his larger map appears for the first time the word "Messasipi." On the map prepared by Randin, this same stream is called, "Rivière Buade." The great map of those early days was that drawn by Franquelin, about 1680. Here the Mississippi is called "Missisipi ou Rivière Colbert"; the Missouri, "Grande Rivière des Emissourittes, ou Missourits"; the Illinois, "Rivière des Ilinois ou Macopins," also "Ilinese"; the Ohio, "Fleuve St. Louis," and "La Belle Rivière." The Illinois River had also been named "Rivière Seignelay," and was so called by Hennepin. The St. Joseph was "Rivière des Miamis"; Peoria Lake is occasionally referred to as "Lake Dauphin" as is also Lake Michigan; Kickapoo Creek was given its Indian name, "Ar-cary"; Chicago on the Franquelin map is spelled "Che-ke-gou"; the Wabash is the "Ouabache," and yet earlier the "St. Jerome."

Along these streams, and upon the storm-lashed lake, many an odd craft, bearing many a strange company, invaded this Illinois wilderness. The earlier *voyageurs*, those first French explorers, whether in priestly vesture bearing uplifted crucifix, or in soldier garb with clanking sword at heel, pressed forward down these unknown water-ways in the lightly built, narrow canoes, such as were used by the Algonquin Indian tribes of Canada. This crank boat, a mere layer of birch bark or of skin stretched over thin framework, capable of upbearing no more than four men and propelled by paddles, was easily transported from stream to stream through forests or over rocky bluffs, and with sharp stern and bow, was quickly controlled by skilled hands in rapids and turbulent water. It was peculiarly a development of river travel through a wilderness country, yet these daring navigators never hesitated to press boldly forth upon the mighty lakes in the stormy Winter season, coasting the rocky shores of Huron, and the wave-lashed beaches of Michigan. Desperate tales of wintry voyaging in such frail canoes have come down to us, and La Salle and Tonty braved more than once terrible peril and suffering along the watery miles of storm-lashed sea between Chicago and the mouth of the St. Joseph. A marked disadvantage in such craft was inability to transport any considerable quantity of provisions or merchandise. Early in their journeys the *voyageurs* were compelled to rely on their rifles for food, on audacity for safety. Then the delicate structure of their canoes was a constant menace; the grazing of a rock, the rasping against a stony bottom, involved delay for repairs. Even on the peaceful waters of the Illinois, Tonty is constantly telling of damages sustained by his canoes.

Yet contracted, frail, uncomfortable, and unsafe as such craft seem, they were sent sternly against the current, or dancing down swift streams propelled by the lusty strokes of skilled Canadian *voyageurs*. Rapids were shot like the flight of an arrow, storms braved in the open sea, and thousands of leagues of dark, unknown water explored and given to the world. Again and again the same delicate canoe would safely thread the intricate water-ways leading from

Montreal to the far-off Mississippi, steering its devious course along Ontario, up the black-fringed Ottawa, coasting the rocky shores of Huron, past the little mission station at Michillimackinac, down stormy Michigan, until at last its venturesome prow would feel the peaceful plashing of the Illinois. It involved months of travel, of peril, of intense loneliness, with the great savage wilderness stretching away unknown, mysterious, on every side, the weary *voyageurs* ever gazing forth on black tangled forests, wide, lorn prairies, or the dreary desolation of uncharted seas.

It was thus that the priest Marquette, his face already stamped with coming death, accompanied by the rugged Joliet and their *engagés*, drifted downward from Green Bay, along the Fox, the Wisconsin, and the Mississippi, every mile opening before them the unknown, every curve of the stream hiding, perchance, some unsuspected peril which would leave them to perish miserably in that gloomy wilderness. It was thus La Salle felt his uncertain way down the reed-strewn Kankakee, along a stream so narrow the slight boat could hardly be forced onward, and it was in just such a canoe he made again and again those heart-breaking trips to repair his fortunes in Canada. Tonty, Boisrondet, Hennepin, all those whose gallant names yet linger in this fascinating story of the Illinois country, trusted their all to such frail boats, and pushed their narrow prows up many an unnamed stream, seeking thus new pathways into the unknown desolation surrounding them. Such daring cost lives in plenty, and many a reckless *voyageur* sank beneath rapid and wave; but the dangers halted none who crept forth alive. What could be more pathetic than the story of Louis Joliet's long and dangerous voyage eastward with his report of discoveries of the far Mississippi? He had been wonderfully successful along all his journey, only to meet with serious accident almost in sight of home. At the foot of the rapids of La Chine, just above Montreal, his canoe caught in an eddy, was capsized and two of his men and an Indian boy drowned, while all of his papers were lost and his own life preserved as by a miracle. He writes to Frontenac: "I had escaped every peril from the Indians; I had passed forty-two rapids; and was on the point of disembarking, full of joy at the success of so long and difficult an enterprise,— when my canoe upset, after all the danger seemed over. I lost two men, and my box of papers, within sight of the first French settlements, which I had left almost two years before."

Later, in this same period of exploration, heavier boats were adopted for use on such broad streams as the Illinois and Mississippi. The large vessel projected by La Salle, the building of which was begun at Fort Crèvecœur, was never completed, owing to the mutiny in Tonty's command. But boats more capacious and stronger, some of hollowed logs, others of heavy skins extended over strong framework, and possibly a few of flat-boat form built from rude planking, were constructed soon after a permanent fortification had been erected at Starved Rock. The increasing trade in furs made such boats a necessity. The canoe, however, remained all through the French regime the favorite for long rapid journeys over all kinds of water-ways. Tonty, on his marvellous trip to the Gulf of Mexico in the vain hope of finding La Salle, used a wooden boat, but his entire journey was made upon broad water. In narrow, shallow streams, like the Kankakee or the Rock or the Fox, paddles were far more serviceable than oars, and when portages were long and numerous the lighter the boat the better. Later, during the French occupancy, troops were frequently transported along the Mississippi and Illinois, between Fort Chartres and Detroit, on huge blunt-nosed flat-boats, operated by sweeps, specially constructed for the purpose. On the larger rivers these had to be warped up against the strong current by means of ropes, a most toilsome process. Such troop-boats were also despatched eastward, especially during the French and Indian War, from Fort Chartres by way of the Ohio, Wabash, and Maumee. Captain Aubray made this journey in March, 1758, with seventeen large boats laden with soldiers and provisions. With the coming into the country of American pioneers, the old-time canoes rapidly disappeared from off the water-ways, and a broader type of wooden boat was substituted. Many settlers arrived in huge log arks, sitting high above the water, laden with household goods, and propelled and guided by long sweeps. These, oftentimes made bullet-proof as a defence against savages along the shores, were easily floated down the Ohio, but the sturdy oarsmen had many a difficult struggle forcing their unwieldy vessels northward against the sweeping current of the Mississippi. Nevertheless, toil conquered difficulties, and not a few of these arks penetrated the water-ways as far northward as Peoria. Rafts were also occasionally used for journeying down stream, and for many years the unwieldy keel-boat was very much in evidence. Many still live who have voyaged on such with produce to New Orleans.

In imagination let us stand at a curve in the Illinois where the eye can follow in wide sweep the gleaming waters of that noble stream, surging downward to its meeting with the Mississippi. Just above, leaning far out across the water, stands a huge tree, the gnarled trunk and distorted limbs evidencing age, a tree which, local tradition claims, was old when red men ruled this fair domain. Resting thus, dreaming idly of those far-away days of history-making and struggle, let there sweep before us a panorama of dissolving views, the sights this old sentinel tree has witnessed in the long centuries of silence. The representatives of races dead and forgotten, with strange faces, peculiar dress, and odd-shaped water-craft, come out from the early morning mist and drift slowly by. Their language is guttural, unknown; their ancient weapons, heavily tipped with copper, shimmer in the sunlight. Scarcely have these rounded the bend below, disappearing for ever from this land which was once their own, when the Indian comes, a stalwart bronze figure, taciturn and silent, his facial outline strong with lines of cruelty and savage instincts. His is a bark canoe, cleaving the waters like a wild duck; beside him rests his spear, flint-tipped; at his back hangs the bow, with quiver of arrows, while his hands grasp the dripping paddle. Like a flash he also is gone, but others of his great race follow swiftly after; solitary hunters, families migrating to distant villages, traders eager for barter among neighboring tribes; war-parties, bedecked and painted, whooping madly as they urge their frail boats forward in a wild race for the goal. But these are not all the same; their dress, their hair, their feathers and war-paint, their very cries, tell of a constant change in tribes, even in races — Illinois, Miamis, Sacs and Foxes, Winnebagoes, Pottawattomies, Kickapoos, Iroquois, and many others, take turns in gliding past in grim and savage procession. But wait; here is something new creeping up against the stream from around that distant point below. There are two boats, canoes unlike those others, battered and stained by months of severe service, and they hug the shore closely to keep away from the sweep of the current. The paddles rise and fall as though the arms wielding them were wearied with long toil. Yet the occupants are different from all those others who have been passing this way for unknown centuries; they are not savages — they are of the white race. As they pass silently, take one glimpse and remember the picture — three men to each boat, two at the paddles, the third resting. Mark him with the broad shoulders and dark beard — it is Louis Joliet; and that other, that striking face, clean-shaven, pale, the deep-set eyes aglow with interest, the thin form hidden beneath a shapeless black robe — it is the Jesuit Marquette. Like shadows, yet clearly foretelling a coming new life to this land of wilderness, they disappear

A HISTORIC WATER-WAY

THE ILLINOIS RIVER, FROM BUFFALO ROCK

into the dim north, and once again floats past the old Indian procession. The obscuring curtain of savagery descends upon river and bluff.

Suddenly hundreds of canoes hurry southward, the paddlers working feverishly with many an affrighted glance cast backward over their shoulders. They are Illinois, and in their boats are huddled women and children crazed with fear. A laden canoe grounds on a mud-bank out yonder, but the others make no pause for rescue. With plashing paddles, and shrill cries of terror, they round the bend below. Scarcely has the last laggard disappeared, when down sweep others — canoes crowded with painted warriors, whooping like fiends, the wild wolves of the Iroquois. As the merciless hawk drops down upon his prey, they come, crushing the disabled boat, and with savage, cruel blows killing every occupant, yet scarcely pausing in their mad pursuit of the fugitives beyond. The days pass, the river rolls onward, silent and desolate. But watch; a solitary canoe swings suddenly into sight, tightly hugging the dark shore shadows. It holds three men, and the anxious faces peering forth from beneath the broad hat-brims are white. Mark that man in the prow, him with the strong, manly face, the stalwart figure, the clothing half soldier, half *coureur de bois* — it is Robert de la Salle. And others come, glance curiously up at this old tree crowning the bluff, and pass on into the silent mystery of the years, and the wilderness. Life and death, hope and despair, the red race and the white, the Indian, the French, the English, the American, each in turn, or intermingled, as the wheel of history revolves, go floating by. The one-armed Tonty, swarthy of face but white of heart, ever the dauntless soldier; Boisrondet, hardly more than a boy; Hennepin, in his gray robe; Durantaye, the first commandant at Chicago, and later still, many a dashing French gallant, and blunt English soldier. More and more the old water-way throbs with life, an ever changing and renewing life, civilization forcing barbarism backward with recurring waves. Priest and soldier, fur trader and settler, press back and forth, each in turn fulfilling that mission with which he is entrusted; the frail canoe changes to the rude boat, the flat scow, the top-heavy ark, the lunging raft, the laden keel-boat, the modern steamer. War and peace rule in turn these sparkling waters, and through it all the old tree gazes down in silence, while the historic river of the Illinois sweeps ceaselessly forward to pour its waters into that greater stream, ever hurrying onward to the Gulf. Who can stand upon its banks unmoved by memory of what it has been — of that dim past when early civilization battled with savagery; of faces and names for ever associated with these silvery waters through historic years? Teeming with romance, every wave a messenger of some forgotten sacrifice in the brave days of old, rolls on still in peerless majesty that ancient highway of the prairies, the historic Illinois.

CHAPTER VIII

OLD PRAIRIE TRAILS AND THEIR TRAVELLERS

IN those years before white men came to Illinois, as well as during the entire period of sparse French occupancy, the virgin prairies of the country, roamed over by wild beasts and as wild men, were crisscrossed by innumerable Indian trails, leading either from village to village, or else to some more distant point of interest. Some of these were distinctly war trails, pointing the way direct toward distant hostile tribes or to some doomed white settlement along the far-off eastern border; others were the outgrowth of the chase, or the bartering of furs amid distant lodges; while the more important, traversed oftentimes by entire villages in their migrations, were the established routes of the aborigines, and remained much the same during many generations of constant wilderness travel.

The Indian mode of journeying when on foot was always in single file, their war parties oftentimes stretching for a great distance in straggling procession. As a result of this peculiarity, their trails leading across the country, if much used, soon cut deeply into the soft, alluvial soil of the prairie, leaving a plainly marked and narrow track, worn by the hundreds of moccasined feet passing that way. As some trails were thus used for possibly centuries of wilderness travel, and by many different tribes, not infrequently this gash became so deeply cut as to make travelling difficult, and consequently others were started close at hand, thus forming parallel tracks running for miles side by side. Like great uncoiled snakes these trails wound here and there across the level plains, and over the low hills, now skirting the edge of a dark forest, or plunging into its depths, here dipping into some silent ravine, or running beside the margin of lake or stream, yet ever pointing directly, and by the most feasible route, toward the selected destination, however far away.

The natural instinct of the savages as path finders was beyond all question, and those main trails which in an early day intersected the Illinois country, so far as they can be traced by modern research, exhibit few mistakes in judgment. The large rivers were avoided so far as possible, but, when they must be met, were crossed at convenient and shallow fords; the high and rocky hills stretching along the southern portion of the State were penetrated by means of their natural passes, while, wherever the trail led, the best of camping-grounds were always found convenient to the end of a day's travel. Several different points within the limits of the present State appear to have been favorite Indian meeting-places, and were seemingly used as such by more than one tribe, judging from the number and widely diverging trails leading thereto. The most clearly marked spot in this respect is Danville. From here, as a centre, narrow Indian paths branched off like the spokes of a wheel to every point of the compass. The Peoria Lake, or rather the *dêtroit* between the lakes, was likewise a favored meeting-place for various tribes, possibly for fishing as well as purposes of barter, while Rock Island and the mouth of the Chicago River were alike largely frequented. From Shawneetown in the far south, numerous well-worn trails led both north and west. During the days of Fort St. Louis, Starved Rock became a centre for widely diverging trails, traversed by many tribes.

Nor, with all these years which have passed since wandering, moccasined feet thus wore away the soft prairie sod, have evidences of these early aboriginal trails totally vanished. The lines were cut, not only across the dreary wilderness, but equally deep have they been impressed upon history.

In the very earliest of those old days of struggle and advance they became the prized inheritance of the pioneers. When venturesome settlers first began to stray cautiously forth from beside those streams, along whose inviting banks they had first made homes, the Indian trails became their natural guides into the unknown interior. They pointed the easier path through the Ozarks, and to spots of fertility and beauty far beyond. Following them, daring adventurers were led far out beyond the uttermost frontier, and thus is accounted for many an isolated settlement, seemingly a mere pin-prick amid the surrounding wilderness. Many of these trails were utilized for years by the earlier settlers as convenient means of communication; not a few afterwards became mail routes, and later still, stage routes, and finally, by the law of long usage, were transformed into permanent roads, which, ignoring all the rigidity of section lines and the authority of government surveys, swept independently straight across the country as the crow flies, as unerring in direction as when first traced thereon by some long dead and forgotten savage. So to-day, in many portions of this State, one can journey for miles along some old-time Indian trail, which would be alive with thrilling memories of that dead past could it only be induced to tell its long-forgotten story. Even railroads speed through the Ozarks, and across the open prairie, under such savage guidance, and passengers are whirled past scenes of barbaric and historic interest, could the rocks only speak, or the old forest trees give voice.

And what strange scenes of war and peace, what oddly attired passing travellers, what peculiar mingling of past and present, some of these old-time trails have witnessed in the speechless years gone by! It would be indeed a motley gathering could the ghosts of the trail again walk, and revisit those populous prairies. The story of them to-day, even in those little glimpses which have descended through the obscuring years, is most fascinating; yet the colors are sadly faded, the trooping men and women but so many spectres, unnamed and unknown. The old Sauk trail; the path leading from the far-away French villages on the Mississippi to Detroit; from St. Louis to Vincennes; and that dim trace extending from the mouth of the Des Moines to the Peoria Lake — all alike are historic and mysterious. About them cluster picturesque memories, legends innumerable, tragedies unspeakable; hardly a mile but has its story of daring endeavor and wild border life. Let us picture, if we can, some of the many who in those other years have passed this way — the lonely Indian hunter, with his primitive weapons, fearful lest any step might plunge him into danger; the entire village on the move to new territory, the grave warriors stalking on ahead, the laden squaws trailing behind, the hardy ponies dragging the tepees, their long poles scratching up the soft turf; the painted and bedecked war party, armed and silent, skulking through the shadows; the black-robed Jesuit, counting his beads as he treads the weary miles, his one thought the salvation of souls; the wandering *coureur de bois*, careless of comfort, and ever at home in the wilderness, singing as he toils; the marching troops under the yellow flag of Spain, the French *fleur de lis*, the cross of St. George, and the American Stars and Stripes; the inflowing settlers, the gay, merry-making French, the grave-faced Americans, and amid them all the sombre-clad nuns of the Ursulines. All this these trails have seen. Here struggled and toiled the early immigrants, seeking spot for a new home in the wilderness; here the dauntless Kentucky hunters passed, their anxious eyes marking each dark covert in search for some skulking enemy; here the infuriated Rangers swept along in hasty pursuit of their savage foe.

History holds in her iron hand no more picturesque story than these trails could reveal were their guarded secrets known. Here met the nations of the Old World and the New — Indian and white, Spaniard, Frenchman, Briton, and

American; priest and nun, soldier and adventurer, settler and outlaw, fair patrician women, and outpourings from the Salpêtrière and other hospitals of Paris. They have echoed to bursts of merry laughter, and to cries of agony and implorations of despair. Great soldiers, famous border-men, mighty warriors and chiefs, have helped to wear away this sod. Pontiac and Black Hawk, Keokuk and Tecumseh, Gomo and Little Bird, have all been here. Marquette and Joliet, La Salle and Tonty, Du Lhut, Clark, Renault, Boisbriant, Dubuque, Crogan, Taylor, Harrison, have all in turn borne part in their forgotten history — have seen and suffered, toiled and conquered, along these trails of the long ago. Here captives — agonized women and children — have been hurried to distant villages, and a fate of slavery; along here men have been driven under the merciless whip to the fiendish torture of the stake. What suffering and hardship, what yearning and heartsickness, what speechless agony and brave hopes these silent miles have witnessed! And amid it all, bold and undaunted hearts were thus steadily shaping the destinies of a nation, laying the foundations of a mighty State, while through the wilderness, and along these blotted traces, they bore their messages of hope and despair, of peaceful greeting or warlike defiance.

Among these earlier trails marking the Illinois country, both Indian and white, although as a rule the latter utilized the experience of the former, it is only necessary to trace a few of the more important historically. That we are enabled to do this with some degree of accuracy is owing to the careful map-making of Rufus Blanchard.

While not the oldest by many years, the Sauk trail is in some respects one of the most interesting and clearly marked. It formed the pathway along which each recurring year the Sacs and Foxes travelled from their great village on the banks of the Mississippi to Malden in Canada, for the purpose of receiving their annuities from the English government.

It was what might be denominated as a broad trail, the large number of men, women, and children passing along it, with ponies dragging their tepees and household equipments, leaving a wide mark across the prairies. This trail followed as nearly a straight line eastward as the nature of the country would permit, and as a great portion of the territory traversed was level, or nearly so, there are reaches where modern section line roads actually follow this old trace for miles. Then the original pathfinder would meet with some early, but now surmountable, obstacle, and swerve aside to avoid it. This broad trail commenced its long, snake-like course at the present town of Milan, near the mouth of Rock River, crossed the more northern portion of Henry County, probably touching the present city of Geneseo, and then followed the pleasant valley of Green River until well into Bureau County, where it entered upon the higher, rolling prairie. The line swerved here more northeasterly, entering the present limits of La Salle County some two miles south of Mendota, and, crossing the Fox River close to the town of Sheridan, swept over the southern portion of Kendall County,— where the old Maramech trails converged, — finding opportunity to ford the Des Plaines slightly below Joliet, and finally traversed Cook County, about two miles north of its present southern limit, until it entered Indiana. It must have formed a sight well worth the seeing, this annual migration of Indians across the unbroken prairies. These were both large tribes, their confederation peculiarly strong, and no doubt they straggled out for many miles along the way as they marched, even while keeping close enough to each other to ward off hostile attack. As they thus passed through country hunted over by both the Pottawattomies and the Kickapoos, it is hardly likely they always escaped without paying toll of blood. As late as 1883, it is said by competent observers, the marks of this passage were still visible in many places, where the prairie sod had remained undisturbed by the plough.

A SCENE ON THE OLD FRONTIER

SHOWING INDIAN TRAIL, AND BUFFALO HERD GRAZING

The old villages of the Peorias, which when the white men first came were established at the mouth of the Des Moines River in Iowa, were from a very early age directly connected by trail with the populous villages of the Kaskaskias — both being of the Illinois stock — situated upon the great bend of the Illinois River, near the present location of Utica. This trail was quite largely travelled by Indian trading parties, and probably at some time formed a portion of a direct line of savage communication, extending between the Mississippi and the Chicago portage. It was considerably used during the French occupancy of the country by the Jesuits, and by French traders settled near the Peoria Lake. As early as 1720 there was a French trading-post on Illinois soil opposite the mouth of the Des Moines. For several years this path was believed to be that followed by Marquette and Joliet on their return eastward, but later investigations have apparently decided that their return was made directly up the Illinois by canoe from its mouth. This old trail held its course across the present counties of Hancock, Warren, Knox, Stark, and Bureau, but so far as known has left no existing trace.

The overland trail between Kaskaskia and Detroit, laid out and used by the French for both trading and military purposes, was very early established. The date when it was first passed over by whites has not been recorded, but it was probably as early as 1705 or 1706. It was undoubtedly formed largely by the uniting together of shorter original Indian trails, although the necessity of transportation would cause white travellers to avoid obstacles to which an Indian would remain entirely indifferent. This trail was in almost constant use for years, wagons even being driven on it, and considerable detachments of troops marching its entire distance. To this day it remains, along part of its course, a legal highway in continual use. As originally laid out it ran almost directly northeast across the State from Kaskaskia to Danville, bisecting the Counties of Randolph, Washington, Marion, Effingham, Cumberland, Coles, Edgar, and Vermilion. The present cities of Elkhorn, Salem, and Charleston lie upon the old route. Rivers of any considerable size seem to have been successfully avoided, although smaller streams were crossed in plenty, Salt Creek and the upper waters of the Embarras being of most importance. For the greater distance in Illinois the line of passage led across high, level prairie land, dotted over with groves, the banks of the streams being generally heavily wooded. It must in that day have been a beautiful country in all its virgin freshness, and as the early French residents were usually on friendly terms with the Indian tribes along the way — the Piankishaws and Miamis, — there no doubt passed over its winding course many a merry party to whom the long trip proved a continual pleasure. Much of romantic interest clusters about the memory of this old-time track across the wilderness. In those far-off days of French ascendency, when Fort de Chartres was the centre of French power in the great valley, and the commandant of the Illinois country ruled as a little king, this old trail witnessed many a gay and glittering cavalcade. Here passed fair maids and merry matrons of France, not a few in the ruffled petticoat and high-heeled shoes of fashion; beside them gallant soldiers rode with bow and smile, their lace-trimmed uniforms gorgeous in the sunshine. Courtiers of the French court, friends of the great Louis, travelled these sombre miles of wilderness, passing the time with quip and fancy, while many an adventurer, his sole wealth the glittering sword at his side, pressed forward hopefully to his fate in the West. Troops, travel-stained and weary, marched it on their way to battle against the English outposts; wild raiding parties swept over it through the dense night shadows, and many a despatch-bearer, lying low upon his horse's neck, speeded day and night with his precious message. Would that the dead lips might open to tell again the thousand forgotten stories haunting every camping spot, every shaded nook, through which the old trail ran.

But the hour came when the French power grew weak, and all this fair country fell into English hands, and they in turn were compelled to deliver up their brief authority to American bordermen. The trail of George Rogers Clark, made in 1778 from near the site of Fort Massac on the banks of the Ohio River to Kaskaskia, marks an epoch in American history of transcendent importance. Nothing ever occurring in the West has resulted in greater permanent benefit to the people of the United States. In later years this faint track became a largely used trail for the early white settlers, pouring in by way of the Ohio. It was long a regular line of communication between Golconda and the settlements in the American Bottom, travelled by many a hardy immigrant into this new land. A puzzled guide caused Clark to wander somewhat ; and to improve the trail by straightening it for a small portion of the way, was a task ably performed in 1821 by Mr. Worthen. A well-marked trail, laid out by the French and distinguished by red signs painted on trees, ran, via the mouth of the Ohio, between Massac and Chartres. Clark's failure to use this was doubtless through fear of discovery on the way.

Clark, with his little band of Kentucky riflemen, left the Ohio River, close to Fort Massac, at the mouth of a small creek just above where the city of Metropolis now stands, and plunged out into what was to him an unknown wilderness. He aimed at first somewhat northeasterly, seeking possibly thus to avoid serious entanglement in the Ozark Hills, until his column had reached to nearly the centre of what is now Pope County, when he swerved more westerly, his course becoming, because of poor guidance, decidedly irregular as they traversed what is now Williamson

County. Their path led across the present site of Marion, whence the direction was straight north until the Perry County line had been crossed. Clark was by this time directly east of Kaskaskia, and his march to that place became as straight as natural obstacles would permit.

The following year he possessed the decided advantage of having competent French guides for his march toward Vincennes. These led him along a path which, for at least a large portion of the way, had been frequently travelled before, it being a connecting trail used by traders since about the year 1710, when Post Vincennes was first established. The mail route between these places, which was opened in 1805, chose a more northern course, thus avoiding the necessity of crossing those streams which gave so much trouble to Clark. This trail, thus utilized by that gallant band of frontiersmen in their desperate midwinter march through the wilderness, and along which they toiled and suffered for so great a purpose in the making of the history of Illinois, ought to be traced with care and marked by suitable monuments along its entire course. To-day its direction can only be approximately given, as the best modern authorities differ somewhat widely regarding details. This much, however, we know beyond probable dispute — it led, in somewhat irregular course, because of natural difficulties, through Randolph County, probably crossing into the northwestern corner of Perry a little west of the present village of Craig, touching Washington County in its southeastern corner, and fording Beaucoup Creek a few miles east of Radom. Jefferson County was crossed very nearly at its centre, the column passing perhaps a mile south of the present city of Mount Vernon, later entering Wayne County close to Keene's Station, just east of which they forded Skillet Fork. Here the course became more northerly, the trail passing some five or six miles north of Fairfield, and striking the overflowing waters of the Little Wabash not far from the immediate vicinity of Maple Grove, in the extreme northwest corner of Edwards County. Richland was crossed near the present site of Parkersburg, the Bon Pas River forded near where the town of the same name now stands, and Lawrence County was entered somewhat east of Henryville. The swollen waters of the Embarras were probably first encountered some four or five miles south of Lawrenceville, from which point these undaunted bordermen waded and swam until they attained the junction of the Wabash.

Crossing over this same territory to-day, driving easily across the high rolling prairies, the seemingly level plains, and through pleasant groves, descending into wide, well-drained valleys, and crossing the slowly flowing streams by means of substantial bridges, the traveller can hardly imagine the innumerable difficulties, the unspeakable hardships, surrounding every mile of that early march. There can come to him scarcely a fair conception of what a freshet meant to this country in that day of the long ago, or of the immense downrush of water which rendered this wilderness advance one of the greatest military achievements of the century in which it took place. Only men of iron, long trained to combat all the hardships of the frontier, animated by the highest conception of duty, and commanded and inspired by an indomitable leader, could ever have accomplished it and gone forward to grim battle at its end. Illinois can well afford to mark with enduring memorials that course along which they so sternly struggled to final victory and the winning of an empire to the United States.

Other trails leading in various directions through this Illinois country are of less historic and romantic interest, and their story may be outlined in few words. One of the most interesting is that lonely track left across the northern counties by James Watson Webb, in 1822. At that time, being an officer stationed at Fort Dearborn at the mouth of the Chicago River (rebuilt in 1816), he volunteered to bear tidings of a threatened Indian uprising to the unsuspecting garrison stationed at Fort Armstrong, which stood at the lower extremity of Rock Island looking down the majestic Mississippi. It was in the midst of a severe Winter, and he travelled alone, without a guide, through unknown territory roamed over by hostile savages. His first point of destination was La Sallier's trading-post, situated on the south bank of Rock River, about on the line now existing between Lee and Ogle Counties, a few miles north of Dixon. This had just been established, and was the sole point of civilization in all that country. From here Webb's course was laid almost directly to the Mississippi. Reaching that river in the vicinity of Fulton, he proceeded down the eastern bank until he arrived in safety at Rock Island, and delivered his warning. It was a most perilous journey, not only on account of the hostiles haunting every mile of it, but also the natural dangers of the way, greatly accented by the severe season during which it was accomplished. The territory covered by this solitary traveller included Cook, Du Page, Kane, De Kalb, Lee, Whiteside, and Rock Island Counties. On his return trip Webb chose a more southern route as being safer, crossing Henry and Bureau Counties, until he reached the Illinois River, when the water-ways were followed back to the mouth of the Chicago.

The route of Governor Edwards into the Indian country during the War of 1812 started at Camp Russell, just above the present site of Edwardsville, in Madison County, and passed directly north through Carlinville, Macoupin County, sweeping somewhat east of where Springfield now stands, and then led about three miles west of the present city of Lincoln. Just across the southern line of Tazewell County, near the present town of Centre, they discovered their first Kickapoo village, and destroyed it. From this point their march was almost directly north, until they came to the second village along the eastern bluffs of the Illinois, which after a skirmish was also destroyed. This must have occurred not far from the post-office of Spring Bay. Hopkins's rather disgraceful raid with his mounted Kentucky riflemen, from Fort Harrison on the Wabash, expecting to coöperate with Edwards's column, succeeded in crossing Edgar, Vermilion, Champaign, and Ford Counties. Livingston was penetrated possibly as far as the town of Strawn, where the sight of distant raging prairie fires caused the soldiers to mutiny and retreat.

General Howard's more important advance into the Indian country the following year started from the same point as did Governor Edwards's, but pursued an entirely different route. His command followed the course of the Mississippi until opposite Fort Madison, Iowa, when it struck directly southeast across Hancock, Macoupin, and Fulton Counties to the Illinois River, opposite the site of Havana. From here, cutting across the sharper bends in the stream, the general course of the river was followed until Gomo's village, where Chillicothe now stands, was reached and destroyed.

The Fort Clark and Wabash trail was a well-travelled road after about the year 1815, and was probably used long before that date. It led from the site of Terre Haute, Indiana, to the north shore of Peoria Lake, and was extensively used by immigrants, as well as traders. Kellogg's trail was the first overland route between Peoria and Galena. It was laid out by an early settler of that name in 1825, and was heavily travelled for many years. It crossed Marshall, Bureau, Lee, Ogle, Stephenson, and Jo Daviess Counties. The first mail route in the State was established in 1805, extending from St. Louis to Vincennes, with a branch to Kaskaskia. It crossed the present sites of Belleville, Carlyle, Salem, Maybury, and Lawrenceville, and much of the road is still preserved. The second ran from where Mount Carmel now stands south to Shawneetown, and was placed in operation in 1807. Chicago possessed a mail route running south to Danville in 1832, and one west to Dixon in 1834. Ottawa and St. Charles were thus connected as early as 1830, and Galena was reached via the Dixon route in 1834. Criss-crossing the State were many other trails of less importance, yet all alike holding much of interest to those who desire information about early frontier life. The old roads growing out of these dim tracks across the wilderness were the arteries through which flowed the life blood of Illinois.

CHAPTER IX

THE FRENCH SETTLEMENTS

THE establishment by La Salle of Fort St. Louis on the summit of Starved Rock attracted to that immediate neighborhood a number of adventurous Frenchmen, *voyageurs*, *coureurs de bois*, soldiers, fur traders, and priests. Some of these were accompanied by women of their own race, or were afterwards joined by such, while others established at least temporary homes by contracting alliances with Indian squaws. This post remained in existence from 1682 until at least 1702, when Tonty seems to have finally abandoned it, and gone south. During those twenty years this changeable population of natural wanderers established small trading-posts at various points convenient to tributary streams, resulting in a considerable development of the fur trade, while the indefatigable priests erected many a rude chapel of logs throughout the near-by wilderness wherein they sought to gather closely their dusky flocks. Yet all this bore little semblance to permanent settlement, nor did it endure any length of time beyond the abandonment of the protecting fort.

The oldest permanent settlement by Europeans, not only in Illinois, but in the entire Mississippi valley, must be credited to Kaskaskia, or, more properly perhaps, Notre Dame de Cascasquias, which was located on the west bank some six miles above the mouth of the river bearing that name, and within the limits of the present county of Randolph. As was commonly the case along the French frontier it was first an Indian village, then a missionary station, but slowly gathered to it a vagrant white population. The original mission from which this later settlement sprung, had been established with the early visit of Père Marquette to the great village of the Illinois (likewise called Kaskaskia), on the river of that name, but was removed when the discomfited tribes fled southward for safety from their enemies. Fathers Gravier and Marest, the latter the priest then in charge at the Illinois town, directed the change which was effected some time prior to 1700, although the exact date is unknown. Marest remained with them in their new home, but was afterwards succeeded by Fathers Binneteau and Pinet. These were all Jesuits. The latter established the mission and village of Cahokia, sixty miles farther north, and was peculiarly successful in his Indian labors, the rude chapel built soon proving too small to contain those seeking his ministrations. The tribes directly under his charge were the Tamaroas and Cahokias. Father Binneteau remained at the original post, and proved himself a zealous missionary. The duties of his office compelling him to accompany his flock of Kaskaskias on one of their long hunting trips to the upland plains of the Mississippi, he met his death. Now stifled in the tall grass, now panting with thirst on the arid prairie, parched by day with heat, and at night lying on the ground exposed to chilling dews, he was seized with a mortal fever, and passed away in true martyrdom. Only a little later his companion priest, Father Pinet, also died.

But however dangerous the work or desperate the hardships, there was never lack of volunteers among these soldiers of the Cross. Father Marest, who had previous to his Illinois labors been telling the Christ story to the ice-bound denizens of the Hudson Bay country, came down the streams from the northward and took up again the heavy burdens of this Illinois mission. A glimpse of what his duties involved appears in his correspondence, where he writes:

"Our life is spent in roaming through thick woods, in clambering over hills, in paddling canoes across lakes and rivers, to catch a poor savage whom we can neither tame by teachings nor caresses."

On Good Friday, 1711, he started for the village of the Peorias, and in his description of his journey writes:

"I departed, having nothing about me but my crucifix and breviary, being accompanied by only two savages, who might abandon me from levity, or might fly through fear of enemies. The terror of these vast, uninhabitable regions, in which for twelve days not a single soul was seen, almost took away my courage. This was a journey wherein there was no village, no bridge, no ferry-boat, no house, no beaten path; and over boundless prairies, intersected by rivulets and rivers, through forests and thickets filled with briars and thorns, through marshes in which we sometimes plunged to the girdle."

Early in the eighteenth century he was joined in his labors by Father Mermet, who had previously founded a separate mission on the Ohio at the site of Fort Massac. Mermet was one of the most remarkable men who ever buried their talents in the wilderness inspired by religious enthusiasm. He became the very soul of the mission at Kaskaskia, and the influence of his life and work was felt throughout the entire Illinois country. To show the condition of the Jesuit mission, as well as a pen-picture of the growing French settlements, we can do no better than quote from Father Charlevoix, who visited there in 1721. He writes:

"We lay last night in the village of the Cahokias and Tamaroas, two Illinois tribes which have been united, and compose no very numerous canton. This village is situated on a very small river which runs from the east, and has no water except in the Spring. On this account we had to walk half a league before we could get to our cabins. I was astonished that such a poor situation had been selected when there were so many good ones. But I was told the Mississippi washed the foot of the village when it was built; that in three years it had shifted its course half a league farther to the west, and that they were now thinking of changing their habitation, which is no great affair among these Indians. I passed the night with the missionaries, who are two ecclesiastics from the Seminary of Quebec, formerly my disciples, but they must now be my masters. Yesterday I arrived at Kaskaskia about nine o'clock. The Jesuits here have a very flourishing mission, which has lately been divided into two. The most numerous one is on the banks of the Mississippi, of which two Jesuits have the spiritual direction. Half a league below stands Fort Chartres, about the distance of a musket-shot from the river. The French are now beginning to settle the country between the fort and the first mission. Four leagues farther, and about a league from the river, is a large village, inhabited by the French, who are almost all Canadians, and have a Jesuit for their curate. The second village of the Illinois lies farther up the country."

The growth of the French population was slow and uncertain, while the wandering character of the men, principally *voyageurs* and fur hunters, tended to constant change with little desire for permanent improvement. Captain Pitman, who visited the Illinois country as late as 1766, during the term of British occupancy, described the condition of the towns as they then appeared. Of Kaskaskia, which contained about one hundred families of French and English, many of the original French inhabitants having gone to St. Louis, he writes:

"It is the most considerable settlement in the country of the Illinois, as well from its number of inhabitants as from its advantageous situation. . . . Mons. Paget was the first who introduced water mills in this country, and he constructed a very fine one on the river Cascasquias, which was both for grinding corn and sawing boards. It lies about one mile from the village. The mill proved fatal to him, he being killed as he was working it with two negroes, by a party of Cherokees, in the year 1764. The principal buildings are the Church and Jesuit's house which has a small chapel adjoining it; these, as well as some other houses in the village, are built of stone, and, considering this part of the world,

THE SITE OF OLD KASKASKIA

FROM A PRESENT-DAY PHOTOGRAPH

make a very good appearance. The Jesuit's plantation consisted of two hundred and forty arpents (an arpent is 85-100 of an acre) of cultivated land, a very good stock of cattle, and a brewery, which was sold by the French commandant after the country was ceded to the English, in consequence of the suppression of the Order. Mons. Beauvais was the purchaser, who is the richest of the English subjects in this country; he keeps eighty slaves; he furnishes 86,000 weight of flour to the King's magazine, which was only part of the harvest he reaped in one year."

The French settlements along the lower Mississippi consisted of several small towns within a comparatively small radius, of which Kaskaskia was the centre and chief, as well as the oldest. In all save locality they were much alike, although the settlers of Kaskaskia largely came from New Orleans, and those of Cahokia from Canada. Prairie du Rocher was fourteen miles from Kaskaskia, and in the immediate neighborhood of Fort Chartres. At the time of English occupancy it contained twenty-two houses, each occupied by a family. Saint Phillipe was about five miles from Chartres on the road to Kaoquias. It contained sixteen houses and a small church, but all the inhabitants, excepting the captain of the militia company, deserted it when the English arrived, and crossed the Mississippi into Missouri. Kaoquias, or Cahokia, was established fifteen leagues from Chartres, and six leagues below the mouth of the Missouri River. The village was directly opposite the centre of Duncan's Island, and thus differing from the other French villages was long and straggling, being three-fourths of a mile from one end to the other. In its best days it contained a church and forty-five dwelling-houses. The situation was poor, as in time of flood it was generally covered two or three feet deep. The land here occupied had been purchased of the Indians by the Canadian inhabitants, many of whom married native women. The dwellers at this point were largely hunters, or interested in the fur trade, paying small attention to agriculture, and making few permanent improvements. The mission of St. Sulpice, however, had a fine plantation near by, with an excellent house and mill. When the English came they sold out at a great sacrifice, and returned to France.

The growth of these isolated settlements during the sixty odd years of French rule was not rapid, nor were many of the settlers who drifted into the country permanent residents. The majority came and went, mere vagabonds of the frontier. Yet not a few enterprising Canadians were attracted thither by the climate, finding homes along the Illinois, Mississippi, and Wabash. Fur-trading stations sprang up everywhere along the principal water-courses, and much commerce of this kind found its way over the long leagues to Montreal. A little later, under the stimulus of individual enterprise, and the advice of military commandants, the course of trade gradually changed, until New Orleans became the great mart of the Illinois country. Regular cargoes of pork, flour, bacon, tallow, hides, and leather were annually transported in barges down the broad Mississippi and sold. On the return trip the boats were often laden with rice, indigo, sugar, and European fabrics. The decade commencing with 1740 and closing with 1750 was the most prosperous.

But earlier even than these, were those first French settlers who came in with La Salle, and were granted concessions of land under his patent. These were largely *engagés*, employed either about Fort St. Louis, or in the fur trade early springing up in that immediate neighborhood. The names of some twenty or more of these earliest colonists of Illinois are preserved in the records of the Superior Council of Quebec, and are worthy of record. Among them Mason gives us the following list: Riverin, Pierre Chevet, François Pachot, Chanjou, François Hageur, Louis Le Vasseur, Mathieu Martin, François Charron, les Sieurs d'Artigny and La Chesnaye, Jacque de Faye, Pierre Le Vasseur, Michel Guyon, Poisset, André de Chaulne, Marie Joseph le Neuf, Michel de Grig, Philipes Osnault, Jean Petit, René Fegeret, les Sieurs Laport, Louvigny, and St. Castin, François de la Forest, Henri de Tonty, and the Jesuit Fathers. Bold *voyageurs* probably the most of them, and loyal to their great leader, every man having back of him a life of strange adventure in the wilderness. But their colony lived only while St. Louis crowned the rock; and when the garrison marched forth for the last time and left only a ruin behind, the scattered settlers were not long in following. Some may have halted at the Peoria Straits and founded De Pé, but no doubt the majority drifted down the rivers to old Kaskaskia.

This latter town, the principal point of colonization as well as of political and social power during one hundred and twenty years, and under the shadow of three flags, was in most respects a typical French village of its age. Nestled as closely as possible to the river, along the banks of which its little houses clung lovingly, it never lost its picturesque character. Many species of architecture fronted the narrow, stone-paved streets, although most of the homes were of the primitive French style, low and broad, with dormer windows, spacious porches, great masses of roses often blossoming to the roofs. Yet there were brick mansions also, the material transported from far down the Ohio, while not a few were constructed of stone, quarried from the neighboring bluffs. The Court-house, the House of the Jesuits, and the spacious home occupied by John Edgar, were perhaps the most notable of these, but across the river, nestling beneath the bluff shadow, were other residences, such as that of Pierre Menard, where many of the more exclusive chose to live. The streets, shaded by trees, narrow, not over straight or regular, but often bordered by beds of flowers, were great meeting-places in the moonlit Summer evenings, and many, indeed, were the types to be met sauntering idly there, the air ringing with gossiping voices and cheery laughter, while back on the broad piazzas, little family groups looked forth on the gay spectacle, chatting volubly over their light wine.

The peculiar characteristics of these French colonists have come down to us in little glimpses from the histories of Governors Ford and Reynolds, who saw something of their last days, and the pictures have been added to by the researches of Davidson and Stuvé. The work of this chapter is but a *résumé* of their combined labor.

There was much that was peculiar and interesting about these early French frontier settlements and their people. Unlike the English colonists who usually established themselves in widely scattered independence, it was the French nature to abide in compact villages. These were generally built on some stream, contiguous to timber and prairie, that they might thus have close at hand the three essentials to such easy living as they loved — water, fuel, and ground for tillage. While brick and stone were occasionally used, their dwellings were commonly of the most primitive sort. The framework consisted of posts planted in the earth for three or four feet, and then strongly bound together by cross ties. The interstices were filled with mortar, mixed with straw or Spanish moss. The walls within and without were covered with white lime, lending an air of cleanliness to the entire village. Nearly every such house had its wide piazza in front where the family found a pleasant spot to while away the sultry evenings. Probably not one of these primitive homes has survived. With ample room for broad streets, they preferred to leave theirs as narrow as possible, and, as a result, the merry villagers could sit on their own porches and talk across with their near-by neighbors. Having no machinery they split trees into slabs for flooring, doors, and other purposes, while their houses were thatched with straw. Everywhere the social instincts of the people found outward expression. As a general rule their dwellings were grouped as closely together as possible. Each settlement commonly contained its patriarchal homestead, which was occupied by the oldest existing member of the family. About this sprung up a cluster of smaller houses, the residence of each child or grandchild. Oftentimes the aged patriarch became the centre of a dozen growing families of his own lineage, and embracing three, four, or more generations. Much was ever made of the family life, and ties of relationship were strong.

All such villages possessed a common field in which every inhabitant was supposed to be equally interested. To each was assigned a portion, the extent being proportioned to the size and needs of his family. Everything in connection with the proper cultivation of this land was decided by the village senate. The time for ploughing, sowing, and harvesting, even the form and arrangement of buildings, were thus decided upon. Besides this common field for tillage, there was also set aside a pasture which was free to all the villagers, as was likewise their supply of fuel. Almost without exception no mechanical means of earning a living was known. Agriculture and hunting were the principal occupations of the permanent residents, although *voyageurs* and *coureurs de bois* were always to be met with on the village streets. Young men of enterprise often drifted out into the surrounding wilderness, as employees of the fur trade or boatmen on the great river, to return only at long intervals with many a romantic tale of the strange sights seen, or adventures encountered. The dance was the principal diversion of the villagers, and was made a part of every festival, while there was scarcely a home but contained its fiddle, and capable performer. Care, indeed, was almost a stranger to these villages, and seldom tarried among them for many days as a guest. Amusements, festivals, and holy days were frequent, almost constant. In the light fantastic dance, marked by thoughtless abandon, the young and gay were active participants, while the more aged, with the "reverend father," looked smilingly on. Nor were these enjoyments confined to any sex or condition. In the dance all participated from oldest to youngest, the bond and the free; even the black slave rejoicing over his master's happiness.

"At the close of each year," in the words of Davidson and Stuvé, "it was a custom among them for the young men to disguise themselves in old clothes, visit the several houses of the village, and engage in friendly dances with the inmates. This was understood as being an invitation for all the family to meet in a general ball, in which to watch the birth of the New Year. Large crowds assembled, carrying their own refreshments, and a merry time was ever the result. Another custom was general on January 6. By lot, four kings were chosen, each of whom selected for himself a queen. These together perfected arrangements for an entertainment known as a king-ball. Toward the close of the first dance the old queens selected new kings, whom they kissed as the formality of introduction into office. In a similar manner these kings chose new queens, and thus the gay time continued during the entire carnival, up to the week preceding Lent."

These dwellers on the far French frontier were largely descendants from emigrants originally coming from Picardy and Normandy. Some had drifted down the long waterways from far-off Canada, pausing often perhaps as they voyaged, while others had found passage up the great river from New Orleans. All were ardent Catholics, looking to their priests for guidance in both spiritual and secular affairs. No regular court was ever held in this country during French control, yet there remains no record of any serious infraction of law. The commandant at Fort Chartres, who exercised almost kingly powers, aided by the friendly advice of the priests, either prevented controversies or quietly settled them. Hospitality was held a duty, always cheerfully performed;

RUINS OF OLD KASKASKIA

FROM A RECENT PHOTOGRAPH

taverns were unknown, for every house supplied the deficiency. In politics they simply believed that France ruled the world, and were content; worldly honors were unknown and uncared for, while, with little commerce, the luxuries and refinements of civilization were held valueless. Thus day after day passed by in perfect contentment and peaceful indolence. Of rank there was little distinction; excepting the priests and military officers, all were upon an equality, all dressed alike, all met on the same social plane.

The frank, social disposition of their natures made the preservation of peace with surrounding Indian tribes an easy matter. In the wigwams and camps of the savages they were at home; they met and mingled with them, not as an alien race, but upon terms of intimate friendship. Marriages between white and red were common, not a few with all the sanctity of church ceremony, and half-breed children soon became numerous in the village streets. Their very manners, habits, and love of ceremony commended these careless French habitants to the good will of their savage allies. Magnificent fighters on occasions of necessity, and ever prompt volunteers at the demand of the King, when the battle ceased they were at once transformed into polite courtiers. As Governor Ford says:

"Separated by an immense wilderness from all civilized society, these voluntary exiles yet retained all the suavity and politeness of their race. It is a remarkable fact, that the roughest hunter or boatman among them could, at any time, appear in a ball-room, or at a council-fire, with the carriage and behavior of a well-bred gentleman. At the same time the French women — unless we except the off-scouring of the Salpêtrière and Hospitals of Paris — were remarkable for the sprightliness of their conversation, and the grace and elegance of their manners."

We are told that their horses and cattle, for want of proper care and food, degenerated in size but seemed to acquire an additional vigor and toughness, so that among the incoming Americans a French pony was a proverb for strength and endurance. These ponies were trained to draw, sometimes one alone, sometimes two together, one hitched before the other, the rude ploughs or carts made entirely of wood. The latter held about double the contents of a common large wheelbarrow. When oxen were used they were yoked by the horns instead of the neck, and in this mode were made to haul heavy loads. Nothing like reins were ever needed for driving; the whip of the driver, having a handle two feet and a lash two yards long, stopped or guided horse or ox perfectly. Each village had its Catholic church and priest. The church was the great place of resort on Sundays and holidays, and became associated with the gayety as well as the spiritual life of the people. The priest was advisor, director, and friend to all his flock.

The costume of these Illinois French, like their manners and customs, was simple and peculiar. In much it was the natural outgrowth of their situation. Too poor and too remote to obtain finer fabrics, the men during the Summer wore pantaloons made of coarse blue cloth, which in the Winter season was supplanted by buckskin. Over their shirts and long vests, a flannel cloak was worn, to the collar of which was attached a hood, to be drawn over the head on the coldest days, but when warmer it fell back on the shoulders after the manner of a cape. It was a blanket garment, called a *capote*. None wore hat, cap, or coat, but the heads of both men and women were covered with madras cotton handkerchiefs, tied about in the fashion of night-caps. *Voyageurs* and hunters wore cloths of a blue color, folded in form of a turban. The fancy head-dresses which the women wore at balls and other festivities were often tastefully trimmed with ribbons, and ornamented with gay flowers. The dress of the matron, although plain and of the antique short-waist, was frequently greatly varied according to the taste of the wearer. Both sexes wore moccasins, which, on public occasions, were variously decorated with shells, beads, and ribbons, yielding them a picturesque appearance. In Summertime bare feet was the rule.

It was in 1720 that Major Pierre Dugue Boisbriant, some of whose descendants yet reside at Prairie du Rocher, accompanied by one hundred men, came up the river from New Orleans, and at a point sixteen miles above Kaskaskia built Fort Chartres. In 1721 Kaskaskia became a parish, and in 1722 the commandant issued the first land warrant known to the records of what is now Illinois. In 1721 Renault brought two hundred miners and five hundred slaves to work the mines he expected to discover, and in this year also the Jesuits established a college and monastery at Kaskaskia, while Fort Chartres became the centre of life and fashion in the West. Here the officers and their ladies held high carnival, and many a gay company made merry till the dawn. The traders in the villages, and at the fort, kept a heterogeneous stock of goods in one large room, where the assortment was fully displayed before the eyes of purchasers. Although poor agriculturists, judged by present standards, they raised not a little for export. In 1745 the Illinois country sent four hundred thousand pounds of grain to New Orleans. At this date the French population was about nine hundred souls all told.

Day by day, year by year, almost the same scenes of indolent contentment were to be witnessed in all their villages — at Kaskaskia, Cahokia, Prairie du Rocher, Prairie du Pont, and St. Phillipe. The peasantry, in their picturesque costumes, conspicuous with coloring, mingled with gentlemen who, even in that wilderness, clung to the Parisian garb, with the French soldiers in their blue uniforms and white facings, the black-robed Jesuits, and the stolid Indian warriors. After 1721 black slaves were numerous throughout the settlements. These were originally San Domingo negroes brought by Renault to labor in his mines, but, twenty years later, sold to the colonists. The missionary Vivier wrote in 1750:

"We have here whites, negroes, and Indians, to say nothing of the cross-breeds. There are five French villages, and three of the natives, within a space of twenty-one leagues, situated between the Mississippi and another river called Kaskaskia. In the five French villages are, perhaps, eleven hundred whites, three hundred blacks, and some sixty red slaves, or savages. The three Indian towns do not contain more than eight hundred souls all told."

Other little settlements were throughout the country, the merest pin-pricks on the great map of the wilderness. At Le Pé, now Peoria, at Chicago, possibly at Rock Island and Quincy, there were small stockaded forts with a few French settlers, largely half-breeds having native women for wives, gathered about them. A somewhat larger settlement, although constantly changing its inhabitants, was that of the lead miners in Jo Daviess County. A trading-post was established on the Missouri side of the river at New Madrid as early as 1740. The region was notable for its bears, and the principal trade of the inhabitants was the sale of bear's grease. Hence the *voyageurs* named it "L'Anse de la Graisse" — Grease Bay. St. Genevieve in Missouri dates from about 1755. Following even more closely in point of time the Illinois settlements, came the occupation of the Wabash country. A stockade was built on the upper Wabash previous to 1712, but that route eastward by water was not greatly used until after 1716. This post was called Ouatanon, and occupied the present site of the city of Lafayette, Indiana, at the mouth of Little River. The fortified trading-post of Vincennes was established in 1722, but did not become a French settlement until about twelve years later. Besides the inevitable water communication existing between all these French outposts, land trails connected most of them, and they were always in comparatively close touch from the constant passing back and forth of *voyageurs* and *coureurs de bois*. In time of need these isolated communities furnished many volunteer soldiers to aid the French struggle to retain the West, the forces moving eastward along water-courses or over the land trails, and being represented in every battle waged upon that long frontier.

Thus in the very heart of the continent, more than a thousand miles from either ocean, flourished for nearly a hundred years these interesting communities of French pioneers. Yet in all that time they accomplished little of permanent value, and to-day the fact of their former occupancy of this land is scarcely more than a dream. Their forts have crumbled into dust, their towns have disappeared beneath the encroaching waters of the great river which was once their highway, or, deserted by their inhabitants, have decayed and disappeared. Only a few remnants have escaped the inflowing tide of American population, and they also are fast losing the peculiarities of their fathers.

CHAPTER X

ON THE SITE OF MARAMECH: A GREAT INDIAN TRAGEDY

WITHIN the present limits of Kendall County, two small streams unite in one, and, in less than a mile, flow into the Fox River. They are known as Little and Big Rock Creeks. Between these was located that famous ancient Indian village of Maramech, described by La Salle, and given prominent place upon Franquelin's map as early as 1684. Near here, many a year later, according to recently discovered French reports, occurred one of the most horrible tragedies of the Illinois country. The victims were Fox Indians, who, from the earliest settlement of this country, were almost the only western tribe with whom the invading French were unable to enter upon permanent terms of friendship. Mr. John F. Steward, in the Illinois Historical Transactions and in a book on the subject, has given the best and fullest account we have of the event.

From the very earliest days of exploration and fur-trading the warriors of this important nation, it seems, exercised sufficient control over the more northern portages leading toward Canada to enable them to collect toll of the adventurous *voyageurs* eager to get their peltries to the far-away Montreal market. This led to constant bickering and trouble, and finally even to bloodshed and a beginning of frontier war. As early as 1712, Mr. Steward's researches tell us, Du Buisson, then commandant at Detroit, saw fit to organize numerous rival Indian tribes into a sort of loose confederacy for the sole purpose of attacking these Foxes, and they were thus driven away from the streams they so long had dominated, after a brief but fierce battle. In 1716 De Lignerie, commander at Mackinac, incensed by some outrage now unknown, once again moved against these same people, who were at that time located along the Wisconsin River, and, at Butte des Morts, wrought wholesale slaughter. Again in 1728 and in 1730 they were attacked, by new combinations of vengeful enemies incited and led by Frenchmen, and finally were forced to fly for safety, their fields of corn destroyed, and their villages burned to the ground.

It is this last expedition, the most important and bloody of all, with which this chapter especially deals, furnishing as it does a vivid and weird picture of the early dealings between the white and red occupants of the land. Harassed continually from every side by implacable enemies, those of their own race being constantly egged on to greater atrocities by the influence of French greed, the dispirited fragment of what had once been the strong Fox nation finally started eastward hoping, it is said, to find an asylum of safety among the powerful Iroquois. On this unfortunate retreat, for such it must be considered, the hastily fleeing tribe, according to Steward's researches, probably followed the old Kishwaukee trail leading southeastwardly, one of the many that centred at what is now believed to have been the former vast Indian town of Maramech. This was a very old track crossing the prairie, worn so deeply by moccasined Indian feet in the long ago as to remain plainly apparent until the land was finally broken up by the plough. In this migration of the Foxes, in their attempt to reach safety in the distant lodges of the Iroquois, probably between two and three hundred warriors, with an unusual proportion of women and children, plodded dejectedly along this ancient, narrow highway.

On the journey they continually suffered attack from small parties of Mascoutins and Kickapoos, yet held grimly forward, beating back their wary assailants until they finally attained to the banks of the Fox, where they were reluctantly compelled to halt by the increasing number opposing passage across the stream, and entrench themselves in crude Indian fashion. This consisted merely of building a large number of temporary shelters by digging shallow holes along the banks of the stream. Finding that they were unable to accomplish unaided the damage desired against these fleeing exiles, the wily Indian allies despatched hasty reports of the situation to the nearest French garrisons, then stationed at Chartres, the fort on the St. Joseph, and Green Bay. St. Ange, at Chartres, was the more prompt to respond, leaving his post for the scene of action early in July, 1730. He moved slowly up the Illinois River, in boats, and pushed forth into the more northern wilderness, having with him about five hundred men all told, including French and Indians from the Kaskaskia settlements.

It was on the twelfth of August that St. Ange's scouts first came into actual touch with the Foxes, who were now strongly fortified in their primitive Indian fashion close to the old site of Maramech. On the seventeenth, forty Fox hunters were encountered in the woods, and after a sharp fight hastily driven back within their little fortification, which consisted of no more than a small grove of timber, enclosed with rude palisades, and situated upon a rather steep slope.

Warned by these fleeing scouts of the fast approach of this new and dangerous hostile force, the Foxes, now completely surrounded by their vengeful enemies and having no opportunity for further retreat, made every preparation possible for a stubborn defence. The warriors busied themselves hunting in an effort to secure sufficient provisions to withstand a siege, while the women and old men worked at strengthening the fort in every way possible with their primitive tools. Within the stockade were crowded a thousand half-starved women and children. St. Ange,

Photo by R. E. Lincoln, Plano, Ill.

ON THE SITE OF MARAMECH

MONUMENT ON THE SITE OF MARAMECH

ERECTED BY JOHN T. STEWARD

as Mr. Steward's careful study would seem to show, immediately approached from the southward, keeping well under cover of the heavy woods along the river bank; De Villiers, accompanied by French and Indians from Fort St. Joseph, was bearing down upon them from the east; while De Noyelles with still others was hurrying over the great Sauk trail from Detroit, eager to be in at the death. At last St. Ange left his partial concealment, and, crossing the river with his men, penned the desperate Foxes more closely within their little stockade of logs, and began the siege, opening fire on every savage whose head appeared above the defences.

A few days later, but before any serious fighting had yet occurred, De Villiers succeeded in joining him, bringing fifty Frenchmen and five hundred Indians to augment the force of besiegers. Assaults were immediately attempted, but these the desperate Fox warriors hurled fiercely back with heavy loss, and the siege continued, the besiegers daily advancing closer against the walls of the fort by use of the spade. In final desperation the now starving Foxes sent forth a peace party, begging for some satisfactory terms of surrender, and De Villiers, who was in command of the attack, was apparently inclined to be merciful, but his purpose was overborne by the influence of the allied savages. It was at about this time that De Noyelles arrived on the scene, having with him ten Frenchmen and two hundred Indians. He brought positive orders that no quarter should be granted the defenders. Under his instructions, the lines were drawn yet closer, and the exchange of fire became constant. Hunger soon reigned on both sides, even the allies themselves, although perfectly free to hunt, being reduced to eating their shields of rawhide. How those cooped up helplessly within the narrow confines of the little fort suffered no pen can tell; the story of their desperation died with them.

Day by day they were pressed harder, the walls being several times assaulted; many of the defenders perished, some from starvation, others in open battle. St. Ange built a small fort, almost within pistol shot, thinking thus to effectually shut off the water supply of the agonized garrison, but the desperate Foxes managed to tunnel through the hard, rocky earth, and thus secured sufficient to keep them alive. On the eighth of September a violent storm arose, which was followed by a dark, cold night. The sentinels of the allied French and Indians, already wearied by the long siege, became careless; vigilance relaxed along the besieging lines, and in the intense blackness of the night the watchful Foxes discovered an unguarded lane, and burst through their enemies unnoticed. The chance crying of a child is said to have been the first sound which alarmed the unsuspecting sentries of the sleeping allies, but amid the intense gloom and uncertainty of the night, they were completely baffled as to the direction of the flight.

With earliest coming of daylight the fierce pursuers, burning now for vengeance, were upon the trail of the hapless fugitives. These latter made every effort to defend themselves, but the mere weight of numbers pressing hard and relentlessly upon their rear was sufficient to ensure defeat. Placing their women, children, and old men in the van of retreat, the despairing warriors remained nobly behind to battle. But the attack was exceedingly fierce, and the overwhelming allies drove through them, hurling them helplessly aside in the mad shock of their assault. The dead and the prisoners, many of whom were remorselessly tortured and few spared, numbered about three hundred warriors, and one thousand women and children.

At the centre of what was probably the original enclosure Mr. Steward has erected a monument, made of a great bowlder, with a suitable inscription carved thereon, in commemoration of this great border tragedy of the old French regime. Nothing could be more impressive, for not only does this granite stand there in memory of a brave people and a heroic deed, but back even of this occurrence within the recorded story of white men, loom the fabled legends of generations of Indian life in this mysterious old town of Maramech, famous in song and story, whose true history can never be written by mortal pen, yet will remain for ever a fascinating romance of the Illinois country.

CHAPTER XI

THE SPANISH INVASION—ILLINOIS IN THE REVOLUTION

DURING the first years of American control of the Illinois country the official neighbor upon the west, separated only by the rolling waters of the Mississippi, was Spain. And more than once in those stirring border days of bluster and bold fighting, were peaceful relations severely strained, and the two nationalities brought to the very verge of serious acts of hostility.

The Spanish capital of what somewhat later became officially known as Upper Louisiana was the little village of St. Louis, which the French had founded in 1764 as a trading-post. Around its scattered houses, because of a predatory attack made by English and Indians in 1780, the Spaniards had erected a log stockade, with a small stone fort or two standing close by. Its commander this year of which we now treat, 1781, was Don Francesco Cruvat, Brevet Lieutenant-Colonel of Infantry. In January of that same eventful year, there marched forth from his little garrison at St. Louis those Spanish soldiers who for the first and only time bore the flag of that nation triumphantly across Illinois territory. It is an interesting and picturesque story, but one apparently not deemed of sufficient historical importance to be given the space it perhaps truly deserves. Certainly until treated by Mr. E. G. Mason, in his interesting "Illinois Sketches," it has remained almost totally ignored.

In this party of adventurers — for they were little more — there were sixty-five militia-men. Of these, thirty are reported to have been Spanish, the remainder probably being of French blood. Sixty Indians, recruited from various Western tribes, accompanied them as allies. Don Eugenio Pourre was the Commander of this company, and probably the only man in the entire party who comprehended fully the purposes of the expedition. He was a Captain in the Spanish line. Next to him in rank stood Don Carlos Tayon, a Lieutenant in the royal service, while the others of importance and some note were Don Luis Chevalier, "a man well versed in the language of the Indians," expected to act as interpreter, and two grave warrior chieftains, whom the Spaniards called Eleturno and Naquigen.

And what was the cause for all this stern and warlike array? Merely this — it was apparently a faint echo from far across the sea, of a great European quarrel, the war then being desperately waged by Spain against England. In this cause the isolated garrison at St. Louis, anxious enough for some excitement, had boldly determined to bear their part, and now planned a swift stroke against the nearest fort over which floated defiantly the hated English banner. This chanced to be the old fort of St. Joseph, situated on the river of that name, in what is now Southern Michigan. The exact spot where this old stockade once stood is scarcely agreed upon by any two historians, the majority of them locating it either at the mouth of the St. Joseph River, where La Salle's Fort Miami probably stood, or else up that placid stream as far as the ancient portage to the Kankakee, near South Bend, Indiana. Mason decides, after most careful study of the various maps of that early day, that this fortification more likely occupied the south bank of the St. Joseph River, and was situated about one mile west of the present town of Niles, Michigan. Whatever may have been its exact site, it was certainly no ordinary journey which now lay before these adventurous Spaniards. As Mr. Mason writes, "Many marches far more famous have been of less extent and with fewer privations." It was midwinter when they started, the ground already covered deeply with newly fallen snow, the forest trees bare of foliage, the rivers locked in ice, and the desolate prairies deserted of game. Four hundred miles and more of Indian-haunted plain and forest stretched between them and their destination, while at the end of that difficult journey an enemy awaited their stealthy approach whose strength was but poorly known. And they started forth unusually heavily laden for such a march, not only bearing necessary provisions for the long journey, and sufficient stores of ammunition for the anticipated battle, but also stocks of merchandise, with which it was hoped to buy safe passage through the many savage tribes then in close alliance with England, across whose country they must necessarily pass on their way.

This march, while possibly in no way intended at the time of its conception to involve the struggling eastern American colonies, led directly across Illinois territory, which had been already won to the American cause by Clark's bordermen, and was hence an armed invasion, which might naturally lead to unpleasant consequences. Moreover, the French settlement at Le Pé had to be avoided, lest an attempt be made here to oppose their progress. As Mason says:

> "Nor could these bold fellows take the most direct route to the point of attack, as preceding expeditions had done, for no man might face the Grand Prairie in midwinter and expect to survive. For shelter, and for water and fuel as well, they were compelled to follow the courses of the streams and the woods which bordered them, and so they journeyed patiently northeastward, pushing forward in the teeth of the wintry blasts which grew ever colder and more dreary. By day they plodded onward, laden with their heavy burdens, having before them only the ice-covered streams on the one hand, and the straggling forests, with glimpses of the vast white plains beyond, on the other."

The light-hearted Frenchmen in that struggling column needed all their natural cheeriness to keep up heart under such conditions, and it was a time when the Spaniards might recall encouragingly the deeds of those daring cavaliers of their race in many a desperate venture of the wilderness. The weather proved more severe than usual even in that Winter-swept country, and their supplies of food soon became distressingly scant. Every mile of advance only added to their sufferings, and they were compelled by fast-increasing weakness to throw aside much of their loads, while those in command continually urged the wearied men to renewed exertion.

The records of this long-neglected march across the Illinois wilderness are exceedingly scanty, so much so that it is impossible to trace with any certainty the route followed. It is supposed, from the recent discovery there of ancient cannon balls of European manufacture, that the present site of Danville may have been crossed, and it is suspected that some trouble was experienced there in getting past an important Indian village; yet all we truly know is that this band of determined invaders actually moved slowly and painfully across the whole of what is now Illinois, buffeted by wintry storms, their general direction being from southwest to northeast, and, leaving the present limits certainly not far from Danville, turned more northerly, and struck through swamp lands straight toward the old Kankakee portage, about where South Bend now stands. All along the latter portion of this wearisome route they bought their safe passage through the English Indian allies by the free use of presents from their fast-depleting stocks, but after finally reaching the banks of the St. Joseph they threw all prudence to the winds, and rushed eagerly forward to win their battle by surprising the English garrison.

Far more easily than they had dreamed as being possible was this end accomplished. Totally unwarned and unprepared, the few English traders and soldiers gathered within the stockade were quickly made prisoners of war, and Fort St. Joseph was held as belonging to the far-distant King of Spain. In Mason's words, "He was the sixth sovereign who had borne sway there, if we include in the list La Salle and Pontiac, who in truth were kinglier men than any of the others." And so, in his turn, Don Eugenio Pourre, Captain of the line, took possession in the name of his Most Catholic Majesty. He lowered the English flag, and floated the glaring Spanish colors proudly overhead during all the brief period of his stay. His men plundered the fort with the thoroughness born of long experience, giving the greater portion of the spoils thus obtained to their own selves, and what they left to those Indians who had permitted them to pass so easily. But they remained on the spot merely the few days sufficient to recruit their strength, knowing full well so exposed a post could never be permanently defended against English reënforcements. They had struck their blow; now discretion was realized to be the better part of valor. The march homeward was accomplished without special incident. Early in March, 1781, Don Eugenio, bearing in his hands the captured English ensign, made formal report in St. Louis to Don Francesco Cruvat regarding the success of his adventure. A full year later this report was received in distant Spain.

There was doubtless more in this expedition than appears upon the surface, and from it the wily Spanish diplomats may have hoped to attain an end to which this marauding trip was merely an incident. Spain had an ambition at that time, as well as later, to grasp as her own the entire Mississippi valley, and this swift raid of Pourre's through Illinois' midwinter may have been planned but as a stepping-stone toward the realization of that fond dream of final conquest. The attempt failed, not through any unwillingness of European allies to assist, but because of the vigorous opposition and protest made by Jay, Franklin, and Adams on the part of the United States. An able commentator says: "Counsellors less wise, less firm than they, might have yielded to these veiled Spanish claims, especially as they were warmly supported by France, and had they done so all this northwestern territory would have become Spanish soil, with the Ohio as the extreme western boundary of the Union." So, not only as a picturesque incident of early border life, but as an illustration of crafty diplomacy, born in European cabals, is it worth while to remember the passing and repassing across the Illinois prairies of this invading flag of Spain. Unwitting and careless, those red and white border soldiers did their little part, mere pawns in the great game of empire which was being played out in the cabinets of far-off Madrid and Paris.

It is indeed odd what an important part this little insignificant stockade situated on the banks of the St. Joseph River played during all the revolutionary struggle in the West, and how there seemed to centre in that particular spot, now so hard to locate, every effort made by Illinois patriots to strike a blow in aid of the cause of Independence. As early as October, 1777, it was surprised and captured by Illinoisans. Tom Brady, a genial Kaskaskia Irishman, better known as "Monsieur Tom," associated with a Canadian half-breed named Hamelin then residing at Cahokia, led a little party of sixteen daring volunteers to the attack. They crept in under cover of night, capturing and paroling the garrison of twenty-one regulars; seized a considerable amount of merchandise, burned what they could not conveniently carry away with them, and, upon leaving, wantonly set fire to the buildings and stockade. Rendered careless from the easy success of their lawless venture, they were promptly overtaken on the Calumet River, not far from the present South Chicago, by those same regulars whom they had just paroled, together with a number of hastily recruited

Indians. A hot fight followed, but at the end of it, several being killed, two after having surrendered, Brady and twelve of his men were held prisoners. He was sent overland to Canada, under guard, escaped, when near Montreal, and, by means of a long toilsome journey, finally found his way back to Kaskaskia, married the famous widow Le Comte, and was later elected sheriff of St. Clair County. Mason pertinently remarks in this connection: "His career illustrates the indomitable character of the Illinois office-seeker. Warfare, imprisonment, exile, hardships, all were unavailing to prevent Tom Brady from returning to his bailiwick and securing an office."

But Fort St. Joseph was not destined to remain long in peace. The failure of Brady's expedition, together with the capture and death of many of his men, served to awaken a spirit of revenge along the entire Illinois frontier. During the Summer of 1778 Paulette Meillet, then residing near the site of Peoria, of which he was credited as being the founder, and a man of note among fur traders, led a force consisting of three hundred French, Indians, and half-breeds from that place along the water-courses of the Illinois and Kankakee to St. Joseph. Reports of his approach flew before him, so that surprise of the garrison proved impossible, but his force was sufficiently large to venture upon an open assault, and the impetuous mob of red and white invaders surged fiercely over the palisades, and once again the English flag came down at a run. The garrison was paroled, the fort once more looted and set on fire, after which the victorious Illinoisans, bearing with them it is said fifty thousand dollars in stores, safely retraced their steps to the security of the Peoria Lake.

Another revolutionary expedition was yet later organized in the Illinois country, but its results were only death and defeat. It is a strange story, and there is wrapped up in it a character that remains one of the mysteries of history.

Early in the revolutionary struggle, a young French officer calling himself La Balme came to this country, presumably for the purpose of joining the Colonial army. That he was a man of refinement and education, as well as some social influence, is evidenced by his journal, which has been preserved. Yet apparently he never united with the Continental troops, nor is there any record preserved showing that he ever held commission or authority from our government, or that of Virginia. Nevertheless, he suddenly appeared in the Illinois country, with plenty of arms and money, and began recruiting a force of volunteers ostensibly to attack the strongly garrisoned British post at Detroit. This occurred quite soon after Clark's conquest of the Northwest, and the French people of the Illinois were naturally in a frame of mind to be easily led into such an enterprise. La Balme certainly became very popular. One of Clark's officers wrote, "The people run after him as if he was the very *Masiah* himself"; but he was unable to discover by what government authority the man was acting.

In spite of his lack of credentials, strong companies of young men were easily enrolled at Kaskaskia and Cahokia, and at the head of these La Balme marched triumphantly across the State to Vincennes, where he gathered nearly as many more to his desperate enterprise. The French girls became enthusiastic, and sang songs of encouragement for the volunteers, urging all the young men of their acquaintance to enlist, and treating lightly those laggards who hesitated. He left Vincennes with a well-equipped force behind him, ascended the Wabash, and, making a sudden attack on an English trading-post called Kekionga, near the present city of Fort Wayne, Indiana, captured it with all its stores. Flushed with this easy success, and as yet independent of all military discipline, that night La Balme's force kept very poor guard over their encampment on the banks of the little river Aboite. The result of this carelessness was their complete undoing. The enraged traders hastily collected the Indians in the neighborhood, and before morning dawned burst impetuously from out the forest upon the unsuspecting Illinoisans, killed La Balme, routed his forces, and recaptured their goods. To this day no one knows by what authority this expedition was organized; but had its leader succeeded in capturing Detroit according to his plans, the name of La Balme might have stood in Illinois history beside that of George Rogers Clark. As it is, he remains merely a memory, and nothing more.

There exist a few other traditional accounts of independent forays and skirmishes occurring along the Illinois frontier, associated with the revolutionary struggle, helping to show that the Illinoisans of that early age, although mostly of French blood, were eager enough to strike a blow for the cause of freedom. Indeed this spirit was evidenced at even a much earlier period. When first the English banner was unfurled above old Fort Chartres, those that remained of the ancient French population immediately demanded their rights as citizens in no uncertain terms. Practically they said to the English authorities sent to rule over them, "We have become English subjects by the terms of the Treaty of Paris, and we want the rights of Englishmen." This spirit of manly independence grew, and the French bordermen of Illinois were not one whit behind their Eastern brethren in boldly asserting their demands. It is an interesting chapter, and one long neglected, until written of by Mr. Mason. In 1771 the scattered people of Illinois met in mass meeting at Kaskaskia, although it is impossible to ascertain by whom the call was issued, and forwarded a peremptory demand to the English government, protesting against the tyranny of those placed in authority over them, asking for institutions like those in the Connecticut colony, and the right to appoint their own governor and all civil magistrates. We must remember in this connection that, at this date,

Connecticut alone of all the Eastern colonies, preserved her ancient charter, and remained comparatively free of English rule.

This demand of the Illinoisans was sent forward through the regular military channels to General Gage, who was then in command at Boston. In transmitting this precious document to the home authorities Gage endorsed it, " A regular constitutional government for the people of Illinois cannot be suggested. They don't deserve so much attention." " I agree with you," added Lord Hillsborough, then at the head of the British colonial office, " a regular government for that district would be highly improper." His successor, Lord Dartmouth, took a similar view, and immediately drew up what he termed " A Sketch of Government for Illinois," and returned it with his compliments, into the western wilderness, trusting thus to settle the whole affair. It was extremely simple and utterly unsatisfactory. It provided in a few terse paragraphs, arrogantly British in every sentence, that all powers should be vested in officers appointed by the Crown, and none left to the selection of the people. Immediately a storm of wrath swept over distant Illinois. With apparently no formally issued call for such a meeting of protest, the entire population of the surrounding country surged into Kaskaskia to vent their indignation in speech. Daniel Blouin, a French-Canadian fur trader, whose name should be preserved in our records with special honor, came to the front as leader. Acting as the mouthpiece of those earnest souls behind him, he sent to Lord Dartmouth a protest against his " Sketch of Government," expressed in no uncertain language. The " Sketch " was rejected " as oppressive and absurd, much worse than that of any of the French, or even of the Spanish colonies." And to this insolence was boldly added: " Should a government so evidently tyrannical be established, it could be of no long duration. There would exist the necessity of its being abolished."

This was away back in 1771, and occurred in the very heart of the Illinois wilderness. There was certainly something heroic and stirring about the defiant attitude of this little isolated band of men, largely uneducated, foreign of birth, who had been transferred by fate of war to the British Crown, yet insisted boldly on every right which that transfer gave them. "They were not born free," in the words of Mason, who has made the most careful investigation of this incident, "but they were determined to die free," and thus early in that great controversy leading up to the struggle of the Revolution, these men of obscure Illinois stood daringly forth, rebels for freedom. It is worth while that we remember it, and write the name of Daniel Blouin, of Kaskaskia, with the deed of these early protestants, high on the roll of honor.

Twice during the continuance of the revolutionary struggle was the Illinois country invaded by hostile British arms. The first invasion occurred in 1779, soon after Clark's conquest, and was directed against the French trading-post of Le Pé, near where Peoria stands. The force used consisted almost entirely of Indians, recruited about Mackinac, but was commanded by Charles de Verville, a Canadian in the British service. He followed the waterway from the Chicago portage, surprised the unsuspecting French settlers, capturing and burning their stockade. No attempt, however, was made to hold the place, and the motley company retraced their steps, laden with spoils and a few prisoners.

The second expedition, which occurred the following year, was planned for more permanent results, but ended in failure because of an evident misunderstanding of orders on the part of the commanders of the separate columns engaged. St. Louis, then a Spanish village, was the principal point of attack, and a horde of Indians, recruited on the Fox and Wisconsin Rivers, and commanded by British officers, was despatched down the Mississippi, expecting to coöperate with a similar body advancing from the south. The latter failed to appear, and the expedition degenerated into a mere raid, the allied Indians being finally scattered and driven back to their northern haunts. Charles de Longlade endeavored to assist in this affair by leading a party of savages into the Illinois country by way of the Chicago portage, but arrived too late. "Old Jean Baptiste Pointe au Sable, the negro trader then living along the Chicago River," comments Mason, "saw them come and go, but was protected by his British commission, and suffered nothing at their hands."

Elsewhere it is stated that probably Clark first unfolded the United States flag on Illinois soil near Fort Massac. It is possible, however, that it was seen here even earlier. In 1778 James Willing, a Captain in the Continental army, built an armed vessel at Fort Pitt, and set out upon a cruise down the Ohio. He certainly skirted the entire boundary of Southern Illinois, captured a number of traders, and greatly alarmed the commandant at Kaskaskia. But Willing turned down the Mississippi, and after a series of adventures was captured at Mobile. It is not at all improbable that at his adventurous mast-head defiantly floated the newly designed Stars and Stripes.

CHAPTER XII

THE EARLY LEAD-MINERS OF FEVER RIVER[1]

AS early as 1659 the French became aware that the Indians procured lead in the neighborhood of Fever River, now the Galena, in the northwestern corner of the present Illinois. Radisson and Groseilliers were the first to make definite mention of this rumor, which came to them from the lips of the Sioux. Hennepin's map of 1687 locates a recognized lead mine near where Galena now stands, while Joutel, visiting that neighborhood the same year, gives definite description of several such mines throughout the region. During 1690, Nicholas Perrot, at that date French commandant of the West, established a small trading and military stockade on the eastern bank of the Mississippi opposite Dubuque, and visited the Indian mines in person, but seemingly this establishment was but temporary. Certainly the Indians frequently brought to the few adventurers then in the country numerous specimens of this lead ore.

But nothing permanent appears to have been attempted regarding development of these finds previous to 1699. Some six years earlier Le Sueur, then commandant at Chequamegon Bay, extended his widening explorations throughout this region, finally erecting a fort of some considerable size and importance on a large island in the Mississippi somewhere between Lake Pepin and the mouth of the St. Croix. While at this work he reports "discovering mines

[1] Much of the historical data in this chapter was long hidden away in the pages of local newspapers and unpublished manuscripts, until dug out, and lately published, by Dr. Reuben Gold Thwaites, to whom the present writer acknowledges his indebtedness for facts.

of lead, copper, and blue and green earth," and as a result of such discoveries went to France hoping to gain permission from the French authorities to work them somewhat to his own profit. On his return he arrived in Louisiana with D'Iberville's second expedition, in December, 1699. Under the King's commission Le Sueur had with him thirty miners, and was accompanied by one Pénicaut, who acted as personal companion and reporter. This latter wrote an account of the expedition, quoted by Dr. Thwing, in his most valuable essay on this subject, and, after describing graphically the rapids in the Mississippi at Rock Island, says:

"We found both on the right and left bank the lead mines, called to this day the mines of Nicholas Perrot, the name of the discoverer. Twenty leagues from there on the right, was found the mouth of a large river, the Ouisconsin."

By United States land survey, Dr. Thwing states, the distance has since been measured at thirty-nine English miles. It was nearly the middle of August, 1700, when these adventurers arrived opposite the mouth of Fever River, which Pénicaut called "Rivière à la Mine." He tells us that up this little stream, only about a league and a half, there was seen "a lead mine in the prairie." Passing farther up the Mississippi, a number of others were likewise discovered, but these latter were within the limits of Wisconsin rather than Illinois. La Sueur passed the following Winter on the Blue River, but for some reason now unknown made no further effort to profit by his valuable discoveries; the following Summer he abandoned the country and returned to France, having accomplished nothing from his concession.

Very little more was heard regarding these deposits for fifteen years, although wandering *coureurs de bois* traded with the Indians thereabout for sufficient lead to supply their own immediate requirements. In 1715, La Mothe Cadillac,

Governor of Louisiana, came up into the Illinois country searching for silver, but had to be satisfied with carrying back some samples of lead ore taken "from mines fourteen miles west of the river," probably those near Dubuque. In 1721, there arrived in the Illinois, accompanied by a numerous company of miners and San Domingo slaves, Philippe François de Renault, newly appointed "director-general of the mines of the Royal India Company in Illinois." His parties of prospectors ranged widely along both sides of the Mississippi, probably as high up as Minnesota and Wisconsin, and during the four years spent in the district made numerous discoveries of lead, but principally within the present limits of Missouri. After the final dispersion of Renault's settlement in Monroe County, the next direct reference to the upper lead mines is given by M. le Guis in 1743, when he describes at some length the methods then employed by "eighteen or twenty" miners he saw operating on Fever River. Mentioning no names he speaks of them as "a fast lot, every man working for himself at surface operations, and extracting only enough to secure a bare existence throughout the year."

His graphic report of these early smelting operations is interesting:

"They cut down two or three big trees and divide them in logs five feet long; then they dig a small basin in the ground, and pile three or four of these logs on top of each other over this basin; then they cover it with the same wood, and put three more logs, shorter than the others, on top, and one at each end crossways. This makes a kind of box, in which they put the mineral, then they pile as much wood as they can on top, and around it. When this is done they set fire to it from under; the logs burn up and partly melt the mineral. They are sometimes obliged to repeat the same operation three times in order to extract all the matter. This matter falling into the basin, forms a lump, which they afterward melt over again into bars weighing from sixty to eighty pounds, in order to facilitate the transportation to Kaskaskia. This is done with horses, who are quite vigorous in the country. One horse generally carries four or five of these bars. It is worthy of remark that, in spite of the bad system, there has been taken out of the La Motte mine 2,500 of these bars in 1741, 2,228 in 1742, and these men only work four or five months in the year at most."

Modern miners, Dr. Thwaites remarks, in quoting this report, will see in this description little difference in method from that followed by later American operators up to the time of the introduction of the Drummond blast furnace in 1836.

Until November, 1762, France was in complete control of both sides of the Mississippi River, and Eastern Missouri and Eastern Iowa were referred to in French reports as being part of the Illinois country. This fact creates some slight confusion as to the location of mines. Little, however, remains of record regarding the development of the mineral deposits constantly being discovered in the real Illinois, although it is evident, from subsequent English writings, that these opportunities were not wholly neglected. In the Journal of Captain Henry Gordon, written in 1766, occurs this mention in proof that the mines were continually operated:

"The French have large boats of twenty tons, rowed with twenty oars, which will go in seventy odd days from New Orleans to the Illinois. These boats go to the Illinois twice a year, and are not half loaded on their return; was there any produce worth sending to market, they could carry it at no great expense. They, however, carry lead, the produce of a mine on the French side of the river, which yields but a small quantity, as they have not hands to work it. These boats, in times of the floods, which happen only in May and June, go down to New Orleans from the Illinois in fourteen and sixteen days."

The earliest application on record for any grant of lead-mining land within the valley of the Upper Mississippi is credited to one Duralde in 1769. It was signed by Belle Rive, the commandant at Fort Chartres. This tract embraced land " three arpents in front, by the ordinary depth" (probably forty arpents), on Le Sueur's River of the Mines (Fever River), " a hundred and sixty leagues, more or less, above St. Louis." Dr. Thwaites decides, from the general tone of Duralde's petition, that he must have been a ne'er-do-well, and certain it is that he never settled on his lands, or operated any mines. So far as Illinois is concerned, the next person of importance to appear in this upper wilderness was Julien Dubuque. The exact date of his entrance to the immediate region remains obscured, but he soon became a man of influence among the surrounding Indian tribes, and proved himself possessed of what the majority of his nationality seemed to lack, business energy. He first obtained, in 1788, permission to work the lead mines undisturbed, from a council of the Sacs and Foxes, with whom he was on the most friendly terms as a trader. The greater part of Dubuque's mining operations were carried on west of the Mississippi near where the city bearing his name now stands. These were known then as " The Spanish Mines," possibly because some of that race had originally discovered them, although Dubuque had made several additional discoveries of his own.

But Dubuque, always full of abounding energy, did not entirely restrict himself to these operations on the west shore. Tradition whispers that at the time of his first location at the Spanish mines, a man named Du Bois was engaged alone in working a lead mine on the Illinois shore nearly opposite — probably a little south of the present village of Dunleith. There had been considerable Indian trouble in that country, originating over the desire of the whites to mine for lead. As late as 1780 it was reported by Lieutenant Governor Patrick Sinclair that the Sacs and Foxes were in active alliance with the Spanish and American (probably meaning French) miners against further British encroachment. The result was that the British in their turn sought savage allies. The Winnebagoes and Menominees assisted them in an open attack on a party of these miners, and seventeen Americans and Spaniards were taken as prisoners to Mackinac. But this state of affairs did not greatly trouble Dubuque, who retained friendship with all the tribes, and his prospectors and miners continued to roam at will over the northern Illinois country. They certainly opened leads on Apple River near the present village of Elizabeth, and in 1805 were operating the Old Buck and Hog leads on Fever River. Undoubtedly there were at this time more white miners in the region than we have any means of tracing.

Nearly all of these oldest mines were originally worked in superficial fashion by Indians. Probably a few had so been operated for fully a century before the arrival of white men. In those earlier times their tools were buckhorns, many of which were found in abandoned drifts by the first settlers. Something of the nature of their operations has been recorded, and described by Dr. Thwaites. The savages would load their ore at the bottom of the shaft into deerskin bags, and hoist or drag it to the surface by means of long thongs of hide. The lower work was performed almost entirely by old men and squaws, the warriors doing the smelting above. Dubuque, through his influence as a trader, made considerable use of the Indians in all his mining adventures. Besides working them in his mines, he employed others in wide prospecting tours, continually seeking new leads. When any were thus discovered and reported to him, he would at once despatch Canadians, or half-breeds, to prove up the claims. "In this manner," comments Thwaites, "almost the entire lead region of Iowa, Wisconsin, and Illinois became occupied by Dubuque's men, before the Americans came in for permanent settlement."

It was a case where possession was fully nine points of the law.

On the east, or Illinois, side of the river he met, however, with some considerable opposition from representatives of the American Fur Company, who, through friendship with the chiefs of the Foxes, obtained considerable supplies of lead, and are even said to have smelted some for themselves. But it was not until after France in 1803 disposed of her rights in all this Western territory to the United States, that Dubuque began to meet with any decided competition, nor was that destined to become serious, as his death occurred in 1810. The first adventurous American of whom we have distinct trace to try his fortune in this region was George E. Jackson, a Missouri miner. He built a rude log furnace as early as 1811 on an island, which has since disappeared. From accounts preserved it lay then near the eastern bank of the river, just below Dunleith, about opposite the mouth of Catfish Creek. Jackson took his store of lead down the river by flat-boat, accompanied by one assistant, and is reported to have had a great deal of trouble with hostile Indians on the way. Indeed all these earlier American miners were greatly harassed by the savages, although the French appear to have had little trouble. A year or so later, one John S. Miller, possibly Jackson's earlier assistant, became associated with him as a partner, but very soon after this the island was abandoned by both men, probably on account of trouble with the Indians. Five years later Miller came back, accompanied by two companions, traded some lead for goods at Dubuque's old mines, and penetrated the country as far as Galena, remaining for some years in the district, but accomplishing little in mining.

Even at this period, and for considerable time following, nearly all the practical lead-mining was performed by Indian labor, although occasionally under white supervision.

Practical white miners penetrated the district very slowly. Nicholas Boilvin, writing to the Secretary of War under date of February, 1811, reports that the Sacs and Foxes on the east side of the river, and the Iowas on the west side had "mostly abandoned the chase, and turned their attention to the manufacture of lead." He reports that in 1810 they manufactured four hundred thousand pounds of the metal and disposed of it to Canadian traders. As early as 1810 Henry Shreeve bought lead of Indian miners on Fever River, taking a small boat-load down the Mississippi. The War of 1812 created a lead demand, and resulted in an unusual output under the supervision of English officers. During the five years between 1815 and 1820 Captain John Shaw made eight trips in a trading boat between St. Louis and Prairie du Chien. At the Fever River mines he saw Indians smelting ore in rude furnaces, and at one time bought from them seventy tons of metal, without in any considerable measure reducing their supply.

Meanwhile the commercial rivalry existing between the French-Canadians, operating by way of the lakes, and the rapidly encroaching Americans pushing up the river, was becoming more acute, even resulting in armed intervention and bloodshed. As these operations were being carried on in the very heart of the Indian country all parties concerned — traders, prospectors, and miners — travelled heavily armed, and any chance meeting of the bitterly warring elements was apt to result in open conflict. Details of such hostile meetings are lacking, but up to 1819 it is known that several American traders, attempting to open negotiations with Indian miners in opposition to the interests of Canadian traders, had been waylaid and killed. In 1815 a crew of American boatmen endeavoring to pole their way up Fever River were stopped by the Indians themselves, probably instigated by Canadian influence. Colonel George Davenport, however, as agent of the American Fur Company, was on most cordial terms with the chiefs of the Sacs and Foxes, and at one time erected a trading-post near the mouth of the Fever, and so far as known, experienced no difficulty. He has the credit of shipping to St. Louis the first flat-boat cargo of lead coming direct from the Fever River mines. This was in 1816, but it is probable others were sent down earlier, but failed of record.

As early as 1804, United States government officials began to evince an interest in this property. In that year Governor Harrison bought from the Sacs and Foxes a tract of land lying contingent to the mouth of the Fever River fifteen miles square. In August, 1816, a treaty was concluded with the Ottawas, Chippewas, and Pottawattomies in which a tract five leagues square on the Mississippi, the exact limits to be afterwards designated by the President, was reserved for the United States, and withheld from settlement. For several years following nothing official was done, but the tide of American immigration became perceptibly stronger. In 1819 a number of miners and traders settled throughout the Fever River district, including Jesse W. Shull, François Bouthillier, Samuel C. Muir, and A. P. Van Metre. These men took Fox Indian women for wives, and thus remained unmolested. Muir has credit for naming Galena.

The largest reported discovery of lead ore up to this date was made about a mile above the Galena site by Indian prospectors. It required the entire force of the band to raise the enormous nugget to the surface. Never preserved in its entirety, it was disposed of to visiting traders in small amounts, so that the true value of the find has never been ascertained. Some time either in 1819 or 1820 there came to this region a man destined to exercise much influence in its future development. This was Colonel James Johnson, of Kentucky, a brother of that Colonel Richard M. Johnson, who was reputed to have slain Tecumseh.

Johnson was a man of brains, energy, and some means. The exact date of his first experiment in lead-trading is unknown, but a traveller in that country in 1821 speaks of meeting his flat-boats on the Mississippi, loaded with ore. Johnson at once prepared to take advantage of those rights offered under government sanction. Just before the date of his arrival Major Thomas Forsyth, on behalf of the government, had reported the number, situation, and quality of all the lead mines lying between Apple Creek and Prairie du Chien. This report was of vast assistance to prospectors, and, coupled with the Act of Congress in 1807, opened the way to extensive operations under form of law. In that year the mineral lands had been reserved from sale, while it was ordered that leases be granted to individuals for terms of either three or five years. Owing to Indian hostility, as well as Canadian intrigue, no immediate advantage was taken of this Act in the Upper Mississippi region. Here the few scattered miners continued to operate independently, and without system. Indeed the first lease in the Fever River country was not issued until 1822, fifteen years later, to four Kentuckians, and there is no record that they ever made any use of it, or even visited Fever River.

But on April 12 of that same year, Colonel Johnson secured a three years' lease, and at once began active operations. He took with him to the mines, from Southern Illinois and Kentucky, a large number of competent workmen, besides some negro slaves, and a complete supply of requisite tools, for operations on an extensive scale. Encamping very close to where Galena now stands, Johnson began mining in a way never before attempted in the lead country. Several French and Indian settlements were close at hand, but his camp being kept under strong military protection was not molested. From this moment may properly be said to date the real advance of lead-mining in the State, as then it definitely passed from out Indian hands, and primitive methods, to more intelligent guidance, and scientific discovery. Colonel Johnson met with almost immediate success, and his example was followed by others, who were thus encouraged to invest capital in the enterprise. Yet at first the change in population and output was extremely slow. The following year only nine lessees are of record, but among them was Dr. Moses Meeker, who established a large colony, and became quite influential in mining operations.

But meantime there flocked into this northern country a horde of squatters and prospectors from Missouri, Kentucky, and Tennessee. These largely arrived by boat via the Mississippi, although not a few travelled overland by way of Fort Clark, at the Peoria Lake, and thence north along an old Indian track, later known as "Kellogg's Trail." The old Lewiston trail across Rock County was also extensively used during this migration. Few of these arrivals possessed any means, and fewer still paid any attention to congressional enactments. Nor were they greatly encouraged to do so. The lessees, then operating, received little if any support in their rights under the law; protracted disputes followed, and much money and time were wasted in legal squabbling. As a result unlicensed plants became more and more numerous, until the leasing system grew so unpopular, and yielded so small a revenue to the government, that in 1846, under another Act of Congress, the lands were placed on the open market and sold.

Here and there throughout the lead country are yet to be discovered many interesting details regarding the adventures of these early pioneers, who won their way through personal dangers and financial difficulties. A report issued to Congress in 1826 by Lieutenant Thomas says there were in the Fever River diggings the first of July the year previous about a hundred persons engaged in mining;

which number increased to four hundred and fifty-three by August, 1826. This refers probably to American miners. The heaviest immigration began in 1829, from which time we may safely date the modern history of this industry, naming all those present previously in that region the real pioneers.

CHAPTER XIII

OLD-TIME FORTS AND THEIR HISTORIES

FROM time immemorial to these piping days of peace, this country of the Illinois has been dotted with fortifications. The remains of ancient works, undoubtedly of this character, are traceable along the valleys of the Rock and Illinois Rivers, as well as in the American Bottom, some antedating even Indian occupancy. With the earliest coming of French explorers the far-reaching plans of La Salle began immediately to take practical form in the erection of forts, and, in a measure, was continued by his successors. Many of these were but temporary, small affairs, mere walls of mud, crowned possibly with log palisades, and intended for resting-places on some route of travel or for the protection of fur traders. The one at Chicago is a fair illustration of the former, that on the present site of Waukegan of the latter. Of Chicago we have but a glimpse, with the testimony of Tonty, that Oliver Morel, Sieur de La Durantaye, commanded there in 1685. The number of his garrison is unknown, but it was undoubtedly small. That at Waukegan was a fur-trading station built for protection against the savages, and was long known as the Little Fort. It was established about the year 1720, and remained in existence until 1760. An easy portage could be made from this point to the Des Plaines, and was probably a well-used water route. Other similar French trading-posts — which by courtesy were called forts — were erected near the present site of Peoria, and on the Mississippi opposite the mouth of the Des Moines. Doubtless there were many more, the locations of which have not been preserved.

The earliest true fortress erected within the present State boundaries by white men was La Salle's Crèvecœur — the "Fort of the Broken Heart"— on the east shore of the Illinois, just below Peoria Lake, in the year 1680. It was a well-conceived defence as against savages ; its general plan is fully described in our chapter devoted to La Salle. It was occupied only a few months, being utterly destroyed by mutineers during the temporary absence of Tonty, who had been left in command. No attempt was ever made at rebuilding, and to-day even the exact site remains a matter of controversy, but it probably stood on the present site of Wesley City, about three miles below Peoria. It constituted the fourth in that long chain of fortifications projected by La Salle to extend from Montreal to the Gulf, for the perpetuation of French power in this vast Western domain.

The truly important French forts erected within the Illinois country were three in number,— St. Louis on Starved Rock, Massac on the Ohio River, and Chartres on the Mississippi. The latter is said to have been the greatest structure of its kind ever built by France on the American continent. La Salle and Tonty, assisted by a few Canadian *voyageurs*, and a number of Illinois Indians, began the erection of Fort St. Louis in November, 1682. This was immediately following their return from the discovery of the mouth of the Mississippi River, and the point selected was an ideal one. Some few miles below the city of Ottawa, but on the opposite side of the Illinois, rises an immense cliff, peculiarly conspicuous for its isolation and inaccessibility. Two years before, it had been selected by La Salle for this purpose, and now, having finally decided upon establishing a permanent colony of Algonquins upon the Utica meadows, he determined to build here a fort for their better protection. Let us mark for a moment that commanding eminence of Starved Rock, as it stood then,— more than two hundred years ago, — and as it stands to-day.

It rises directly from the river, as steep on three sides as a castle-wall, to the height of one hundred and twenty-five feet. Its beetling front overhangs the stream washing its base, so that water could be drawn up by a cord and bucket from below, while its western brow looks dizzily down upon the tops of vast forest trees beneath. To the east opens a wild gorge, or ravine, nearly two hundred feet across, choked with foliage, a little brook creeping down through the rocky depths. On the other side is a wide valley. This cliff, in those old days, was accessible only from behind, where a man might toil up, although not without great difficulty, along a steep, narrow passage. The circuit of its top measured six hundred feet. From this summit, once attained, the magnificent valley of the Illinois is seen spreading out, as far as the vision will extend, in a landscape of exquisite beauty. The river beneath sweeps along amid a number of heavily wooded islands, while farther away it meanders through vast meadows, until it disappears like a thread of light in the dim distance.

On this ideal spot, as inaccessible as an eagle's nest, these indomitable Frenchmen began the erection of their wilderness fort. They cut away the forest crowning the summit, utilizing the timber thus obtained for the building of storehouses and dwellings for officers and men, including a warehouse for peltries, and a chapel. Then, with immense labor, logs were dragged up the steep pathway at the rear, and the rock completely encircled with a palisade fifteen feet high. A parapet covered with earth protected the rear, and this was crowned with wooden spikes, iron pointed. Scarcely was the work completed before a vast Indian village began to grow up about it, and the hardy adventurers soon looked down upon thousands of black tepees scattered far away along the banks of the river. Representatives of almost every tribe in that country flocked there, to dwell in supposed safety beneath the promised protection of the *fleur de lis;* Fort St. Louis became instantly the Mecca of the distressed Algonquins. It is estimated that in less than three months fourteen thousand Indians were encamped within sound of the morning and evening guns. High above, the little garrison of Frenchmen looked over their palisades, and felt themselves indeed masters of the wilderness.

The scope of the work confronting La Salle, and particularly his political and financial difficulties in Canada, permitted his passing but little time in carrying out those gigantic plans which he had centred about Fort St. Louis. Its command had to be early entrusted to others, Henri de Tonty, M. de la Durantaye, M. de Forest, Sieur de Boisrondet, and Bellefontaine. During one entire Winter, Tonty, and an officer of dragoons, the Chevalier de Baugy, ruled there in unison, the one representing La Salle, the other La Barre, the new Canadian governor. When Spring came they were obliged to rally their men to a common defence of the rock against a sudden attack of the invading Iroquois. After six days of fighting, during which several desperate attempts were made to storm the defences, the savages were obliged to retreat. We know comparatively little of what occurred within or without during the existence of this fort, or of the personnel of its constantly changing garrison. Probably little of soldierly pomp was ever observed, the men employed being mostly *voyageurs* and *coureurs de bois*, more deeply interested in profitable fur trading or adventurous exploring than in military exercises. In a letter written by La Salle from the Chicago portage June 4, 1683, he states that the garrison then consisted of but twenty men, having scarcely a hundred pounds of powder, while at another time he claims to have accomplished his entire work in the Illinois country with the help of only twenty-two Frenchmen.

From this centre, however, many an exploring expedition set forth along the water-ways, or pushed forward into that unknown country away from the familiar water-courses. Various tribes were visited in their far-off encampments, and a quite profitable fur trade rapidly established, apparently greatly to the discomfiture of La Salle's enemies in Canada, and the envious traders at Mackinac. Numerous missionaries, mostly Récollets, though with an occasional wandering and inquisitive black robe, made headquarters on the rock, roving far among the tribes in their efforts to convert the savages. Of the presence of white women at Fort St. Louis there is little record, although we know there were such, while many members of the garrison found sufficient solace among their red neighbors. While often obliged to yield command temporarily to others, Henri de Tonty remained practically supreme at St. Louis until its final abandonment in 1702, when he was ordered to remove to the Mississippi. The old fort was later reoccupied by the French, although not in a military way, and as late as 1718 a number of fur traders were still making it their headquarters. Three years after this date it was again entirely deserted, and Charlevoix, passing the spot, saw only the remains of its fast-decaying palisades. To-day nothing remaining there tells the patient, heroic story of that past, excepting the same grim rock towering high above the well-tilled fields surrounding it.

Fort de Chartres was for forty-five years the seat of French power and authority in the upper Mississippi valley, and for the seven years following was a British stronghold. Its history from beginning to end is fraught with unique and romantic interest. In December, 1718, Lieutenant Pierre Dugué de Boisbriant, a Canadian, holding a French army commission, accompanied by several officers and a considerable detachment of troops, arrived at Kaskaskia by boat from New Orleans. Having selected a fort site eighteen miles above, and north of the village, by the end of Spring, 1720, it was practically completed. This fort stood on the alluvial bottom, three-quarters of a mile distant from the Mississippi, close by the site of a still older fortification said to have been erected by adventurers under Crozat. It was constructed entirely of wood, and is described as a stockade fort, strengthened with earth between the rows of palisades. Within the enclosure were the commandant's house, the barracks, and a storehouse, all constructed of hewn timber and whip-sawed plank.

A village almost immediately sprang up along the bottom land between the fort and the river, settled by French immigrants, and the enterprising Jesuits built the church of St. Anne de Fort Chartres. This first Fort Chartres remained occupied by different bodies of troops until 1756. During these thirty-six years it was the scene of many stirring events, of much important history. Here in 1720 came Philippe François de Renault, as Director-General of Mining Operations, bringing with him into this wilderness two hundred white miners and five hundred San Domingo negroes, thus introducing slavery into the Illinois country. Renault, however, succeeded in accomplishing little in the way of mineral discovery, except to uncover a few scattered lodes of lead ore. He was granted a large tract of land in Monroe County, on which he laid out the small village of St. Philippe. About the same time Lainglois, a nephew of Boisbriant, established the still existing town of Prairie du Rocher. In 1721, the post was visited by the famous priest, Father Xavier de Charlevoix, who was accompanied on his travels by an armed escort, and received with a salute of honor. In his train was a young Canadian officer, Louis St. Ange de Belle Rive, who decided to remain in the country, and afterwards twice held command at the fort. He was a typical French soldier, gallant and debonair, ever ready either for fight or frolic.

In 1725, owing to Bienville's recall to France, Boisbriant became acting Governor of Louisiana, and his former position as Major-Commandant at the Illinois was given over to Sieur de Liette, a captain in the royal army. His administration was principally notable for trouble with the Fox Indians, during which the French settlements were harassed, and troops from the fort took part in several skirmishes. In 1730 Belle Rive succeeded De Liette, holding the position for four years, during which little occurred of any military or political importance, other than Indian expeditions, although Chartres, under his inspiration, became a centre of social gayety, the scene of much ceremony and military pomp. In 1734 Belle Rive was transferred to Vincennes, while Captain Pierre d'Artaguette was given command at Chartres. Almost immediately tragedy took possession of the boards. D'Artaguette was ordered, with every soldier who could possibly be spared from the garrison, to take part in the expedition planned against the Chickasaws in Northern Mississippi. In February, 1736, he left Fort Chartres accompanied by thirty regulars, one hundred volunteers, and two hundred Indians, in a great fleet of *bateaux* and canoes. At the third Chickasaw Bluff, he was joined by the Sieur de Vincennes with twenty Frenchmen and one hundred Indians from the Wabash. Marching inward, his undisciplined command became so impatient for action, that the Indian stronghold was attacked before Bienville could arrive with additional forces from New Orleans. Although seemingly successful at first, the final result was a severe and disastrous defeat. D'Artaguette was badly wounded and captured, together with De Vincennes, Father Senat, a Jesuit priest from the Illinois, and about fifteen other Frenchmen, including young St. Ange. The prisoners were held for some time by the Chickasaws in the hope that Bienville would offer a satisfactory reward for their release. He failed to respond to their messages, and, at last, the hapless victims were burned to death by slow fires. The news cast a gloom over the entire country of the Illinois, and was never forgotten by the inhabitants, the name of D'Artaguette remaining a household word among the French for years.

Alphonse de la Buissouiére was the next commandant at Fort Chartres. In 1739 he led a second expedition from the Illinois country into the land of the Chickasaws, being somewhat more successful in his operations, and escaping without serious loss of life. The following year he was succeeded in office by Captain Benoist de St. Clair, who continued in command of the post for over two years, with nothing occurring outside the ordinary routine of garrison life, and an occasional grant of land. In 1742, the Marquis de Vaudreuil became Governor of Louisiana Province, and immediately appointed the Chevalier de Bertél to the command of the Illinois. He had a somewhat stormy time of it, owing to the early breaking out of war between France and England. Many of the old-time Indian allies of the French along the border were early won over by British agents, and much fear of armed invasion was felt throughout the territory. The fort was by this time greatly out of repair, was poorly supplied with war material, and its small garrison depleted by desertions. De Bertél anxiously urged an increased efficiency upon his superiors at New Orleans, yet little appears to have been done except the enrolment of several companies of militia in the surrounding French settlements, and a slight increase in the regular garrison. Fortunately no British appeared so far in the wilderness, and the fort remained unmolested by enemies. In 1749, De Bertél relinquished his command, and Captain St. Clair once again came into control. He celebrated his return to the post by marrying the daughter of a Kaskaskia citizen, and reigned until the Summer of 1751, when he in turn was superseded by the Chevalier Macarty, by descent an Irishman, by profession a French Major of Engineers. He was accompanied by nearly a full regiment of grenadiers. During his term as commandant the second Fort de Chartres was erected.

Of the old fort no relic now remains, nor is it possible to determine its exact site.

This second fort, one of the greatest ever built in America up to that date, and the most costly ever erected on this continent by France, was constructed according to plans prepared by an engineer officer, Lieutenant Jean B. Saussier. It was begun in 1753, and occupied by troops toward the end of the Summer of 1756. The site chosen was about a mile above the old fort, and half a mile back from the river. The spot selected would seem to have been a strange one for so important a structure, being low and exposed to inroads of water, but was apparently in accordance with French practice. Here, at the great expense, for those days, of one million dollars, was erected a vast fortification. It is generally believed that large profits went to the commandant and others interested in its construction. The fort was built of limestone, quarried from the bluffs four miles east, where to this day the quarry may be seen, while the finer stone with which the gateways and buildings were all faced came from beyond the Mississippi. Altogether it covered an area of four acres, and was capable of sheltering a garrison of three hundred men. The most complete description of its interior arrangement is that given by Captain Pitman, who visited it ten years after completion, and while it was under British control. He wrote as follows:

"The fort is an irregular quadrangle; the sides of the exterior polygon being four hundred and ninety feet. The walls are two feet, two inches thick, and pierced with loopholes at regular intervals, with two portholes for cannon in the faces, and two in the flanks of each bastion. The ditch has never been finished. Within the walls is a banquette raised three feet for men to stand on when they fire through the loopholes. The buildings within the fort are a commandant's house and a commissary's house, the magazine of stores, *corps de garde*, and two barracks; these occupy the square. Within the gorges of the bastion are a powder magazine, bakehouse, and prison, on the floor of which are four dungeons."

As early as Captain Pitman's visit the river current had already cut the bank away to within eighty yards of the fort. The great freshet of 1772 produced such havoc that the west walls and two bastions were precipitated into the water. Soon after this the British garrison were obliged to desert it entirely, and took up their quarters at Fort Gage on the Kaskaskia. Since then it has become a total ruin. In 1820 sufficient remained to permit the making of a very careful drawing of the original plan. By 1850 a dense forest covered the site. To-day the sole existing memorial of the old fort is the powder magazine, which remains in a good state of preservation, an object picturesque and venerable.

To resume the story of this fort: in 1760 Macarty gave up command to Neyon de Villiers, who commanded the French and Indians against Washington in the fight at Great Meadows, a large part of his force on that occasion coming from Fort Chartres. During his incumbency, Pierre Laclede Liguest arrived at Fort Chartres from New Orleans, with a great store-boat deeply laden with miscellaneous goods. After wintering at the fort, Laclede proceeded up the river in February, 1764, and landing on the west shore, established St. Louis. In June, 1764, Captain de Villiers, becoming impatient over the delay of the British to take possession, by terms of the Treaty of Paris signed the previous year, finally resigned his position, and retreated down the river, accompanied by several officers, a company of soldiers, and a number of the French inhabitants, who were unwilling to remain in the country under English rule. The veteran St. Ange de Belle Rive travelled from Vincennes and assumed command. With the very few soldiers remaining, his task of preserving peace proved a difficult one, but was successfully accomplished, and on October 10, 1765, he finally surrendered the fort to Captain Thomas Stirling, who came from Fort Pitt with one hundred Highlanders of the 42nd British Regiment, to take formal possession. After ninety-two years of French control the white banner of France was lowered, and the Red Cross of St. George took its place. St. Ange, with his little remaining garrison of thirty men, crossed the river to St. Louis, where he took service under the King of Spain. Captain Stirling remained only until December 4, when Major Robert Farmer, with a detachment of the 34th British Foot, arrived from Mobile, and assumed command. Others followed rapidly until the final abandonment of the fort in 1772 — Colonel Edward Cole, Colonel John Reed, Lieutenant-Colonel John Wilkins, and Captain Hugh Lord each commanding in turn. In the Spring of the last mentioned year, a great freshet tore away the entire river wall, the water rising to the height of seven feet inside the fort, which was hastily abandoned, the garrison retiring to Kaskaskia.

Thus passed away old Fort Chartres, its memory still locally preserved in the name of the river landing and ferry near where it once stood. "It is much to be regretted," says a writer well versed in the subject, "that so few of the records and official documents of old Fort Chartres have been preserved to reveal to us the story of its various occupants in the daily life, and of the stirring events, and strange thrilling scenes that transpired there."

On the banks of the Ohio, just without the confines of the city of Metropolis, are the ruins of Fort Massac, the third important French fortification built in the Illinois country. Its story, while involving no especial memories of bloodshed or of war, is connected with many stirring events, and associated with numerous historic names. Tradition marks the site as having been used by De Soto in 1542, and, whether this is true or not, this spot has in turn been occupied by Spaniards, French, English, Indians, and Americans. The old earthworks, yet partially preserved, have a brave tale to tell. Here Juchereau traded, and

Father Mermet preached; here the southern Indians came in their bark canoes to hear the story of the Christ; here the French, falling rapidly back in retreat from Fort du Quesne, halted, and St. Ange de Belle Rive stopped every pursuing expedition down the Wabash and the Ohio. Here Tecumseh hunted; here Wilkinson, Sebastian, Powers, and others, with Spanish, French, and Creole women as companions, plotted to dismember the American Union; here Aaron Burr rested, and planned treason, here the beautiful wife of Blennerhasset first learned of her husband's connection with the plot, and here Lieutenant Zebulon Pike once held command.

In August, 1702, M. Juchereau de St. Denis, with thirty-three Canadians, and accompanied by Father Jean Mermet as chaplain, left Kaskaskia to form a settlement and build a fort on the Ohio. His purpose was fur-trading with the southern Indians, and his license came directly from Versailles. On this site he erected a palisaded cabin or two, and a storehouse for his goods. A short distance away, the zealous priest built his little mission chapel of logs. This latter was called "Assumption," but if Juchereau ever named his trading-fort, all record has been lost. In later years it was commonly referred to as the "Old Cherokee Fort." Two years later the commandant died, and in 1705 the establishment was completely broken up through difficulty with surrounding Indians, the French fleeing hastily to save their lives, leaving behind all their stores, together with thirteen thousand buffalo skins. Tradition has it that this small trading-fort was reëstablished by adventurers in 1710, but remained unimportant until the French and Indian War of 1756.

It was during this latter war that the defeated French came floating down the Ohio on their retreat of nearly a thousand miles. Reaching the site of Assumption, M. Aubry, who was in command, halted and landed his troops. Many among them had been previously stationed in the Illinois country, and knew it well. This spot was one hundred and twenty miles by land from Kaskaskia, and but little farther to Fort Chartres. It was four days' journey to the mouth of the Illinois. And here they proposed to stay on guard over the mouth of the Ohio, thirty-six miles below. They occupied the old site, throwing up earthworks, and erecting over it a stockade with four bastions, upon which they mounted eight pieces of cannon. Quarters were furnished within for one hundred men. Henceforth, in French records, it was known as Fort Massac.

Four years later, M. de Macarty rebuilt and strongly fortified the place. In 1763, by the terms of the Treaty of Paris, Massac was surrendered into the hands of the English, but the French garrison, although small in numbers, remained in possession until the Spring of 1765. The English, during the thirteen years they held control of the Illinois country, never occupied the fort with troops. Had they done so, an important chapter of Western history might have been differently written, for it was on this unguarded spot that the flag of the newly united Colonies was probably first unfurled above Illinois territory, and George Rogers Clark began his daring march of conquest.

Indeed, Fort Massac was not again held by troops until the United States was threatened with trouble by both Spain and France in 1794, when it was hastily rebuilt and occupied, under special orders from President Washington. Major Thomas Doyle was its first American commander, and it remained a post of some importance, the scene of many stirring events, until after the collapse of the Burr conspiracy. In 1797, about thirty families were settled in the neighborhood; Captain Zebulon Pike was in command, having a garrison of eighty-three men. At different times Generals Anthony Wayne and James Wilkinson occupied the fort as their headquarters. As late as 1812, it was repaired, being gar-

SITE OF FORT GAGE, FROM KASKASKIA

PRESENT ASPECT OF THE EARTHWORKS OF OLD FORT GAGE

risoned at that time by a Tennessee volunteer regiment. In 1855 Governor Reynolds visited Fort Massac, and thus describes its appearance. The outside walls were one hundred and thirty-five feet square, and at each angle bastions were erected. The walls were palisaded, with earth between the wood. A large well was sunk within the fortress, and the whole appeared to have been strong and substantial in its day. Three or four acres of gravel walks were made on the north front of the fort, along which the soldiers paraded. These walks were arranged in exact angles, and beautifully decorated with pebbles gathered from the river. The site was one of the most lovely on La Belle Rivière, commanding a charming view. There were remains of the unstoned well near the centre. The ditch surrounding the earthworks was then some three feet below the surface, while the breastworks were raised about two feet above the inner level. The gravelled sentry-walk could be plainly traced. To-day the site has been transformed into a State park, and the Illinois Daughters of the American Revolution are restoring the old fort, so far as possible, to its former dimensions and form.

Other forts within the State limits were numerous, but not of great historic importance. Fort Dearborn, on the site of Chicago, has its tragic story told in another chapter. Rebuilt in 1816, it was garrisoned for about twenty-five years by United States troops. Fort Gage, to which the British soldiers retired when the crumbling walls of Chartres would no longer shelter them, was built on the bank of the Kaskaskia. In shape, it was an oblong parallelogram, 280 by 251 feet, constructed of large squared timbers, built upon earthwork. It was never heavily garrisoned, the occupants in 1772 consisting of one officer and twenty soldiers. In the village of Kaskaskia at this time were two small companies of well-disciplined French militia. In 1778, when Clark reached Fort Gage, there was not a British soldier on duty, and a Frenchman, M. Rocheblave, was in command. Fort Clark was erected in 1813 on the present site of Peoria, about where the Rock Island depot now stands, and gave name to the place for several years. It was a strong palisade structure of logs, similar in form to many others, although larger and mounting cannon, and was garrisoned by both rangers and United States troops, and successfully sustained one severe Indian attack. Fort Armstrong was erected upon a rocky bluff at the lower extremity of Rock Island, in 1816, and from its situation was a very conspicuous object to travellers on the Mississippi. It was garrisoned by United States troops, and attained considerable prominence during the Black Hawk War, but was never the scene of any historic events of importance.

In 1811, great numbers of block-house forts were built, extending from the Illinois River to the Kaskaskia, thence across to about the present town of Equality, following up the Ohio and the Wabash, thus protecting nearly all existing settlements. Among the more important of these may be mentioned, one on the site of Carlyle; one just above the town of Aviston, known as Journey's Fort; two on the east side of Shoal Creek, called Hill's and Jones's Forts; one a few miles southeast of the present town of Lebanon, on the west side of Looking-glass Prairie, known as Chambers's Fort ; on the Kaskaskia River were Middleton's and Goring's Forts; one on Doza Creek, known as Nat Hill's; two in the Jourdan settlement, eastern part of Franklin County, on the road to the salt works ; one at the mouth of the Illinois River ; while a little later, John Campbell, a United States officer, erected a small block-house nineteen miles up the Illinois, on its west bank. More pretentious military stations were established opposite the mouth of the Missouri, and on Silver Creek, near Troy. But the main depot was built a mile and a half northwest of the present Edwardsville, and called Camp Russell.

Most of these were very simple, temporary affairs, consisting of a single house of a story and a half, or occasionally two stories, built of logs, with the corners closely trimmed to prevent scaling. The walls below were provided with loopholes ; the door was made of thick puncheons, and strongly barred on the inside. The upper story usually projected over the lower three or four feet, with loopholes through the floor. These were merely single-family forts, and were very numerous. The stockade forts, garrisoned by rangers, consisted of four block-houses, such as described above, or larger, placed one at each corner of a square piece of ground, of dimensions ample enough to accommodate all the white residents of the neighborhood. The intervening space was filled in with timbers, or logs, set firmly on end in the ground and extending upward twelve to fifteen feet. This formed the stockade, and along it upon the inside was a raised platform for riflemen to stand upon. Loopholes cut in the projecting walls of the corner block-houses commanded the entire stockade from without. Within, cabins were erected for the settlers, and a well was dug, unless the site selected contained a spring. Usually there were two heavy entrances, large enough to admit teams, and strongly barred. In times of special peril, horses and cattle were driven within the enclosure. If the fort stood in the woods, the trees were cleared away on every side, so as to give an open firing-space for the defence.

The most notable, as well as the largest, strongest, and best equipped of these stockade forts, was Camp Russell, established early in 1812, near Edwardsville, then the extreme northern frontier. The old cannon of Louis XIV, which, for many years, had done service at Fort Chartres, were taken there and mounted on the walls, adding little to the defensive strength, but much to military appearance, and being especially important on days of festivity, or dress parade. This stockade was made the main depot for military stores, and became a general rendezvous for volunteers, rangers, and regulars, while from here departed the various expeditions northward into the Indian country. The only United States regulars, however, camping here during the war were a small company under command of Captain Ramsey. It was here that Governor Edwards established his headquarters, and gathered about him the beauty and chivalry of the Illinois country. Here were much entertaining, many brilliant balls and glittering dress parades, for the Governor dearly loved display, and presided with courtly grace and stately dignity over scenes of frontier merry-making and military pomp.

At various periods in its earlier history, defences were erected in the Illinois territory that might be mentioned in this connection. During the short-lived Black Hawk War numerous temporary forts were built in the northwestern portion of the State, and held by parties of volunteers, such as Fort Hamilton in Stephenson County, Fort Paine in Du Page, Fort Beags in Will, and Gray's Fort in Kane, and Apple River Fort in Jo Daviess; but these were of small historical interest. Traders also, pushing forward ahead of civilization, erected numerous defensive stockades, which later became centres of influence, and occasionally of military importance. Among these may be mentioned, La Sallier's Trading Post on Rock River in Lee County, established in 1822, Hubbard's in Iroquois in 1822, and one unnamed in northern Knox County, established in 1828. Shull had such a trading-fort on the Mississippi near Galena as early as 1819. All of these possess local interest, and about them doubtless hover stories of adventure in those early days of danger worthy of preservation. Illinois has been a continuous battle-ground, and every fort evidenced a stern advance toward civilization and peace within her borders. They were the footprints of her daring pioneers.

CHAPTER XIV

THE FOOTSTEPS OF GEORGE ROGERS CLARK

IN June, 1778, the entire country of the Illinois was under English control, as it had practically been since the Treaty of Paris, in 1763. But to the eastward the struggle of the United Colonies for independence had caused the steady draining of troops from this far frontier, so that by this date not a British regular remained on guard along the Mississippi valley. The scattered forts, with their small stores of military equipment, were left to the uncertain protection of French militia, the depth of whose allegiance to England's interests was extremely doubtful. It was the time to strike on behalf of the Colonies for all this great expanse of western territory, and fortunately the leader for just such an emergency had discovered means for action.

George Rogers Clark, born of a good Virginia family, was at this time twenty-six years of age. His education was fair, but from childhood he had been a restless rover of the woods. Six feet in height, stoutly built, with red hair and black penetrating eyes, he was courageous to audacity, but of quick temper. In many ways Clark early became a marked character along the Kentucky frontier—"a land of heroes and desperadoes, saints and sinners." He had served in the Dunmore war as a boy, and later won rank with Boone, Kenton, Logan, and other famous bordermen in Indian fighting. He had taken part with the revolutionary forces in the East, but had early conceived the importance of wresting the territory bordering upon the Ohio from British control. Presenting this project to Virginia officials, including his personal friend, Patrick Henry, and overcoming many obstacles, he at last, heading a little party of determined frontiersmen who had volunteered for the desperate service, floated down the Ohio, and found landing on Illinois soil just above old deserted Fort Massac. Altogether, he had with him for this daring enterprise one hundred and fifty-three followers. It was a motley gathering. There was no attempt at military dress, the officers being in nowise distinguished from the men by their apparel. Personal prowess alone determined the permanency of command. They were all alike volunteers, recruited from along the frontiers of Virginia and Kentucky. On their feet were moccasins; the majority wore loose, thin trousers of homespun or buckskin, having a fringe of leather thongs down the outer seam of each leg; some were attired only in leggings of leather, and were otherwise as bare of knee and thigh as a Highland clansman. Common to all was the fringed buckskin hunting-shirt, a garment hanging loosely down from neck to knee, and girded about the waist by a broad belt, from which was suspended tomahawk and scalping-knife. On one hip hung the powder-horn, on the other a provision pouch. A home-made hat, or cap of fox or squirrel skin, having the tail dangling behind, protected the head, while in the hand was held the rudely constructed flint-lock rifle, a long clumsy appearing weapon, but deadly enough in the hands of such cool, expert marksmen, trained to rely upon it in time of need. Of these men Clark held the complete confidence, binding them to him by strong personal influence, unquestioned daring, and cool self-control. Perhaps no other man on the border could at that time have governed them as completely as did he. His force at the commencement of the expedition was divided into four companies, commanded by Captains John Montgomery, Joseph Bowman, Leonard Helms, and William Harrod. They first stepped on Illinois soil at the mouth of Massac Creek, a mile above the old fort, then without occupants, June 30, 1778. It is most probable this was the first time the flag of the United States was ever unrolled so far in the West, as there is every reason to believe Clark carried such a banner, just adopted, with him on his expedition.

With no possibility of receiving further reënforcement, a thousand miles of trackless wilderness stretching between them and their base of supplies, uncertain regarding the defences fronting them, these undaunted men of the border determined on pushing boldly forward across unknown country, trusting to make surprise accomplish the work of numbers. Meeting by chance, when but a few miles from the river, a small party of Kentucky hunters, the latter were easily induced to act as guides for their countrymen, and with one John Saunders in advance, the little army set forth on its daring and toilsome march. It was one hundred and twenty miles as the crow flies, from Massac to Kaskaskia. The country to be traversed was marked by no signs of guidance save a few dim, winding Indian trails, while the route selected led through swamps, amid the low mountains of the Ozarks, and across level plains beyond. Their success depended altogether upon swiftness and secrecy ; but on the third day of travel, while within the present limits of Williamson County, the bewildered guide lost his way. Much confusion resulted, the exasperated bordermen threatening him with death, but fortunately in time to save himself from such fate, Saunders recognized a distant point of timber, and from there led directly forward to Kaskaskia.

On the afternoon of July 4, with their garments worn and soiled, and their cheeks covered by beards of three weeks' growth, the invaders cautiously stole down into the Kaskaskia River valley, and concealed themselves along the east bank, in a thick wood, to wait for the coming of night. They were at this time about three miles above the town, which was situated on the opposite shore. Reconnoitring parties were cautiously despatched, through the early dusk, who learned something regarding the situation in the village, and fortunately secured sufficient boats with which to transport the command across the stream. Clark's plan of attack was extremely daring and simple. His small force was divided into three parties consisting of about fifty men each. Two of these were directed to cross the river and take position opposite different portions of the town, moving forward as silently as possible through the darkness, guarding against discovery. The third, under his own immediate command, was to advance directly down the east bank, climb the steep bluff, and dash in upon Fort Gage. He was to make the first attack ; the others being expected to await his signal of success before charging the town.

Lovers of romance have woven many an interesting legend about the stirring events of that dark night, most of them melodramatic and improbable.

"We have been told," writes Dr. Thwaites, in his exhaustive essay, "that, as Clark and his men lay there by the postern gate, they could hear the sounds of French fiddles squeaking a quadrille, and now and then gay shouts of laughter. The officers of the post were, it is related, giving a ball to the inhabitants in the large assembly room with its puncheon floor. The outlying houses were deserted. Men and women, villagers and garrison, Indians and *coureurs de bois*, were, without regard to rank or race, crowded into the hall, heeding nothing save the dance. Even the sentinels had deserted their posts to join in the festivities, and Kaskaskia, a victim to the irrepressible gayety of the French, was unguarded. Leaving his men at the gate, says the story-teller, Clark, alone with his guide, strode across the parade, and leaning against the doorpost, with folded arms, watched the gay scene — a patch of light and color in the heart of the gloomy wilderness. As he calmly stood there, an unbidden guest, an Indian, lying curled in his blanket on the entry floor, started and gazed intently upon him. Another moment, the savage sprang to his feet and sounded the war-whoop. In the midst of the general consternation, Rocheblave, and his brother officers, hurried to the door, but Clark, unmoved, bade them go on with the dance, but be pleased to remember that they were now holding revelry under the banner of Virginia, and not that of Great Britain."

The truth, while smacking less of romance, is scarcely less stirring, when we consider the isolation of these gallant men, and their utter uncertainty regarding the force opposing them. Clark's immediate party, which numbered scarcely more than a dozen, lay, during the early evening, under the river bank, where they were barked at by dogs. The scouts pressing up the steep hill and finding the fort gate open, those behind pushed on through the darkness to Rocheblave's house, and succeeded in capturing that surprised commandant in an upper room. Hauling him downstairs, they gave the signal for general attack. Yelling like mad, the united bordermen surged through the fort, in which they found not a single soldier to oppose them, and up and down the streets of startled Kaskaskia, and within fifteen minutes were in full possession without the necessity of firing a gun. Armed with the knowledge — which had just reached this country before he left the East — that France was already in open allegiance with the American Colonies, Clark made judicious use of this important fact to win to himself the confidence of the French inhabitants. His moderation and kindness toward them also tended to immediately restore quietness. Their spirits rose when they learned that instead of being made slaves by these bloodthirsty Virginians, the "long knives" they had been taught so long to fear, they were, upon taking an oath of allegiance to the Republic, to be allowed to go at their pleasure, and meet in their little church as of old. All the Creoles, Clark reported, took the oath of loyalty, as thus prescribed, but Commandant Rocheblave had been exceedingly violent and insulting in language, and for punishment was sent to Virginia as a prisoner, and his slaves sold, the money thus obtained being divided among his riflemen.

A small party, accompanied by a few eager French volunteers under command of Captain Bowman, promptly took possession of Cahokia, sixty miles north, making the trip on horseback. Meanwhile Father Pierre Gibault, the Kaskaskia priest, now thoroughly devoted to American interests, was despatched overland to Vincennes, to learn something of the situation at that post, and returning about August, reported to Clark that through his influence the American flag had been hoisted above that fort, the small squad of British soldiers in possession deeming it safer to withdraw before the threatened uprising of the French inhabitants, and fearing the approach of Clark and his "long knives." Captain Helm was at once sent to this post to assume command of the French militia, taking with him as companion a single American by the name of Henry.

Successful as Clark had thus far been in carrying out all his plans, he was still in a most perilous position. His little band stood utterly alone in the heart of an immense wilderness. French loyalty to the new Republic was at best doubtful, while the surrounding Indian tribes were restless, and easily swayed by either British or French adventurers. West of the Mississippi, the Spanish influence prevailed, and must be kept friendly to insure his future safety and success. His force was far too insignificant for any serious thought of armed conquest, or to enable him to carry out his original project of a quick military advance against the important British post at Detroit, yet while that remained in English hands, all he had yet accomplished was in peril. Fortunately in this emergency Clark proved himself diplomat as well as soldier, winning the interest of the Spanish officials, the friendship of surrounding Indian tribes, and cementing more firmly the confidence of the French inhabitants to his cause. So passed the busy days of that Summer and Fall, the American commander strengthening his position in every possible way, while despatching urgent messages eastward begging for reënforcements to aid him in carrying forward his further plans of conquest.

Meanwhile, General Hamilton, the British commander at Detroit, was far from being idle. Seeking for allies among those Indian tribes already pledged to the English service, he gathered together a formidable war party for the purpose of re-garrisoning Vincennes, and for the reëstablishment of British influence throughout the Illinois country. By the seventh of October he had departed in person for the scene of action, accompanied by one hundred and seventy-seven whites, largely Creole volunteers, and about three hundred Indians, of various tribes. Because of storms and icy streams they were seventy-one days in reaching Vincennes. Here Captain Helm and his single American soldier attempted resistance, but on the prompt desertion of the French militia finally surrendered after obtaining "all the honors of war."

The news of this easy recapture of Fort Sackville, and the town of Vincennes, which it commanded by its guns, did not reach Clark on the distant Kaskaskia until fully a month later. The entire Illinois country was soon plunged into wild alarm by the persistently circulated rumors of British advance, aggravated by raiding parties of Indians, incited by Hamilton. Clark's personality alone sufficed to hold his motley following firm, and gradually confidence was restored to the excitable French, while he waited with what patience he could command for more definite information regarding the exact situation on the distant banks of the Wabash. This did not reach him until the evening of January 29, when Colonel Francis Vigo, a Spanish merchant, just arrived from Vincennes, furnished him with complete details as to Hamilton's force and plans, informing him that all but about eighty of the British force, with one hundred Indians, had returned to Detroit, while the commander was busily planning a campaign for the coming Spring.

Above all else, Clark was a man of action, and in this emergency realized at once that any further hesitation meant defeat. Desperate as the venture then appeared, he decided to attack the British at once, rather than await any invasion on their part. Hastily he had a large bateau, which was named "The Willing," constructed, armed it with two four-pounders, and four large swivel guns, manned it with a crew of forty volunteers, largely French Creoles, under Lieutenant Rogers, and on the evening of February 4 despatched this rude vessel down the Mississippi with orders to patrol the Ohio and ascend the Wabash as far as possible, so as to coöperate with his land force. Then he turned energetically to the organization of this overland expedition. Persuaded by the enthusiastic Creole girls, the principal young men of the section flocked to the call of the tall Virginian. On the very day following the departure of "The Willing" southward, he marched out of wildly cheering Kaskaskia, at the head of his little volunteer army of one hundred and seventy bold fellows, both American and French, their flags fluttering, and their drums beating merrily.

Scarcely in the pages of manly endeavor will be found any record of a more truly desperate venture than this mid-winter march across the untracked wilderness to battle against overwhelming odds. The distance to be covered by these invaders was some two hundred and thirty miles, across a little-known country beautified by alternating lakes, rivers, groves, and prairies. In Summertime it would have been a continuous scene of beauty and peace, while in the cold of Winter the frozen plains and ice-bridged streams would have offered comparatively easy travelling. But this was February; the temperature was that of early Spring, and great freshets sweeping down the broad valleys had completely inundated all the lowland. The ground under foot became more sodden as they advanced; progress was

GEORGE ROGERS CLARK

FROM A COPY BY EDWARDS OF JARVIS'S PORTRAIT; THE COPY BEING IN POSSESSION OF THE WISCONSIN HISTORICAL SOCIETY

necessarily slow; hardships increased. The little band were without tents or protection of any kind, the floods had driven away the expected game from along the route of march, and Clark and his officers were soon at their wits' end to devise methods for keeping up the flagging spirits of their wearied, hungry men. The first week passed amid constantly increasing toil and exposure. At the end of it, they arrived at the "drowned lands" of the Wabash, a broad stretch of low, level country, lying entirely submerged, and extending almost the entire distance from the valley of the Little Wabash to Vincennes. The opposite banks of this stream were five miles apart, with water sweeping tumultuously down, and in no place less than three feet deep. Here, drenched by the constant rain, hungry, and becoming somewhat disheartened before such obstacles, these men, encouraged by their leaders, managed to construct a rude raft, or flat-boat, and ferried their baggage across to the opposite shore, which was distinguished merely by a fringe of trees. The stronger among them waded and swam across, aided by the few horses in the party. Occasionally sinking in the mud and water as high as their shoulders, the toiling soldiers were cheered to new exertions by every device which the officers could conjure up. An Irish drummer, of exceedingly small stature, but with rare talent as a singer of comic songs, was hoisted on the head of the tallest man in the company, and thus led the way, stirring those behind with his wit and music.

Almost worn out by fatigue, hunger, and exposure, the heroic, struggling band attained to the banks of the Embarras River on the twelfth day out from Kaskaskia. They were now so close to Vincennes that they dare not discharge their guns for fear of alarming the unsuspecting garrison, whom they yet hoped to surprise. The Embarras was a raging flood, utterly impassable. The very best they could do was to find a small swampy hillock in the midst of the tumultuous waters. Here amid a constant drizzle soaking them to the skin, they huddled closely together for the night, shivering from cold, and having neither food nor fire with which to warm themselves. The next morning they were aroused from their discomfort by the sound of the sunrise gun at Vincennes, then scarcely nine miles away. But it boomed to their ears across a wide and desolate waste of waters. The dismal surroundings, coupled with ever increasing hardship and danger, greatly depressed the French volunteers, but the Americans remained undaunted. They remained in camp that day, but despatched a detail on a rudely constructed raft, in an endeavor to either steal boats from near the town, or open communication with their own bateau. Two days later, these returned unsuccessful in their endeavors. As Captain Bowman wrote, "There was not one foot of dry land to be found. No provisions of any sort now for two days." On February 20, a boat was brought in containing five Frenchmen belonging to Vincennes. These villagers reported to Clark, greatly to his encouragement, that Hamilton and his men had no suspicion of any attack being threatened, and that the native inhabitants of Vincennes were all well-disposed toward the American cause.

The twenty-first it rained violently all day, but the desperate invaders felt that they could remain quiet no longer. Every moment of delay increased the peril of discovery. Facing the steady downpour at daybreak, the little band was safely ferried on rude rafts, aided by a few canoes, across the raging waters to the eastern side of the Wabash on which lay Vincennes. There was no river bank to be found in all that desolation of down-pouring flood, and their slow advance was made in the face of imminent peril. All around them extended a vast swamp, without a spot of dry land appearing for leagues above its surface. The icy water oftentimes rose to the chins of the struggling soldiers, yet they pushed resolutely forward, the stronger wading, their rifles held high above their heads, while the weaker and more famished were borne in the few canoes. No nobler incident of heroic toil and self-sacrifice is recorded in American history. With infinite labor and suffering scarcely three miles of that awful journey toward battle had been completed when darkness again overtook them, and they were obliged to seek refuge for another night. Fortunately at that critical moment a little boggy island was discovered lifting its water-soaked surface above the stream, and there, for their seventh night of suffering and exposure, within sound of the evening and morning guns of the fort, those men of iron slept, hungry, and in clothes sopping wet.

They awoke once more with the dawn to confront the same deadly prospect. Without food to afford strength for the undertaking, the gallant fellows plunged into the freezing flood, moving forward in Indian file, the strongest man of each company leading the way. Occasionally some brave heart would start a song, which others would take up in the straggling column behind, and thus all through those hours of misery they stumbled blindly on, determined still to find and grapple with the enemy. That night they were within six miles of Vincennes, their camping-spot a maple grove on a hillock. It was bitterly cold ; when the reluctant morning dawned, ice half an inch thick covered the smooth water, while the sodden clothing of the men was frozen stiff. But the sun breaking through the lowering clouds promised a bright day, and brought with it renewed courage. Clark, facing his famishing, half-frozen men, pledged his word that the next night should find them within striking distance of the foe, and then, dashing into the water at the head of the column, sternly ordered his officers to close up the rear, and shoot down any man who refused to follow him.

The road forward grew constantly more difficult, while the increasing weakness of the men made the advance desperately slow. The lowland, now known as Horseshoe Plain, across which they struggled, had been transformed by the constant downpour of weeks into a shallow lake fully four miles wide. Not the slightest point of land uplifted above the water, but far away a distant fringe of woods fortunately hid their movements from sight of both the town and the fort. Near the centre of this lake, the prolonged hardships of that toilsome struggle began to tell most seriously. Man after man fell in the ranks exhausted, and the few canoes they possessed were paddled frantically back and forth in an endeavor to save the poor fellows from drowning. Soldier clung to soldier in support, staggering forward scarcely able to keep his feet, while the lion-hearted Clark urged, commanded, implored them to renewed exertion. The water deepened until it reached the shoulders of the tallest, and when finally the despairing, suffering column attained to the edge of an island grove, the men flung themselves sobbing on the sodden ground, so thoroughly exhausted that to rally them was almost impossible. But in this moment of utter despair, a little ray of hope came as encouragement. From a party of Indian women who chanced to pass in a canoe, some food was obtained. Fires were lighted, the weakest given broth, and thus all were inspired to renewed determination.

But at the best it would be hard to conceive of a situation more utterly desperate, more apparently hopeless. The merest handful of weakened, famished men, fronting an unknown but superior force, pressing sternly on to attack a strongly garrisoned fort in the very heart of the enemy's country, without a single piece of artillery, their scanty rifle ammunition wet and useless, — it was a scene of fact stranger than any fiction ever penned. From where they now rested, breathless and shivering from cold, they could distinguish, only two miles away, through scattered woods, and across yet another wide lake, the distant log houses of the little town.

A scouting party brought in a Creole who was discovered hunting ducks in the swamp, and he furnished them with both food and bad news. Hamilton and his British garrison were still unconscious of their approach, but two hundred additional Indian allies had just arrived at Fort Sackville. Those staggering, almost unarmed, bordermen realized now that immediately before them, entrenched, provisioned, thoroughly equipped with small arms and cannon, there awaited a force — British, French, and Indian — fully four times their own. It was a moment when any but the most heroic souls would have quailed in utter despair. But Clark was emphatically the man for such an emergency, and at his back that day were the men of iron to support him in desperate deed. His simple plan was that of audacity and daring, the usual strategy of the border. Despatching the captured Creole directly to his own people of the town bearing a letter, requesting their secrecy and assistance, he prepared at once to impress them with his power and ability to make good his threats of vengeance if they failed him. His camp, while in plain view from the village, was luckily concealed from the fort. Taking advantage of the peculiar lay of the land between, Clark marched his little band of men back and forth just within the edge of a wood, every banner unfurled to the breeze, every rifle shining in the light, thus deceiving the watchers into the belief that he had behind him a thousand armed followers. Such an exhibition of military strength, coupled with Clark's reputation for daring along that frontier, and the mystery of his sudden appearance from out the waste of those surrounding waters, completely overawed the French population, and not one among them even dared to steal away to the unsuspecting British fort and warn the garrison of the danger threatening.

At sundown, Clark divided his party, now eager for battle, into two small bands. Of one he assumed personal command ; the other was entrusted to Captain Bowman. At seven o'clock the latter pushed silently forward and surrounded the town, while the former hurried directly through the village toward the unsuspecting fort. The excited inhabitants greeted the advancing column with cheers as it swung rapidly along the single street of the village, and handed out to the men hidden stores of much-needed ammunition. The surprise of the fort was complete. Hamilton believed the first stray shots heard were fired by drunken Indians, nor did he fully awaken from confidence until, in the brilliant moonlight, his officers discovered that the stockade was already completely surrounded by American bordermen. There was no hesitancy in the swift and deadly attack. Those gallant fellows had not marched and hungered all those long leagues to play at war, and they realized fully the vast odds opposing them. The palisaded fort was a strong frontier defence, having large block-houses at the angles, the second floors towering eleven feet above the ground, and each containing both cannon and swivel guns. Clark possessed not a single piece of artillery, but he had with him the most expert riflemen of the border. Sheltered behind houses, palings, and ditches, as coolly as though they were hunting game in the backwoods, these men poured such a constant, deadly fire through the narrow loop-holes of the fort as to utterly silence the British guns. Not a gunner dared remain at his piece, and before sunrise it became plainly evident that the garrison was already seriously crippled, although the return fire of small arms continued briskly.

At nine o'clock that morning the Americans paused in their attack just long enough to eat breakfast, that being the first regular meal they had enjoyed in six days. Clark, taking advantage of the pause, sent in to Hamilton an invitation to surrender, but that officer refusing, the firing was at once hotly resumed. Soon after this parley occurred, a party of French and Indian scouts, not understanding the situation, burst into the town. They were loaded down with scalps and provisions from a recent raid upon American settlements. Instantly the enraged borderers burst from their coverts and charged them, killing two and wounding most of the others. Six were captured, deliberately tomahawked in sight of the horrified garrison, and their bodies thrown into the river. Whether justified by circumstances or not, this act overawed the surrounding savages, and struck terror among the French volunteers within the fort, many of whom refused to fight longer. For two hours the fighting continued unchecked, the firing from the concealed American riflemen proving constant and deadly. A number of men in the fort were struck by shots entering through the narrow loopholes, and finally, in despair of any relief from without, Hamilton sent forth a white flag, requesting a three days' truce, for the purpose of arranging satisfactory terms of surrender. To this Clark responded in the following note, thoroughly characteristic of the man and the times :

"Colonel Clark's Compliments to Mr. Hamilton and begs leave to inform him that Colonel Clark will not agree to any Other Terms than that of Mr. Hamilton's Surrendering himself and Garrison, Prisoners at Discretion.

"If Mr. Hamilton is Desirous of a Conference with Colonel Clark he will meet him at the Church with Captain Helm.

"February 24th, 1779. G. R. CLARK."

Finding no escape possible, Hamilton agreed to this conference, where he sought in vain to have the terms of capitulation modified. At last articles of agreement were signed, and the time set for the formal surrender of the fort to the Americans. At the appointed hour, on the morning of the twenty-fifth, Lieutenant-Governor Hamilton, with his garrison of eighty men, marched forth from the stockade, past Bowman's and Mac Carty's companies, the latter entirely Creole volunteers, while the Americans under Captains

Williams and Worthington entered the fort, relieved the sentries, and hoisted the American flag above the palisade. Thirteen guns were fired as a national salute, during which an accident occurred, greatly marring the deep joy of victory. By a premature explosion of cartridges, Bowman, Worthington, and four privates were severely burned. The captured fort was promptly re-christened "Patrick Henry."

It is almost impossible in words to express fitly the importance of this achievement. In many respects it stands unique and alone among the daring deeds of war. Clark, in the midst of Winter, isolated amid the wilderness, fronting an unknown but largely outnumbering enemy, had conducted a forced march of two hundred and thirty miles, through leagues of icy water, often rising to the shoulders of his struggling men. With only a small party of ragged, famished, half-disciplined militiamen, a large proportion Creole, he had boldly advanced into the very heart of a strange and hostile country, and, without the aid of artillery, had captured a strong stockade fort, containing cannon and swivels, and manned by a trained garrison, largely outnumbering his command. The conception and execution were alike heroic, and, with all honor to those gallant men who so boldly followed him, the meed of praise belongs for ever to George Rogers Clark. And the result was well worthy the action, for by this means the great Northwest was won to the United States.

CHAPTER XV

PIONEER LIFE AND ADVENTURE ALONG THE ILLINOIS BORDER, 1782–1812

IT was these romantic exploits, performed by General Clark and his frontier followers in the years 1778–1779, which made known the fertile Illinois country to Eastern bordermen. The result was an almost immediate emigration to the banks of the Mississippi and the Wabash. Among these earlier arrivals not a few of Clark's soldiers returned, and settled upon lands which had been allotted them as a reward for army service. By nature adventurous, and of a fearless spirit, cut off by a widely unsettled region from any civilization, and completely surrounded by savage tribes, it is surprising that these earlier settlers escaped with so little trouble. Fighting there was in plenty, and Indian massacre, yet no such continuous bloody incidents as mark the pioneer history of Kentucky and Ohio are to be found in the early annals of Illinois. Nevertheless, these first adventurous settlers, who invariably founded their primitive log homes along the banks of streams and within the shadow of the woods, fearful lest the temptingly open prairie land should prove unproductive, were never left for long undisturbed by their troublesome red neighbors. They held to their exposed positions for many years through constant vigilance, and the readiness of their deadly rifles.

Of all the Illinois Indians, the Kickapoos proved themselves during this period the most formidable and dangerous. Since 1763, when they were forced southward from about the great lake where they had formerly ruled supreme, this tribe had occupied a portion of the territory lying along the

Mackinaw and Sangamon Rivers, having their principal villages on Kickapoo Creek, and at Elkhart Grove. For some reason their intense hatred of the inflowing American settlers was implacable, and they were ever the first among Illinois tribes to commence hostilities, the last to submit and enter into treaties with the whites. During the ten years extending from 1786 to 1796 this tribe alone, recruited possibly by young and adventurous warriors from other near-by villages, kept the isolated white settlements in a continual state of alarm. For protection, the hardy bordermen of that day had no power to look to but themselves. Laboring in the corn-field or the forest, they never laid aside the trusty rifle, while oftentimes at night the tired worker was compelled to stand guard about his own home. It was a time of continual alarm, of ever-haunting peril, and no family enjoyed for a moment the feeling of perfect security.

The earlier of these white settlers to arrive drifted in naturally from the south, arriving on flat-boats, or huge family arks, like floating forts, by way of the Ohio and the Wabash, and later advanced gradually farther into the interior, attracted by the fertile lands discovered during their hunting expeditions along the smaller streams. These pioneers were mostly from Kentucky, Virginia, and Pennsylvania, of the rough, adventurous border type, largely incapable of enjoying life unspiced by danger, while among them were to be found a few, oftentimes of more sober and settled purpose, claiming birthplace in far-off New England, or New York. Vigorous and athletic, accustomed to all the privations and hardships of the open, these pioneer backwoodsmen of Illinois were remarkable for their physical strength and courage, which was naturally increased by their continual struggle against a savage, skulking foe. Under such conditions as confronted these men, the weakling could not long survive.

They early adopted a costume not unlike that worn by

the Indians surrounding them, a fur cap, or rude home-made hat of leather, buckskin leggings, together with a loose hunting-shirt, within the capacious bosom of which they could conveniently store away jerked beef and bread or almost any other of the necessities requiring transportation upon the trail. About the waist was worn a belt, to which were attached knife and tomahawk. Moccasins were worn upon the feet, and the necessary rifle seldom failed to adorn the shoulder. The universal habitation was a log hut, generally set in a little clearing, and containing but a single room, to be increased in size as the need arose or prospects brightened. Not infrequently this would be surrounded by palisades of sharpened logs set firmly in the ground, and projecting upward fifteen feet or more, as a further protection against their Indian foes, and, whenever possible, these scattered cabins were erected in close proximity to some strong central block-house, to which the harassed occupants might retreat in times of grave emergency, or where they could leave their women and little ones in safety while the fathers tilled the fields.

Considering the difficulties to be overcome, immigration into this new land was rapid. The distance from the nearest Eastern settlements was considerable, yet three hundred family boats were reported to have arrived at the falls of the Ohio in the Spring of 1780 alone. The larger number of these, however, were destined for Kentucky. Among the immigrants to Illinois whose names have since become familiar in State history, may be mentioned James Moore, Shadrach Bond, James Garrison, Robert Kidd, and Larkin Rutherford. Accompanied by their families these made the perilous journey across the Alleghanies, on foot and by wagon down the Ohio and up the Mississippi by flat-boat, until they finally landed at Kaskaskia. Of these Moore, who was the leader of the party, with a few others, soon located on the hills near Bellefontaine, while Bond and the remainder settled in the American Bottom close by Harrisonville, near what was afterwards known as the block-house fort. It was this early settlement which gave to this region its peculiar name. James Piggot, John Doyle, Robert Whitehead, and a Mr. Bowen arrived shortly afterwards, and settled permanently within the State. These are believed to compose the list of the earliest American settlers, although it is quite probable others went in fully as early by way of the Wabash, and it is not impossible that there were arrivals even in this neighborhood, overlooked by the historians of those days. Among those mentioned, Doyle taught school, and was, perhaps, the first professional teacher in Illinois. Speaking French and Indian, he became very useful as an interpreter. Not until 1785 was this little band of pioneers reënforced by new arrivals. Then came Joseph Ogle, Joseph Warley, and James Andrews, all from Virginia, and each having a large family accompanying him. The following year witnessed the arrival in the country of James Leman, George Atcherson, and David Waddell, with their families, in huge arks hauled laboriously up the river, besides several others whose names have not been preserved.

It is extremely difficult to picture in the mind the lonely isolation, oftentimes the seemingly desperate surroundings, of these first American invaders of the Illinois wilderness. About them stretched the primitive forests, the virgin prairie, dominated over by the jealous Indian, and inhabited by all manner of wild beasts. Roads were unknown, trails merely those used by the savages, the streams alone forming means of communication between the widely scattered settlements. These latter were even more thoroughly separated by reason of the rough, mountainous nature of that southern portion of the State, where these earlier settlers found homes. We can bring the picture before the mind — a small French village or two along the Mississippi, with a few more, mere huddled groups of huts, upon the distant banks of the Illinois.

Farther south, scarcely as yet venturing to push forth from the protecting shadows of the Ozarks, the Americans had cleared a few patches in the dense forests, and erected their block-houses at the confluence of convenient streams. Adventurous hunters wandered back and forth, keeping up some measure of communication between these settlements, but forest, plain, and river were all Indian-haunted, and there was no trade, no social intercourse. Each little body of pioneers lived alone, the merest pin-prick in that desolate wilderness which they had come to conquer.

Their surroundings were primitive, their wants extremely few. Following the first year or two of struggle, during which they frequently felt dire want, on their rude tables might be found johnny-cake, or *journey* cake, made of coarse corn-meal, hominy, or pounded maize, thoroughly boiled, with other savory preparations of flour and milk, in addition to a rich variety of game afforded by the chase. In season, the forests and the banks of streams offered much in wild fruit, while bee-trees, with their welcome sweets, were not uncommon. Their furniture was ever of the roughest description, being usually hewn out with the axe, and fashioned with a knife. Most articles in common use were altogether of domestic manufacture, although a few opulent families transported treasures from the East. The table utensils were largely of wood, those of metal being extremely rare, if not entirely unknown to the earliest comers. Bedding consisted of the skins of bear, deer, or buffalo. Stoves were not thought of, and the huge fire-places, rudely constructed of stones, plastered with clay, piled high with blazing logs, were favorite haunts on those long Winter evenings, when the storm howled without, and the forest trees overhead swayed to the blast. It was a rough, hard life, a life of toil, exposure, privation, and continuous danger. The nearest neighbor was usually miles away, the trail toward his dwelling the merest dim foot-track through forest and across prairie. Opportunities for the education of children were extremely scanty, even as regards the rudiments. If by any chance the mother could read, while the father was at work in the partially cleared field, his rifle slung to his back, she would barricade the door against prowling savages, gather the little ones about her, and teach them as best she could from out the treasures of her own memory.

During this entire period — that is, from 1786 to 1796 — these small, scattered settlements were nominally under the jurisdiction of the Northwestern Territory. Not until the organization of the county of St. Clair by Governor St. Clair in 1790, was there any adequate administration of law, indeed, no pretence at such administration. No courts were in existence, and no civil government worth mentioning. The people were a law unto themselves ; their manners were rude, but their morals were simple and pure ; the grosser vices being exceedingly uncommon. Uncouth as they were in language, dress, and action, crime of any kind was most infrequent. They were proverbial for hospitality and kindness to strangers ; with no tavern in the whole country, every home was wide open, every passing traveller welcome to the best they had to offer, which was, indeed, scanty enough. Among the earlier families of distinction as pioneers there was a record of unblemished morality and rectitude of conduct. Not a few had come to this far land impelled thereto by a love of freedom which the East would not satisfy. Yet a common poverty made brethren of them all.

In 1791, by special Act of Congress, four hundred acres of land was granted to each head of a family who had made improvements in Illinois prior to 1788, except village improvements. A list of names, entitled to these donations, shows a total number of two hundred and forty-four, eighty of whom were Americans, the others being French or French half-breeds. By allowing the estimated number of five souls to a family, we have a total population in that

A TYPICAL LOG HOUSE OF THE ILLINOIS COUNTRY

year of 1,220. This was exclusive of negroes. Another side-light comes from the fact that before 1791, under the then existing militia law, the muster roll gives about 300 men capable of bearing arms, of whom only sixty-five were American. This illustrates better than words the paucity of the population and their defenceless condition.

"In the year 1797, a colony of one hundred and twenty-six persons — the largest which had yet arrived — was fatally stricken with disease," says Davidson and Stuvé's history, quoting Western annals. "They were from Virginia, had descended the Ohio in the Spring, and landed at Fort Massac, from which they made their way across the country to New Design. This place, situated within the present limits of the county of Monroe, was first established in 1782. It was located on an elevated and beautiful plateau, barren of timber, overlooking both the Kaskaskia and Mississippi Rivers. The season chanced to be exceedingly wet, the weather extremely warm, and the trails heavy with mud. The colonists, burdened with women and children, toiled for twenty-six days through the woods and swamps, covering a distance of one hundred and thirty-five miles. They arrived at their destination completely worn out, sick, and almost famished. At New Design they found the old settlers — who had long been harassed by Indians — poorly prepared to accommodate them. There was no lack of hospitality, but generosity of heart could not enlarge the cabins, seldom containing more than one room, into which three and four families were now crowded, sick ones and all. Food was insufficient, salt very scarce, and medical aid out of the question. A putrid and malignant fever broke out among the newcomers, attended by such fatality as to sweep half of them into the grave before the coming of Winter. No such fatal disease ever appeared before or since in the country."

Nor did it affect any of the older inhabitants, yet the report being borne eastward tended greatly to retard immigration for several years.

Wherever the adventurous foot of a white man trod in the Illinois country, that was the day of hardship, danger, and death. Every forest covert, every concealing tuft of prairie grass, every sharp bend in the stream, might hide some skulking red enemy. In the little cleared fields, even within those log enclosures called home, no man felt safe from attack. Parties of vengeful warriors would burst from the dark woods, work their hellish deeds, and vanish, leaving death and destruction behind. But if this was the day for deeds, it was not the time for proclaiming them. The majority of the earlier settlers were illiterate men, they seldom came in contact with others of their own race excepting their more immediate neighbors, and no newspaper flourished to reward heroism. But few out of the many deeds of adventure, of desperate peril and suffering, have survived, and these are set forth in the fewest words possible. We will make mention of some of those as recorded in the "Annals of the West," pages 700 to 705. Multiply these a hundred fold, and they may afford a faint mental picture of those ten years of continuous horror along that battling Illinois frontier.

At first that section known as the American Bottom — the rich strip of low land lying between the Ozarks and the Mississippi, and extending northward until nearly opposite St. Louis — seemed the chosen field for Indian foray and destruction. As early as 1783 one James Flannery was murdered by a marauding party of savages while on a hunting expedition. A few years later the Indians openly attacked the American settlement at Bellefontaine, in what is now Monroe County, killed James Andrews, his wife and one daughter, together with James White and Samuel McClure. Two daughters of Andrews were taken prisoners, and borne by their captors as far as Peoria Lake. One died in the Indian village, the other was later ransomed by French traders, and as late as 1850 was still living in St. Clair County, the mother of a large family. Most of those in this settlement had built, and retired into, a large block-house, but these were recklessly taking their chances outside. Not long afterwards, and near the same place, William Biggs was taken prisoner. While himself, John Vallis, and Joseph and Benjamin Ogle, were passing from the station on the hills to the block-house fort in the bottom, they were suddenly attacked by Indians. Biggs and Vallis were a few rods in advance of the others. The latter was instantly killed, and Biggs captured. The others escaped in safety. Biggs was taken across the prairies to a Kickapoo town on the Wabash. The Indians treated him kindly, offering him the daughter of a brave for a wife, and proposed to adopt him into their tribe. He was finally liberated by the French traders, and later became a resident of St. Clair County, a member of the territorial legislature, and judge of the county court. He published a narrative of his captivity among the Indians. During this same year, James Garrison and Benjamin Ogle, while hauling hay from the bottom, were attacked. Ogle was shot in the shoulder, where the ball remained, but Garrison sprung from the load and escaped unhurt into the woods. The horses took fright, and running away carried the helpless Ogle safely into the settlement. Later, while engaged in stacking that same hay, Samuel Garrison, and a man named Riddick, were killed by the Indians, and both scalped.

The year following the savages became exceedingly bold, devoting their attention particularly to the killing of cattle and stealing of horses. Nor were they satisfied entirely with this species of mischief. A party of them attacked three boys, only a few yards from the Bellefontaine block-house, one of whom, David Waddell, was struck with a tomahawk in three places, and scalped, yet he recovered. The others succeeded in escaping unhurt. About this same time a young man named James Turner, while out hunting along the American Bottom, was waylaid and shot. Two men travelling to St. Louis were ambuscaded, killed, and scalped. Two other men were attacked while on a load of hay, one being killed outright, while his companion was scalped, but recovered. During this same reign of terror throughout what is now Monroe County, John Ferrel was killed, and John Dempsey was scalped but afterwards made his escape.

During the year 1790 the Indians seemed also to concentrate their depredations against the scattered settlers along the American Bottom, and Bellefontaine became again the centre of their hostile operations. During the Winter, when the pioneers usually felt more secure from attack, a party of Osage Indians from Missouri, previously peaceable, suddenly crossed the Mississippi, and stole a number of their horses. The Americans rallied, took their trail, and overtaking them, exchanged fire. James Worley, one of the oldest among the settlers, getting somewhat in advance of the others, was shot and scalped, his head being cut off and left upon a sand-bar, beside his mutilated body. Somewhat later in the season, James Smith, a Baptist preacher from Kentucky, who was on a visit to these frontiers, was taken prisoner by a roving band of Kickapoos, and had a most unpleasant experience. While in company with a Mrs. Huff, and a Frenchman whose name has not been preserved, he was riding on horseback from the block-house to a settlement then known as Little Village. The savages fired upon them from an ambuscade near Bellefontaine, killing the Frenchman's horse at the first shot. They then sprang upon the woman and her child, whom they despatched with the tomahawk, and Smith was taken prisoner. His own horse having also been shot, he at first attempted to escape on foot, and having some valuable papers in his saddlebags managed to throw them into the bushes, where they were found the next day by a friend. He might possibly have gotten away in safety, but being very zealous in good works, he suddenly stopped and fell on his knees in prayer for the poor woman being butchered, who had been seriously impressed for some days under his ministration about religion. The Frenchman, unhurt, escaped into the thicket, but the Indians soon had Smith, and loaded him up with numerous packs of plunder they had collected during their raid. They then took up their line of march through the prairies. Smith, who was a large, heavy man, soon became exhausted under his load and beneath the hot sun. Several consultations were held by the Indians as to how best to dispose of their prisoner. Some among them were for despatching him at once, being fearful lest the whites pursue them from the settlements. Frequently they pointed their guns at him with this purpose in mind. But Smith, understanding something of the Indian character and superstitions, would bare his breast in defiance, and point upward to signify that the Great Spirit was his protector. Seeing him frequently on his knees in prayer, and hearing him singing hymns on the march, which he did to relieve his own mind of despondency, they came to the conclusion that he must be "a great medicine," holding constant intercourse with the Great Spirit, and that it would not be safe to kill him. After reaching this decision, they relieved him of his burden, and treated him with extreme kindness. He was taken to the Kickapoo towns on the Wabash, where after a few months' captivity, he obtained deliverance, the inhabitants of New Design, who greatly valued his ministerial labors, paying one hundred and seventy dollars for his ransom.

Meanwhile there was no cessation in the Indian troubles along the border. Raids were constantly being made on exposed settlements, nor were the settlers in sufficient numbers at any one place to retaliate in force. It was a continual record of skirmishing, the savages apparently not so anxious to take human life as to procure for their own use the horses of the bordermen. To these, however, this was always a most serious loss, and certain to provoke a fight, if the red thieves could be overhauled. In May, 1791, while endeavoring to protect his horses, John Dempsey was attacked, but succeeded in making his escape. He was a man of some importance in that young settlement, and, as soon as the matter was reported, a party of eight men started promptly on the trail of the marauders. The Indians outnumbered the whites two to one, and coming into contact, both sides immediately took to the trees. A running fight was kept up for several hours, the Indians retreating, the whites remorselessly pursuing them from tree to tree, until night finally put an end to the conflict. Five of the Indians were killed, while none of the whites were injured. This company of settlers was composed of Captain Hull, Joseph Ogle, Sr., Benjamin Ogle, James N. Semen, Sr., J. Ryan, Wm. Bryson, John Porter, and D. Draper.

The success of this expedition had a quieting effect for some time, so that little occurred to disturb the peace of the border excepting a few desultory cattle raids, until the beginning of the year 1793. Then followed a period of contention and alarm wherever a venturesome white settler had cleared his little patch of ground in the heart of the backwoods. The few earlier settlers were greatly strengthened this year by the opportune arrival of a band of emigrants from Kentucky. These were nearly all bordermen, and among them was that famous family of Indian fighters named Whiteside. It was not long before their energy and courage were put to severe test. In February an Indian, skulking in ambush, succeeded in severely wounding Joel Whiteside, although he escaped with his life. Others, however, were not so fortunate, and in quick succession, John Moore, Andrew Kinney, Thos. Todd, and several others whose names are now unknown, were killed and scalped by various raiding parties. Finally, a party of Kickapoos, supposed at the time to be headed by the celebrated war-chief, Old Pecan, made a predatory excursion into the American Bottom. Near where is now the residence of S. W. Miles, in Monroe County, they succeeded in stealing nine horses, and began their retreat. A number of settlers rallied and commenced a vigorous pursuit, but of these many dropped out, unwilling to venture so far into the Indian country, until finally all had abandoned the desperate undertaking except eight men. This little band was led by Wm. Whiteside, a borderman of unquestionable bravery and great prudence. Those with him were Samuel Judy, John Whiteside, Uel Whiteside, Wm. L. Whiteside, Wm. Harrington, John Dempsey, and John Porter.

This little band of intrepid frontiersmen followed closely on the trail of the retreating savages, passing near the site of the city of Belleville, toward the Indian encampment on Shoal Creek, where they succeeded in recovering three of the stolen horses, without permitting their enemies to become aware of their presence. The band of pursuers, small as it was, now divided into two parts, consisting of four men each, and prepared to approach the unsuspecting Indian camp from opposite directions. The signal for attack was to be the discharge of the leader's gun. Stealing cautiously forward through the timber lining the bank of the stream, they succeeded in getting within firing-distance unobserved, and poured in a withering volley. One Indian, a son of Old Pecan, was instantly killed, another mortally, and several others slightly, wounded ; then the uninjured savages fled in confusion, leaving their guns behind them. Such unexpected courage on the part of the whites, together with the attack on two sides at once, convinced the Indians that they were being followed by a large force, and the wily old chief approached, intending to beg for quarter. Discovering, however, how few there were of the whites as opposed to the number of his own warriors, he determined instantly on resistance, and called aloud to his braves to return, and retrieve their honor. He had surrendered his own gun to the whites on first coming up, and now seized the gun in the hands of Captain Whiteside, striving to wrest it from him. Whiteside was a powerful man, and he forced the enraged Indian back, permitting him to go to his people unhurt, deeming it dishonorable to destroy an unarmed man, after he had surrendered. But this little band of eight men was by this time in a most perilous position. They stood alone in the very heart of the Indian country, where hundreds of warriors could be raised in a few hours' time. Captain Whiteside, who was as prudent as brave, decided at once upon retreat. With those horses they had recovered, they immediately plunged into the wilderness, heading for home. They travelled night and day, neither eating nor sleeping, until they arrived in safety at Whiteside's station in Monroe County. The extreme narrowness of their escape was made manifest that same night, when Old Pecan, with seventy warriors, pressing hot on their trail, reached the vicinity of Cahokia. From that time the very name of Whiteside ever struck terror among the Kickapoos.

Whether right or wrong, this action brought swift retaliation on the part of the Indians along the border. In revenge for the death of Old Pecan's son, a young man named Thomas Whiteside was shot and killed close to the station, and a little later a son of Captain Whiteside was tomahawked, and died of his wounds. Mr. Huff, one of the oldest settlers, was also waylaid and killed while on his way to Kaskaskia. The year following, two white men and some French negroes were killed on the American Bottom, and several others taken prisoners. About this same time, several members of the family of Mr. McMahon were killed, and himself and daughter taken prisoners. This man lived upon the outskirts of the settlement. Four Indians attacked his house in daylight, killed his wife and four children before his eyes, laid their bodies in a row on the floor of the cabin, took him and his daughter, and departed hastily for their towns. On the second night of their march, McMahon, discovering the Indians asleep, slipped on their moccasins and made his escape. He arrived at the settlement just as the neighbors were about to bury his family. They had already enclosed the bodies in rude coffins, and were covering them with earth. He looked at the closing graves, and raising his eyes to Heaven said in pious resignation, "They were lovely and pleasant in their lives, and in their death are not divided." His daughter, later Mrs. Catskill, of Ridge Prairie, was ransomed by the charitable contributions of the people. A short time after this occurrence, the Whitesides and others, to the number of fourteen, made an attack upon an encampment of Indians, of greatly superior force, which was situated at the foot of the bluffs, just west of the present site of Belleville. Only one Indian out of the entire party returned to his tribe to tell the story of the battle. The graves of the remainder were to be seen only a few years ago in the border of the thicket near the battle-ground. During the heat of the skirmish, Captain Whiteside was severely wounded,— he thought mortally,— having received a shot in the side. As he fell he called to his sons to keep on fighting and not to yield an inch of ground, or permit the savages to touch his body. Uel Whiteside, who had also been shot in the arm, so that he could no longer use his rifle, hastily examined his father's wound, discovering that the bullet had glanced along the ribs, and lodged against the spine. With that daring and disregard for pain so often characteristic of bordermen, he immediately whipped out his knife, gashed the skin, and extracting the ball, held it up, crying, "You're not dead yet, father." The old man leaped to his feet, and renewed the fight, bearing his full part to the end. Many such instances of desperate intrepidity, and warlike heroism, distinguished the men who in those days of peril were called upon to defend the frontiers of Illinois.

The defeat of the confederated Indians in 1794, on the Maumee, by General Anthony Wayne, brought peace to these long-harassed settlers along the Illinois border. A few horses were occasionally stolen, and in 1802 two Americans were killed, but no open attack was made upon the settlements. Families again took up their abode on the open prairies, and began pushing out farther into the unoccupied wilderness. Emigrants from the States came clustering around them, and the cultivation of the soil was pursued without fear of molestation. During the period extending between 1802 and 1810, nothing occurred to interrupt the quiet routine of peace upon the frontier.

While what is now Illinois was thus a portion of the Northwestern Territory, it had been divided into two counties, Randolph and St. Clair. In 1800, by an Act of Congress the whole of the Northwestern Territory, with the exception of the State of Ohio, was named Indiana, and Wm. H. Harrison, later President of the United States, was appointed its Governor. Illinois continued thus as a part of Indiana until February 3, 1809, when, by another Act of Congress, all that portion of the Indiana Territory which lies west of the Wabash River and a direct line drawn from that river and Fort Vincennes due north to the territorial line between the United States and Canada, was formed into a separate territory by the name of Illinois. Ninian Edwards, then Chief Justice of Kentucky, was named as Governor. In 1810, new settlements had been formed in Gallatin, Johnson, Union, and Jackson Counties, and the census gives the population of the territory at that time as 12,284 inhabitants.

CHAPTER XVI

THE TRAGEDY AT FORT DEARBORN

IN 1812 this pleasant peace of the Illinois border was destined to be rudely interrupted by sudden wild Indian foray. The breaking out of a second war between England and the United States immediately involved the savages of the West, already restless from the constant encroachment of settlers, and stirred by the harangues of dissatisfied chiefs. Almost without exception, the various tribes allied themselves promptly on the side of the redcoats, and began depredations along the entire exposed American frontier. The war itself opened within the present limits of Illinois with most pathetic tragedy. But it was not those long-time battling settlers of the southern counties, whose advance settlements now extended as far north as Edwardsville, in Madison County, upon whom this first shock fell. It was reserved for a little isolated garrison of regular soldiers, stationed at the extreme northeast corner, upon the very spot where to-day Chicago proudly looks forth across the blue waters of Lake Michigan.

It is comparatively easy to stand in the open, amid the surroundings of unchanged nature, and recall some grim event of history which has taken place upon that spot. The mind responds happily to the summons, and quickly weaves the recorded details about those hills and valleys, woods and ravines. It all stands out once again, a clear mental picture of that other day long past. But it is far different when a great city has sprung up there, and buried deep, beneath its mass, all evidences of former tragedy or heroic struggle. The great buildings rising on every side fetter imagination, and the obstructing curtain of time refuses to rise, to permit of our beholding things as they really were a brief century previous. We are too closely imprisoned within the stone walls of the present,— the wild, little understood, former life returns to us as the merest dream, the actors in it but shadows, unreal and indistinct.

There are few busier spots in any city than that which Chicago presents at the southern approach to the Rush Street bridge. It is typically illustrative of commercial enterprise, and ever alive with business activity. During the hours of daylight the street is thronged with hurrying figures, and oftentimes blocked by a multitude of teams. It composes the centre of a vast wholesale district, and various interests constantly swirl and battle here for mastery. Out in the dull-colored river, huge passenger and freight steamers are continually churning past, while the great walls of business blocks, teeming with thousands of workers, rear themselves story upon story into a sky black with smoke. To stand there, amid such a throng, and read the inscription graven upon a tablet embedded within the red brick wall of a wholesale grocery opposite, is like being suddenly awakened from a dream. The mind cannot at once compass the vast vista between. It seems unreal, untrue, so far a call from now to then, from this scene of feverish activity and money-getting, to that other day of frontier loneliness and heroic self-sacrifice.

Let us walk slowly and thoughtfully from this spot southward on Michigan Avenue, one of the most stately boulevards of the world, past the sombre-hued business-houses, the magnificent hotels, the great buildings dedicated to art, music, and drama, until we arrive where the green park stretches along upon one side, smiling back upon rows of pleasant houses. It all forms a city scene to be remembered, to be long treasured in the mind, with its panorama of ever-changing natural and architectural beauty, its constantly recurring suggestions of refinement and wealth. Let us drift eastward as we approach Fourteenth Street, and select for our farther promenade one of those avenues running closer to the lake shore, avenues beautified by large and tasteful homes, rendered attractive by every device of wealth. At Eighteenth Street, we may pause and contemplate the bronze monument erected there. If we have done this thoughtfully, then we have lived over once again within our own minds one of the great tragedies of the Illinois frontier, for we have been walking upon historic ground, ground once reddened with blood, along a path marched over by soldiers, women, and children, to their fate beneath the dripping knife and tomahawk of savages.

It seems now so far away, so unreal in the midst of all this glamour and show. Yet here it was that the unspeakable horror was perpetrated. Here the hordes of painted savages skulked behind the sand-ridges, and leaped forth to kill and mutilate; here Wells died, as became a fearless soldier; here Ronan gave up his young life ungrudgingly ; here women and little ones, whose names have been forgotten, fell shrieking beneath the savage blows. Let us see if out of that dim past we cannot paint again, in fresher coloring, that old historic picture against the background of this busy city life.

It is August of the year 1812. This is the uttermost frontier, and the northern Illinois country is a wilderness of prairie and wood, almost untouched by the venturesome foot of the explorer. A few scattered French settlements — their inhabitants largely half-breeds — dot the distant banks of the Mississippi and the Illinois. A little fringe of white settlers has pushed northward from the Ohio as far as the confines of the present county of Madison, but that is hundreds of miles distant. All communication, if any is had, must be by means of water-ways or dim Indian trails, while to the eastward only a single path leads through leagues of forest land to the distant outpost at Fort Wayne. So Fort Dearborn stands, a silent, isolated sentinel of civilization, in the very heart of a wilderness, the full extent of which no white man knew. Picture this spot — here at busy Rush Street bridge — in that month of August, 1812. Nine years previous, Lieutenant Swearingen, with his little company of regular soldiers, had landed on the desolate shore of the lake. Proceeding up the bank of the river,— a narrow stream, having but slight current, from where it then emptied near the present foot of Madison Street,— they finally selected this spot, where the river swerved southward, as being best fitted for purposes of fortification. Here the ground, generally flat and level, rose into something of a mound, yielding from its summit a clear view far away across the plains of sand and prairie. It was a magnificent expanse of primeval nature outspread on every side, yet desolate in its unspeakable loneliness. And upon this spot these army pioneers erected a rude, typical frontier fort.

This consisted of a simple stockade of logs, standing each upon end, firmly implanted in the ground, extending upward some fifteen feet, and sharpened at the top. This outer stockade, which was built perfectly solid (excepting for one entrance facing southward, protected by heavy gates of oaken timber, and another, a subterranean one, leading out beneath the north wall to the river), was sufficiently large to contain a small parade ground, together with the requisite buildings for the expected garrison, such as officers' quarters, troop barracks, guard house, and magazine. These were alike roughly constructed of logs, while two block-houses, each erected so that the second story should overhang the first, were built as an additional protection, one standing at the southeast, the other at the northwest, corner of the palisaded wall. A narrow elevated walk, or banquette, of wood enabled defenders to stand within

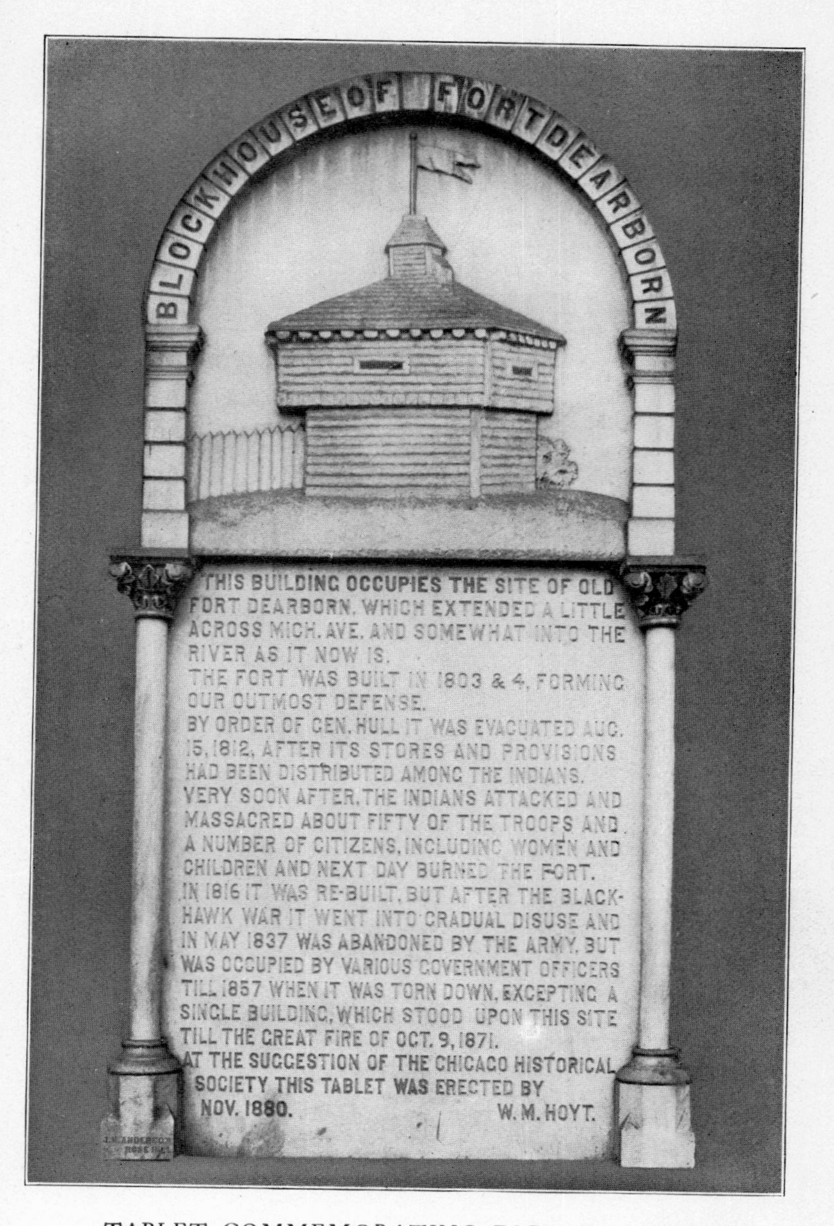

TABLET COMMEMORATING FORT DEARBORN

ERECTED ON THE WALLS OF THE BUILDING NOW OCCUPYING THE SITE

the enclosure, and look out across the sharpened pickets at the scene beyond.

In August, 1812, this primitive structure contained a garrison of four officers, with fifty-four non-commissioned officers and privates of the First Regiment, United States Infantry. The commandant was Captain Nathan Heald, an experienced soldier in the prime of life. Associated with him were Lieutenant Linus T. Helm, an officer who had much frontier service to his credit ; Ensign Ronan, a young, smooth-faced lad in his first command, and Surgeon Van Voorhees. The wives of the two senior officers were with them, Mrs. Helm, a bride but seventeen years of age, the step-daughter of John Kinzie, a much-respected Indian trader, who had his home almost directly across the river from the fort. A number of the soldiers also had their families with them, so that altogether the stockade contained twelve women and twenty children.

If possible, let us throw aside our present environment, and imagine ourselves soldiers at that isolated spot a century ago. Stand beside me for a moment, and glance out across those sharpened palisades upon that scene of unvexed wilderness, stretching away upon every hand. It is hardly conceivable now, amid the mighty buildings and the restless activity of these city streets, that such a picture could then unroll itself. A narrow, sluggish river, its low banks reed-bordered, moved slowly lakeward just beneath the northern wall. Across its waters a rope ferry connected the fort with John Kinzie's rather pretentious cabin on the opposite bank. In all that wide domain of sea and sand and prairie, only four other scattered settlers' homes appeared within view. These were occupied by Ouilmette, Burns, and Lee, the last named possessing also a second cabin, situated farther out upon the south branch of the little river, and occupied by a tenant named Liberty White. These were alike, one-story, single-roomed huts, and were the sole visible evidences of advancing civilization. Just west of the fort stood a two-story log house, which had been erected as a trading-store for the Indians, so as to obviate as much as possible all necessity for their entering the fort itself. The southern bank of the river, both above and below, was fairly honeycombed by caves dug in the soft earth, in which the soldiers stored the vegetables raised in their gardens.

Such were the more immediate surroundings. But what of that wider view, sweeping to the far horizon? It was then the profound loneliness of such a situation must have rested like a weight upon the most buoyant spirit. Westward the dull level of the plains swept out into unknown, unexplored mystery, roamed over by strange races of savages; to the north the land was more broken, and somewhat heavily wooded, yet no white man dwelt there for hundreds of leagues; to the east, and only a few yards away, the waves of the great lake broke moaning upon the wide, sandy beach, the restless water stretching in tumultuous loneliness to their distant juncture with the arching sky; southward, the almost level prairie, brown and sun-parched, merged swiftly into rounded heaps of drifted sand, the only relief being found in a few straggling groups of wind-racked cottonwoods. Beautiful as it may have been in its variegated coloring and extended vista, it was so utterly desolate, so still and solemn, as to leave behind a feeling of depression difficult to withstand. None of that little garrison could fail to realize to the full how isolated they were from all others of their race.

Early during August of that year 1812, there came drifting to the ears of the garrison, by means of Indian runners, rumors regarding the approaching struggle with England, and of a growing uneasiness among the surrounding tribes, especially the Pottawattomies and the Wyandots. On the ninth the first direct, and official, news reached them, and proved to be of the gravest character. On that date an Indian named Winnemeg, or Catfish, a friendly warrior of the Pottawattomies, arrived directly from Detroit, bringing word of the English capture of the garrison at Mackinac, together with orders from General Hull, in command of the American troops in that territory, to "evacuate the fort at Chicago if practicable, and in that event to distribute all the United States property in the fort, or factory, to the Indians in the neighborhood, and repair to Fort Wayne."

The situation at Dearborn at that time was such as to test severely the judgment of any man. If Captain Heald failed to decide promptly and for the best, it was no more than many a gallant commander has done both before and since. Already rumors of the condition of affairs had gone abroad, and the Indians, many of them hostile and threatening, began to gather around the stockade, in constantly increasing numbers. These made permanent camp somewhat to the westward of the fort, near where the river forked, perhaps at the present intersection of Clark and Lake Streets. Their scouting parties were to be met with along every trail leading to the south and west. This condition, which almost amounted to a siege, as the soldiers dared not venture without the walls except in large parties, was greatly aggravated by the situation within. An unusually large number of the little garrison were upon the sick list, and unfit for duty, while the perilous task of conveying women and children over that long trail, stretching through woods and swamps to Fort Wayne, every mile of it traversing the hunting-grounds of hostile savages, was not to be lightly considered. In truth, it was a situation so filled with peril as to make the boldest hesitate. Heald seemingly quailed before it, and, unfortunately, hesitated far too long in deciding what was his duty. The delay merely served to aggravate matters, bad enough from the start. It brought new courage and numbers to the allied Indians, and aroused, among the officers of the garrison, a spirit almost akin to mutiny.

But through all this internal dissatisfaction and outside threatening, Captain Heald apparently remained firm in his determination to obey orders, as well as in his confidence relative to the friendliness of the Indians. These increased rapidly in numbers and insolence, there probably being fully five hundred in their encampment by August 12, while many others were hurrying toward them along the trails. They held frequent councils in the black shadows of their lodges, and upon the evening of that day the commandant attended one, although every one of his officers refused to accompany him. Word had been brought them that treachery was intended, and when Captain Heald left the protection of the fort, and walked forth upon the open prairie, those left within trained loaded cannon in the direction of the distant encampment. This evidence of watchfulness, coupled with the absence of so many whom they had hoped to entrap, induced the wily savages to postpone their planned attack, and the Captain was permitted to return in safety. During this council, Heald proposed to the chiefs to distribute among them the stores and ammunition belonging to the garrison, provided they would agree to furnish him with safe escort to Fort Wayne. The assembled Indians were profuse in their pledges, and there is much reason to believe that these were at the time honestly made.

Yet here enters in the strange, inexplicable, yet entirely natural vacillation, leading up to a most deplorable tragedy. Alarmed, no doubt, by the imminent danger surrounding them, influential members of the garrison began urging the impolicy of thus furnishing the Indians with arms and ammunition, which they might later use against the retreating whites. Heald appears to have been overborne by the force of this argument, so that on August 13, in direct opposition to his promises, he had all the extra ammunition thrown into an abandoned well within the stockade, while the store of liquor was broken open and poured into the river. This deceit, being early discovered by the watchful savages, merely served to increase their resentment, and contributed much to the carrying forward of plans of treachery.

The fourteenth was rendered notable by the unexpected arrival of a small reënforcing party, who approached by way of the land trail, leading along the lake shore from the east. Although severely worried by the enveloping hordes of angry Indians, who sought to obstruct their progress, these latter finally succeeded in reaching the gates of the fort, which were thrown open for their admittance. The despairing garrison, eager for any news from without, surged about them, with anxious questioning and vociferous welcome. They proved to be a party of thirty Miami warriors, induced to accompany Captain William Wells, a white man of life-long experience upon the border, and the adopted son of Little Turtle, the famous war-chief of the Miamis. Wells was, in many respects, a remarkable frontier character. Captured while but a mere child, he had spent many years in Indian camps, rising among them to the dignity of a warrior, and taking personal part in more than one wild foray. Later in life, his white blood asserting itself, he had returned to his own people, serving gallantly as a scout under Wayne's command, and at this time held the important position of Indian Agent at Fort Wayne. At that remote post he had learned by chance of the order to evacuate Fort Dearborn, and comprehending fully the hostile purposes of the Indians, had made a forced march through the wilderness, hoping thus to arrive in sufficient time to protect his niece, Mrs. Heald, as well as to assist the beleaguered garrison. But his coming was already too late. The grave mistake had been made, and was beyond rectifying. The worst passions of those encompassing savages had been aroused, and although they succeeded in partially concealing their intended treachery, the trap of death was already laid for its unsuspecting victims. On the evening of this same day a second council was held; but, if anything, this proved less satisfactory than the other. The Indian spokesmen were vehement in their indignation over the wanton destruction of ammunition and liquor, and their manner was insolent and threatening. Nevertheless, they reiterated their pledge of protection to the garrison, if they would desert the fort, and, in spite of bitter opposition on the part of his officers, Captain Heald determined to put these pledges to the test.

That little stockade of logs, erected on the southern bank of the Chicago River, within sound of the booming waves of the lake, the great silent plains stretching all around it, was an animated scene that night of final preparation. John Kinzie had brought his family within its walls, while other settlers of the neighborhood, some twelve in number, had likewise sought its protection, so that sinewy backwoodsmen mingled with the soldiers and the women and children, in hurried preparation for the fateful march of the morrow. Wagons were loaded with the necessities of the trail, and preparations made for the transportation of the sick, and those others unable to travel on foot. Then the reserve ammunition, twenty-five rounds to each man, was distributed, and the wearied workers finally flung themselves down for whatever sleep was possible. Above them, on the narrow platforms, the sentries gazed anxiously forth into the black night shrouding the prairie, where many a warrior skulked and gloated in fiendish anticipation of the morrow. Beyond, at the Indian village, great fires blazed, about which dark forms leaped in wild and threatening dances.

At nine o'clock in the morning the little party left the

MONUMENT MARKING THE SITE OF THE FORT DEARBORN MASSACRE

fort. It was a beautiful August day. The sun shone with unwonted splendor, and Lake Michigan "was a sheet of burnished gold." As the fugitives filed slowly out of the fort gate, the company of infantry, in light marching order, took the advance on foot. Following them closely was a caravan of wagons, piled high with camp equipage, upon which rode the wives and children of the soldiers, together with those too sick to travel otherwise. The officers' ladies were mounted, while the few white settlers travelled as best suited themselves. The rear of the column was guarded by a portion of Wells's Miami escort. By some strange fortune, as the little party thus emerged from the stockade, on the commencement of their desperate trip through the wilderness, the band began playing "The Dead March," but were instantly ordered to substitute a more cheering tune.

Captain Wells, who, having no faith in the pledges made, had blackened his face, in accordance with the custom of those Indians among whom he had lived so long, led the van, accompanied by a few of his Miami scouts. To the right and rear of the column straggled along the escort of nearly five hundred Pottawattomies. In this order the company travelled slowly southward, along the shining sand of the level beach, with the smiling waters of the lake close beside them upon the left. Some among them undoubtedly felt distrust of those red warriors, skulking along at their side, their cruel eyes gleaming beneath matted hair, as they furtively contemplated their destined victims. But in the hearts of most was merely a rejoicing that they were again bound eastward, toward their old homes. Children looked forth from behind the wagon covers, and clapped their hands in innocent glee at the unusual spectacle, while the mothers watched them and smiled. As these two columns, the white and the red, approached in their southward march a low range of sand hills which separated the beach from the prairie, probably at about what is now the foot of Twelfth Street, the Indians silently defiled to the right, thus bringing these slight elevations of sand between them and the whites, who continued toiling along nearer the shore. No one thought anything of this act at the time ; it seemed perfectly natural, and engendered no feeling of suspicion. Only a little farther down the beach this intervening ridge terminated, and there it was supposed the two diverging columns would reunite for the continuance of their long journey together around the head of the great lake.

In this way the march of the fugitives continued uninterrupted for perhaps a mile and a half. The low walls of the deserted fort, already overrun by a howling mass of savages, quarrelling over the spoils left behind, were still visible, when the advance files of that sturdy column of infantry reached the spot that is now the foot of Eighteenth Street. Suddenly there was a halt of the scouts in front. Then Wells wheeled his horse, and rode back furiously, shouting as he came: "They are going to attack; form instantly, and charge them!" These hasty words of warning were barely uttered, when the savages, concealed behind the sand ridge, poured a deadly volley into the close ranks of the troops. Totally surprised, and for the instant almost panic-stricken, the dead and wounded lying at their feet, the officers succeeding in holding their men in something like order, swung them into hasty battle line, and, with inspiriting cheers, led them in impetuous charge against their concealed assailants. At the summit of the sand ridge, they were met with so hot a fire, they were barely able to hold their position. A number fell, including one veteran soldier of seventy years. The action became fierce and general, rapidly extending down the entire line. The Miamis fled with almost the first fire, their chief pausing barely long enough to hurl his defiance at the Pottawattomies before joining his cowardly companions. The troops, although poorly prepared for battle, fought with great gallantry, forcing at first the savages in their front to give way, and gaining a foothold on the open prairie beyond the sand ridge. But they were soon overwhelmed by the numbers hurled against them. The Indians outflanked their short line, and in less than fifteen minutes from the first attack had gained possession of the horses, with the provisions and baggage wagons. Here commenced their murderous work upon the helpless women and children.

At once it became a terrible scene, seldom equalled in all the bloody annals of the frontier. Dr. Van Voorhees, who had been wounded at the first fire, was, while in a paroxysm of fear, cut down by the blow of a tomahawk. Ensign Ronan, although mortally wounded, continued to struggle bravely against a powerful savage who had seized him, until he finally sank beneath the cruel thrust of a knife. The young wife of Lieutenant Helm was attacked by a savage, who sought desperately to cleave her skull. Springing aside quickly, the blow merely grazed her shoulder, and in self-defence she wound her arms tightly about his neck. In the midst of the struggle which ensued, another Indian grasped and forcibly bore her away, plunging her into the water of the lake, and held her firmly down, almost concealed from sight. Discovering that he had no immediate intention of drowning her, she ventured to look up, and, through his disguise of paint and war feathers, recognized the well-known face of the friendly young chief, Black Partridge, whom she had known from childhood. As the fierce *mêlée* began to slacken, he bore her safe to the shore, and protected her from the others. The wife of one of the soldiers fought with such desperation that she was literally cut to pieces, and her mangled remains were left on the field. Mrs. Heald also fought for her life like a heroine, and received several wounds. After she had been captured, a savage assailed her with his tomahawk, but she was saved by the interposition of a friendly chief.

Scattered by the fierce fire, their formation broken, their officers wounded or dead, the troops fought bravely until only twenty-seven out of sixty-six remained, when, on receiving pledge of protection, the helpless remnant surrendered. Scarcely had they ceased resistance when a brutal savage assailed one of the unprotected baggage-wagons, and twelve children fell beneath his murderous tomahawk. Captain Wells, maddened at the awful sight, shouted, "If that is your game, I can kill too!" and instantly breaking away from his guards, rode furiously toward the Pottawattomie camp, where the Indian squaws and children were. For a brief time in his swift flight, he succeeded in avoiding the deadly aims of the pursuing savages, by lying prone on his horse's neck, but finally the animal was killed, and the rider once more made a prisoner. Winnemeg and Wabansee, both of whom were friendly to the whites, interceded to save his life, but Peesotum, a Pottawattomie chief, gave him his death-blow, by a stab in the back. His body was terribly mutilated, the heart being cut out and torn in pieces, for distribution among the tribes as a token of bravery. On the following day, Billy Caldwell, a half-breed Wyandot, gathered up the scattered fragments of his body, and gave them decent burial in the sand. Wells Street, in Chicago, perpetuates his name.

So ended the unequal struggle, the total Indian loss not exceeding fifteen, while of the whites, twenty-six infantry-men, twelve settlers, two women, and twelve children were killed. Captain and Mrs. Heald, Lieutenant and Mrs. Helm, with twenty-five non-commissioned officers and privates, besides eleven women and children, were made prisoners. Of these, more than half were wounded, many seriously. Unfortunately, in the hurry and excitement of the moment, the wounded were not particularly referred to in the stipulation of surrender. This was immediately taken advantage of by the treacherous savages. Such helpless sufferers, on being conveyed to the Pottawattomie camp, were regarded as proper subjects for the most savage and cowardly brutality, and several were given over to torture, while during the night following the battle, five were tomahawked.

In this connection, the recollections of Mrs. Helm, as afterwards recorded in a book written by Mrs. John Kinzie, are particularly graphic. Saved, as narrated, by Black Partridge, she was conducted from the water to the sandy beach. It was a hot August day, and walking through the loose sand in her drenched condition became inexpressibly painful. She stopped, and took off her shoes to free them from the sand, when a squaw seized and carried them off, compelling her to limp along without them. When they finally gained the prairie, she was met by her father, who brought her the good news that her husband was safe, and but slightly wounded. Arriving at the wigwams, Mrs. Helm saw the wife of Wau-bee-nee-mah, a chief from the Illinois River, standing near. Seeing her exhausted condition, this squaw seized a kettle, dipped up some water from a stream close at hand, threw into it some maple sugar, and stirring it up with her hand, offered it to the lady to drink. This unexpected act of kindness touched her deeply, but her attention was soon directed toward another matter. The fort had become a scene of plunder ; the cattle were shot down as they ran at large, and now lay dead or dying around. Suddenly an old squaw, infuriated by the sight of so much blood, grasped a stable-fork, and assaulted a wounded soldier, who lay groaning and writhing in agony under the heat of the sun. With delicacy of feeling hardly to be expected at such a time and place, Wau-bee-nee-mah stretched a mat across two poles, so as to hide this dreadful scene from Mrs. Helm.

In the battle, Captain Heald had received two wounds, and his wife seven. Her captor, being about to pull off her bonnet so as to scalp her, young Chaudonnaire, an Indian of the St. Joseph tribe, who knew her, came to the rescue, and offered a mule he had just taken, for her ransom, to which he added ten bottles of whiskey. The latter temptation was too strong to be resisted. Captain Heald was made prisoner by an Indian from the Kankakee River, who, seeing the pitiable condition of Mrs. Heald, generously released his captive, that he might accompany his wife. Chaudonnaire, with some others, placed both in a bark canoe, which a Pottawattomie chief paddled for three hundred miles along the eastern coast of Lake Michigan until they reached Mackinac, where they were kindly received by the British commander, and on being sent to Detroit were exchanged. Mrs. Helm received a slight wound in her ankle, besides having her horse shot under her, and, after passing through the scenes already described, was permitted to accompany the family of her step-father, Mr. Kinzie, to Detroit, they being spared from the threatened general massacre by the intervention of Billy Caldwell, Black Partridge, and other friendly chiefs. Her husband was taken to the Au Sable, thence to St. Louis, and finally liberated by the aid of Thomas Forsythe, then Indian agent at Peoria. The other captive soldiers, with their wives and children, were dispersed among the tribes along the Illinois and Wabash Rivers, some few among them being sent north along the lake shore. The majority were ransomed at Detroit the following Spring, although a number remained in captivity for another year, but were not unkindly treated.

And all this took place within the very business limits of what is now Chicago. At the foot of Eighteenth Street, marking the probable site of this sanguinary contest, stands the beautiful memorial monument, a representation of the saving of Mrs. Helm by Black Partridge. Close at hand are palatial residences, while all about are the evidences of modern wealth and refinement. Standing there now, and dreaming of the past, one can scarcely realize the awful scene of that fifteenth of August, 1812, when this frontier tragedy was enacted — when men, women, and little children went down to death together beside the unruffled waters of the lake. It makes a grim foundation-stone upon which to build a mighty city, nor should it be forgotten by the citizens in the passing years.

CHAPTER XVII

ILLINOIS IN WAR OF 1812

SANGUINARY and ominous in Illinois history as was the opening of the War of 1812, the events following were far less dramatic. At that time constituting the far frontier, sparsely settled in its southern portion, the remainder of it a mere wilderness, Illinois remained untouched by the main forces of both sides. Indian fighting and massacre, with constant alarm along the border, was the portion borne by Illinois settlers, and while their Eastern comrades were battling manfully along the coast, and amid the snows of Canada, or earning the plaudits of the world upon the sea, the hardy frontiersmen of the Ohio and the Mississippi were struggling to hold their own against a savage, skulking, relentless foe.

The beginning was prompt, for immediately following the massacre at Chicago, British representatives descended the Mississippi River as far as Rock Island, and making that their headquarters, began distributing loads of goods as presents among the Indians, the special agent employed being one Girty. To clear the West of such enemies and revenge the Fort Dearborn disaster, two thousand volunteers assembled at Louisville, Kentucky, under command of General Hopkins. October 14, 1812, this little army crossed the Wabash near Vincennes, and began its march over the prairies of Illinois. It was an ill-disciplined body of volunteers. The country traversed abounded with wild game, and no orders issued by the officers could prevent the men from constantly firing. Their insubordination increased with the difficulties of the march. In this manner they succeeded in getting some eighty or ninety miles within the Indian country, when they encountered a large prairie fire, and became at once frantically alarmed for their own safety. In spite of the remonstrance of their General and the efforts of their officers, they at once turned about and returned to their homes, without so much as striking a blow, or even coming within sight of the enemy. This constituted one of the most ignominious failures recorded in Western history.

Meanwhile other movements were being planned elsewhere. Governor Edwards collected a body of Illinois frontiersmen, three hundred and fifty strong, at Camp Russell, near the site of Edwardsville, in Madison County, then the most advanced of the border settlements. These were organized as mounted riflemen, and were soon reënforced by Colonel Russell with three companies of United States Rangers. These troops moved almost directly north toward the Illinois River, expecting to coöperate with Hopkins's column, then reported as advancing from the East. Disappointed at the retreat of the latter, Edwards's men nevertheless persevered in their enterprise, and succeeded in destroying one of the Indian towns, pursuing the frightened savages into a swamp, and killing about twenty of them. The whites, who were the assailants, had but one slightly wounded. Their subsequent retreat to the protection of the settlements, however, was reported as being extremely rapid.

Early in the year 1813, the country was placed in such state of defence as was possible with so sparse a population. Block-house stations and stockade forts were repaired along the entire frontier, and the more remote settlers and feebler garrisons were removed to the better-defended settlements. New companies of rangers were organized, and so distributed as to patrol the frontier thoroughly. From the present Alton to Kaskaskia, twenty-two family forts were scattered along, yet even this was insufficient to keep out all Indian marauding parties. Breaking through these lines of guard, savages fell upon the family of a Mr. Lively, living four miles southeast of Covington, in the present Washington County, and slew four. The bodies of the two women were shockingly mangled; a little boy of seven years was borne away from the house, and his head severed from his body. The body of Mr. Lively was also mutilated. A son, and a stranger who was stopping there, were out on the prairie in quest of their horses, and from a distance witnessed the attack on the house. During their retreat to the nearest settlement, they made camp in a grove six miles southeast of Fayetteville, along the banks of the Kaskaskia River, which perpetuates the name of the murdered family. Captain Bond's company of Rangers at once took up the pursuit, but as the Indians had had four days' start, they easily escaped. On the banks of the Kaskaskia, near the present town of Carlyle, a Mr. Young and a minister named McLean had a desperate encounter with a party of savages. Mr. Young and both horses were killed, and McLean, who was unarmed, escaped by plunging into the river and swimming to the other shore. Several murders were committed on Cache River, in the present Alexander County. On the Wabash, thirty miles above Vincennes, near Fort Lamotte, the wife of a Mr. Houston and four children were killed. On a small prairie, two or three miles from the present town of Albion, in Edwards County, a settler named Boltenhouse was slain. The prairie on which he lived still bears his name.

Meanwhile another expedition northward was projected. Large numbers of hostile Indians were known to be gathered in the neighborhood of the Peoria Lake, whence marauding parties were despatched to harass the exposed settlements of both Illinois and Missouri. A joint expedition from these two sections was therefore organized to penetrate this

Indian stronghold and break it up. Some nine hundred men were collected, and General Howard, of the United States Army, given command. The Illinois troops rendezvoused at Camp Russell, and marched up the Mississippi by companies, as far as the Illinois, which they crossed some two or three miles above its mouth. The movement was slow ; in Calhoun County, attracted by bee-trees, several rangers wandered away from the main column and got into a skirmish with Indians, but escaped with no more serious injury than the smashing of a gun-stock by a bullet. Meanwhile, the Missourians marched a hundred miles north on the west side of the Mississippi to Fort Madison, where they swam the river, mounted naked on their horses, while their clothing was rafted across on a platform upborne by two canoes. This latter force was under command of Colonel McNair, afterwards Governor of Missouri. The troops, uniting together, continued their march up the Mississippi. Near the site of Quincy, they passed a recently deserted Indian village, which apparently had contained not far from a thousand Sac warriors. Reaching a point called Two Rivers, they struck out directly eastward, across the open prairies, toward the Illinois, which they reached near the mouth of Spoon River. Here their provisions boat joined them, and took on board the sick. The slow march was continued up the banks of the Illinois as far as Peoria, where there was a small stockade, probably built on the bluff near the straits, in charge of Captain Nicholas, of the United States Army. Two days before, the Indians had made an attack here, but had been repulsed. All the way along since leaving the Mississippi, the troops had crossed fresh trails, from which they inferred that the savages, alarmed at their advance, were fleeing northward. Yet at no time did they obtain sight of any hostiles.

The invading army was marched up the lake as far as Gomo's village, on the site of Chillicothe, but found the enemy already flown. The deserted village was reduced to ashes, and the troops began retracing their steps. At the outlet of the lake, where Peoria is situated, they remained in camp several weeks, building Fort Clark. Major Christy, with two fortified keel-boats, was despatched up the river as far as the rapids, while Major Boone was sent up Spoon River to scour the country toward the valley of the Rock. Neither saw anything of the enemy, except deserted villages. The army then returned by direct trail to Camp Russell, where it was disbanded. This campaign, although bloodless, was well conducted, and was of great benefit to the frontier, which was, in consequence, spared from Indian raids during all of the following Winter.

But 1814 opened with horrible Indian atrocities. Our naval victories on Lake Erie, the recovery of Detroit, together with the defeat of the British at the battle of the Thames, where Tecumseh fell, caused the savages to retreat from Canada and concentrate in large numbers along the upper banks of the Mississippi, whence marauding parties swept swiftly down upon the exposed Illinois settlements. Space can be taken to mention but a very few of the well authenticated incidents that occurred at this time, as reported by Davidson and Stuvé and Ford and Reynolds. In July, a band of savages, raiding the Wood River settlements, six miles east of the present Alton, massacred a Mrs. Reagan with her six children. The husband and father, being absent at the time, was the first to discover the slaughter. Reaching home at nightfall and opening the door of his cabin, he stepped into the blood of his loved family and beheld their stark and mangled remains. Captain Samuel Whiteside, with his company of Rangers, at once took up pursuit, following the savages closely as far as the Sangamon, where all succeeded in escaping, amid a dense thicket, excepting the chief, who was shot dead out of a tree-top. At his belt was dangling the scalp of Mrs. Reagan. In the western part of Clinton County, where the Ohio and Mississippi Railroad now crosses a stream, Jesse Bailes and wife were out one Sunday evening, looking for some stray stock in the creek bottom. The dogs baying at a thicket, it was supposed the fugitives were found, but on approaching closer they were fired upon by Indians concealed within. Mrs. Bailes was shot down, and died shortly after. In August, while a company of Captain Short's Rangers were encamped at the Lively cabin, they discovered a trail which, being followed, led to the starting up of a party of seven Indians with fourteen stolen horses. Following these, a skirmish resulted in which the whites were worsted, one man being wounded, another saved from death by a twist of tobacco in his pocket, and a horse killed. William Stout made a swift ride to camp for reënforcements. Captain Short, with thirty men, at once started on the trail, following it all night, and the next morning overtook the savages on a fork of the Little Wabash. On discovering the whites, the Indians at once prepared for battle, assured, no doubt, by their former victory, and not realizing the force opposing them. They were soon surrounded, and upon discovering their situation, sang their death-songs, shouted defiance, and fought bravely to the end. All were killed. The only white man who fell was William O'Neal.

On August 21, 1814, occurred the most desperate single-handed combat ever fought on the soil of Illinois. A little fort, or block-house, had been erected about twenty miles from Vandalia, and some eight miles south of the present town of Greenville. It was considered an important point, and Lieutenant Journey and eleven men were stationed there as garrison. Governor Reynolds's account of what occurred there is as follows:

"Among these Rangers was Tom Higgins, a young fellow of twenty-five, of muscular and compact build, not tall, but strong and active. Discovering Indian signs near the fort, the company early the next morning started out to investigate. They had not gone far when they were fired upon from ambush by a much larger party. At this first fire, the commander, Journey, and three men fell. Six immediately retreated toward the fort, but Higgins stopped 'to have another pull at the red-skins,' and taking deliberate aim at an approaching savage, shot him down. Higgins's horse had been wounded, he supposed mortally; but coming to, he was about to effect his escape when he heard the familiar voice of a comrade named Burgess calling to him from the long grass, 'Tom, don't leave me!' Higgins told him to come along, but Burgess replied that his leg was smashed, so that he could not move. Higgins immediately dismounted; but in attempting to raise the wounded man on the horse, the animal took fright and ran off, leaving them both behind. 'This is too bad,' said Higgins, 'but don't fear; move off as well as you can, and I 'll stay behind and keep back the Indians. Get into the tall grass, and crawl as near the ground as possible.' Burgess did so, and succeeded in thus getting away unobserved.

"It would have been much easier and safer for Higgins to follow the same plan, but believing if he did so it would endanger his friend, the gallant fellow chose a different direction, endeavoring to conceal himself within a thicket. A moment later, he discovered a stout savage near by, with two others approaching. He immediately started for a small ravine, hoping thus to separate the party, and permit him to fight them one at a time. In this attempt at retreat, he was horrified to find one of his legs fail him, he having been wounded in the first encounter, without before realizing it. The larger of the pursuing Indians pressing him closely, Higgins endeavored to get a shot at him, but the wily savage at once halted, and danced about so it was impossible to obtain sure aim. He then resolved to take his chances, and permit the Indian to have the first shot. The savage raised his rifle, and Higgins, intently watching the fellow's eye, wheeled suddenly as he pulled the trigger, and received the ball in his thigh. He fell to the ground, staggered to his feet again, receiving the fire of the two others, and once more fell, this time severely wounded. The Indians, now feeling certain of their victim, flung aside their empty guns, and rushed eagerly toward him, spears and knives in hand.

Lying there almost helpless on the ground, the wounded man succeeded for a short time in holding them back by aiming first at one and then another as they approached. As he did not fire, the heavier Indian came to the conclusion his gun must be empty, and was advancing boldly when Higgins shot, and the savage fell dead.

"It was by now a most desperate situation. The undaunted Ranger lay helpless on the ground, his gun empty, and four bullets in his body. About him circled two Indians unharmed, while a large party of others were in a ravine only a few steps away. Yet even then Higgins did not despair, and when the two Indians rushed upon him, raising the war-whoop as they came, a fierce and bloody conflict ensued. They inflicted upon him numerous flesh-wounds, but, fortunately, none of these were deep, as their spears were only thin poles, hastily prepared for the occasion, and bent whenever they struck a rib or muscle. At last one of the savages flung his tomahawk, which struck Higgins on the cheek, severing his ear, laying bare his skull to the back of his head, and stretching him out upon the prairie. Again the two Indians rushed at him, but the Ranger kept them off with his feet. Getting hold of one of their spears, the Indian, in attempting to pull it from him, raised Higgins up from the ground, when with one blow of his rifle he dashed out the savage's brains, but broke his gun, the barrel only remaining in his hand. The other Indian now attempted to stab the exhausted man with his knife, but Higgins succeeded in warding off the blows, and the savage gradually fell back from before the glare of his untamed eye, evidently seeking to reach the spot where his discarded rifle was lying. Higgins knew that if the fellow once recovered that, his case would be hopeless. Drawing his hunting-knife, and summoning every remaining power to his aid, he staggered forward and closed with his foe. A most desperate struggle followed, during which deep gashes were inflicted on both sides. Faint and completely exhausted by loss of blood, the battling Ranger was no longer a match for his adversary, who succeeded in throwing him off, and at once started for his rifle. To add to his despair, the main body of Indians could now be seen advancing toward him from out the ravine, and Higgins gave himself up for lost.

"Almost the whole of this unequal contest had been witnessed from the fort. But, not knowing how many Indians were in the party, the little garrison were fearful of venturing forth in rescue. At this moment Mrs. Pursley, the wife of one of the Rangers, urged them to make the attempt, but failed to get the men to comply. Exasperated at their refusal, she taunted them with cowardice, snatched her husband's rifle from out his hand, and declaring that so fine a fellow as Tom Higgins should not be lost for want of help, mounted a horse and rode out alone. The Rangers, being thus shamed galloped hastily after her, reached the spot where Higgins had fallen and fainted, and, before the main body of Indians came up, succeeded in bearing their wounded companion in safety to the fort. For several days his life was despaired of. In the absence of a surgeon, they extracted two of the balls, and a third Higgins subsequently, with his usual hardihood, cut out himself with a razor. The fourth he carried with him to his grave. Open-hearted, generous, and brave, this noble specimen of borderman finally recovered, and survived to a great age, honored and respected by all who knew him."

During this same year on the waters of the Mississippi, just above Rock Island, occurred one of the most gallant actions recorded in the annals of the West, or, indeed, in the entire history of warfare. General Howard, who still remained in military command of this department, desired to strengthen a small garrison then stationed at Prairie du Chien, in what is now Wisconsin. With this purpose in mind, he despatched reënforcements to the number of one hundred and eight men, under command of Lieutenant Campbell of the regular army, in three keel-boats, up the river. Of this force, sixty-six men were Illinois Rangers under Captains Stephen Rector and Riggs, who occupied two of the boats. The remainder of the party were with Campbell in the third boat. Arriving at Rock Island, they remained there unmolested for one night, camping near the foot of the island, but the next day, at the bottom of the rapids just above, great numbers of the Sac and Fox Indians came out in their canoes to the boats, the savages making

PRESENT ASPECT OF CAMPBELL'S ISLAND

THE SCENE OF RECTOR'S GALLANT FIGHT IN 1814

many professions of friendship. Several of the French boatmen, who were employed at the paddles, were known to these Indians, and well liked. The visitors endeavored to warn these that there was danger ahead, by squeezing their hands with a pull down the river, thus plainly indicating that it would be well for them to leave in that direction. Believing an attack on the flotilla was planned, several of these Frenchmen spoke to Lieutenant Campbell in warning, but, feeling confident in the number of his force, and not being greatly accustomed to Indian warfare, that officer disregarded these indefinite suspicions, and ordered the savages to leave, commanding the boats to press forward against the swift current. The sutler's and contractor's barges, with the two boats containing the Illinois Rangers, succeeded in working safely past the more dangerous rapids, and had arrived at a point some two miles ahead of the others, when Campbell's barge was suddenly struck by a fierce gale of wind tearing down from the west, across the wide waters, so strong as to force it almost helpless against a small island which lay not far from the Illinois shore. Believing it would prove safer to remain sheltered there until the really dangerous wind-storm abated, he immediately stationed sentinels at the edge of the wood, while some of the men went ashore to cook breakfast. Scarcely had the fires been lighted under the camp-kettles, when a large body of Indians, under command of Black Hawk, who had been lying concealed along the main shore, waiting some such opportunity, commenced a fierce attack. Springing into a number of canoes made ready for just such an emergency, the hordes of savages passed rapidly across the narrow water-way between the mainland and the island, and, giving vent to the war-whoop, rushed out of the forest upon the few disembarked men, driving them on a run back to the protection of the barge. The surprise was complete, several falling before they could rejoin their companions. Immediately the battle burst forth in fury, a brisk fire of musketry being exchanged between the few regulars partially protected aboard the stranded barge and the hordes of Indians who had immediately taken shelter behind the trees on the island. Meanwhile, Captains Rector and Riggs, ahead with their boats, which were tossing on the storm-lashed river, seeing the smoke of battle and hearing the distant report of guns, endeavored to return, but so strong was the fierce gale which buffeted them, that Riggs's boat became utterly unmanageable, and finally stranded helplessly on the rapids. Rector, endeavoring to avoid a similar disaster, which seemed inevitable, let go his anchor. The anxious Rangers, however, were by this time within long range of the scene of action, and they at once opened with their rifles on the distant savages, forcing them to fall backward somewhat from the shore.

In this way the unequal conflict raged for considerable time, the exposed occupants of the stranded barge suffering severely, but totally unable to get away from the bank. Finally, with numerous wounded and several dead on board, among whom Campbell himself was very badly hurt, defensive firing had almost ceased, when the boat was discovered to be on fire. Far out in the stream, the distant Rangers saw the smoke and understood the meaning. It was at this desperate juncture when Stephen Rector and his gallant crew of Illinoisans, comprehending the horrible situation of their helpless comrades, performed as cool and heroic a deed as ever imperilled the life of man. Deliberately, in the teeth of that howling gale, in full view of hundreds of infuriated savages lining the near-by shore, and within easy range of their deadly rifles, these frontier heroes raised their anchor, lightened their barge by casting overboard nearly all their stock of provisions, and then guided it with the utmost labor and amid tremendous danger down that madly racing current, actually forcing it to the windward of the burning barge and into the very blaze of the Indian guns. Holding it there, in spite of the galling fire fairly scorching their faces, these men coolly rescued the survivors, removing wounded, dying, and all to the security of their own vessel, and then swept with them in safety down the river. It was as heroic a deed of daring as was ever performed in war. The island was later named for Campbell, but with Captain Rector and his Illinois Rangers remains the true glory of the action. The manner in which it was accomplished only serves to illustrate the desperate need for haste, and the quick response of brave minds, in moments of extreme peril. The provisions once cast overboard, the crew, largely composed of experienced French boatmen, at once leaped into the swirling water on the windward side of the heavy barge, which brought the boat between them and the direct fire of the enemy. Partially sheltered in this manner, they were enabled to guide their heavy boat, in spite of the raging storm beating against them, until it rested close beside the disabled barge, and to hold it there securely until the removal had been effected, when they hauled it against the wind far enough out into the wide stream to be safe. The loss suffered during this brisk action was twenty-five: nine killed,— four Rangers, three regulars, one woman, and one child,— sixteen wounded, including Lieutenant Campbell and Dr. Stewart, both severely. Rector's boat was now uncomfortably crowded for the wounded, but the force on board being large, they rowed night and day until St. Louis was reached. Riggs, with his company in the other boat, exchanged shots with the Indians all day, but at night succeeded in slipping past, and finally arrived at St. Louis without the loss of a man.

A little later, another expedition was despatched by boat to the upper Mississippi, where British agents continued active among the Indians. It was fitted out at Cape au Gris, an old French hamlet on the left bank of the river, a little above the mouth of the Illinois. It consisted of three hundred and thirty-four effective men,— forty regulars, the remainder rangers and volunteers,— and was under command of Major Zachary Taylor, afterwards President of the United States. Nelson Rector and Samuel Whiteside were in command of the boats containing the Illinois troops. This force passed Rock Island, as well as the rapids above, without molestation, or seeing anything of the enemy. But about this time they learned from scouts sent ashore that the entire country around them swarmed with hostile Indians, while a number of English were there in command, having a detachment of regulars, and possessing artillery. Feeling it unsafe to proceed, the three boats in advance turned about, and began the descent of the rapids, seeking to rejoin the others below. These were commanded by Rector, Whiteside, and Hempstead; and no sooner had they rounded the foot of the island before they were at once plunged into a severe fight, large numbers of the concealed enemy pouring heavy volleys into them from all along the shore. A little way above the mouth of Rock River, and not far from some small islands covered with willows, which have since disappeared, Major Taylor finally succeeded in anchoring all of his flotilla of boats close together. During the darkness of the following night, the English planted a battery of six pieces close to the water's edge, but well concealed behind underbrush, hoping thus to sink and disable the frail boats out in the stream, while remaining themselves beyond rifle range. Indians in large numbers were posted in concealment upon the willow-islands for the purpose of butchering any who might escape the cannonading and reach their shelter alive. But Taylor's prompt action frustrated this plan. Almost at break of day he ordered his entire force, with the exception of only twenty boatmen left as a guard on each vessel, to the upper island for the purpose of dislodging the enemy, whom he believed to be posted there in considerable force. It was accomplished with great gallantry, the island thoroughly scoured, a number of the skulking Indians killed, and the remainder driven to the shelter of the smaller island below. Meanwhile the British cannon opened fiercely upon the fleet, the shots piercing the sides of many of the exposed vessels, and causing several to leak badly. As soon as possible, the men engaged on shore rushed back, and the boats were promptly dropped down stream beyond range of the artillery. Captain Rector was next ordered to take his company of Rangers, and clear out the savages hiding on the lower and smaller island. He attempted it, forcing the Indians back among the willows, but they, being heavily reënforced from the mainland, charged in turn and hurled his men back upon the open sand-beach, where they were exposed to a galling fire. At this time, through some misunderstanding among the officers, the boats out in the stream began to retreat down the river. Rector attempted to follow, but his barge grounded when just off shore, and the savages with wild yells of triumph surged madly about them. A most desperate hand-to-hand fight followed, the Rangers using their clubbed guns and hunting-knives to beat back their fierce assailants. For a moment it looked as if all must perish, but Whiteside, with his Illinoisans, hurried to their rescue, driving back the savages until the Rangers could be released from so perilous a position. Taylor immediately returned southward, and reported his loss as eleven men wounded, of whom three afterwards died.

This failure practically ended all effort to open the upper Mississippi River to American occupancy. The enemy remained in undisputed possession of the entire country north of the Illinois River, nor was there any force in the West sufficiently strong to drive them out. With the approach of Winter, however, Indian depredations almost wholly ceased along the frontier, and the Peace of Ghent, signed December 24, 1814, closed the war.

CHAPTER XVIII

THE STRUGGLE WITH BLACK HAWK

THE fifteen years following the close of our second war with England was a time of grateful peace within the Illinois borders, and was distinguished by a large influx of immigration from the East. Settlers came to the new country both by way of the rivers and lakes, the Northern States beginning for the first time to be well represented, and yielding a new complexion to the growing settlements. More chose sites for farms on the open prairies, and beyond the main water-courses, while little towns sprang up, as if by magic, in midst of the surrounding wilderness. Numerous colonies, many from New England, some from across the sea, populated in a day entire districts. The outer fringe of white settlement swept swiftly northward and westward, so that by 1831, while many counties yet remained unorganized, there were few, indeed, utterly devoid of permanent white occupants. North and west of the Illinois River, however, the country remained very sparsely settled, the few scattered villages far between, the sole means of communication those dim trails leading across the unbroken prairies and through the dark woods. Indians still hunted wild game throughout nearly all of this region, but were being steadily pressed backward into narrower confines by the advance of white invaders.

In the lead regions of the far Northwest were several trading-posts and small mining settlements. A coach-road, known as "Kellogg's Trail," first opened in 1827, connected Galena with Peoria, and was largely travelled. Here and there along this road were a few scattered settlers, thus located by Dr. Thwaites: "Old Man" Kellogg at Kellogg's Grove, Winter on Apple River, John Dixon at Dixon's Ferry on Rock River, "Dad Joe" at Dad Joe's Grove, Henry Thomas on West Bureau Creek, Charles S. Boyd at Boyd's Grove, and several others. Between Galena and the Illinois River, the most important settlement was on Bureau Creek at Bulbona, where some thirty families were gathered. There were also small collections of cabins at Peru, La Salle, South Ottawa, Newark, and Holderman's Grove, with a cluster of eight or ten along Indian Creek. Chicago, at this date, contained, perhaps, three hundred people, who were housed in primitive cabins nestled beneath the shadow of Fort Dearborn. Scattered between these settlements were a few widely separated farms, squatters being far more numerous than homesteaders. Such is a brief description of Northern Illinois in the year 1831.

Under these conditions, trouble was inevitable, and it finally broke forth in fierce conflict with the closely allied tribes of the Sacs and Foxes, whose seat of power was within the present county of Rock Island. As early as 1804, General Harrison negotiated a treaty with these Indians, whereby they ceded all their claims east of the Mississippi River to the United States, but in this they reserved a right to both reside and hunt thereon until the land should be actually sold for white settlement. This treaty was again ratified in 1822, in a "full council" held at Fort Armstrong, on Rock Island. About 1828 the country immediately around the mouth of Rock River was surveyed and sold, and the next year was taken possession of by American families. At this time, in accordance with the terms of these treaties, the United States gave due notice to the Indians residing there to leave the territory. Keokuk, then chief of the Sacs, at once withdrew across the Mississippi, accompanied by the majority of both allied tribes. Meanwhile, Black Hawk, a man then sixty years of age, and long a pensioner of the

British government, becoming dissatisfied, endeavored to rally all the Western Indians into a confederation with which to resist further encroachments of the whites. His success was only partial, yet he succeeded in gathering about him most of the young and restless of the two tribes, over whom he exercised a species of chieftainship, warranted by his long leadership in war.

In 1830, a sort of informal arrangement seems to have been agreed upon between the few Americans who had already purchased and occupied land near the mouth of Rock River, and those Indians still remaining in the neighborhood, by which the latter were to continue undisturbed cultivating their old fields. This, of course, added nothing to the legal rights of the savages, yet undoubtedly encouraged them greatly in their schemes for resisting final removal. With headquarters on the high bluff, since known as Black Hawk's Watch Tower, they cultivated in a feeble way a portion of the rich valley lying below. Their enclosures consisted of stakes stuck in the ground, having small poles tied with strips of bark between. During the Summer and Fall the Indians appeared sullen toward their white neighbors, but did no damage, other than to allow their loose horses to range at will throughout the unprotected cornfields. After the winter hunt was over, the Indians again collected in a body at their old camp, under the immediate guidance of Black Hawk, and at once began a series of petty depredations along the immediate frontier, which greatly exasperated the widely scattered settlers, who, from lack of numbers, were unable to retaliate. Black Hawk, in these proceedings, exhibited his shrewd cunning, for he had evidently instructed his party to commit all injury possible to property, while never attacking or killing any of the whites. His policy, apparently, and judged from results, was to provoke war, but to compel the Americans to take the first openly hostile step, and thus enable him to call upon his

Indian allies among other tribes for help in defence of ancient rights, and the "graves of their fathers."

The stories of these numerous depredations and midnight raids were quickly spread throughout the near-by settlements, creating much excitement and alarm; many fled the country, while others gathered together for defence. Black Hawk, at this time, had about five hundred well-trained Indian warriors under his immediate command. They possessed numerous horses, and were well armed; every report reaching the State officials bore evidence to their hostile purposes. In consequence, Governor Reynolds cannot be said to have acted hastily or improperly, when, with all these facts before him, on the 27th of May, 1831, he issued a call for volunteers to guard the frontier, and requested of General Gaines the assistance of regular troops to expel the invaders from Illinois. Legally, and under the terms of a treaty repeatedly ratified, the State was practically being invaded by a hostile band of savages, under the leadership of an openly avowed enemy of the United States.

In answer to this call for volunteers, the settlements made quick response, the entire border throbbing with a desire to repay in kind many a real or fancied injury. More than sixteen hundred men, most of them on horseback, were in rendezvous at Beardstown by the 22d of June. Meanwhile, all over the region threatened with trouble, stockade forts were hastily erected, the scattered inhabitants forming themselves into garrisons. Among those in Illinois, the more important were situated at Galena, Apple River, Kellogg's Grove, Buffalo Grove, Dixon's, South Ottawa, Wilburn (about opposite the present Peru), West Bureau, Hennepin, and Peoria. Fort Armstrong, on Rock Island, became a busy scene, ten companies of regular troops being at once ordered there, with large quantities of war equipment. General Atkinson, widely and favorably known to the Indians as "White

Beaver," was in command at this post, and acted promptly, despatching stern orders to the invading Sacs and Foxes to withdraw at once from Illinois territory. To these Black Hawk, rendered confident by the advice of his prophet, who assured him success in the struggle, returned defiant answers, meanwhile travelling up Rock River accompanied by his braves, as far as Prophetstown, in what is now Whiteside County, but attempting no depredations on the way. The very act of advance, however, could not be construed in any other way than a challenge to conflict.

To temporize longer with the savages was only to invite additional danger to the exposed settlements. A second gathering of volunteers at Beardstown was hastily organized into four regiments, under command of Colonels John Thomas, Jacob Fry, A. B. Dewitt, and Samuel M. Thompson. A scouting company under Major James D. Henry, and two odd battalions, commanded by Majors James and Long, were also in the field. In command over all was Brigadier-General Samuel Whiteside, who had previously won honors as an efficient Indian fighter. Accompanied by Governor Reynolds in person, with rank as Major-General, this little army made their slow way to Fort Armstrong, where they were duly mustered in as United States Volunteers. Lieutenant Robert Anderson, later the gallant defender of Fort Sumter, became inspector-general of the Illinois troops.

May 9, 1832, this combined force of regulars and volunteers took up Black Hawk's trail clearly marked along the east bank of Rock River. Whiteside, with his mounted frontiersmen, led the way on land, while Atkinson followed closely with the main body in boats, transporting provisions, cannon, and baggage. The command of the latter consisted of three hundred volunteer infantry, and four hundred regulars, these last under Colonel Zachary Taylor, afterwards President of the United States. The travelling proved decidedly bad, both by water and land. For many days the toiling troops were drenched to the skin, being almost constantly swept by pelting rains. The trail became a quagmire, and the river a torrent. Whiteside, however, was able to outdistance Atkinson in the advance. He reached Prophetstown, only to find it completely deserted of Indians. But, the signs of their departure being fresh, he pushed forward after them as far as Dixon's. Here his force was augmented by two additional battalions, under Majors Stillman and Bailey, which had been organized in that upper country. Not yet being regularly sworn into United States service, these men demanded to be employed as scouts, or on detached service, and were finally, on the 13th, sent ahead of the slowly advancing column under Stillman's command, as Whiteside was anxious to use them in any manner possible, thus relieving his better-disciplined force.

Black Hawk, meanwhile, after tarrying a week at Prophetstown in persistent but vain council with the assembled Winnebagoes, from whom he gained little encouragement, had pushed on, accompanied by his motley following, to the mouth of Sycamore Creek, in Ogle County. Here, in council with the Pottawattomies, his schemes of a great Indian alliance were again defeated through the personal influence of the chief Shaubena, who remained an avowed friend of the whites. Utterly discouraged by this second rebuff, although a few hot-heads had joined him, the Sauk leader was now ready to meet any overtures of peace which might have been made him by the whites, but, unfortunately, in that very moment of readiness, circumstances suddenly arose which made the continuation of war inevitable. Major Stillman's force of undisciplined scouts had made unsuspecting camp within a clump of open timber only three miles southwest of where the Indians were still holding council; about them on every side stretched the open, undulating prairie. Black Hawk learned of the near presence of these troops about sunset. He had with him at that time only some forty or fifty warriors,— a mere personal body-guard,— the remainder of his band, together with the hostile faction of the Pottawattomies, being encamped on the Kiskwaukee, some seven miles distant. Supposing these advancing soldiers to be under command of Atkinson, whom he knew well, he sent forward three of his young men to open parley with them, and bearing an offer to meet with "White Beaver" in council. The Sauk chief afterwards stated that his sole purpose in this was the seeking for terms of peace.

That which followed on the part of the whites was full of disgrace and humiliation to the entire border, and remains a blot on frontier history. Stillman's troopers, totally undisciplined, and, as many report, in liquor, were busily making camp, when the three Indian flag-of-truce bearers suddenly appeared on the summit of a little prairie knoll nearly a mile distant. Instantly a yelling mob of excited whites, without waiting any command, dashed out upon them, driving the three helpless and surprised savages into the camp amid curses, blows, and threats. Black Hawk, in precaution against failure, had despatched a small party of five braves to watch the reception of his truce-bearers. These were likewise observed by the crazed soldiery, and fiercely charged upon by about twenty troopers, who had hastily mounted their horses. Two were killed, the other three succeeding in escaping to the council grove, where they reported that the truce-bearers were also slain by the whites. The old Sauk war-chief rose up with indignation, and, determining at once to avenge such foul treachery, sallied forth, his little party mounted on ponies, to meet the enemy. Even as they thus emerged onto the open prairie, Stillman's force, over three hundred strong, came rushing toward them like an undisciplined mob. The Sauks, withdrawing behind a fringe of bushes, remained firm, but at sight of the Indians thus making a stand, the troopers came to a sudden

BLACK HAWK

FROM AN OLD PORTRAIT

halt. Instantly, inspired by anger to the performance of so desperate a deed, Black Hawk sounded the war-whoop, and his little band of savages, scarcely forty all told, sprang forward, firing fiercely as they advanced. Without even returning the volley, the terrified militia turned and fled. All night long, although the Indian pursuit is said to have ceased at dark, those frightened volunteers of Stillman's plunged wildly onward in their mad retreat, through swamps and creeks, for twenty-five miles to Dixon's. Nor did all of them pause even there, but kept on to their distant homes, alarming the entire border with their wild and fanciful tales of Black Hawk's force and savagery. The whites had in this unfortunate affair eleven killed. Besides the two scouts, and one truce-bearer wantonly murdered, the Indian loss remains unknown.

While the story of this skirmish remains a blot of disgrace on the military records of Illinois, one redeeming incident occurred at Old Man's Creek, a small stream rising in Ogle County, and flowing into Rock River. It is now known as Stillman's Run. Here Major Perkins, Captain Adams, and about fifteen men made a determined stand, and by hard hand-to-hand fighting held back the savage pursuers until their companions had found opportunity to escape. Captain Adams sacrificed his own life for this purpose, his body being found the next day lying near two Indians he had slain in personal combat. Everything pointed to a most desperate struggle. Their guns were broken into fragments, and their bodies covered with the scars of knife and tomahawk wounds. Major Hackleton also had a single-handed fight, but succeeded in killing his antagonist and escaped.

Nevertheless, it was now to be war beyond question, while this easy, unexpected victory greatly encouraged Black Hawk and his gathering warriors. The abundant stores of provisions which Stillman left behind were also of much assistance in holding his braves together, and encouraging others to join his standard of revolt. Realizing that it would not be safe to tarry long in so exposed a position, the wily savages, after gathering up their spoils, hastily retreated northward to the head-waters of the Rock, near Lake Koshkonong, across the Wisconsin line, a land of swamps and inaccessible hiding-places. Here Black Hawk was soon joined by parties of Winnebagoes and Pottawattomies, mostly young braves eager for renown, and began immediately despatching his raiding parties down into Northern Illinois to harass the more exposed settlements with all the atrocities of border warfare.

Meanwhile, Whiteside, with his fourteen hundred men, startled by the news of this defeat, advanced to Stillman's battle-field, only to discover it deserted of all save the dead. The sadly mutilated bodies, disfiguring the prairie, were buried with military honors, and on the 19th the entire army, now under command of Atkinson, with the exception of Stillman's discomfited corps left at Dixon to guard stores, began its slow march up the Rock in pursuit of Black Hawk's retreating braves. But scarcely were they well out of sight when news reached them that Stillman's men had deserted their post at Dixon and returned to their homes. Atkinson, with his regulars, hastily turned back to protect the exposed stores, leaving Whiteside alone to press forward on Black Hawk's trail. But almost immediately the volunteers who composed his force, refusing to leave the State, demanded their discharge from service. Unable to control them, the column was finally turned about, marched to Ottawa and the men disbanded, the whole campaign having proved a most miserable failure.

Immediately the path was thus made clear by retreat, Black Hawk's eager warriors swarmed down upon the exposed settlements. The chief led in person the larger division, about two hundred strong, and, like unchained fiends thirsting for blood, they swept the entire border. Small scalping parties, principally composed of Winnebagoes, coöperated with them, while about a hundred Pottawattomies, led by Mike Girty, were guilty of terrible atrocities. While these raiders wrought sad havoc also throughout Southern Wisconsin, in Illinois they swept unchecked clear to the Illinois River, and the entire northern half of the State was in a tumult of alarm, every settler in peril. Stock was wantonly slaughtered, cabins fired, settlements raided, and men, women, and children killed in sudden midnight forays. Many of the latter were borne away captives. No one knew where the fiends would break forth next, or who would fall beneath merciless knife and tomahawk. On the 22d of May, a party of thirty Pottawattomies and three Sacs, under Girty, surprised and slaughtered fifteen men, women, and children at the Davis farm, on Indian Creek, twelve miles north of Ottawa. Two daughters of William Hall, Sylvia and Rachel, were captured, but a month later were surrendered to the whites. On the 14th of June, eleven Sacs killed five white men on the Pecatonica River, and a little later the same band murdered two more a few miles east of Galena. They were, however, fiercely pursued by a party of volunteers under General Dodge of Wisconsin, and, during a hot fight, the entire eleven were killed, the whites losing three in the affair.

About this same time, Captain Stephenson, with a portion of his Galena company, unexpectedly came into contact with an Indian raiding party somewhere between Apple River and Kellogg's Grove. The savages took refuge within a clump of trees, and after considerable firing had been exchanged, the Americans charged them three times, but were repulsed with the loss of six men killed, and Stephenson seriously wounded. On June 24, Black Hawk's own party made a desperate attack on the Apple River Fort, situated fourteen miles east of Galena, and a quarter of a mile north of the present village of Elizabeth. He had with him more than a hundred and fifty warriors. Fortunately, word of their stealthy approach reached the threatened neighborhood in time for the firing of guns as a signal to those engaged on various work without. From every direction these flocked immediately to the safety of the fort, a log stockade, with strong block-houses at the corners, and the heavy gates were closed. As soon as the Indians arrived within firing distance, the action began with fury. It continued unabated for fifteen hours, during which the savages made several attempts to burn and storm the fortification. They took possession of near-by dwellings in the village, knocked holes through the walls, and, thus safely sheltered, poured a galling fire upon the besieged. Others devoted themselves to destroying property in full view of the garrison. There were only twenty-five men inside the fort, but they fought with desperate daring, believing death in battle preferable to surrender and subsequent butchery. The mothers and children united to help, moulding bullets and loading guns, and at length the Indians drew off, convinced of their inability to capture the place. The white loss was but one man killed; that of the assailants is unknown.

On their retreat, this band of Black Hawk's very unexpectedly ran into Major Dement's battalion of volunteers, one hundred and fifty strong, who were encamped at Kellogg's Grove, about nine miles south of the present village of Lena. A spirited fight ensued on the open prairie, which finally resulted in a stampede of the ill-disciplined American forces, until they found shelter within a block-house situated within the grove. Here, however, they made a firm stand, and succeeded in driving back their fierce assailants and holding their position until reënforcements arrived, before which the Indians sullenly retired. The whites had five killed, while the Indian loss was fifteen. Other skirmishes, but of less importance, occurred about this time at Plum River Fort, Burr Oak Grove, Sinsinawa Mound, and Blue Mounds.

Meanwhile neither Governor Reynolds nor the United States authorities remained idle. Pursuant to another call, two thousand volunteers gathered at Beardstown, June ten, while a thousand regulars, under General Winfield Scott, were ordered westward. Among these volunteers, General Whiteside, previously in command, enlisted as a private, while among the three hundred mounted rangers, as a private, was Abraham Lincoln. In less than three weeks after Stillman's defeat, these State troops were gathered together at Fort Wilburn, near Peru, and made ready for the field. They were divided into three brigades, headed by Generals Posey, Alexander, and Henry. With Dodge's Rangers, already waiting in the northwest to coöperate with them, and the available regulars, the entire force numbered nearly four thousand effective men. With the scouting battalions kept well in advance, and occasionally having brief skirmishes with fleeing raiding parties, the main column marched slowly forward up the east bank of the Rock, leaving Dixon's for the unknown wilderness beyond on the afternoon of June 27.

On the 30th they crossed the Illinois border, about a mile east of the present city of Beloit, following closely the fresh trail of the retreating Sauk raiders. Every precaution was taken to guard against surprise; whenever possible, the troops being encamped at night within timber and protected by hastily erected breastworks. The sentinels were frequently fired upon by savages skulking in the darkness, but no attempt was made in force to obstruct their progress. At the outlet of Lake Koshkonong, which was attained July 2, deserted Indian camps were found, with white scalps dangling from the tepee-poles. No one in the struggling column chanced to be acquainted with the country they were now traversing, while the few Indians captured gave misleading information, and consequently progress became daily more slow and difficult and uncertain. Food was so scarce the army had to be divided in order to search after provisions. For this purpose, General Henry was despatched with a considerable detachment in the endeavor to reach Fort Winnebago, about eighty miles distant. While on the way, learning through his scouts that Black Hawk's band was in the immediate vicinity, he promptly took up pursuit, sending back word by courier to Atkinson's camp, by that time some thirty-five miles distant, of his purpose, and requesting reënforcements. Throughout the entire volunteer force this news was received with manifestations of joy, while every discomfort was instantly forgotten in an awakened eagerness to overtake the savages. Filled with enthusiasm, the troops pressed sternly forward across a country made most difficult for travelling by deep swamps and innumerable sink-holes. Frequently the men were compelled to dismount, and wade up to their armpits in mud and water. At last, on the 21st, at three o'clock in the afternoon, after an advance so rapid that forty horses succumbed between the Catfish and the Wisconsin, the eager soldiers came finally into contact with the fleeing enemy. Skirmishing began at once, until at last the Indians came to a final stand within a mile and a half of the river. The savages made the first charge, but were repulsed with heavy loss, and, after a half-hour of hot firing on both sides, and a steady advance by the whites, were driven back to the refuge of the high bluffs. Here darkness put an end to the fight. This was the battle of Wisconsin Heights, which occurred opposite Prairie du Sac. The Indian loss was heavy, that of the Americans slight.

After the battle, Black Hawk loaded a large raft with women, children, and old men, and sent it down the Wisconsin River, hoping that the soldiers on duty at Fort Crawford would permit these non-combatants to safely cross the Mississippi in peace. He reckoned on a humanity which did not exist. Lieutenant Joseph Ritner, with a small body of regulars, intercepted these helpless fugitives, and, firing on them, killed fifteen men, capturing four men and thirty-two women and children. Nearly as many more were drowned, while of those who escaped to shore, all but a mere handful perished in the wilds.

During the night following the Wisconsin Heights battle, Neapope, who was Black Hawk's chief lieutenant, endeavored vainly to address the whites from a high eminence, in the Winnebago tongue, begging mercy. Unfortunately, no one then in the camp understood his language, and he retired, feeling that he had been rebuffed. Meanwhile the Indians succeeded in crossing the river, fleeing down the western bank. Atkinson, as soon as he could procure sufficient provisions, energetically took up the pursuit. By the 28th the troops were also across the Wisconsin, all the commands united together, and had struck the trail of the fugitives, which, trending to the north of west, pointed directly toward the distant Mississippi. It was a hard road to travel, but the troopers were constantly encouraged to press grimly on by the large number of dead Indians found along the way, who had perished either of wounds or starvation. Everywhere were abundant evidences that the fleeing wretches were eating the bark of trees, and the flesh of their fagged-out ponies. On the first of August, Black Hawk with his starving remnant succeeded in reaching the Mississippi, about two miles below the mouth of the Bad Axe. Close behind them toiled the relentless pursuing troops.

At this time Black Hawk had no thought except to save himself and his people from these relentless pursuers. His one remaining hope was to cross the broad river before Atkinson and his men could come up.

Only two or three canoes were discovered along the shore,

but with these, and a large raft, hastily constructed, the exodus was begun. The raft, laden with women and children, was despatched, but in mid-stream capsized, and nearly all its occupants were drowned. Scarcely had this occurred when an army supply-steamer, the "Warrior," suddenly appeared on the scene. John Throckmorton was captain, and he had on board fifteen regular soldiers and six volunteers under Lieutenants Kingsbury and Holmes. As soon as this steamer appeared, Black Hawk hailed it, requesting that a boat be sent ashore, as the fugitives desired to give themselves up. This request was understood plainly, but the Captain, apparently fearful of treachery, refused, and, instead, ordered Black Hawk to come aboard in one of his own canoes. This the chief could not do, as they were then filled with fleeing women and children. Immediately upon his stating this fact, and refusing to come, those on board discharged three rounds of canister-shot into the unsuspecting group of Indians huddled on shore. Instantly a fierce fire of musketry burst forth on both sides, during which twenty-three Indians were killed, one white being wounded. The boat then steamed away to Prairie du Chien.

During the night following, a few more Indians escaped across the river. Amid the darkness, even Black Hawk's heart failed him, and, accompanied by ten warriors and a number of squaws and children, he fled eastward, seeking a hiding-place amid the dalles of the Wisconsin. But when day dawned, his conscience smitten at thus deserting his people in their time of need, the old chief turned back, and from a distant bluff witnessed the tragic scenes of the final struggle; for by this time Atkinson and his toiling men were upon them. After a hard march, beginning at two o'clock in the morning, the head of that remorseless pursuing column burst forth from the bottom timber, and came into full view of the fugitives. Brigadier-General Henry's command was first to come into contact with them. Swinging his entire force straight down the face of a steep bluff, and dashing recklessly forward on foot, his eager soldiers came suddenly face to face with three hundred desperate warriors. A fierce struggle ensued, the savages being steadily forced back from tree to tree by relentless bayonets, while frightened women and children plunged into the river, seeking escape, and many of them were drowned. Much of the fighting here was hand to hand. In the midst of it, Atkinson, with the main body, came up hurriedly, and plunged headlong into the *mêlée*. The carnage became greater than ever. The Indians fought with the desperation of despair, and, although weak from hunger, died like warriors. A few escaped, fleeing down a broad slough to a willow-island, which the steamer "Warrior," now returned, raked from end to end with canister. Henry's and Dodge's volunteers also charged it fiercely through mud and water, and finally swept completely across it. Some fugitives succeeded in swimming the river, but many, attempting it, were drowned on the way, or picked off by riflemen, who, in their excitement, exhibited no mercy to men or women or children. So, after three long, horrible hours of continuous slaughter, ended the battle — or shall we call it massacre? — of the Bad Axe. One hundred and fifty Indians were killed outright, an unknown number drowned,— probably fully as many,— and only fifty taken prisoners. Perhaps three hundred succeeded in attaining the west shore. The loss of the whites was but seventeen killed and twelve wounded. No one can consider the incidents of this war — its unnecessary beginning, its cruel ending — without realizing that it is a dishonorable chapter in border history and a black blot on Illinois.

The remainder is soon told. Black Hawk was delivered up by the Winnebagoes, among whom he sought refuge, and after being held in prison until the early Summer of 1833, was finally delivered over to the guardianship of his old rival,

Keokuk. Feeling this insult keenly, he nursed it bitterly through his few remaining years, which were passed on the Des Moines River, in Davis County, Iowa. Here he died, October 3, 1838, at the age of seventy-one.

General Winfield Scott, with his Eastern regulars, did not arrive on the field to assume command until all fighting was over, and nothing remained for him to do but discharge the volunteers. Cholera among his troops had detained him at Detroit, Chicago, and Rock Island, nearly a fourth of his detachment of a thousand men having died of the pestilence. Beyond these, the entire American loss in the war was probably not to exceed two hundred and fifty.

CHAPTER XIX

THE MORMONS AT NAUVOO

IN April, 1840, large numbers of a religious body, known as Latter-Day Saints, or Mormons, removed from Missouri to Illinois. They had purchased a considerable tract of land located on the east bank of the Mississippi, in Hancock County. Nowhere along the great river is there a more picturesque and attractive spot. The succession of terraces ascending from the water until the high land is reached, furnish a gradual slope of remarkable beauty; noble groves of tall oaks, interspersed with winding vistas, clothe the ground to the summit, from which point the eye looks forth over a green, undulating prairie. Near the river, in that early day, stood the spacious residence of Dr. Isaac Galland, who had combined art with nature in forming a most delightful country-seat. On this fine tract of land, in 1834, he had laid off the little town of Commerce. This land having been sold to Mormon agents, preparations were immediately made to build here a great city of their faith, which was named Nauvoo, signifying either "peaceful," or "pleasant."

So well did they succeed in these early plans, that at the end of no more than five years the entire scene was changed. Nauvoo by that time already contained a population approximating fifteen thousand, while accessions were pouring in from all parts of the world, and several smaller villages and settlements, entirely Mormon as to inhabitants, had been started within the limits of the county. Nauvoo itself was very irregularly built, being scattered over six square miles, a part lying down upon the flat skirting the river, but the major portion extending higher up, and crowning the bluff. The most conspicuous building in the place was the "Temple," never thoroughly completed until too late for occupancy, which, standing upon the highest brow of the bluff, overlooked the surrounding country for twenty miles in Illinois and Iowa. It was built of compact, polished limestone, quarried within the limits of the city, but no order of architecture was observed, the Mormons asserting that they built day by day through direct inspiration. It was one hundred and twenty-eight feet long, eighty-eight feet wide, sixty-five feet to the top of the cornice, and one hundred and sixty-five to the summit of the cupola. The basement was a huge apartment, and contained a baptistry supported by twelve oxen hewn out of limestone. In the main story was the audience-room, the second contained another room, while in the third was a hall for educational purposes. Besides these, the building also contained numerous smaller apartments for the use of the church officials.

Upon the peculiar religious tenets of the Mormons we need not dwell. Their stormy career while in Illinois is the theme of this chapter, and it is only necessary to briefly consider that peculiar faith on which all else was founded. Joseph Smith, a native of Vermont, obscure, without money or education, or even respectability, professed to have received a special revelation, engraven on brass plates hidden in a box, which he had discovered on a hillside near Palmyra, New York, in 1827. Thus he became the founder and leader of this persevering body of blindly believing men and women. In twenty years the disciples of this "prophet" increased to six hundred thousand. The first distinctive Mormon settlement was established at Kirtland, Ohio, in 1831. From here a mission was soon despatched into Missouri, and, after a disgraceful failure of the Mormon bank at Kirtland, the leaders of the sect, including Smith and Rigdon, his principal lieutenant, likewise sought

Joseph Smith

FROM A RARE PHOTOGRAPH

refuge in the West. Soon after their Missouri advent, a military corps, called the "Danite Band," was organized, ostensibly as a protection to the disciples from all "Gentiles," as those unconnected with them were called. It was a secret organization, with password and grip, the members bound by a solemn oath to "do the prophet's bidding," and to drive off, or "give to the buzzards," all who dissented from Smith's revelations. This organization was undoubtedly at the bottom of nearly all subsequent trouble.

As a result of illegal and violent acts soon following this settlement, the aroused people of Missouri compelled them to depart from the State, and in 1840 twelve thousand of them arrived in Illinois in a destitute condition. Their tale of distress and persecution touched the hearts of neighboring settlers, who kindly assisted them in every possible way to obtain a new start at Nauvoo. The State legislature passed several special acts for their benefit, conferring on them powers and prerogatives which later became exceedingly dangerous to the surrounding community. With its intensely industrious population, which was constantly augmented by fresh arrivals, Nauvoo thrived wonderfully, and in the short space of two years a city was built, containing every known form of architecture, from humble mud hut to stately stone mansion. By this time, also, under special legislative enactment, they were permitted to organize the "Nauvoo Legion," a body of four thousand well-drilled Mormons, with the prophet as general.

To understand something of the danger of such a situation as this, it is necessary to comprehend to some extent the character of this rapidly increasing Mormon population. Governor Ford, in whose administration these troubles occurred, has sketched their peculiarities clearly. It really consisted of two distinct classes — the rulers and the ruled. The one was characterized by shrewd knavery, the other by credulity. Few moral distinctions were ever made in that community, and none socially; the mass of converts were drawn from the lowest social stratum, and many a well-known criminal found safe hiding-place from the law at Nauvoo. All that the leaders apparently cared for was the strengthening of their individual power, and the constant increase of their revenues. The majority of the ruled were simply fanatics, whose credulity made them the faithful followers of self-appointed leaders, among whom Smith continued chief. There was a wide difference among them in education and industry. The many toiled, while the few enjoyed the results of that toil. The more polished portion of the Mormons is said to have been a merry set of fellows, fond of music and dancing, dress, and gay assemblies. They had their regular parties and balls, from which, however, no one was ever known to be barred on the score of character. In short, it was a community of rich and poor, drone and worker, ruled over arbitrarily by twelve apostles, with Smith at their head, ever seeking new power, and growing more and more indifferent to all considerations, excepting their own selfish interests. In the very nature of things, a clash between such a community and the State must inevitably occur.

From the date of first settlement until 1844, Mormonism prospered unchecked in and about Nauvoo. It was during this period that the prophet is said to have received his revelation permitting the chiefs of the Mormon hierarchy to have as many wives as they could support. This new privilege led to the first serious division in the ranks of the "faithful," resulting in the establishment of a rival newspaper at Nauvoo, called the "Expositor," in May, 1844. This immediately provoked trouble, as the "Expositor" in its first, which was also its last, issue began exposing certain questionable acts on the part of the prophet and his advisers. As a result, a party of Mormons, presumably acting under direct orders from those high in authority, made a sudden cowardly attack on the offending printing-office, broke the press into pieces, and flung the type by the handfuls into the street. This outrage led the rebels against Smith's dictatorial power to unite their influence with the rapidly increasing number of Mormon opponents living in the outside country district, and warrants were finally sworn out for the arrest of Joseph Smith, his brother, Hyrum, and several others then prominent in the church government. The leader in this rebellious movement was William Law, who declared that personal wrongs had been done him at the hands of Smith. Those arrested were merely taken before the municipal court of the city (of which Smith was likewise mayor) and, on *habeas corpus* proceedings, immediately discharged. The seceding disciples were soon after compelled to leave Nauvoo, and retired to Carthage, the county seat. Meanwhile, Smith was constantly engaged strengthening his civil authority. By means of his common council, and without the slightest authority of law, he established a recorder's office at Nauvoo, in which alone the titles to property could be recorded. So he also established a department of marriage licenses, and proclaimed that none in the city should purchase real estate for the purpose of selling again, excepting himself. These acts, however, affected only the resident Mormon population, but the "Saints," encouraged thereby, immediately took other and far more radical steps, which tended to awaken outside antagonism, and suspicion as to their ultimate purposes. A law was enacted providing that no writ issued from any other place than Nauvoo should be executed within the limits of that city, unless countersigned by the mayor. As a result, robberies could be, and were, committed elsewhere, the culprits fleeing for safety to Nauvoo, where full protection was assured. It became a Mecca for criminals throughout that entire section, counterfeiters being especially numerous. About this same time, petitions were sent to Congress asking the organization of a separate territorial government, of which Nauvoo should be the centre, and Smith actually announced himself as a candidate for President of the United States, sending forth nearly three thousand missionaries to advocate his claims before the people. These acts awakened much uneasiness throughout the State, and served to crystallize public sentiment against any further encroachment on the part of the Mormon leaders. Inflamed by such rapidly increasing arrogance, those in the immediate neighborhood of Nauvoo, and especially the settlers of Hancock County, felt that they rested in close proximity to a powder-magazine, which needed but a spark to produce an explosion.

The spark was early forthcoming. So persistent were rumors of evil intention upon the part of the Mormon population, coupled with their persistent ignoring of State laws, that Governor Ford, whose account of these events is most complete, and generally correct, paid a personal visit to the county for purposes of investigation. Whether rightfully or not, the militia in Schuyler and McDonough Counties were called out, and assembled at Carthage to aid in the enforcement of civil processes throughout the Mormon community. Hearing of this, Smith at once proclaimed Nauvoo to be under martial law; his followers throughout the country were summoned to the defence of the city against invaders, and the legion assembled under arms. Yet, when the constable with his deputies appeared, no armed resistance was attempted, although much delay occurred. Through the influence of the Governor, final surrender was made, and on June 24, 1844, Joseph Smith and his brother, Hyrum, with the members of the Nauvoo city council, went unattended to Carthage, and there surrendered themselves prisoners to the county authorities on the simple charge of riot, as nothing more serious had been formally alleged against them.

They were confined in the jail, which was a stone building

THE JAIL AT CARTHAGE, AS IT WAS AND AS IT IS

FROM THE UPPER WINDOW JOSEPH SMITH MET HIS DEATH

of considerable size, furnished with a suite of rooms for the jailer, cells for the close confinement of dangerous prisoners, and a large apartment, not so safe, but far more comfortable. The Mormon leaders were first confined in the cells, but later transferred to this larger room, where they were allowed many liberties. No apprehension whatever was apparently entertained by the officials in charge of any attack being made on the jail from without, nor was it believed the prisoners would endeavor to escape, as the charge against them was not a serious one. The Governor, anxious to smooth over the difficulty, proceeded with a small escort to Nauvoo, that he might better understand the situation, while apparently every necessary precaution had been taken to safeguard the prisoners confined at Carthage.

But by this time the entire anti-Mormon population of Hancock County was at fever-heat. A large number of men, principally from Warsaw, assembled in and about Carthage, ready for any desperate deed, if only the opportunity and a leader arose. Who their leader was will probably never be definitely ascertained, but the opportunity soon appeared in the rumor rapidly spreading that the "Carthage Grays," the only military organization then remaining on duty, were encamped in the public square, with only eight men left as a guard over the jail. Suddenly, with all plans apparently perfected, the assaulting mob, which was composed of scarcely more than fifty men, many of these Missourians, having blackened their faces to prevent recognition, scaled the slight fence surrounding the jail enclosure, and made a rapid rush for the building. The few soldiers on duty, having no heart in the defence, fired in the air, and were promptly disarmed, the assailants surging up the stairs toward the room wherein the Smiths were known to be confined. At the time, two other prominent Mormons, Richards and Taylor, were with the prisoners. Hearing the shouts of the advancing mob, and the rush of feet on the stairs, the imperilled men within instinctively flung themselves against the door in a vain effort to bar the way. Finding the door would not yield to their first blows, the leaders of the mob fired through the light wood, one bullet passing through Hyrum Smith, who fell, exclaiming, "I am a dead man." Taylor was struck in four places, almost at the same time, and Richards, who remained unhurt, caught him up in his arms, and ran with him to one of the inner cells. Joseph Smith, armed with an old pepper-box pistol, but already slightly wounded, fought bravely in defence of his life, wounding four of the assailants before the overwhelming rush of numbers and the bursting in of the door forced him to flee. Finally, his weapon exhausted, he rushed to a window on the east side, raised the sash and leaned partially out, probably with the intention of jumping, when several balls, fired from below, pierced his body, and he fell to the ground close beside the well-curb. It is believed not another shot was fired after Smith was thus killed. This occurred about five o'clock in the afternoon, and the mob immediately dispersed, many of them fleeing eighteen miles across the prairie to Warsaw. Much apprehension was felt lest the Mormon population of the country should rise in vengeance, but nothing of the kind occurred. Instead, the tragedy seemed to stun them with despair. A delegation travelled sadly to Carthage for their dead, and the bodies were buried at Nauvoo with all the honors of the church. Nine men, Levi Williams, Jacob C. Davis, Mark Aldrich, Thomas C. Sharp, Wm. Voras, John Wills, Wm. N. Grover, — Gallagher, and — Allen, were later indicted for this crime, tried, and by the sympathetic jury declared "not guilty."

The principle that the death of the martyr is the seed of the church proved true in regard to Mormonism. Instead of perishing with its prophet, it received new life. Rigdon, who had been Smith's principal lieutenant, finding himself unable to obtain chief rule, retired with a small remnant of the

HOUSE OCCUPIED BY JOSEPH SMITH AT NAUVOO

HOUSE OCCUPIED BY BRIGHAM YOUNG AT NAUVOO

"saints" to Pennsylvania, while a council of twelve apostles took charge at Nauvoo and elected Brigham Young leader. Missionaries were despatched everywhere to preach their faith, and new disciples began pouring into Nauvoo from all over the world. With this rapid increase in membership, and consequent political power, the feeling of antagonism among the surrounding anti-Mormon population became more intense and dangerous than before. Outrages occurred on both sides, houses were fired, property destroyed, and lives sacrificed in a species of guerilla warfare extending throughout the entire extent of Hancock County. Within this limit no man's life was safe, while depredations were committed both up and down the river by bands of ruffians. Which side might be justly named the aggressor it would now be difficult to decide. Courts were invoked in vain by both parties; feeling ran so intensely high that justice by jury was impossible, and, as a result, Mormon and Gentile resorted to the arbitrament of the rifle to settle their disputes and obtain their rights. Time and again the Governor despatched large forces of militia into the field to avert what had every appearance of civil war, but the moment these forces were withdrawn the conflict burst forth afresh, and new atrocities were committed. At Lima and Green Plains one hundred and twenty-five Mormon houses were burned, the occupants having to flee for their lives in the darkness. In retaliation for this act, the Mormons, several hundred strong, and well armed, took forcible possession of Carthage, and swept in destruction across a large portion of the county, destroying a number of lives. General Hardin, at the head of three hundred and fifty militiamen, succeeded in checking these ravages, and the scattered Gentiles returned to their homes.

But now the adjoining counties, becoming fearful of invasion, took up the matter in earnest, demanding of the Governor, in no uncertain tones, that the entire body of Mormon believers be driven from the State. This, as necessary to peace, was finally agreed upon, but, through the pacifying efforts of General Hardin, the distressed "saints" were given until the following Spring to effect arrangements for final removal. A small force of soldiers as guards, under Major Warren, was stationed at Nauvoo to keep peace in the meanwhile. By this time the Mormon leaders fully realized the spirit of stern opposition arrayed against them, and the utter futility of attempting any longer to combat it by force of arms. Nothing remained but complete withdrawal from the State, with whatever was possible of their property. That Winter of 1845-46 was the scene in Nauvoo of stupendous preparation for the coming exodus. All the principal dwellings, including the Temple itself, were converted into workshops, and before Spring came, twelve thousand wagons had been completed. Unfortunately, rumors early reached the place that United States regular troops were on the way up the river to enforce certain writs long-ignored, and to escape these the movement westward was begun before all necessary preparations had been completed. As early as February 15, poorly provisioned and poorly clothed for such a journey, the leaders, accompanied by two thousand of their followers, crossed the wide Mississippi on the ice, and took up their weary journey through Iowa. By the middle of May, fully fourteen hundred more followed, with their flocks, their wives and little ones, the intention being to seek some safe spot in the far-off mountain wilderness of the West where they could remain utterly alone to work out their destiny. Possibly a thousand Mormons, who had thus far been unable to dispose of their property, remained behind in desolate Nauvoo. This remnant was almost immediately plunged into serious and increasing difficulties with the surrounding population of fast-encroaching Gentiles, eager enough to profit by the necessities of the "saints." Some were whipped, and otherwise tortured, by mobs, while others suffered heavy property losses. Retaliation naturally followed, and writs for arrest were freely sworn out on both sides. The trouble terminated in an armed attack on Nauvoo, made by hastily gathered forces under command of Thomas S. Brockman, at one time a Campbellite preacher, of poor reputation, consisting of eight hundred volunteers, and five pieces of small artillery. The Mormons had barely two hundred men remaining for defence, yet succeeded in holding off their assailants until a self-appointed committee from Quincy interfered, and granted them fair terms of surrender. In this affair the Mormons lost one killed and nine wounded, their assailants three killed and four wounded. The Mormon remnant, thus finally banished from the city they had built, were thrown homeless on the Iowa shore, to get away as best they could, without either money or conveyances. Many died from hunger and exposure, but later, those who survived were aided on their journey by the awakening of a better public spirit among their enemies, which was exhibited in numerous acts of charity.

The story of the Mormon exodus, after its advance had crossed the Mississippi, does not form part of Illinois history, but so thrilling are the incidents of that long march, and so vitally are they connected with the driving forth of the participants from this State, that the tale of it cannot be entirely ignored. That first company, which had crossed the river on ice in midwinter, had their families with them. The first night in camp, nine children were born. For days the cold was intense, the keen winds sweeping down across the bare prairies ; the nights becoming so many struggles to keep from freezing. Wood was scarce, the stock of food inadequate, and large numbers became permanently crippled from exposure. The long-wished-for Spring found them not half-way to the Missouri, and facing fresh difficulties. Snow, sleet, and rain combined to make the prairie soil, across which they must travel, a sea of black mud almost impassable; heavy downpours so swelled the streams as to result in weeks of delay. The winds of March brought more sickness than the storms of Winter. Coffins, formed of tree-bark, were made, and in these men, women, and children were laid away to rest. Such graves continually marked the progress of Mormon travel.

Want developed disease; yet, in all their suffering, brotherhood was constantly in evidence. Self-denial was the rule, and each scrap of food any possessed was shared equally. Young men gave up their places in the column, walking back to portions of the frontier where they were unknown, and hiring themselves out for wages, that they might thus purchase provisions for the aged and destitute. Others halted in their pilgrimage, broke the prairie sod, and raised grain for the sustenance of their brethren.

Nor during these months of trial among the vanguard were those left behind in Nauvoo any less burdened. Constantly harassed by their Gentile neighbors, as already described, their property sold for a song, or taken from them by fraud and force, their power of self-protection constantly waning, strange as it may seem, these zealous fanatics devoted the greater portion of their remaining energies to the completion of that Temple, which they already realized must immediately be deserted to its fate. Never since the dispersion of the Jews does history afford any parallel to the Mormon attachment to this quaint and beautiful edifice. In every stone it was associated with, and symbolical of, their religion. Its erection had been enjoined upon them as a sacred duty, by their first prophet and his successors. From the beginning it was a labor of love; hardly a Mormon woman but had truly denied herself to make gifts in its behalf; scarcely a Mormon man who had not served the tenth part of his year upon its walls. Therefore, in this stress of their final lingering on Illinois soil, even while they were parrying the sword

THE TOWN OF NAUVOO

FROM THE IOWA SHORE

thrusts of their advancing enemies, this little remnant continued to labor upon it, until they completed even the gilding of the angel and trumpet on the apex of its lofty spire. As a closing work, they placed on the entablature of the front, like a baptismal mark on the forehead,—

"*The House of the Lord;*
Built by the Church of Jesus Christ of Latter-Day Saints.
Holiness to the Lord!"

As Colonel Kane wrote:

"For that one day the Temple stood resplendent in all its typical glories of sun, moon, and stars, and other abounding figured and lettered signs, hieroglyphics, and symbols, but that day only. The sacred rites of consecration ended, the work of removing the sacrosancta proceeded with the rapidity of magic. It went on all through the night, and when the morning of the next day dawned, all the ornaments and furniture, everything that could provoke a sneer, had been carried off, and, except some fixtures that would not bear removal, the building was dismantled to the bare walls. It was this day that witnessed the departure of the last elders and the largest band that moved in one company together. The people of Iowa have told me that from morning to night they passed westward like an endless procession. They did not seem greatly out of heart, they said; but at the top of every hill, before they disappeared, they were to be seen looking back, like banished Moors, on their abandoned homes, and the far-seen Temple with its glittering spire. After this consecration, which by outsiders was construed to indicate an insincerity on the part of the Mormons as to their stipulated departure, or at least a hope of return, their foes set upon them with renewed bitterness."

This Temple, upon which had been bestowed so much of labor and love, was, only two years later, October 19, 1848, totally destroyed by the torch of an incendiary.

By this time of the final departure of that lingering remnant from Nauvoo, the advance of the remarkable column of pilgrims was at Grand Island, on the distant Platte. No picture of that great march through the wilderness can exceed the one sketched by Colonel Kane, before the Historical Society of Pennsylvania.

"From the first formation of the camp, all its inhabitants were constantly and laboriously occupied. Many of them were highly educated mechanics, and seemed only to need a day's anticipated rest to engage them at the forge, loom, or turning-lathe, upon some needed chore of work. A Mormon gunsmith is the inventor of the excellent repeating-rifle, that loads by slides instead of cylinders; and one of the neatest finished firearms I have ever seen was of this kind, wrought from scraps of old iron, and inlaid with the silver of a couple of half-dollars, under a hot July sun, in a spot where the average height of the grass was above the workman's shoulders. I have seen a cobbler, after the halt of his party on the march, hunting along the river bank for a lapstone in the twilight, that he might finish a famous boot sole by the camp-fire; and I have had a piece of cloth, the wool of which was sheared and dyed and spun and woven during a progress of over three hundred miles.

"At this time, say two months before the final expulsion from Nauvoo, there were already, along three hundred miles of the road between that city and our Papillon Camp, over two thousand emigrating wagons, besides a large number of nondescript turnouts, the motley makeshifts of poverty; from the unsuitable heavy cart that lumbered on mysteriously with its sick driver hidden under its counterpane cover, to the crazy two-wheeled trundle, such as our poor employ for the conveyance of their slop-barrels—this pulled along, it may be, by a little drugged heifer, and rigged up only to drag some such light weight as a baby, a sack of meal, or a pack of clothes and bedding. Some of them were in distress of losses upon the way. A strong trait of the Mormons was their kindness to their brute dependents, and particularly to their beasts of draught.

"Besides the common duty of guiding and assisting these unfortunates, the companies in the van united in providing the highway for the entire body of emigrants. The Mormons have laid out for themselves a road through the Indian Territory, over four hundred leagues in length, with substantial, well-built bridges, fit for the passage of heavy artillery, over all the streams, except a few great rivers where they have established permanent ferries. The nearest unfinished bridging to the Papillon Camp was that of the *Corne à Cerf*, or Elkhorn, a tributary of the Platte, distant, maybe, a couple of hours' march. Here, in what seemed to be an incredibly short space of time, there rose the seven great piers and abutments of a bridge, such as might challenge honors for the entire public-spirited population of Lower Virginia. The party detailed to the task worked in the broiling sun, in water beyond depth, and up to their necks, as if engaged in the perpetration of some pointed and delightful practical joke. Their chief sport lay in floating along with the logs, cut from the overhanging timber up the stream, guiding them until they reached their destination, and then plunging them under water in the precise spot where they were to be secured.

"Inside the camp, the chief labors were assigned to the women. From the moment when, after the halt, the lines had been laid, the spring wells dug out, and the ovens and fireplaces built, though the men still assumed to set the guard and enforce the regulations of police, the Empire of the Tented Town was with the better sex. They were the chief comforters of the severest sufferings, the kind nurses who gave them in their sickness those dear attentions with which pauperism is hardly poor, and which the greatest wealth often fails to buy. And they were a nation of wonderful managers. They could hardly be called housewives in etymological strictness, but it was plain that they had once been such, and most distinguished ones. Their art availed them in their changed affairs. With almost their entire culinary material limited to the milk of their cows, some store of meal or flour, and a very few condiments, they brought their thousand and one receipts into play with a success that outdid for their families the miracle of the Hebrew widow's cruse. They learned to make butter on a march, by the dashing of the wagon, and so nicely to calculate the working of barm in the jolting heats, that as soon after the halt as an oven could be dug in the hillside and heated, their well-kneaded loaf was ready for baking, and produced good leavened bread for supper."

It was thus that, day by day, this wonderful advance was

conducted. In the early Spring of 1847, a body of one hundred and forty-three picked men, with seventy wagons drawn by their best horses, left Omaha to make the trail for those who were to follow. They carried little with them but seeds and farming implements, relying almost wholly on their rifles for food. They made long daily marches, moving as rapidly as possible. Behind them toiled on more slowly a second party with five hundred and sixty-six wagons, carrying a large quantity of grain. By the last of July, these hardy pioneers reached the valley of Salt Lake, and choosing this for their final halting-place, began, that same day, their labor with the plough. Behind them, struggling sternly on across a thousand miles of desert, streamed the seemingly endless procession of Mormon wagon trains; while yet farther away in distant Illinois, the deserted Temple looked down from its high bluff on the waters of the Mississippi, a desolate memorial of a community passed away for ever from its shadow.

CHAPTER XX

EARLY AMERICAN SETTLEMENTS

NEITHER English nor American settlers flowed into the Illinois country during the brief period of British control, the few soldiers stationed at Fort Chartres, and later at Fort Gage, together with some scattered fur traders, along the rivers, being the only evidence of their possession of this territory. Possibly the first of English lineage to touch the soil of Illinois was Lieutenant Frazer, who, in the early Spring of 1765, was despatched a thousand miles down the Ohio from Fort Pitt to prepare the Western Indian tribes, who had been associated with Pontiac, for the coming of Major George Croghan for a peace conference. Lieutenant Frazer's reception, however, was so threatening, that he abandoned his purpose, and fled to the French at Kaskaskia for protection, later going down the river to New Orleans. Major Croghan closely followed his distressed ambassador, accompanied by a small party of soldiers, and on the 6th of June reached the mouth of the Wabash. Here they discovered a breastwork, supposed to have been erected by the Indians. Six miles farther on, they made camp at a place called the "old Shawnee village," probably the site of Shawneetown. Here they remained six days, seeking to learn some news of Frazer. Starting once again down the Ohio, at their first landing the party was suddenly attacked by eighty Kickapoos and Mascoutins, and after five of his men had been killed, Croghan, with the remainder, was made prisoner. Taken up the Wabash to Vincennes, the Englishman was promptly released, through French influence, and after holding a brief conference with Pontiac, in a council-meeting somewhere near the northwestern corner of what is now Edgar County, he completed his long journey through the wilderness by travelling along the old French trail to Detroit.

Undoubtedly, during the time intervening between Croghan's brief visit and the invasion of the Americans under Clark, a few adventurous Kentucky hunters roamed over this region. Some, indeed, may have found their way there even earlier. They were not numerous, or warmly welcomed by the French, and no establishment of settlements was attempted. But that such wanderers were already in the field is clearly evidenced by Clark's encounter with just such a party almost immediately after landing with his command at Massac. At the first coming of the British, the exodus of the old Canadian French was very large, the greater portion removing across the river to St. Genevieve, or Laclede's new hamlet of St. Louis. It is believed that scarcely two thousand souls remained within the territory of the Illinois. But Clark's returning soldiers made the charms of this new country widely known throughout the Eastern colonies, and almost at once the tide of American emigration set bravely in. Men who had served under Clark returned, accompanied by their families, having been granted land liberally as reward for their army experience. Others came with them, lured by their descriptions of this new wilderness land, and, within the short space of a single year, permanent settlements of American pioneers sprang up on the American Bottom and in the fertile valleys of the protecting Ozarks.

Nor was Government lax in taking control. In October, 1778, the Virginia Assembly, under whose orders Clark had conducted his expedition, organized all the territory lying northwest of the Ohio into the county of Illinois, and appointed Colonel John Todd, who, when under Clark's command, had been the first man to enter Fort Gage, as Lieutenant-Commandant. By the Spring of 1779, Todd was at Kaskaskia, organizing a temporary government for the rapidly arriving colonists. At this period, with the exception of the few remaining French in their small villages along the Mississippi, and some families scattered upon the banks of the Illinois and the Wabash, all within the present boundaries of the State was the abode of the nomadic savage. It was not until the years 1779–80 that American immigration became at all apparent. All migrations are inclined to follow along certain lines of latitude, and the first arrivals in the Illinois country, taking advantage of the natural highway afforded them by the Ohio, were originally residents of Virginia and Pennsylvania, although not a few of them had made temporary halt within the confines of Kentucky. They were invariably of the frontier type, imbued with strong Southern sentiment, and not a few brought with them black slaves to aid in the future development of this new land. Either crossing the wilderness through Kentucky on foot or on horseback, constantly harassed by Indians along the way, or floating slowly down the beautiful stream in great, awkward family-boats, which were frequently attacked by hostile savages upon the shore, these daring settlers, most of them poor and nomadic in habits, began streaming into this newly opened country. Three hundred such family-boats were reported as arriving at the falls of the Ohio in 1780, although comparatively few pushed on to the Illinois. Meanwhile, for thirty-six years, Northern Illinois remained an almost untrodden wilderness. In 1812 possibly a dozen settlers were about the present site of Chicago, hovering within the protecting shadow of old Fort Dearborn, but no influx of colonists from the Northern States, arriving by way of the great lakes, and spreading out over the rich prairies of the more northern counties, occurred until after the close of the second war with England. Even then the advance was slow beyond the main water-courses, several counties being without a single settler as late as 1840.

So far as known, the honor of being the first permanent American settlement in Illinois lies undecided between Bellefontaine and New Design, both in Monroe County, where James Moore and a small party, including Shadrach Bond, James Garrison, Robert Kidd, and Larkin Rutherford, made their home in either 1780 or 1781. New Design was certainly settled by 1782, and Piggot's Fort was built only a year later. The little band then in the country, not more than a dozen men all told, a few accompanied by their families, were not reënforced until 1785, when perhaps as many others joined them, seeking homes in the American Bottom. For some reason these early incoming Americans did not readily mix with the remnant of French population occupying the older settlements in Randolph County. They either halted below the Kaskaskia River, or else worked their unwieldy arks farther north against the swift current of the Mississippi, leaving the French entirely alone.

During all these earlier days the Illinois borders were not only constantly harassed by Indian raiders, but the incoming settlers were compelled to fight their passage along almost the entire length of the Ohio, which was lined with hostile savages. In consequence, the colonists were few, and those only of the most adventurous spirit. Colonel Todd, the first Virginia commandant, spent but little time in the Illinois country; he lost his life at the battle of Blue Licks, Kentucky, August 18, 1782. He was succeeded by a Frenchman, Timothée de Montbrun, of whom little or nothing is known. He naively writes himself, "Lt. Comdt. Par interim," and land grants bearing his signature were among the archives at Kaskaskia. March 1, 1784, Virginia formally ceded her claim to all this territory lying north of the Ohio to the United States, but it was not until October, 1787, that Major-General Arthur St. Clair was elected by Congress as Governor of the Northwest Territory, of which the Illinois country then formed part.

This interim proved a slow transition period in the history of the Illinois settlements; colonists were few, while those already in the country, besides being constantly on the defensive against Indian attacks, were in great uncertainty as to their land titles. Nothing, indeed, seemed established upon a permanent basis; adventurers were many and speculation rife. Until the final organization of the county of St. Clair in 1790, there was a very imperfect administration of the law, which consisted of an odd mixture of French and English precedents. There were no regular courts, and, indeed, no civil government worthy of mention. The settlers were a law unto themselves, and to their honor be it said, little occurred demanding serious punishment. A land speculation, instituted by a territorial court named by Governor Todd, did much to demoralize the earlier settlements. This court was appointed at Post Vincennes in 1779, and Colonel J. M. P. Legras acted as president. Adopting the custom of the French commandants, this court began to grant tracts of land to both French and American settlers, as well as to civil and military officers. Before 1783 nearly twenty-six thousand acres had thus been conveyed to different individuals, and by 1787, when the practice was stopped by General Harmar, the total grants amounted to forty-eight thousand acres. Indeed, so far did they venture as to grant to themselves, as members of the court, all that scope of country extending on the Wabash from Point La Coupée to the mouth of White River, seventy-two miles in length, and extending westward into Illinois for one hundred and twenty miles. This shameful transaction was early taken advantage of by swindlers, and great numbers of incoming settlers were duped into buying land to which the seller possessed no legal right, although the original titles had been duly executed under the seal of Virginia. It was not until after 1802 that these sharp practices were entirely discontinued.

In February, 1790, Governor St. Clair, accompanied by Secretary Winthrop Sargeant, arrived at Kaskaskia. At this time there were not more than three or four small scattered American settlements in the entire region, and probably not more than twenty-five actual American settlers. The country extending from the conference of the Ohio to the mouth of Little Mackinaw Creek, on the Illinois, was organized into the county of St. Clair. This magnificent but desolate domain was divided into three judicial districts, and John Edgar of Kaskaskia, John Baptiste Barbeau of Prairie du Rocher, and John de Moulin of Cahokia, were named as judges. Of these, De Moulin was a Swiss, possessing a good education and some knowledge of law; Barbeau was Canadian French, and a merchant; while Edgar was an Englishman. Cahokia became the county seat, with William St. Clair clerk and recorder, and William Biggs sheriff. Immigration, however, remained almost stationary for four years longer, being retarded by constantly recurring Indian wars, until after Wayne's great victory on the Maumee, August 20, 1794. From that date we may trace a steadily increasing influx of American settlers, pouring in by way of the Ohio. In the year 1791, only sixty-five Americans capable of bearing arms were in the Illinois country, with three hundred all told. By 1809 the population amounted to above nine thousand.

As early as 1795, St. Clair County was divided by running a line through the New Design settlement, in the present Monroe County, due east to the Wabash — all lying south being established into the new county of Randolph. For nine years following May 7, 1800, the Illinois country was known as a part of Indiana Territory, with the seat of government established at Vincennes. This was a period of continuous growth in population and extension of settlements. By the end of this period, colonists had advanced as far north as Wood River, in the present Madison County;

eastward on Silver Creek, and some miles up the Kaskaskia; south and east from Kaskaskia about fifteen miles out on the old Fort Massac road were frequent settlements; the Birds had located at the mouth of the Ohio; at Old Massac and the Ohio salines were small settlements ; Shawneetown, which, after 1813, and for a quarter of a century following, was the principal town in Illinois, had contained a few straggling houses since 1805 ; along the west side of the Wabash a number of families had made their homes, one McCawley having penetrated inland as far as the crossing of the Little Wabash. By 1804 an Irish colony had established itself near Cave-in-Rock, on the Ohio River, in Hardin County; one Daniels built a stockade fort in Jackson County a year later, and by 1807 a considerable settlement had gathered near the mouth of Skillet Fork, in the present White County. Chilton had a stockade fort as far north as the southeastern corner of what is now Madison County as early as 1803, while the Goshen settlements, established in 1802, and the Judy settlement, in 1801, were within the same county limits. Edwardsville was established in 1805. Turkey Hill, just east of the present Belleville, had settlers as early as 1798, but the most exposed and advanced post to the northward, previous to the second war with England, was Jones's stockade fort, established in western Bond County in 1809. This point marks the extreme advance of the American frontier when Illinois was first organized into a separate Territory. A glance at the map will reveal the wide, untracked wilderness stretching between these few, small, isolated settlements. Far to the northeast, where Chicago now stands, were a few settlers, chief among them being the fur trader, John Kinzie, all clustering about Fort Dearborn, established in 1804. At the Peoria Lake a number of French traders resided. In 1810, the census returns showed the inhabitants to number 11,501 whites, 168 slaves, and 613 of all others, except Indians — an increase of four hundred per cent during the preceding decade. Nine-tenths of what is now Illinois remained, however, an almost unknown wilderness over which red savages held undisputed dominion, outnumbering their white neighbors at least three to one.

February 3, 1809, all this country, including the present State of Wisconsin as well, was reorganized under the name of Illinois Territory, and Ninian Edwards of Kentucky was appointed Governor. The next seven years, while exceedingly eventful along the Illinois frontier on account of the war with England, were not years of colonization or growth. The settlers already on the field were almost continually under arms in defence against Indian foray, while new arrivals were few in number. Large numbers of block-houses were erected, as described in a previous chapter, while the military campaigns, extending to north of the Illinois River, made the soldiers taking part in them acquainted with this remote country, and thus stimulated an advancement of settlers immediately following cessation of hostilities. Even while the struggle continued, some few were bold enough to push farther northward into the very heart of the hostile Indian country. T. Carlin erected a cabin in 1815 in the southern portion of Green County, while the Macoupin settlement was established a year later. Vandalia had settlers as early as 1813, while still farther east, within the present borders of Effingham County, G. Lippsword erected a lonely cabin in 1815. September, 1812, the counties of Madison, Gallatin, and Johnson were organized, making at that date a total of five.

With the close of the war, the tide of immigration at once set in with renewed volume, the more northern States now being largely represented, their contingent arriving by way of the lakes, and scattering out from Chicago. An Act of Congress, passed in 1813, granting the right to settle by preëmption upon the public domain, contributed largely to this desire for settlement. Previously, emigrants in four cases out of five had merely "squatted" on the land, acquiring no right or title. Small and inferior improvements were the natural result; but now matters immediately began to assume a more permanent appearance. Moreover, about this same time, a better means of communication was inaugurated between the Illinois country and the East, not only stimulating emigration, but commerce as well. The keel-boat, with its six months' voyage to New Orleans, or the slow wagoning across the Alleghany Mountains, was superseded by the steamboat. The first boat to ascend the Mississippi under its own steam was the "General Pike," which reached St. Louis in August, 1817; the "New Orleans" had come down the Ohio as early as 1811.

In the year 1818, Illinois, with its present boundaries, was admitted to the Union as a State, having then an estimated population of forty thousand. The first election was held on the third Thursday of September, when Shadrach Bond was elected Governor. Fifteen counties were at this time duly organized, the most northerly of these being Bond, laid out the year previous. Only about one-fourth the actual territory of the new State was embraced within these organized counties. The settled portions of the State were at that time almost entirely south of a line drawn from Alton via Carlyle, to Palestine, on the Wabash, and even within this area there were large tracts of wilderness country several days' journey in extent; the settlements being mostly scattered along the borders of the principal streams. Nineteen-twentieths of the residents were Americans, and except a few from Pennsylvania, were nearly all of Southern origin. These indelibly stamped their peculiar characteristics upon all of Southern Illinois. By 1821, the counties of Greene, Fayette, Montgomery, Lawrence, Hamilton, Sangamon, and Pike were established, the latter including all of the State lying north and west of the Illinois River. This vast and hitherto unoccupied territory was by this time beginning to receive its pioneer settlers. J. A. Perrigo had taken land in the present Adams County; Scott had a small settlement established in 1820; and the same year saw the starting of the Diamond Grove colony in northern Morgan, while north of the river a few settlers had established homes in Fulton. From this date the progress of the pioneers was rapid. In the counties as now organized, C. Hobart was in Schuyler by 1823; Carter's settlement, in McDonough, in 1826; Yellow Bank, in Henderson, in 1827; Knox had settlers by 1828, and Stark the same year. Peoria was never wholly deserted by Americans after the erection of Fort Clark in 1813. Menard had a settlement as early as 1819, and Beardstown was founded that same year. The more eastern counties seem to have been somewhat slower in attracting immigration, although McLean had two settlements — Funk's and Randolph's Groves — as early as 1824. Coles was first settled in 1824, while Edgar was invaded in 1817. In Vermilion several settlements were started by 1820.

The Summer of 1825 witnessed much change in population. A great tide set in toward the central portion of the State. Through Vandalia alone, we are told, two hundred and fifty wagons were counted in three weeks' time, all bound north. Destined for Sangamon County, eighty wagons and four hundred people were counted in two weeks' time. The census of that year gave the State a population of 72,817. By 1830 the census returns reached 157,447. There were at this time fifty-six organized counties, but those in the northern portion of the State were mere skeletons, and unwieldy in size. Fully a third of the domain now constituting Illinois yet remained a wilderness. All that portion, with the exception of a few remote frontier settlements and traders' stockades lying between Chicago and Galena, and stretching southward to the Illinois River and even beyond, was hunted over by Sacs and Foxes, Winnebagoes, and Pottawattomies. What settlers there were hugged the outskirts of the timber bordering the rivers and creeks, or the edge of groves, scarcely any venturing forth upon the open and, as they still believed, unproductive prairie. Along the Mississippi and the Illinois, settlements were scattered at distant intervals, while on Fever River were congregated about a thousand all told, mostly employed at lead-mining. In 1825, Mr. Kellogg laid out a trail between Peoria Lake and this settlement of distant lead-miners at Galena. It ran through an unbroken wilderness, crossing Rock River a few miles above the present Dixon, and passing through West Grove. Winnebago Indians assisted the travellers to cross the stream, by forming a ferry-boat of canoes, while the horses swam. A year later Bolles trail was established, and the river ferried at Dixon, about where the Illinois Central bridge now stands. This was a more direct route, and became at once popular. In the Spring of 1827, within the space of a few days, two hundred teams passed at this point. The Lewiston trail, still farther west, crossed the Rock at Prophetstown, in Whiteside County.

A glance at the map will show the location of the few points north of the Illinois occupied at this time by American pioneers. In La Salle County were three small settlements, including Ottawa; Bureau likewise contained three, the most northerly being at Dad Joe's Grove, a famous stopping-place on the old Galena trail; in northern Lee was La Sallier's trading-post, established as early as 1822, while a man named Ogee had operated a ferry just above Dixon since 1827. Savannah, on the Mississippi, had inhabitants in 1828, and Rock Island in 1826. In Ogle, old man Kellogg held down an isolated claim about the grove perpetuating his name; in Stephenson, O. W. Kellogg settled in 1827, and there were a cabin or two amid the wilds of Kendall and Will Counties. Chicago was the merest village, almost lost in mud.

Up to the close of the Black Hawk War, Illinois, in

all essential features, remained the far frontier, while her population exhibited every characteristic of the border. Among the common people, the niceties of dress and manners were given little attention. But after this date a new era dawned, and the population rapidly changed their customs to conform with fast advancing civilization. The original dress of the territory, which had been a raccoon-skin cap, linsey hunting-shirt, buckskin breeches, and moccasins, with a belt around the waist, to which were attached knife and tomahawk, gradually disappeared, until it was rarely seen. The costume year by year grew more to conform to that worn in the Eastern States. The women changed in this respect even more rapidly than the men. The old cotton and woollen frocks, spun, woven, and made with their own hands, and striped and cross-barred with blue dye and turkey red, gave place to boughten gowns of calico, or even silk. The head, formerly uncovered, or decorated by marvellous sun-bonnets, became crowned with wonders of millinery art. With this pride of appearance came a desire for comforts, and even luxury, in the home life. The log cabins were abandoned in the little timber openings, and better houses, of plank, or stone, built on the previously despised open prairie. Villages, springing up more thickly, began at once to exercise refining influences over the manners and habits of the previously isolated settlers.

During all these years of slow pioneer advancement, the pursuits of the people, other than the professional hunters, were entirely agricultural. A very limited number of merchants supplied those few necessities not produced or manufactured at home, while far apart small mills were operated. The settler raised his own provisions; tea and coffee were almost unknown in the newer settlements. Ford writes of those days:

"The farmer's sheep furnished wool for his winter clothing; he raised cotton and flax for his summer clothing. His wife and daughters spun, wove, and made it into garments. A little copperas and indigo, with the bark of trees, furnished dye-stuffs for coloring. The fur of the raccoon made him a hat or cap. The skins of deer, or of his own cattle, tanned at a neighboring tanyard, or dressed by himself, made him shoes or moccasins. Boots were rarely seen, even in the towns. And a log cabin, made entirely of wood, without glass, nails, hinges, or locks, furnished the residence of many a contented and happy family. The people were quick and ingenious to supply by invention, and with their own hands, the lack of mechanics and artificers. Each settler, as a rule, built his own house, made his own ploughs and harness, bedsteads, chairs, stools, cupboards, and tables. The carts and wagons for hauling were generally made without iron, without tires or boxes, and were run without tar, and might be heard creaking as they lumbered along the roads, for the distance of a mile or more."

In this connection, Governor Ford relates an anecdote regarding James Lemon, an old-time Baptist preacher of Monroe County. Mr. Lemon eked out his somewhat meagre salary by farming, and made all of his own harness. While breaking a bit of stubble-land, he turned out for dinner, leaving his harness on the plough-beam. His son, thinking thus to avoid an afternoon's hard work, hid one of the horse-collars. But the old man proved fully equal to the emergency. Returning, and not being able to find the missing collar, he mused for a moment, and then, to the great disappointment of Lemon, junior, deliberately pulled off his leather breeches, stuffed the legs with stubble, straddled them across the neck of his horse, and ploughed the rest of the day as bare-legged as he came into the world.

Previous to 1818 there was no commerce between other settlements and the Illinois, except the small traffic carried on by the French in their unwieldy barges along the rivers. It made but little progress during the period extending from that date to 1830. Steamboats became somewhat numerous on Western waters by 1816, and a few years later one or two small ones were operating along the Illinois River as far as

Peoria, and possibly farther. The old keel-boats rapidly disappeared, yet there was so little trade that steamboating was for considerable time far from profitable. The merchants in the little villages, having usually exceedingly small capital, were mere retailers of dry-goods and groceries; they purchased for shipping nothing excepting a few skins, and a little tallow and beeswax. These men rarely paid cash for anything, but traded for the goods carried in stock. Indeed, they possessed neither capital nor talent for any more liberal line of trade, the development of which had to wait patiently until the country became older and more thickly settled. New Orleans remained the principal market for the early Illinois country, but it was only a small city, and was easily glutted by any over-production. Because of this lack of merchants, the Illinois producers early became traders on their own account. Several would collect a quantity of articles believed to be salable, build a flat-bottomed boat, load their wares into it, and float down to New Orleans and a market. The journey home was usually accomplished on foot, and such ventures seldom proved profitable. Among all these earlier settlers who made homes remote from the French villages, the great want was mills. The simplest modes of trituration, as Governor Reynolds depicts them, were by means of the grater and the mortar. The first consisted in the brisk rubbing of an ear of corn over a piece of tin closely pierced or indented. The mortar was extemporized by excavating with fire the butt of a good-sized short log, up-ended, sufficiently deep to hold a peck or more of corn. Over this was erected a sweep to lift, by countertraction, a piston with a firm, blunt end, which pounded the corn into a coarse meal. To these primitive and laborious processes succeeded, in order of their simplicity, and in due time, hand-mills, band-mills, horse-mills, and last, water-mills.

After the close of the War of 1812, the new arrivals from

the Eastern States brought some money and property with them; the earliest pioneers had had little or none. Before this time money was scarcely ever seen in the country, skins being used as a circulating medium. The money thus brought in, together with that which had been paid to the volunteers during the war, awakened the people to new ambition, so that by 1819 the entire country was in a perfect rage for speculating in land and town lots. The Government was then selling land at two dollars per acre ; eighty dollars on the quarter-section to be paid down on the purchase, with a credit of five years for the remainder. Everyone on hand began to invest, expecting to reap a fortune from future-arriving immigrants. The two independent banks then organized — at Edwardsville and Shawneetown — invested all their surplus in this way, and loaned freely to others for the same purpose. New towns were laid out all over the country, and by 1820 nearly the entire population were deeply involved. But the expected immigrants failed to arrive, and, consequently the whole financial structure fell like a house of cards, tying up the entire business of the country, and for years following money was almost as scarce an article as in the earliest days.

It was not until 1857 that the last county — Douglass — was defined and organized. This was in the eastern-central portion of the State, and had contained settlers, at the Ashmore settlement, near its southern boundary, from an early date. Moreover, the old French trail from Kaskaskia to Detroit crossed this territory, as did the later trail running from Terre Haute to Fort Clark. The picturesque days of the frontier had by this time almost wholly vanished, and the typical bordermen, who, through suffering and danger and privation, had won this broad domain from savagery, had either entirely passed from the earth, or drifted on, ever in advance of civilization, across the Mississippi. The age depicted, the movements traced, poorly picture this continuous struggle against nature and barbarism, which was so strongly fought out through seventy-seven years, by these iron hearted men and women in the midst of the vast wilderness. From the moment when James Moore and his adventurous companions first set foot on the soil of Monroe County, down to the final organization of Douglass, there was no halting in the steady, determined advance of that skirmish-line of American pioneers. Through wars with Indians and white antagonists; through months of dreary Winter and parching Summer; through danger and death, hardship and deprivation, they toiled sternly, each year witnessing newly conquered country, settlements, and solitary cabins planted ever farther out into the surrounding wilderness. Where neighbors were near at hand, as in the colony settlements or about the stockaded forts, much of frontier merriment prevailed, and toil was made sweeter through companionship. But in those many solitary cabins, sunk deep within the heart of the timber, which from time to time dotted the banks of every stream from the Wabash to the far-off Fever, who can picture the intense loneliness of their inhabitants, or compute the price they paid for what is ours to-day? These were the men, women, children, who, through self-sacrifice and toil, peril, and desperate loneliness, won this great domain from savagery to civilization.

CHAPTER XXI

THE STORY OF THE CAPITAL

THE Illinois country had been duly organized into a Territory by the Ordinance of 1787, but for nearly four years following no attempt was made to select or convene any legislative body. By reason of extraordinary powers, conferred upon him through special Act of Congress, the Governor was not only an executive, but likewise to a great degree the law-making power of this sparsely occupied region. Under the terms of that justly celebrated ordinance — a curiosity still to the student of republican institutions — the private citizen was apparently considered as of no particular account. He was not permitted to exercise the elective franchise, unless he was a freeholder of fifty acres, nor could he hope for election to legislative honors, without possessing two hundred acres. All the Territorial officials not directly named by the President in person were to be appointed by the Governor. The latter was permitted the privilege of convening a legislature whenever he became fully convinced that a majority of the freeholders desired it. Judging from results, no Governor was ever so convinced, for, in spite of a continuous and increasing clamor, amounting almost to an uproar, on the part of the settlers, no such call was issued until Congress once again took hold of the matter, and thus afforded partial relief to the perplexed and disfranchised citizens.

By the Act of May 21, 1812, Illinois was duly advanced to the second grade of Territorial government. By this action the right of suffrage was specifically extended to any white male person, twenty-one years old, who had paid a

Territorial tax, and resided in the Territory for one year preceding any election. Property qualifications were abolished. For such purposes of voting the Governor was required to apportion the Territory. A vote to get an expression from the people for or against entering upon this second grade of Territorial government was held during three successive days, beginning on the second Monday in April, 1812. The question was decided in the affirmative by a large majority. At once the Governor, assisted by the judges, organized the new counties of Madison, Gallatin, and Johnson, which, with the two old counties of St. Clair and Randolph, made a total of five. September 16, a proclamation was issued, publishing their establishment and boundaries. On the same date, a call was issued for the election of five members of the new Legislative Council, seven representatives, and a delegate to Congress. The time set was the eighth, ninth, and tenth days of October, in each county. The voting-places were: Madison County, the house of Thomas Kirkpatrick; St. Clair County, at the Court-house in Cahokia; Randolph County, the Court-house of Kaskaskia; Gallatin County, at Shawneetown; and for the county of Johnson, at the house of John Bradshaw. By the resulting vote of the people, Shadrach Bond, one among the earliest settlers of the Territory, a nephew of that Shadrach Bond who first came to New Design in 1783, and later the first Governor of the State, was elected to Congress. The members chosen to the Legislative Council were Pierre Menard, of Randolph, selected to preside; William Biggs, of St. Clair; Samuel Judy, of Madison; Thomas Ferguson, of Johnson and Benjamin Talbot, of Gallatin. Those elected to the House of Representatives were: George Fisher, of Randolph; Joshua Oglesby and Jacob Short, of St. Clair; William Jones, of Madison; Philip Trammel and Alexander Wilson, of Gallatin; and John Grammar, of Johnson.

From Davidson and Stuvé's "History of Illinois" we take the following brief pen-pictures of these pioneer legislators for this infant Territory:

"*Pierre Menard*, a Canadian Frenchman, settled at Kaskaskia in 1790. He was a merchant, and enjoyed an extensive trade with the Indians, over whom he exerted a great influence, and was for many years the Government Agent for them. He was well informed, energetic, frank, and honest, and was very popular with all classes. *William Biggs* was an intelligent and respectable member, who had been a soldier in Clark's expedition, and ten years afterwards had been a prisoner for several years among the Kickapoos. He wrote and published a complete narrative of his Indian captivity, and, in 1826, Congress voted him three sections of land. He was for many years County Judge. *Samuel Judy* — the same who, in the Fall preceding, commanded the corps of spies in Governor Edwards's military campaign to Peoria Lake — was a man of energy, fortitude, and enterprise. Some of his descendants now reside in Madison County. *Joshua Oglesby* was a local Methodist preacher of ordinary education, who lived on a farm, and was greatly respected by his neighbors. *Jacob Short*, the colleague of Oglesby, removed to Illinois with his father, Moses, in 1796, and pursued farming. During the War of 1812, he distinguished himself as a ranger. *George Fisher* possessed a fair education, and was by profession a physician. He removed from Virginia to Kaskaskia in 1800, and engaged in merchandising, but at this time he resided on a farm. *Philip Trammel* was a man of discriminating mind, inclined to the profession of arms. He was the lessee of the United States Saline in Gallatin County. His colleague, *Alexander Wilson*, was a popular tavern-keeper at Shawneetown, of fair abilities. *William Jones* was a Baptist preacher, grave in his deportment, and possessed of moderate abilities. He was born in North Carolina, removed to Illinois in 1806, and settled in the Rattan prairie, east of Alton. This was the first appearance in public life of *John Grammar*. He afterwards represented Union County frequently during a period of twenty years. He had no education, yet was a man of shrewdness. After his election, it is related that, to procure the necessary apparel to appear at the seat of government, he and the family gathered a large quantity of hickory nuts, which were taken to the Ohio Saline and traded off for blue strouding, such as the Indians usually wore for breech-cloth. When the neighboring women assembled to make up the garments, it was found that he had not invested quite enough nuts. The pattern was measured in every way possible, but was unmistakably scant. Whereupon it was decided to make a bob-tailed coat, and a long pair of leggings. Arrayed in these he duly appeared at the seat of government, where he continued to wear his primitive suit for the greater part of the session. Notwithstanding his illiteracy, he had the honor of originating the practice, much followed by public men since, of voting against all new measures — it being easier to conciliate public opinion for being remiss in voting for a good measure, than to suffer arraignment for aiding in the passage of an unpopular one."

By proclamation of the Governor, this interesting and pioneer legislative body convened at the seat of government in Kaskaskia on November 25. The two houses met in a large, rough, old building of uncut limestone, having a steep roof and gables of unpainted boards, with dormer-windows, situated in the centre of a square, and which, after the partial ruin and abandonment of Fort Chartres, had been utilized by the French as headquarters for the military commandant. Some able historians assert that this building, rather than Fort Gage, was the British military headquarters captured by General Clark in 1778. The lower floor, which consisted of one large, cheerless room, with very low ceiling, was roughly fitted up for the use of the House, while a smaller upper chamber was given over to the deliberations of the Council. The latter body chose John Thomas as their secretary, while the House elected for clerk William C. Greenup. The two bodies possessed a doorkeeper in common. All the twelve members, we are solemnly informed, boarded with one family, and, it is suspected, lodged in a single room. The difference exhibited here in comparison with more modern legislative customs is very marked, and was scarcely less conspicuous in other matters. History tells us that these primitive law-makers of Illinois addressed themselves diligently to the business in hand, making no effort at delay or circumlocution. Windy speeches and violent contentions were unheard of, and parliamentary tacticians, if any such were present, met with sudden squelching. It has been naively remarked that not a lawyer appears on the roll of names. It is reported, possibly by political enemies, then as now extremely active, that at the conclusion of each legislative session the long table was promptly cleared, and the weary statesmen regaled themselves by playing the popular game of bung-loo.

The scope of this charter makes any extended review of laws enacted impossible, but it may be well to mention a few of the more stringent and peculiar. Beginning with a totally blank legislative page, attention was early addressed to criminal affairs, and a degree of punishment for crime adopted strange to these later and more fastidious days. For felonies and misdemeanors, whipping on the bare back, confinement in stocks, standing in the pillory, and branding with hot irons, were the penalties prescribed, in addition to fines, imprisonment, and loss of citizenship. The number of stripes to be inflicted was prescribed with painful accuracy: for burglary, 39; perjury, larceny, etc., 31; horse stealing, first offence, 50 to 100; hog-stealing, 25 to 39; defacing brands, 40 ; bigamy, from 100 to 300. Besides in cases of treason and murder, death by hanging was pronounced against arson, rape, and second-offence horse-stealing. In case of debt, if the property found was not sufficient to liquidate the obligation, the body of the debtor might be seized and cast into prison. The Territorial revenue was raised by a tax on lands; the county revenue, chiefly by a tax on personal property, including slaves. Able-bodied single men, owning two hundred dollars' worth of taxable property, were assessed one dollar each. The entire Territorial revenue from November 1, 1811, to November 8, 1814, amounted to but $4,875.45, while of this less than half had been actually paid into the treasury, the remainder being in the hands of delinquent sheriffs, of whom there were apparently a large number. In 1816, an act was passed preventing Indiana attorneys from practising in Illinois, while in 1817 the Territory was carefully parcelled out between the medical doctors — all newcomers to be examined by the old practitioners, and then, at their discretion, on the payment of ten dollars, possibly allowed to practise. This delightful condition prevailed until the Territory was made into a State, when it was promptly corrected.

During the Territorial existence of Illinois, three such general assemblies were elected by the people — the Council holding over the second term. In 1817, Colonel Benjamin Stephenson was selected as delegate to Congress, and in 1816 Nathaniel Pope was given similar honor. Ten new counties were meanwhile organized, and their boundaries defined.

By the year 1818 Illinois had sufficiently increased in population to aspire to a position among the sisterhood of States. Nathaniel Pope, then delegate in Congress, presented the necessary petition to that body, and in due time a bill was reported for the admission of Illinois with an estimated population of forty thousand. This was probably an over-estimate. In defining the permanent boundaries of the new State, it was owing to the vigilance of Mr. Pope that we are to-day indebted for the coast on Lake Michigan, the site of Chicago, the northern terminus of the Illinois and Michigan Canal, and the lead mines of Galena. By the language of the Ordinance of 1787, all this region should have remained a portion of Wisconsin. In pursuance of this enabling act, a convention was called to draught the first constitution of the new State. The meeting was held at Kaskaskia, in the same old building used for nine years previous by the Territorial legislature, beginning in July, 1818, and completing its labors on the twenty-sixth of August following. Of this body, consisting of thirty-three members, Jesse B. Thomas was chosen president, and William C. Greenup named as secretary.

The constitution thus adopted was never submitted to any ratifying vote of the people, nor by it were they left very much choice, even in the selection of their more important State officers. While the election franchise was extended to embrace all white male inhabitants above twenty-one years of age, yet these electors were not trusted to vote except for governors, the General Assembly, sheriffs, and coroners; all other State and county officials being appointive with the General Assembly. The first election under this constitution — the defects of which were early apparent — was held in September, 1818; and Shadrach Bond was selected as Governor, with Pierre Menard, Lieutenant-Governor. There was no other ticket in the field. Their period of service was for four years. By the terms of the document issued by the State Constitutional Convention, the seat of government was to remain at Kaskaskia until the General Assembly should otherwise direct. With this change in view, that body was required at its first session to petition Congress to grant to the State a quantity of land, to consist of not more than four and not less than one section, or to give to the State the right of preëmption in the purchase of that quantity, the land to be situated on the Kaskaskia River, and, as near as might be, east of the third principal meridian, on that river. Should this request be granted, the General Assembly, at its next following session, was required to appoint five commissioners to make selection of the land and provide for the laying out of a town upon it; which town, it was declared, should remain the seat of government for a term of twenty years. From outside reports it appears that when this subject was being considered by the convention, two points were contemplated and debated upon. One was Carlyle, just located on the Kaskaskia River by two Virginia gentlemen; the other an elevated spot, higher up the river, known as Pope's Bluff, the property of Nathaniel Pope. Ford writes:

"He [Pope] and his friends were, of course, extremely anxious that the seat of government should be located there, while the proprietors of Carlyle were fully as desirous that their position should find favor. In midst of the discussion which ensued over these conflicting interests, a well-known hunter and trapper, named Reeves, who had a lonely cabin still higher up the river, wandered in, and became deeply interested. In glowing terms he depicted the superior beauty of Reeve's Bluff, insisting warmly that 'Pope's Bluff, er Carlyle neither, wasn't a primin' ter his bluff.' Such was the force of his representations that the language of the original bill was sufficiently altered to admit of his site. Strange to say, when, in 1818, commissioners were finally appointed to select the land which had been granted by Congress they fixed upon the home of the old hunter at Reeve's Bluff."

It was, indeed, a most attractive spot, a heavily wooded tract, covered by gigantic trees, well elevated, and sightly. The only seeming disadvantage of this position for the State capital was, that, at that early day, it was in the midst of an almost untouched wilderness, lying considerably northeast of the principal settlements of the country. However, with abundant faith in the future, work upon the new site was at once begun, and the town laid out with a handsome square and broad streets. Governor Ford records:

"After the place had been selected, it became a matter of great interest to give it a good-sounding name, one which would please the ear, and at the same time have the classic merit of perpetuating the memory of the ancient race of Indians by whom the country had first been inhabited. Tradition says that a wag who was present suggested to the commissioners that the Vandals were a powerful nation of Indians who once inhabited the banks of the Kaskaskia River, and that 'Vandalia,' formed from their name, would perpetuate the memory of that extinct but renowned people. The suggestion pleased the commissioners, the name was adopted, and they thus proved that the name of their new city (if they were fit representatives of their constituents) would better illustrate the character of the modern than the ancient inhabitants of the country."

Indeed, the first workmen on the site were sufficiently vandals to cut down and saw into cord-wood every one of those magnificent forest trees, leaving not a single specimen to sigh in the Summer wind, or bend to the blast.

In Judge Caton's address reviewing these interesting events, he says of this new town:

"Lots were sold at public auction on credit, at fabulous prices, few of which were paid in full. The enterprising and scheming came to it, some from the Old World, and soon the nucleus of a town was formed. Measures were inaugurated for the erection of a State House, which culminated in a plain two-story frame building, of rude architecture, set upon a rough stone foundation, and placed in the centre of the square, the lower floor of which was devoted to a passage and stairway to the upper story, and a large, plain room, devoid of ornament (for the accommodation of the House). The upper floor was divided into two rooms, the largest for the accommodation of the Senate, and the smaller one for the office of Secretary of State, the Auditor and Treasurer occupying a detached building, hired for that purpose. No ceremonies were observed in laying the corner-stone of this unsightly structure; no music disturbed the solitude of the forest, then in its primeval beauty; no crowd in pageantry lent excitement to the scene; no sound was heard save the rap of the mason's hammer, and the sharp clicks of the trowel."

Soon after this indifferent building was completed, final steps were taken for the removal of the seat of government from old Kaskaskia, where, under French, English, and American rule, it had been located for more than one hundred and fifty years. In one small wagon, and at a single load, the entire State archives were transported to Vandalia.

Undoubtedly, much of great historical value was lost at this time. Sidney Breese, clerk to the Secretary of State, and Mr. Kane, had them in charge, and the road being poor, at several points a path had to be cut through the woods. When they arrived at the new Capitol, they found the building occupied as a temporary home by the Auditor, Elijah C. Berry, with his family. These, however, were soon induced to remove to an adjacent cabin, and a little later, the first session of the legislature convened at Vandalia. This structure in which they met was totally destroyed by fire, breaking out at 2 A. M., December 9, 1823. So rapidly did the flames spread, that not a single article of furniture was saved. Besides most important State documents, some of inestimable value, all the books, and papers belonging to the office of the United States Land Receiver, were likewise destroyed. The cause of the fire was never ascertained. A subscription paper was immediately started, to which the citizens of Vandalia contributed liberally, and in three days three thousand dollars was raised. To take the place of this destroyed capitol, a commodious brick building was constructed, which still stands, for many years containing the county offices for Fayette County. It may be of interest to note, in this connection, the pay of State officials at this time. The salaries of the Governor and the supreme judges were one thousand dollars each; Secretary of State and Auditor, five hundred dollars; all payable quarterly. The allowance to legislators per diem, was four dollars, while presiding officers received five dollars.

Long before the twenty-year term assigned to Vandalia had expired, numerous ambitious cities throughout the State were in the field, anxious to be selected as the new and permanent capital. Under the pressure thus constantly exerted for a change, a commission was appointed to consider the matter, and, when a new legislature was being voted for, the people themselves were requested to express their preference at the ballot-box regarding the six different cities diligently seeking the choice. Much interest was taken, the result of the vote being as follows: Alton, 7,514; Vandalia, 7,148; Springfield, 7,044; the geographical centre (Illiopolis), 744; Peoria, 486; Jacksonville, 272. This election was held in August, 1834, and from its results Alton was plainly designated as the choice of the majority of the voters. But it requires something more than votes to construct a capital; the legislature took no action, and consequently nothing resulted. But the question of removal would not down, and it became more and more plainly apparent that the unfortunate situation of Vandalia made it impossible to retain the seat of State government at that place much longer. In those days of overland journeys, it was convenient to comparatively few, and becoming less so with every year, because of the increase of immigration northward.

Springfield, greatly encouraged by the unexpectedly large vote received in 1834, never let up in agitating the matter of a change; and two years later there was in the House a delegation from Sangamon County of unusual influence and ability. The delegates were nine in number, popularly known as the "long nine" because they averaged six feet in height, some more and some less — there being precisely fifty-four feet in their combined stature. These men were able, persistent, and dextrous political manipulators, a unit upon all questions appertaining to the welfare of Sangamon, and they pushed the Capital bill strongly for the benefit of Springfield. These men were: A. G. Herndon and Job Fletcher, Senators; Representatives, Abraham Lincoln, Ninian W. Edwards, Dan Stone, John Dawson, W. F. Elkin, Andrew McCormick, and Robert L. Wilson. By February 28, 1837, they had actually forced the reluctant legislature to final action, and a vote was taken much after the manner followed in the selection of United States Senators. Twenty-nine places were presented and voted upon.

Springfield started with thirty-five votes, but on the fourth ballot it reached seventy-three, which was a strong majority. The location having thus been definitely determined, fifty thousand dollars was at once appropriated for the erection of a State House on the new site, but the act was to be null and void unless an equal amount should be subscribed by individuals prior to May 1. Springfield agreed to donate two acres of ground, in addition, without expense to the State. This being satisfactorily arranged by the date set, the legislature met first in Springfield (in extraordinary session) December 9, 1839; but as the new Capitol was then far from being completed, the House convened in the Second Presbyterian Church, and the Senate in the First Methodist, which was an old frame structure. The Supreme Court held its sessions in the Episcopal Chapel.

It was not until the War of 1812 that the attractions and fertility of what has since been named Sangamon County began to be known to the earlier Illinois settlers, who up to that date had hardly penetrated north of Madison County, excepting along the rivers.

The Indian name applied to all this region was "Sangamo," meaning "the country where there is plenty to eat," and the volunteers marching wearily across it in Edwards's advance to Peoria Lake, on returning home, scattered widely among their neighbors vivid descriptions of the beauty of this newly discovered land. The "St. Gamo Kedentry," as it was pronounced in the vernacular, immediately became famous, and scarcely had the war ceased before hardy, adventurous settlers began to erect their little log cabins along the timbered streams. In the Autumn of 1819, a family of emigrants, originally from North Carolina, by the name of Kelly, encamped on the right bank of Spring Creek, in the western part of the present city of Springfield. Here they decided upon making their future home, and thus became the earliest settlers. Two years later, the county was

ILLINOIS STATEHOUSE

THE OLD AND THE NEW

organized, the county seat being fixed at Kelly's; and in recognition of his field and Spring Creek,— at least so the story goes,— the embryo city was given its rather unhappy name of Springfield. Even in this choice of a county seat the fate of the future capital hung for a while in the balance, and was finally decided by a somewhat dubious trick, according to a volume of the "Springfield City Ordinances." A previous election to the legislature had turned entirely upon this question of location. W. S. Hamilton, son of the great Alexander Hamilton, favored Sangamo Town, a beautiful elevated bluff on the river, in which he was personally interested, lying seven miles northwest. Jonathan H. Pugh was the Springfield candidate, and Hamilton, receiving the majority of votes, was elected. It seemed then as if Springfield's hopes were finally doomed, but, as a last resort, a sufficient fund was raised, and the defeated candidate, Pugh, despatched to Vandalia to labor in the lobby. So well did he perform this task that Hamilton not only failed to get his beloved Sangamo Town named as county seat, but a legislative committee was appointed to visit both sites and decide on a location. The committee chanced to reach Springfield first; were most royally entertained by the hopeful citizens, and loaded into carriages to be driven to Sangamo Town. It is to be feared the drivers selected were rabid Springfield partisans, as they chose a road leading across much low, wet land, through sloughs and mudholes. The way became particularly horrible as they drew closer to the proposed site, and in utter disgust the committee left the ambitious Sangamo to its former obscurity.

At the time of the selection of Springfield as the future State capital, the village contained a population of 1,100, and was little more than a straggling frontier hamlet, the buildings small and unpretentious. The corner-stone of the State Building was laid July 4, 1837, E. D. Baker being the orator of the occasion. The estimated cost of the structure was only $130,000, but, as usual in such cases, the actual cost was nearly one hundred per cent more. At first it was the wonder of all the country around, settlers travelling for long distances merely to gaze upon it in speechless awe, but this feeling, before many years, died away, as the citizens began to realize that it was far from being large enough to meet the fast-growing requirements of the State. In less than a quarter of a century, public demand was aroused for a new building. Population had increased marvellously,—in 1840 to 476,183; in 1865 to 2,141,510. It was during the legislative session of this last-mentioned year that a bill was introduced advocating the removal of the seat of government to Peoria. Other cities began at once to join in the clamor, urging their own superior claims, and Springfield became justly alarmed. Much dissatisfaction with existing conditions was in evidence all over the State, but it apparently centred in Springfield's miserable hotel accommodation and exorbitant charges.

The citizens of the capital city rose to the emergency, building the magnificent Leland Hotel, and, at the next legislative meeting, made to the State most liberal offers; the county of Sangamon agreed to purchase the old State House and square for $200,000, to be converted into a courthouse, while the city council offered a seven-acre lot, in the very heart of the city, at a cost of $62,000, as a site for the new Capitol. Feeling ran extremely high, and the ladies of Springfield thronged the visitors' gallery, and vied with each other in extending social courtesies to the legislators. With all these latter gentlemen, at last, apparently in a proper frame of mind for favorable action, a bill for a new State House to be erected at Springfield was diplomatically introduced, and finally forced to a passage, February 25, 1867. It limited the cost of the new Capitol to $3,000,000. This result, however, was not accomplished without opposition and extended debate; one extremely humorous speech by Mr. Voris advocated the dislocation of the Capitol, and the holding of a peregrinating legislature by railroad, which should stop at every place where a notice appeared that it was wanted.

The work of building was hurriedly begun; but opposition throughout the State was far from being dead, and much delay was occasioned by the acts of rival cities, and the unwillingness of the legislature to be liberal in expenditure. Decatur sued out a writ of *quo warranto* directed against the building commissioners, and the case was threshed out in the Supreme Court to Decatur's final defeat. The constant necessity of increasing appropriations to meet the cost of construction led Peoria to make a munificent offer for the seat of government — she pledged herself to reimburse the State to the full amount already expended, donate a beautiful ten-acre lot, and furnish, free of rent for five years, suitable accommodation for the legislature. This offer aroused the interest of the State to fever heat, and the two houses accepted a free excursion to Peoria, where they were royally entertained by the enthusiastic citizens, and carefully shown every point of interest thereabout. For a time the fate of Springfield hung once more trembling in the balance, everything resting upon the passing of the appropriation bill. This was fought to the last possible moment with great bitterness and with every device known to parliamentary law; but, finally, at ten o'clock at night, June 7, 1871, it was passed by a vote of one hundred to seventy-four. Peoria's apple of hope was turned to ashes, and Springfield remained the capital of Illinois. The Capitol Building was completed in 1887, at a cost of over $4,000,000.

CHAPTER XXII

THE BATTLE AGAINST SLAVERY

AS far back as 1720 the spectre of the black slave began to cast its baleful shadow across the Illinois country. Previous to that date a few red slaves, prisoners of either war or debt, were held in bondage among the French colonists, yet the number was small, and would never have proven of any political consequence. It remained for Renault, business agent for the "Company of St. Philippe" to bring here the first African slaves, and thus lay the foundation for a bitter struggle, destined to last for more than one hundred years. Renault left France in 1719 with a cargo of mechanics, miners, and laborers, numbering some two hundred, and on his way stopped long enough at San Domingo to purchase five hundred black slaves. Accompanied by this extensive company, he voyaged slowly up the Mississippi, finally arriving in Illinois, where he established headquarters at the village of St. Philippe, in what is now the southeast corner of Monroe County. From there his parties of prospectors scattered widely, in a vain effort to locate precious mineral. In 1744, completely discouraged by lack of success in his mining ventures, he returned to France, but before going sold his remaining slaves to the surrounding French colonists.

By French law, under date of April 23, 1615, slavery in the American colonies had been duly legalized, and later, by the terms of the Treaty of Paris in 1763, the French inhabitants of Illinois were by England confirmed in their right to this species of property. When the United States came into possession of all this territory in 1784, the following stipulation in the deed of cession was naturally construed to imply the continuation of such enslavement, and practically so resulted: "That the French and Canadian inhabitants, and other settlers of the Kaskaskias, St. Vincents, and the neighboring villages, who have professed themselves citizens of the State of Virginia, shall have their possessions and titles confirmed to them, and be protected in the enjoyment of their rights and liberties." Later, when this question came up directly before Congress, in a bill providing "that after the year 1800 there shall be neither slavery nor involuntary servitude in any of the said States," to be formed out of this territory, it met with decisive defeat. At this time Indiana Territory, which included the Illinois country, contained a slave population of one hundred and thirty-three. In 1810, Illinois Territory alone had one hundred and sixty-eight slaves; in 1820, nine hundred and seventeen, probably including indentured and registered servants; and by 1830 these totalled seven hundred and forty-six.

The situation of Illinois, as well as the character and training of the earlier settlers, were alike conducive to the extension of slavery, at least throughout the more southern counties. Hence through all the earlier days it flourished, but was finally checked by a strong opposition sentiment sweeping down from the North, brought by incoming settlers from New England. It seems strange now that this pro-slavery sentiment was not even more strong and abiding than it proved to be in time of final test. Geographically, Illinois projects far southward, and during all the earlier years she was in direct commercial contact with slave States; her first and more influential settlers came from such States, while the soil was adapted to the production of crops making profitable slave labor. To south and west were situated slave Territories, while Southern Indiana was strongly pro-slavery, both in sentiment and practice. Yet, from the first incoming of American pioneers, anti-slavery advocates were very much in evidence, and an earnest effort was made toward anchoring Illinois among the free States. Both parties took the matter to Congress, besides bringing it up in various forms before the legislature; but for a number of years no important change was effected, and Illinois practically remained pro-slavery. Not until as late as 1845 was the rightfulness to hold slaves in Illinois directly passed upon by any State Supreme Court. The first decision bearing upon this question occurred in Indiana. In this case the mother of the plaintiff had been a slave in Virginia, was removed to Illinois before the Ordinance of 1787, the sixth article of which prohibited slavery in those territories lying northwest of the Ohio River, held in bondage there both before and after its passage, and there the plaintiff was born after that date. It was held that she was free. The second case was passed upon by the Missouri Supreme Court, it being the case of Menard *vs.* Aspasia. The mother of the latter was born in Illinois before the ordinance, and held as a slave from birth. Aspasia, born after the ordinance at Kaskaskia, was likewise held as a slave. The Missouri Court held that she was entitled to freedom; upon a writ of error the question reached the United States Supreme Court, and its decision was similar — slaves born since the Ordinance of 1787 could not be held in slavery in Illinois. In 1845 this question came squarely before the Illinois Supreme Court in the case of Jarrot *vs.* Jarrot, when it was decided that descendants of the old French slaves born since 1787 could not be held in slavery. Many other similar decisions followed, which largely cleared the air, and aided ultimate freedom.

In the years between these dates a continuous and bitter warfare had raged over this important matter. Partially estopped by Congressional enactment, the advocates of slavery in Illinois resorted to various expedients to avoid the law, the most effective of which found expression in a Territorial enactment passed in September, 1807, which permitted slaveholders to have duly recorded an indenture between themselves and their slaves for a term of years, the children of said indentured slaves likewise to serve, the males until thirty, the females until twenty-eight years of age. Such servants might also be sold by an assignment of the indenture, thus practically making their condition one of absolute bondage, while technically avoiding the precise language of the Congressional ordinance. It is impossible here to follow in any specific detail the various subterfuges adopted from time to time to avoid what seemingly was the plain law of the land; courts were invoked, and legislatures convened for the sole purpose of handling this one absorbing question; but in the path of all further reform stood the absolute veto power of the Governor, and, on this matter, Governor Edwards, who was himself the owner of a number of indentured slaves, never failed to act promptly. Through these methods of administration the indentured slave became a recognized institution in Illinois, the slaves steadily decreasing in numbers, it is true, yet the institution was never wholly abolished until the adoption of the Constitution of 1848.

The " Black Laws," as adopted by the legislature in 1819, were very stringent, not to say barbarous. No negro or mulatto could reside in the State until he produced a certificate of freedom under court seal, which must be entered of record in the county where he settled. If he changed residence, the certificate had to be refiled. To emancipate slaves, an owner was required to execute a bond of one thousand dollars; neglecting to do this rendered him liable to a fine of two hundred dollars. To harbor any slave, or hinder the owner in retaking his runaway slave, was declared a felony; every black without proper certificate was held as a runaway subject to arrest, and could be publicly sold at the end of a year. Any slave, or servant, found ten miles from home without the written permit of his master was liable to arrest, and could be whipped on order of a justice; or if he appeared at any dwelling, without leave of his master, the owner of the place thus visited was authorized to administer ten lashes on his bare back. For being lazy, disorderly, or misbehaving generally, he could be corrected with stripes, and for every day he refused to work he was compelled to serve two. In all cases where free persons were punishable by fines, slaves and indentured servants were to be chastised by whipping, at the rate of twenty lashes for every eight dollars of fine, not to exceed forty stripes at any one time. Thus was the free State of Illinois provided with a complete slave code.

The most odious feature of this entire slave code, however, was the kidnapping clause, which, unfortunately, had been so worded as to make capture and punishment for this crime almost impossible. The inevitable result in so new a country, overrun with desperate men, many of them criminally inclined, was to make such kidnapping of free negroes and indentured servants a regular and profitable business. They were seized everywhere by force, or inveigled by strategy upon river boats, and taken South into the cotton States, to be sold to the highest bidder. No crime can be greater or more revolting than this, yet for many years southern Illinois afforded a safe retreat to these kidnapping outlaws, who became more and more numerous and bold. In some instances they were organized into regular bands, having rendezvous and passwords, leaders, and methods of distributing the spoils of their nefarious trade in human suffering. The rough hill country lying between the Ohio and the Mississippi witnessed in those days much of crime and sorrow never to be recorded. Very few case, indeed, ever found permanent mention. The earliest conviction for this crime was that of Jephtha Lambkins, in Madison County, November, 1822, but the details have not been preserved. On the night of May 25, 1823, a free colored man named Jackson Butler, his wife, and six children, residing in Illinois, a few miles from Vincennes, were kidnapped by a band of raiders from Lawrence County, in this State. Butler had belonged to Governor Harrison in Kentucky, had been brought to Indiana, had been indentured, and had faithfully worked out his term of service. His wife was born free, which rendered the children also free. They were taken down the Wabash to the Ohio, and from there disappeared farther South. Harrison, learning of the outrage, at once offered a large reward for the capture of the perpetrators. His name gave the matter wide publicity, and the Butlers were rescued at New Orleans, just as they were about to be shipped to Cuba.

This was merely one out of hundreds of similar instances, although few had so satisfactory an ending. The entire southern portion of the State was overrun by professional kidnappers, and free negroes were kept in constant terror. The Shawneetown "Mercury," as late as 1851, contains an account of a peculiar case illustrative of the class of men engaged at this work. A Mrs. Prather, of Tennessee, emancipated her slaves, and the latter removed to Gallatin County, Illinois. They were followed by a party of kidnappers, who conspired for their arrest as fugitive slaves. Judge Pope, of the United States Circuit Court, before whom the case came, decided that the Tennesseeans had not a shadow of a claim to them. While endeavoring to get hold of these negroes, a well-known Kentucky kidnapper, named Newton E. Wright, came to this State, and became acquainted with two Illinoisans in the same trade, — Joe O'Neal, of Hamilton County, and Abe Thomas. A little later, O'Neal stole three children from a negro named Scott, living in that county, ran them off, and sold them, partly on credit, to Wright, who immediately resold them to one Phillips at New Madrid. When O'Neal's note matured he sent Abe

Thomas to collect, telling him that Wright had some other business for him to attend to, for which he would be well paid. Arriving at Wright's, the desperado was offered one hundred and fifty dollars to go to Hicco, Tennessee, and kill a Dr. Swayne, who had sued Wright on a note. This job was undertaken, and Thomas went to Hicco, gained Swayne's confidence, and endeavored to carry out his contract, but merely succeeded in fracturing the Doctor's arm by a hasty shot fired from behind. Thomas escaped, although closely pursued. A year later, an unexpected clew to the discovery of the felon was obtained. Two residents of White County, Illinois, chanced to meet Dr. Swayne, and heard him describe the man who shot him as having a nose flat at the base, projecting forward like a hawk's bill. These Illinoisans at once recognized Abe Thomas, and a short time afterwards the fellow was seized by a party of Tennesseeans, taken to that State, tried, and convicted.

In 1824 a desperate effort was made to change Illinois into an openly slave State. There can be little question that from 1818 until this date, whenever the voice of the people found expression, they were strongly in favor of slavery. The subject was constantly kept astir, not only by local agitators, but by the continuous stream of Southern emigrants passing through on their way to Missouri. Many who had lands and property to sell looked upon the good fortune of Missouri with envy, while the lordly immigrant, as he passed along with his money and droves of negroes, took a malicious pleasure in increasing it, by pretending to regret the short-sighted policy of Illinois, which prevented him from settling there with his slaves, and purchasing the land travelled over. This growing dissatisfaction culminated in the fierce election contest of 1822, when slavery was practically the one great issue upon which votes were cast. Edward Coles was elected Governor by a small majority. He was openly opposed to slavery, and thus, apparently, the anti-slavery party won; but this was accomplished merely because there chanced to be two pro-slavery candidates in the field,— Phillips and Brown,— and the total pro-slavery vote polled was nearly two thousand in excess of that given Coles. Moreover, the legislature elected was strongly pro-slavery, and counteracted the best efforts of the executive.

The two radically opposed parties locked horns almost immediately, Governor Coles directing attention to this important question in his first communication to the assembled Legislature, and in clear, forcible language urging immediate emancipation. This served merely to fan into flame all opposition, and the pro-slavery advocates, confident in their apparent strength, determined then and there to fasten slavery permanently upon the State. There was but one legal way in which this could be accomplished — by an amendment to the Constitution. To attain this required first a two-thirds vote in each house passing the proposition submitting the question to a final vote of the people. In the Senate, this necessary two-thirds was easily found, but in the House just one vote proved to be lacking. To remedy this, an anti-slavery member, Nicholas Hanson, of Pike County, was unseated, and a contestant for his position, in the person of John B. Shaw, promptly given his place. His vote, thus easily secured, carried the day; but the unscrupulous manner in which it had been acquired later proved a boomerang, and contributed largely to influence the people in their decision at the polls. There followed a most desperately bitter campaign for votes, lasting nearly eighteen months, conducted violently by both parties throughout the entire inhabited portion of the State. In some respects the pro-slavery element had, at the start at least, a decided advantage because of the unequal apportionment of the State into representative and senatorial districts, pro-slavery sentiment being peculiarly strong in the old

French settlements and along the Ohio, while farther north the people were numerically far in advance of the ratio of representation accorded them. The anti-slavery leaders perceived clearly that if they were to win at all it must be through the direct vote of the people, for if the question should be ever left with a chosen convention of delegates as the districts were then apportioned, slavery would unquestionably be fastened upon the State. Nerved by this knowledge, they devoted every effort to defeat the convention call before the people.

Never was such a canvass before made in the State. Young and old, without regard to sex, entered madly into the party strife; families and neighborhoods became divided, and entered into bitter, and at times violent, controversy. Detraction, personal abuse, acrimonious retorts were heard everywhere, and hand-to-hand combats were frequent. The entire country was on the verge of a resort to physical force to settle the angry question, and both threats and open intimidation were freely indulged. Newspapers were established by both parties to the controversy, and their columns teemed with incendiary utterances. Pamphlets were published and scattered broadcast; Governor Coles gave his entire salary to the cause; under the leadership of the Rev. Dr. Peck, anti-slavery societies were organized throughout the State, the headquarters being in St. Clair County. The ministers of the gospel took active part in the canvass, for the moment forgetting their theological differences to unite against this one great sin. Tracts and handbills fluttered everywhere, and almost every stump held an impassioned orator, while the rank and file of the people wrangled and argued wherever they met. All commerce ceased, all work waited, while this great question was being fought out to a finish.

A glance over the array of names prominent in this campaign makes it evident that the more talented, influential,

LIBERTY LINE.

NEW ARRANGEMENT---NIGHT AND DAY.

The improved and splendid Locomotives, Clarkson and Lundy, with their trains fitted up in the best style of accommodation for passengers, will run their regular trips during the present season, between the borders of the Patriarchal Dominion and Libertyville, Upper Canada. Gentlemen and Ladies, who may wish to improve their health or circumstances, by a northern tour, are respectfully invited to give us their patronage.

SEATS FREE, *irrespective of color.*

Necessary Clothing furnished gratuitously to such as have *"fallen among thieves."*

"Hide the outcasts—let the oppressed go free."—*Bible.*

☞For seats apply at any of the trap doors, or to the conductor of the train.

J. CROSS, *Proprietor.*

N. B. For the special benefit of Pro-Slavery Police Officers, an extra heavy wagon for Texas, will be furnished, whenever it may be necessary, in which they will be forwarded as dead freight, to the "Valley of Rascals," always at the risk of the owners.

☞Extra Overcoats provided for such of them as are afflicted with protracted *chilly-phobia.*

FAC-SIMILE OF UNDERGROUND RAILWAY ADVERTISEMENT

FROM "THE WESTERN CITIZEN," JULY 13, 1844

and better-known men then in Illinois public life were enlisted on the side of the convention party, but in energy and zeal, enthusiasm and determination, the opposition proved the stronger. Moreover, they were better organized, and enjoyed the advantage of being able to press home on the individual conscience a great moral issue, to which the minds of the common people made response. Their attacks were based directly upon the merits of slavery; they dodged nothing, while their opponents endeavored to avoid the issue, and befog it. The open, straightforward, manly methods of the anti-slavery advocates inspired respect everywhere and won votes, while, in spite of aid extended to the pro-slavery forces from sympathizers without the State, the very length of the campaign was favorable to the steady growth of anti-slavery sentiment among the common people. On the day of election every possible effort was made to poll a complete vote. The aged, the crippled, the sick, all who could possibly be induced or even dragged from their homes, were brought to the polls. The result was that the convention scheme was emphatically defeated by some eighteen hundred majority. It was a notable victory for the cause of freedom, showing a distinct gain, exceeding thirty-five hundred votes over the gubernatorial contest of only two years previous. The total vote cast was 11,612, while at the Presidential election the November following, the total vote cast was but 4,707. Strange as it may seem, the angry feelings engendered by this prolonged and bitter contest for supremacy died rapidly away, and six months later, it is said, it would have been difficult to find a politician in the State who would openly favor the introduction of slavery. The people's will was supreme. The victory thus won decided forever the position of Illinois on this momentous question.

But the liberty of men is more than a political question, and can never be settled until it is settled right. Illinois, by this decisive act of her voters, was indeed safely removed from the list of avowed slave States, but the curse of virtual slavery yet continued to cast its baleful shadow throughout the settlements. To the south lay Kentucky, a slave State; to the west, Missouri, a slave State, while nearly half of her own population were from birth and habit firm believers in the "peculiar institution." Kidnapping of free Illinois negroes became a recognized trade, in which many prospered. Regular routes were established leading southward, with convenient stations established along the way, by which men, women, and children were hurried into slavery. There are times when fire can best be fought with fire, and as arriving settlers from the New England States, men nurtured in the religion of abolitionism, began to flow into the more northern counties, they planned a somewhat similar scheme for the running away with colored folks, but for a nobler purpose. The Southern kidnappers stole the free, to sell them into hopeless slavery; the Northern abolitionists took the slave from his master and guided him into liberty. It was a dangerous service in those days, when the feeling between the factions was extremely bitter, and one could hardly be certain of the true sentiments of a neighbor. Yet little by little a trustworthy chain was formed the entire length of the great State; then another and another, until soon after 1835, and from then until the breaking out of the Civil War, an almost constant stream of black fugitives was passing along from station to station of the famous "Underground Railway" to ultimate safety in far-off Canada. We know little regarding those old secret routes now; they have left only dim traces, although a few hoary-headed men yet linger, who can tell thrilling stories of that little section on which they once faithfully served. It may be none were acquainted with the entire distance traversed; certain it is that all that any station-keeper needed to know was the location of the next station lying east or north of his own. The

Elijah P. Lovejoy

FROM A RARE SILHOUETTE PORTRAIT

fugitives came to him in the dark hours before dawn; all that day they lay hidden securely from prying eyes, and when night again darkened he led them swiftly onward to another similar place of safety. No record was ever kept of the number that passed, but many a hundred, including men, women, and children, thus won their weary way to freedom across the night-enshrouded prairies of Illinois. One old settler in Knox County, pointing the present writer to the great attic in his quaintly fashioned house, said that often he had hidden there more than twenty fugitives. Sometimes it was but one, trudging painfully along on foot, to be followed a few nights later by a trembling band loaded upon lumbering wagons.

We know little of the details; it is doubtful if anyone now living could accurately trace the old routes along which these fleeing blacks travelled in the dark. There were three of these secret trails leading out from Missouri, across Illinois — one starting at St. Louis, and veering north until it intersected another having its western terminus at Alton, from which point it tended north of east, probably never far away from the present line of the Big Four Railway. A third route led directly northeast from Quincy, passing through Knox, Henry, Bureau, and La Salle Counties on its way toward Lake Michigan. Galesburg in Knox, then Wethersfield in Henry County, were stations on this line, the next beyond being Princeton in Bureau, thirty-six miles distant.

Out of such conflicting interests as slavery engendered, from the suspicion rampant on all sides, and the intense bitterness of party strife, the mob spirit was naturally born. Violence was not uncommon during all of these formative years, and occasionally the smouldering fire burst forth into dangerous flame. Neighborhoods, churches, even families, were divided; the very word "Abolitionist" was hated by many lovers of liberty; yet so subtly did the spirit of abolitionism creep in that no man felt certain of his nearest neighbor. Suspicion filled the air, and stimulated men to acts which under saner conditions would have been impossible. Such, we may safely say, led to the Alton riots and the death of Elijah P. Lovejoy. This occurred in the Fall of 1837, soon after the formation in upper Alton, at the house of the Rev. Mr. Hurlbut, of the first openly avowed Abolition Society in the State. Mr. Lovejoy, who may justly be named Illinois's first martyr to liberty, came to Alton from St. Louis, July 21, 1836. He was then thirty-four years of age, and had been for three years editor of a paper in the latter city, in the columns of which he had so fearlessly expressed anti-slavery views, as to make it necessary for him to flee from the place by night. Determined to be heard, he shipped his press to Alton, where he proposed reëstablishing himself. It chanced to be Sunday, and consequently his goods were left lying unguarded on the wharf, no one supposing any trouble would occur. That night the boxes were broken open, and the printing-press was thrown into the river.

This act aroused great indignation in Alton, and a meeting of protest was held in the Presbyterian Church, at which Mr. Lovejoy and others spoke. In this address the declaration was clearly made that he was not an Abolitionist, but looked to colonization as the best means of ridding the country of the curse of slavery. He stated his desire to establish a religious paper in Alton, and used language which his listeners interpreted to be a personal pledge that its columns should be kept free from all future discussion of the slavery question. As a direct result of this meeting, funds were raised, another press was sent for, and on September 8, 1836, the first number of the Alton "Observer" was issued. It was a success from the start, and soon gained a wide circulation, but it was not long before its editor again boldly attacked slavery. It could hardly be otherwise in that day

LOVEJOY MONUMENT, ALTON

when no true man could long remain neutral or indifferent. In the issue of June 29, 1837, he favored a petition for the abolishing of slavery in the District of Columbia, and in the next advocated the organizing of an anti-slavery society in Illinois. A committee communicated with the editor, warning him to desist, to which he replied somewhat tartly, denying the right of anyone to dictate to him what he should discuss, and offering them the use of his columns to answer his arguments.

They chose, however, a different method, and on the night of August 25 a mob suddenly stormed down upon the office, wrecked it with bricks and stones, drove out the employees, and completely demolished the press. The anti-slavery party at once rallied about their champion, and a third press was sent for; but when it arrived in September, Mr. Lovejoy chanced to be away, and it was immediately seized by another mob, and promptly thrown into the river. Again and again during these weeks of continued excitement the life of the editor was threatened, and twice he was the victim of vicious assaults. But his friends sent for a fourth press, and he remained undaunted at his post.

November 7, 1837, the boat arrived bearing the fourth press, which was at once removed to the stone warehouse of Godfrey, Gilman & Co. Mr. Lovejoy and a number of friends assembled with arms for its defence. No trouble occurred until night, when a mob of perhaps thirty persons, mostly intoxicated, demanded that the press be surrendered to them. Refused this, they at once commenced a fierce attack on the building with stones, brickbats, and guns. Those within fired, killing one of the mob and wounding several others. Soon after, the city bells were rung, horns were blown, and a maddened multitude surged down toward the besieged warehouse. Ladders were placed against the windowless sides, and a number ascended to set fire to the roof. Mr. Lovejoy, with a few others of the defenders, fired upon these, and drove them away, returning below to reload their guns. Shortly after, he again stepped out on the roof to reconnoitre. But this time concealed members of the mob were watching ; a number fired, and five bullets entered his body. He fell, crying, " My God, I am shot!" and instantly expired. With his death, the others surrendered, and the mob broke the press into fragments, and flung them into the river.

The day following, a grave was dug on a high bluff, in the southern part of the city, and the body, without any religious ceremony, was thrown into it and hastily covered up. Some years later this spot was chosen as the site of a cemetery, and the main avenue chanced to pass over the neglected grave of Lovejoy. To obviate the difficulty, his remains were removed to a new locality, and, later still, a simple monument erected over them, bearing the inscription: "*Hic jacet Lovejoy; jam parce sepulto.*" Punishment for his murder seemed to follow without human intervention: the leader of the mob became a prisoner in the Ohio penitentiary, the person most instrumental in the committing of the crime was killed in a brawl at New Orleans, while many others are reported to have ended their lives in violence and disgrace.

But great questions, like the issue of slavery, are not to be settled by mob action. The death of Lovejoy merely fanned the flame, and made agitation more aggressive. Illinois became a battle-ground, nor did the gigantic struggle cease until the surrender of the Confederacy at Appomattox. To the last, pro-slavery sentiment remained strongly entrenched throughout all the southern counties, and from them many a volunteer went forth to don the gray and battle for his faith. But Illinois stood firm for freedom, and during that awful struggle, which broke the last chains from off the limbs of black slaves, she gave of her best manhood 29,588 lives in sacrifice. In that hour of supreme trial she saw her duty, and performed it.

CHAPTER XXIII

THE CODE DUELLO

UNDOUBTEDLY, personal encounters between Indians were never uncommon in the days beyond the reach of historical research, and many a desperate combat was waged in the Illinois country over some dusky maiden, or some grievous injury. But the *code duello*, as known to us, was introduced with the coming of the Frenchman. They were fighting men, those who built and garrisoned Forts St. Louis, Chartres, and Massac, and it is scarcely probable that all those years of frontier isolation passed without many a controversy and bitter word. Yet, few details have come down to us. Rumor speaks of a fierce struggle fought with knives beside the boat-landing at Massac, but no one can tell now the name of either participant. In 1765, when the troops of Britain came into possession of Fort Chartres, a quarrel is said to have ensued between two young officers, one French, the other English. At the bottom of it was a bright-eyed lass of Kaskaskia, and for her favor these two fought with small swords one Sunday morning, close beside the fort. The Englishman was killed, and his opponent escaped down the river, but neither name has been preserved.

The earlier American settlers, coming in from the more southern States, brought with them the duel as the most fit mode for settlement of personal difficulties. The lack of law in this new region would also, very naturally, inspire each man to right his own grievances by force of arms, in a time when every settler bore knife at belt and gun at shoulder. There is no record of long-standing feuds between families, such as have been a curse to the mountain regions of Kentucky and Tennessee; but, amid the rocks of the low mountain range of the Ozarks, dark deeds were done, and ambuscading parties were not entirely unknown even up to the time of the Civil War. So far as the code proper was concerned, while meetings were frequent, they proved, generally, more farcical than serious, and became a source of continual ridicule throughout the State, until a fatal encounter resulted in a stringent law aimed at putting an end to the practice. That fierce and implacable passion, upon which the continuation of duelling must rest, never found congenial surroundings on Illinois soil, and the custom died rather of laughter than of law.

The first meeting of which we have historic mention occurred in 1809, on an island midway between Kaskaskia and St. Genevieve. It was itself a bloodless affair, but became notable because of the angry quarrel growing out of it, which later developed into the dastardly assassination of one of the principals. This duel was between Rice Jones, a young lawyer of great promise, and Shadrach Bond, afterwards the first Governor of the State. The controversy between the two young men originated over political differences, and waxed so warm and personal that a challenge was sent and accepted. The weapons were hair-trigger pistols, and as the men were taking their positions on the field, the one in Jones's hand was accidentally discharged. A quarrel thereupon ensued between the seconds, Bond's representative claiming that Jones having had one shot, it was now the turn of his principal to fire. Bond, however, refused to do so, and his manly insistence on fair play so touched Jones that the two men immediately became reconciled and quitted the field. But this left a bitter feeling existing between Jones and Bond's second, who was named Dunlap. Hatred grew, until one day, when the former was standing on the street in Kaskaskia conversing with a lady, Dunlap crept up behind, and like a coward shot him down. The murderer escaped to Texas, and was never captured, but in 1810 a law was adopted by the Governor and judges making a fatal result in a duel murder, and all taking part in it principals to the crime.

Reynolds, in his "History of Early Illinois," makes mention of another combat between Illinoisans, which occurred during the war period of 1812. His words are: "Thomas Rector, one of the younger brothers (of the famous pioneer Rector family), had a duel with Joshua Barton, on Bloody Island, opposite St. Louis, and was as cool in that combat as if he were shooting at a deer on the prairie. These young men espoused the quarrel of their elder brothers, and Barton fell in the conflict." The easy manner in which this meeting is thus referred to, with its fatal consequences, leaves the impression that such combats were not then uncommon in spite of the existing law. Bloody Island, which was within Illinois jurdisdiction, was for long a convenient and safe battle-ground, often resorted to, but the majority frequenting it were from the Missouri side of the river, especially St. Louis. It was this custom that bestowed on the island its name of horror.

The last fatal duel occurring within the State limits was fought at Belleville, in February, 1819, between Alonzo C. Stuart and William Bennett. It arose from a drunken quarrel, the participants being urged on by their companions, who desired some wild sport, and to make a butt of Bennett. A sham duel was planned, Stuart being informed but Bennett kept in the dark. Nathan Fike and Jacob Short officiated as seconds, the weapons selected being rifles, but these were loaded merely with powder. In the words of Davidson and Stuvé, whose descriptions largely form the basis of this chapter, "The combatants took position at forty paces, and at the signal Bennett fired with good aim, while, to the horror of all present, Stuart fell, shot in the breast, and mortally wounded. The latter, to heighten the merriment, had not discharged his piece at all, but Bennett, either suspecting some trick, or inspired by malice, had secretly slipped a ball into his rifle." The two seconds, together with Bennett, were arrested and indicted for murder. Separate trials being granted, Fike and Short were acquitted; but the evidence was so strong against Bennett that he broke jail and made his escape into Arkansas. Two years later, by means of a rather dishonorable trick, he was inveigled back into Illinois, again arrested, tried at a special term of court in Belleville, convicted of murder, sentenced, and executed.

In 1829, Galena gave to the State the most unique duel ever fought within its limits. Galena at that time was a town containing a motley collection of men, representing almost every nationality of the civilized world, together with a considerable sprinkling of Indians and negroes. On Sunday, when the lead-miners were idle, the place was exceedingly lively, with preaching of the gospel, dancing, all manner of open gambling, and horse-racing under the hill. The miners were just the kind to invent a new form of *duello*. This was no less than a fight between two stone-throwers,—a desperate struggle, apt to inflict even greater injury than the exchange of bullets. The name of only one of the participants has been preserved, he being that famous ranger, Thomas Higgins, whose Indian battle in 1812 has already been described. A quarrel between him and some unknown borderman resulted in this cruel and unusual wager of battle. A pile of stones, carefully assorted as to number and size, was placed within easy reach of each combatant, and they took their positions, ten paces apart. It was a fierce struggle for a moment or two, but proved of short duration, for Higgins's adversary soon turned and fled for his life.

All other hostile meetings within the State were of political origin, and generally resulted in some ludicrous ending, which constantly tended to bring the habit of a resort to arms into greater and deserved contempt. Doubtless, such farces exercised as marked an influence toward the complete suppression of duelling as did the law. The legislative session of 1840–41 was filled with bellicose bluster, and fruitful of numerous "affairs of honor," even yet apt to awaken a smile as we read of them. So intense was the fighting spirit, that one honorable member, Mr. Hacker, solemnly moved the suspension of the duelling law for two weeks, to accommodate all the doughty and chivalrous gentlemen who desired to settle their personal difficulties on the field. The special occasion of this was a quarrel between two senators, — E. D. Baker and Judge Pearson,— in which the former challenged the latter to a "fist-fight" in the public street; this pleasantry the Judge indignantly declined, but expressed a willingness to meet with weapons. Numerous challenges were exchanged at this time, but, so far as known, no actual hostile shots were fired. Sometimes friends interfered, and occasionally courts were invoked as a last resort to keep the peace, while many a good story was circulated regarding the unconscious belligerents, and their warlike propensities were turned into themes for jest and laughter.

In 1842, Abraham Lincoln became involved in one of these affairs of honor, which is perhaps fairly illustrative of a great many others. The origin of this difficulty was political. Mr. Lincoln, in an article published in the "Sangamo Journal" of September 2, 1842, made a bitter attack on some actions of the State officials, relative to the collection of taxes. The article was decidedly rough in language, and written in a jesting style, apt to cut deep. Special reference was made to State Auditor Shields, and he was held up to ridicule personally, as well as officially. Mr. Shields, being of Irish blood, was very easily aroused. Seeking the editor of the paper, he demanded the name of the anonymous writer of the objectionable article, and it was given him. Notes were interchanged, Shields's note bristling with the desire to fight, Lincoln's somewhat defiant in tone, but non-committal as to action. Finally, Shields despatched a formal challenge, naming General Whiteside as his personal friend, to which Lincoln immediately replied, with Dr. Merriman as his representative. The two friends met, and secretly pledged themselves to agree upon some terms by which a hostile meeting should be avoided. To procrastinate as much as possible, all parties concerned were persuaded to go to Springfield, and then, to prevent arrest (for rumors of the coming duel were already afloat in the air), Mr. Lincoln departed hurriedly for Jacksonville, leaving written instructions behind for the guidance of his second.

In this memorandum he explained at some length his connection with the article in the "Journal," but disclaimed any intention of reflecting personally upon Shields, stating that his object was entirely political, and that he possessed no personal pique, and knew of no cause for any. If this was not satisfactory, and a meeting could not be avoided, the arrangements for the fight were to be:

"First, *Weapons* — Cavalry broadswords of the largest size, precisely equal in all respects, and such as are now used by the cavalry company at Jacksonville.

"Second, *Position* — A plank ten feet long, and from nine to twelve inches broad, to be firmly fixed on edge on the ground, as the line between us, which neither to pass his foot over on forfeit of his life. Next a line drawn on the ground on either side of said plank and parallel with it, each at the distance of the whole length of the sword, and three feet additional from the plank; and the passing of his own such line by either party during the fight shall be deemed a surrender of the contest.

"Third, *Time* — On Thursday evening at five o'clock, if you can get it so; but in no case to be at a greater distance of time than Friday evening at five o'clock.

"Fourth, *Place* — Within three miles of Alton, on the opposite side of the river, the particular spot to be agreed on by you."

With our later knowledge of Abraham Lincoln's propensities, one is tempted to perceive a joke cropping out in the position thus gravely prescribed for the combatants, for it looks as though "both were thus placed safely out of harm's way, where they could beat the air with their trenchant blades for ever and do no damage." But it might be well to remember, in this connection, the unusual length of Mr. Lincoln's arm, and feel some sympathy for his opponent. However, Shields was determined to fight, regardless of terms, and all parties concerned left for the supposed field of carnage, taking a physician — Dr. Bledsoe, a most suggestive name — along, to minister to the wounded. Later a Dr. Hope — possibly selected as an offset to his more sanguinary medical brother — joined the party, and the entire company crossed the river to the safety of the Missouri shore. But peace was already hovering in the air above them. Outside friends, uniting with the distressed seconds, succeeded in harmonizing all difficulties, and the ridiculous affair was ended without the exchange of a blow.

But other complications followed, proving scarcely less farcical. Mr. William Butler had officiated during this *fiasco* as a special friend of Lincoln's. He was strongly favorable to a fight, and, immediately upon returning from the bloodless field, in his disgust at the result, wrote an account of the affair to the "Sangamo Journal," which again fired Shields's Milesian blood to fever heat. A challenge promptly followed, was as promptly accepted, and again Whiteside and Merriman became seconds for an "affair." The preliminaries were bloodthirsty enough, being submitted at 9 P. M. the same day, October 3, 1842, as follows: *Time* — sunrise the following morning; *Place* — Colonel Robert Allen's farm (a mile north of the State

House); *Weapons* — rifles; *Distance* — one hundred yards. It was stipulated that the parties were to stand with their right sides toward each other — the rifles to be held in both hands horizontally, and cocked, arms extended downwards, together with other details. These conditions were indignantly spurned by Shields's second as palpably unfair; both time and place were objected to, while it was claimed the position to be assumed gave Butler a decided advantage, he being left-handed. The seconds failed to find each other during the night, and consequently no meeting took place the following morning; as a result Butler decided the matter closed, thus ending the affair.

Yet, in one sense, it was not even yet done with, for now the two seconds, Merriman and Whiteside, promptly broke out. Whiteside's reply to Merriman's challenge on behalf of Butler had been so curt and abrupt in its language as to arouse that gentleman's animosity to the fighting-point. A letter, so expressed as to be tantamount to a challenge, was at once despatched to Whiteside, the bearer being Abraham Lincoln. He brought back a single line, reading: "I have to request that you meet me at the Planter's House, in the city of St. Louis on next Friday, where you will hear from me further." Other notes passed briskly back and forth, one man insisting on a meeting at St. Louis, the other equally strenuous for Louisiana, Missouri. In this way both parties managed to keep at a safe distance from each other, until finally the whole controversy died out, and from all these bellicose manifestations not a single blow was struck nor shot fired. However, the combined "affairs" added much to the gayety of the State at large; the newspapers of the day commented widely upon them, and thus they helped greatly to bring duelling into disrepute.

During the Mexican War two Illinoisans of prominence — Drs. Hope and Price — met on the field of honor near San Antonio, Texas, and exchanged shots, Price being badly wounded in the abdomen. But in Illinois proper, so far as known, there was but one other attempt to put into practice this barbarous method of settling differences, and that led directly to fixing in the State Constitution of 1848 the stringent clause relating to duelling. The two parties involved in this affair were O. C. Pratt, from Jo Daviess County, and his colleague in the House, Thompson Campbell. The difficulty between them arose over a political question, but intemperate language indulged in upon both sides soon brought forth mutual invitations to meet at St. Louis, and have the matter out according to the code. Alike willing, Campbell put up at the Planter's Hotel, and Pratt at the Monroe, while their respective seconds busied themselves with the preliminaries of conflict. Unfortunately for the cause of sport, their bloodthirsty purposes were not kept sufficiently secret; one Blennerhasset, a St. Louis alderman, made affidavit to the challenge, and late on the night preceding the proposed meeting both parties were arrested and placed under heavy bonds to keep the peace. It was even whispered about the State that this outcome was in accordance with a carefully prearranged scheme to attain a name for bravery, while running comparatively little danger of sustaining personal injury. The gentlemen involved returned to Illinois, and calmly resumed their interrupted legislative duties.

The Harris-Henry affair, which, however, was one entirely of words, occurred also about this time, being likewise political in its origin, but harked back to incidents in the Mexican War. During the heat of the election campaign of 1848, Dr. A. G. Henry delivered a speech at Beardstown, in which he charged Major Thomas L. Harris, candidate for Congress, with "skulking at the battle of Cerro Gordo; that he could prove this, and would repeat it to his face the following week." Harris at once took it up, demanding an interview with the Doctor. That gentleman's response to this seemingly natural request was: "I have no business with Major Harris, and do not desire a personal interview." Harris then demanded that he make good his Beardstown statement, to which the Doctor denied having spoken just as reported, and offered to refer the matter to a committee, but added that he must leave town that morning to keep his speaking appointments. Major Harris then proved by four good citizens, in a published card, that Henry had made the statement in the exact language given, whereupon he denounced him to the world as a liar, a scoundrel, and a coward — and that was the last of the trouble.

By the old law of the State, as already referred to, the penalty for duelling, if the issue proved fatal, was death, the same as in a case of murder, but for mere "affairs" not having fatal termination, it was disability for holding any office of trust, honor, or emolument, together with small fines. There was no restraint, and there had never been a conviction for the lesser offence, because the law was easily evaded by parties going outside the State to do their fighting. The Pratt-Campbell affair, however, was given wide publicity, and the legislators endeavored to find a remedy, framing an oath of office, and incorporating it in the constitution, so broad in terms of disfranchisement as to cover not only Illinois, but all the world besides. Of course no such jurisdiction was possible, yet in a moral way it had its appreciable effect. This form of oath passed in the convention by a vote of seventy-four to forty-four; and it may be remarked that both Pratt and Campbell refused to vote, while the still belligerent General Whiteside was numbered among the nays.

Since this passage, with the exception of parties coming into the State for the express purpose of settling difficulties arising elsewhere, no duels, or attempts at duels, have occurred in Illinois. Missourians frequently resorted to the small islands in the Mississippi for duelling purposes, and a number of notable meetings have thus occurred, the most famous probably being that between Governor Reynolds of Missouri and B. Gratz Brown. Duels between Illinois citizens, or in which former Illinoisans were involved, were fought, however, two occurring in California, with fatal results. Another meeting, or threatened meeting, was of sufficient importance to be given space in this review. It occurred under these circumstances: Mr. Bissell, who had been Colonel of the Second Illinois Volunteers in Mexico, was a new member in Congress, when Mr. Selden, of Virginia, in the course of a rather bitter attack on Northern courage, awarded the entire credit of saving the day at Buena Vista to a Mississippi regiment, of which Jefferson Davis had been Colonel. Mr. Bissell promptly took the matter up, claiming that special honor for the Second Kentucky, Second Illinois, and a portion of the First Illinois Regiments, and stating that at the moment referred to the Mississippi regiment was not within a mile and a half of the scene of action. Determined to crush any Northerner who ventured on such boldness, Mr. Davis at once challenged Mr. Bissell. To the surprise of the Southern fire-eaters, this challenge was immediately accepted. There was not a moment's hesitancy. The Illinoisan left the preliminaries for friends to arrange, stipulating only as to weapons and distance. These were common army muskets, loaded with a ball and three buckshot; the combatants to be stationed at forty paces, with liberty to advance to ten. This so evidently meant business, and a determination to fight to the death, that the fire-eaters were thoroughly amazed. Nevertheless, the meeting was definitely arranged for the following day, February 28, at an appointed rendezvous. But at a late hour that night friends of both parties got together and arranged a satisfactory compromise, by having inserted in Mr. Bissell's reply to Colonel Davis, in speaking of his command, the words, " but I am willing to award to them the credit due to their gallant and distinguished services in that battle."

This was held as full satisfaction to all concerned, and the matter was dropped.

As late as 1856 another Illinoisan was involved in a somewhat similar controversy, the party challenged being Senator Stephen A. Douglas, and his challenger General J. H. Lane, well known in Kansas for fighting propensities. The difficulty originated over a forged memorial, which Mr. Douglas, as chairman of the committee on Territories, denounced in severe terms. The newspapers took it up eagerly, and between them and hot-headed friends, General Lane, who was personally connected with the presentation of the memorial, was urged to hostile action. Under date of April, 1856, he addressed a letter to Douglas, asking for " such an explanation of your language as will remove all imputation upon the integrity of my action or motives in connection with that memorial." Again had a grievous mistake been made in judging a man. Douglas replied at once, and in scathing terms reiterating all the facts in the case, concluding: " My reply is, that there are no facts within my knowledge which can remove all imputation upon the integrity of your action or motives in connection with that memorial." There was nothing more said about a duel, "although General Lane, sixty days later, published an abusive card in the Washington papers, which injured its author more than it did Senator Douglas."

Thus in ridicule and disgrace, scourged alike by the law and by public sentiment, the *code duello* passed for ever from the State.

CHAPTER XXIV

SOME PECULIAR COLONIES

EVEN in the earliest days of American settlement colonies became a special feature of Illinois' growing population. The very first American settlement, that about Bellefontaine and New Design, was made by a party of neighbors migrating to the new land in a compact body, while many others, similarly bound together by ties of friendship or religious faith, continued to follow. In the more northern counties, when New England began adding her quota to the incoming throng, this community interest became especially noticeable. In Henry County alone, Andover, Wethersfield, Geneseo, Morristown, La Grange, and Bishop Hill all originated in well-organized colony movements, the emigrants coming generally in a body, and settling upon land previously selected for occupancy by an agent or committee. In many cases religious belief was the principle binding the colony members together, entire churches migrating to this new region, bringing their pastors with them, as was the case with the earlier settlers of Princeton.

Nor were foreign colonists altogether lacking from the earliest days. As far back as 1808, Samuel O'Melvany, an Irishman who soon became well known and popular the full length of the frontier, led a colony of Irish families down the Ohio River until they made permanent settlement near the present town of Elizabeth, in the county of Hardin. Here for many years they prospered as an organized colony, mutually helpful to each other, and through the compactness of their settlement remained largely immune from Indian attack, although surrounded by the fierce Shawnees.

Soon after the War of 1812, Morris Birbeck, an Englishman greatly interested in democratic institutions, paid an extended visit to Illinois, seeking a spot for the location of a selected colony of his own countrymen. While travelling through this section he contributed freely to English newspapers, and being a man of keen observation and scholarly attainments, these letters were widely read and commented upon abroad. Not long after, he and George Flower, both being men of independent wealth, the latter imbued deeply with the community idea then prevalent among religious enthusiasts in the old country, who dreamed of an ideal State in the wilderness, brought out a large colony from England. Several hundred families, representing almost every industrial pursuit, were included in this body, which located within the present limits of Edwards County. Mr. Flower, with his more direct followers, established the town of Albion, now the county seat, where the community idea was put into successful operation, and continued to flourish for some years. About a mile west of this site, Mr. Birbeck established another town, called Wannock, which, however, proved a failure. Considerable rivalry existed between the two places for several years, and as, besides the leaders, there was much wealth and refinement in both colonies, no little attention was paid to social matters. Mr. Flower, unfortunately for the future development of his colony along the lines originally projected, lost his fortune by the breaking of the United States Bank, and soon after removed to Mt. Vernon, Indiana. Several of his descendants yet continue to reside in Edwards County. Mr. Birbeck became Secretary of State under Governor Coles, and was very prominent in the fight against slavery. He was drowned in a bayou of the Wabash, called Fox River, which was swollen by rain. Accompanied only by his son, while on his way home from New Harmony, Indiana (then in charge of the famous Robert Owen communists), where they had been visiting, he attempted to cross the stream, but the rapid current swept the horses aside into deep water, and both horses and Mr. Birbeck perished. His son barely escaped the same fate. It may be possible that in Albion to-day a few of the original settlers yet reside ; certain it is their descendants are quite numerous throughout Edwards County.

Some time about 1815, two German families, named Markee and Germain, first settled in a deep gorge of the Mississippi bluff, in St. Clair County, which soon became known throughout the surrounding region as Dutch Hollow. These two families became a nucleus for the present large German population of St. Clair and the counties adjoining. Another English colony, but Roman Catholic, and bringing their own priest with them, settled as early as 1817 in Prairie du Long Creek, Monroe County. This company was composed of from fifteen to twenty families, originally from Lancaster, the names of the founders being Thomas Winstantly, Bamber, Threlfall, and Newsham. They prospered, and became a thrifty settlement. A third English colony settled in Green County in 1820, and were successful. In 1819, Ferdinand Ernst, who was a gentleman of wealth and literary taste, having his home in the kingdom of Hanover, brought to Vandalia, then just selected as the State capital, a thrifty German colony of about thirty families. Later, in 1822, Bernard Steiner settled a small Swiss community, consisting originally of ten families, in the southeastern part of St. Clair County. Their location was on a beautiful and commanding eminence soon known as Dutch Hill. Others of their race followed, and it became a large and influential settlement.

But the two colony schemes of most interest, whether from a religious or a communistic point of view, working out their destinies in Illinois, were those at Bishop Hill, in Henry County, and the settlement of the Icarians at Nauvoo. The founder of the former colony was Eric Jansen, a man of about forty years of age, a native of Sweden. Although of strong religious faith, he abjured the Lutheran Church, which exercised theological domination in his native land, and by precept and preaching gathered about him some eleven hundred adherents to his independent belief. Controversy and persecution followed, during which Jansen and many of his followers suffered imprisonment and other hardships. For more than three years this unequal struggle for liberty of conscience continued, but the opposition was too strong to be overcome, and a decision was finally reached to emigrate in a body to America. One of the principal tenets of their religion was that all things should be in common, so that no poor should go unprovided for, and none suffer from lack of means. Among the earliest converts to this belief were Messrs. Hedine and Olsen, both men of wealth, who gave freely to aid the needy.

The ordinary authorities refusing passports, the King was appealed to in person, and he permitted them to depart from the country. Under this authority, eleven hundred people set sail from Sweden in the Summer of 1846, reached New York in October of the same year, and a month later some seven hundred of them arrived at Bishop Hill, in this State, for settlement. About four hundred of the original colonists shifted to other locations on the route, many of these latter proving impostors, who had joined the colony for no higher purpose than to get their passages paid to America.

Mr. Jansen, who had come in advance of these others, had been compelled to escape from Sweden into Norway, leaving that country under an assumed name. At New York he met his people, and guided them to the location already selected for settlement. Olof Olsen, a brother of the man of wealth already mentioned, had been the *avant-courrier* of these colonists, selecting the spot for their occupancy. While here on his first visit of exploration, he purchased a farm at the east end of Red Oak Grove, this becoming the nucleus for those to follow. The colonists first settled along the south bank of South Edward Creek, a small, sluggish stream. The site was a beautiful one, sparsely covered with a small growth of oaks. Possessing neither material for building, nor means to purchase any, they were content to erect tents and coverings of brush for immediate protection. These soon proving inadequate, caves were dug in the hill-side, wherein many of the colonists, with their families, managed to pass their first Winter in America. These caves were where the village park is now laid out. The hardships following such conditions of life proved greater than many of the members had resolution to endure. Some stole away singly, others in little squads, leaving the stronger and more resolute to fight it out to the end.

These were, indeed, in most lamentable stress. The journey had nearly exhausted the funds of the society, and they possessed no credit. Yet one thing was certain, by some means provisions for a year must be secured, or the entire company was doomed. Not a man among them, except a sailor who had picked up a few words, could speak any English, but John Olsen, who seemingly was gifted with the faculty of sign language, undertook to provide the necessary food, and succeeded tolerably well while money lasted. After that the struggle was truly desperate, yet was bravely lived through until Spring brought sufficient amounts from Europe to relieve their more pressing needs.

Little by little the mud caves gave way to houses laboriously constructed of unbaked brick, with an occasional small frame structure. These were all very inferior ; but in 1849 a four-story brick house was erected, about one hundred feet in length and forty-five in width. The basement of this building was intended for a general dining-room, while the upper portion was arranged into apartments for families. In 1851 this structure was extended another hundred feet, and is still occupied by newcomers in the community who are unable to provide their separate homes. A large frame building, the upper part being designed for a church, while the basement was partitioned off for families, was erected as early as 1849, the religious enthusiasm of the colonists leading them to prepare a house of worship even before securing their own personal comfort. This building still stands, and is used for the purposes for which it was originally erected.

An English school was established here in January, 1847, a Presbyterian minister, Rev. Mr. Talbot, teaching a class of thirty-five in a mud cave. Many lines of industry were followed by the colonists, much attention being given to orchards and the cultivation of small fruits, but with indifferent success. A brewery for the manufacture of small beer, a favorite beverage of the Swedes, was early started, and by 1851 a commodious brick building for this purpose was erected. A grist-mill on a small scale was soon in operation on Edwards Creek, and two sawmills soon followed upon the banks of the same stream. A steam grist-mill was commenced as early as 1849. Flax was the staple crop for several years, which was principally woven into linen of various grades, the coarsest being used for carpeting. Up to 1857, after which little was manufactured for sale, the aggregate amount of linen sold was 130,309 yards ; of carpeting, 22,569 yards. Some of this linen was quite fine, but the coarser kinds proved to be most in demand ; large quantities were peddled from house to house through the surrounding districts. The necessary spinning and weaving were performed almost entirely by the women, children doing the spooning. In early years, looms being scarce, the work was kept running night and day.

The correct conduct of these people, the purity of their lives, and their industry, soon won the respect of their immediate neighbors, yet they suffered greatly from the strange climate and the exposure of those earlier years. Great numbers sickened and died; mortality among the children was fearful. During the cholera scourge of 1849–52, men would go to their work in the morning in good health, and lie dead before sundown. This cause, coupled with desertion, at one time reduced the colony to four hundred and fourteen souls, but this remnant hung on with grim courage. In their pathetic struggle against want and death, in their frugality and industry, in their unselfish efforts to serve each other, in the vitality of their faith, during these years of poverty and sickness and death, they exhibited a fortitude almost unequalled in the history of Illinois settlement.

At this time, and up to the year 1860, everything the colony possessed was held in common. Families lived apart, generally in substantial brick buildings, subdivided so as to give separate accommodation to from eight to twenty families each; many of these buildings are yet standing and occupied. But all worked together, and at meal-time partook of the same food in the huge dining-rooms. Every member was required to perform a certain amount of labor, and, after receiving sufficient clothing and food from the products, all that remained was used for the purchase of more land, or the erection of additional buildings. Drones, however, early began to appear in this line of industry, and after only fourteen years of effort, it became clear that the beautiful theories of Mr. Jansen must fail in practical life, and the colony became divided.

Two parties formed, one known as the Johnson (Jansen) party, the other rallying under the leadership of Olsen. The former was the more numerous, and in the division of property which followed obtained about two-thirds of the land and personalty. No serious difficulties arose over this division, and the individual affairs of the colony continued undisturbed, but a year later the Johnson party made another step toward the final disruption of the commune by making an individual distribution of all their farm and town possessions. This was accomplished as follows. To every person, male or female, who had then attained the age of thirty-five years, a full share of all lands, timber and town lots, and personal property was given. A full share consisted of twenty-two acres of land, one timber lot, — nearly two acres, — one town lot, and an equal part in all barns, horses, cattle, hogs, sheep, farming implements, and household utensils. All under that age received a share corresponding in amount and value to the age of the individual, no discrimination being shown between the sexes. The smallest share was about eight acres, the other property in proportion. Thus a man over thirty-five, having a wife of that age, and several children, would receive many acres of land, and considerable property to manage. He held that of the wife and children simply in trust, the deeds to all the property being made in the name of the family head. This division is still maintained, and its wisdom was long ago demonstrated by results. The Olsen party meantime continued to cling to the old colony system, but, in little less than a year, they also were convinced of its weakness, and divided their property on the same basis with the others. Their shares, however, were not quite so large.

One tragedy came into this peaceful colony life to mar the fraternity marking its years of existence, and that cost the life of its founder, Eric Jansen. In the Fall of 1848, an adventurer named Root, the son of a wealthy family of Stockholm, made his appearance at Bishop Hill. Expressing a desire to become one of the fraternity, he was admitted without opposition. Soon afterwards he contracted marriage with a cousin of Eric Jansen, which was agreed to under a special restriction, that if Root ever decided to desert the colony, he should go alone, leaving his wife to the full enjoyment of her colony rights. Root proved an utterly worthless fellow, constitutionally opposed to labor of

RUINS OF ICARIAN BREWERY AT NAUVOO

COLONY HOUSE AT BISHOP HILL

any kind, and desiring nothing but to roam the woods with his gun. His treatment of his wife was tyrannical, and when he finally decided to leave, she was not regretful of the separation. Several months later, however, and soon after his wife had given birth to a son, Root reappeared, and insisted upon her leaving the colony with him. This the woman did not desire to do, and was sustained in her decision by Jansen, whom the infuriated husband threatened with a drawn bowie-knife.

Unable to persuade, Root determined to resort to force. Obtaining the services of a young man named Stanley, who belonged at Cambridge, he stationed him with a horse and buggy near town, and, while the community were at dinner, succeeded in forcing the woman to accompany him, and drove rapidly away. Pursuit was prompt, and Root and Stanley were overtaken within two miles; but being heavily armed, they stood off the brethren for some time, until finally Stanley surrendered, and Root yielded up his wife to her friends. Legal proceedings followed, during which Mrs. Root was conducted to Cambridge under the custody of the sheriff. Here Root stole her the second time, driving across country to Rock Island, and taking her to Chicago, where she was later recovered by the colonists and safely returned to Bishop Hill. At the May term of court in 1850, Root and Jansen met at the court-house in Cambridge, and just as the court adjourned for dinner, the former shot the latter, who expired in a few hours. Root was tried for murder, received a penitentiary sentence, and died shortly after its expiration. The old buildings at Bishop Hill remain, and many of the old customs, to tell the story of a beautiful dream of fraternity which was not practical enough to survive the continued strain of experiment.

Soon after the last remnant of Mormon population disappeared from Nauvoo on their long journey to Salt Lake, there appeared on that historic spot the advance agents of a new colony, seeking opportunity to exploit other peculiar theories of social life in this far western country. Nauvoo, in its pathetic desolation, with empty buildings awaiting occupancy, and property held cheaply, was apparently an ideal site for such an experiment, and the agents returned hastily down the river to the waiting colonists at New Orleans, with a favorable report, and an option on the land. These new arrivals were the Icarians, a considerable body of communists, organized in France, under the leadership of Etienne Cabet, the brilliant son of a cooper of Dijon, then fifty-one years of age. The foundations of his dream of absolute equality, as typified in a democratic republic to be called Icaria, were laid as early as 1830, and by 1847 four hundred thousand names were reported as signed to the Social Compact. A year later, having obtained a large tract of land in Texas, an *avant-garde* of sixty-nine chosen men sailed from France to take formal possession. Others followed, but, from various causes, more particularly the nature of the country and the prevalence of malarial fever, this first colonization was an utter failure, so that when, in 1849, Cabet reached New Orleans and took personal command of the entire force,—then numbering five hundred, including many women and children,— agents were despatched up the Mississippi seeking a more suitable location for permanent settlement.

In March, 1849, the remnant of the colony, still firm in the belief in their dream, began their journey up the river. It proved a fearful one. Cholera broke out and many died. On reaching Warsaw, twenty miles below Nauvoo, ice blocked further passage northward by steamer, and they were compelled to tramp the remainder of the way knee-deep in snow and slush, carrying children and sick as best they could. At Nauvoo they found some comfort, in the houses still standing as the banished Mormons had left them, yet much suffering remained. The climate was severe, water unwholesome, food costly, indeed nearly impossible to obtain at any price. For months they subsisted almost entirely upon beans. But in the midst of all this hardship the spirit of the Icarians remained unbroken. Slowly they built their little commonwealth, a mere child's toy compared to the stately city of their leader's enthusiastic plan, yet ruled by the same laws, controlled by the same ideals, which had made them exiles. Six directors, elected annually, controlled the administration ; the laws were made by a general assembly including all men over twenty. Cabet was elected president year after year, yet exercised little authority, as the title was merely one of honor.

The colony was purely communistic, the members putting their every possession, even to loved books and heirlooms, into the common fund. Furniture, tools, and cooking utensils were equally divided; tasks and hours of labor were so arranged as to be evenly proportioned. Homes were indeed separate, each family occupying its own house, but the colony school reared the children in communion, and removed them as far as practicable from all home-making influences. All ate at one common table, and in every way possible individualism was crowded into the background, and treated as unworthy.

And for a while this strange community on the Nauvoo Bluffs flourished and increased. It became fairly prosperous. By 1855 they had, with vast industry and self-denial, erected mills and workshops ; their farms were well tilled ; their school ranked among the very best in the infant State. A well-selected library of choicest literature had been established, containing over six thousand volumes, while an orchestra, well organized and trained, was the marvel of the neighbors. The colony even published for some time a weekly magazine, which won a wide circulation both in this country and in Europe, being printed in three different languages. New members were constantly arriving, and the later years saw a higher grade of newcomers — men and women of gentle birth and refined culture. Katharine Holland Brown — to whom acknowledgment is made for the facts of this connected story — in her sympathetic article in "Harper's Magazine," speaks of several accomplished musicians ; two painters of wide reputation; a famous civil engineer ; a physician who had stood at the head of his profession in Vienna ; Dadant, the authority on bee-culture ; Piquenard, afterward architect of the capitol buildings of both Iowa and Illinois ; Vallet, the sociologist ; and Von Gauvain, nobleman, officer, and teacher. Surely here was the foundation for a noble state, and Icaria's prospects for the future were bright with promise.

Yet with this very moment of highest possibilities the fatal step was taken which led direct to ruin, and Cabet, the founder, that remarkable man whose mind had dreamt the dream of this realization, was himself the cause of failure, even as he had been the inspiration for success. Late in 1855 he seemingly became tired of being president only in name, and made an ineffectual effort to have the constitution of the colony so revised as to give him almost dictatorial powers. This was so utterly opposed not only to the original purpose of the colony but to Cabet's previously avowed principles, that for a brief while the astonished commune remained bewildered. Then the members rose to the issue, every man taking either one side or the other in the ensuing contest, until the entire town was rent into two bitterly hostile camps, but the majority opposing the new project.

The election which soon followed deposed Cabet entirely, but, trusting to the veneration in which he had long been held by his followers, he appealed personally to the assembled voters, in a dramatic scene, withdrew his demands for new powers, and the people again conferred upon him the title of president. A brief peace followed, but in August the smouldering flames burst forth anew, when Cabet, again becoming impatient for power, commanded his old officials to refuse to vacate their positions to those who had been newly elected. The new directors were, however, put in by force, the majority of the communists rallying about them, and immediately all of Cabet's loyal followers in the colony dropped their tools, and refused to work any longer. It was a strike almost modern in the form as well as the way in which it was carried on. Both parties were extremely foolish in their anger and vindictiveness. They would not speak on the street, and turned their backs in passing. Those of the opposing party so arranged their tables in the long dining-hall as not to face Cabet while eating, while even the children took up the quarrel in the commune school.

Neither side would yield an inch to the other, while, after several weeks of this enforced idleness, the majority party seized the storehouses, declaring that those who would not work should not eat. For a while the Cabetists held firm, but the suffering of the women and children finally drove them to reluctant submission. This was made as humiliating as possible, Cabet and his followers being contemptuously lined up before the steps of the phalanstery to receive their dole in silence. As they turned away, one of the number, angered by a sneer, flung his bread upon the ground, and trampled it into the dirt. The others followed his actions to a man, cursing the majority as they did so. No blood was shed, but after this occurrence any reconciliation between the factions was manifestly impossible.

The majority met in secret council, burned their copies of Cabet's *Icaria*, which up to this period had been their creed; then a legal division of the community property was decided upon, and Cabet by vote expelled from the commune. When he finally left Nauvoo in November, one hundred and eighty disciples accompanied him into exile, while eight hundred remained behind. A week later he was smitten with apoplexy while in St. Louis, and died suddenly. His immediate followers located six miles below that city, prospered for a while as a community, but later broke up and scattered. The others, the dominant majority, had no better fate awaiting them. Little by little they drifted away from fateful Nauvoo, which has witnessed so many high hopes wither and die, to a tract of land owned by the commune in Iowa. Here their story was one of splendid effort, but utter failure. From the start all was drudgery, their lives harsh and dull ; yet they sought earnestly to attain to that high ideal of socialism which had originally brought them across the seas. By 1875 they reached the height of their prosperity, and then a second division occurred, this time the younger members pitting themselves against the elder. Once more the colony was rent asunder, most of the younger people drifting to California, the others still clinging in pathetic loyalty to their old Icaria. Year by year they became fewer, less enthusiastic, seeking no longer to win new recruits to their theories of life. They had no cause left to champion, and the end was not far off. By 1895 the last vestige of the great Icarian movement had perished. As the writer above quoted aptly says, " Perhaps no other reform has so stirred a continent at its beginning, only to sink without a ripple at its end."

CHAPTER XXV

HUMORS OF THE FRONTIER

FRONTIER humor is quite apt to prove of the boisterous kind, finding its more common expression in rude practical joking and horse-play. The virtues of the border are Homeric, the sports rough, the play coarse and somewhat animal. Refinement seldom dwells between log walls, and those who invade new lands, fronting daily peril, and breasting the hardships of a wilderness they must conquer, have little time to waste on the small amenities of life. They meet things in the rough, and the seriousness of their environment inevitably stamps itself on countenance and manner. In those rare times when neighbors congregated together, border sports were entered upon with zest, wrestling, rifle-shooting, or horse-racing being the chosen order of the day, and proud indeed was the sturdy pioneer who bore home with him some memento of prowess from such hard-fought fields. These were likewise the sports of the volunteer soldiery, and every house-raising, or gathering of neighbors for any purpose, was certain to witness some test of physical strength.

Yet in numerous ways, along the rather devious course of Illinois history, there crops out an innate sense of humor, sufficient to awaken smiles even now as we contemplate those happenings of the long ago. Historians are not often humorists, yet the pages of those who have told in all seriousness the earlier story of the State have sketched here and there scenes, incidents, and characteristics which tend to relieve the sombreness of border struggle, reminding us anew that the names we read belonged to living men, as human in their time as are we to-day. Politics and political controversy, always intensely interesting in a new land, furnish many glimpses of those strenuous times. Political campaigns were intensely personal, the questions of public policy involved, if any there were, being relegated to the background, while voters selected their choice for office from personal like or dislike of the candidate. Whiskey likewise figured largely in results, and was extremely conspicuous in each campaign. Ford tells us gravely that in the political battle of 1830 William Kinney, a Baptist preacher, who was a candidate for Governor, made his campaign with a Bible in one pocket and a bottle of liquor in the other. Thus armed, he was prepared for any emergency. Treating by candidates for office was in those days an indispensable element of success. In some sections the seeking politicians would hire all the groceries at the county seats, and, on certain days, serve liquor free to all who came. To such places the voters would swarm, riding in from their distant clearings to hear the news, and frequently before night would be drunken enough to engage in many a rough-and-tumble fight. If candidates were present, as was usually the case, speeches were certain to be made, the ambitious orators mounting on convenient wagons, logs, or tree trunks, advocating at length, and with much fervid eloquence, their claims to office. The "vital questions of the day" discussed at such backwoods meetings were seldom measures, but generally men, and the speeches consisted in bitter personal arraignment of opponents. The more intemperate the language employed, the better pleased were the crowd, the greater the influence of the orator. When this was over, inflamed by passion and liquor, the gathering would disperse on their horses, galloping through the town, reeling, huzzahing, and yelling for their favorite, or groaning, cursing, and berating the opposition.

In early political contests, those who were known as the

old pioneers were very much in evidence. Having been first upon the ground, they claimed peculiar privileges for themselves, which were usually granted. This found illustration in other matters as well. Judge Blackwell relates a professional call which one of this class once paid to him. In the older days, bee-trees were held as common property, the finder cutting one down and appropriating the honey, irrespective of boundary lines. As settlements grew, however, this rather lawless privilege had to be curtailed, and consequently this particular pioneer was being proceeded against for trespass by a neighbor whose property had been thus tampered with. Blackwell told him the law, and advised an attempt at compromise, but the indignant old fellow stomped out of the office, declaring, "This country is getting too damned civilized for me; I'll make tracks fer Oregon, where the old pioneer kin git justice." Unfortunately, in politics, as in much else, ignorance and prejudice largely ruled this class, and they bitterly opposed every public policy which tended toward a betterment of conditions; nor were their immediate descendants much improvement over the original stock. As a rule, they were prone to brawling, loud-mouthed, and quarrelsome. They arrayed themselves conspicuously in buckskin breeches, leather moccasins, raccoon caps, and red hunting-shirts belted at the waist, in which they carried a huge knife, which gave them the popular name of "butcher boys." Profane and rough when in liquor, they would swagger through a crowd, loudly proclaiming themselves "half-horse, half-alligator," and seeking to provoke a quarrel.

Such citizens were not likely to vote into office a very high grade of manhood, and as a result, many of the earlier legislators were little worthy of honor. The interests of the people received slight consideration, while all manner of combinations were formed for the parcelling out of fat jobs for personal benefit. Governor Ford describes Samuel Crozier,

Senator from Randolph, as "a remarkable example of pure, kind, and simple-hearted honesty"; then he tells us that after serving two sessions, and after he had been bought and sold a hundred times without even knowing it, the old Senator said that he "really did believe that some intrigue had been going on." From top to bottom, corruption was the rule. And in the elections the "butcher boys" held for a long while the balance of power throughout the settlements. When the knife became finally tabooed as an article of dress, the same class of voters held on in other forms. They became known as "the barefooted boys," the "flat-footed boys," or the "huge-pawed boys," names with which they were greatly tickled; and their influence continued so long as physical force dominated the polls.

In the courts, the judges, even those of the Supreme bench, were not appointed because of any superior legal acumen. Indeed, few possessed even a rudimentary knowledge of the law, and some were not, like Cæsar's wife, above suspicion. For instance, Foster, who was named as one of the Supreme judges, resigned within a year. He was, in the language of Ford,—

> "Almost a total stranger in the country. He was a great rascal, but no one knew it then, he having been a citizen of the State only for about three weeks before he was elected. He was no lawyer, never having either studied or practised law; but a man of winning, polished manners, and withal a gentlemanly swindler from some part of Virginia. He was believed to be a clever fellow in the American sense of that phrase, and a good-hearted soul. He was assigned to hold courts on the circuit of the Wabash; but, being fearful of exposing his utter incompetency, he never went near any of them. In the course of one year he resigned his high office, but took care to pocket his salary, and then removed out of the State."

Governor Reynolds tells, with considerable humor, how he chanced to be selected as a member of that same exalted tribunal. At the time he resided at Cahokia, and had no intention of visiting the session of the legislature, which was disposing of so many fat offices while first organizing the State government. He wanted nothing, and had no axe to grind for anyone else. But, being urged by friends, he went along with them on a visit to Kaskaskia. Upon arrival they found much excitement and commotion at the capital, incident to the selection of the new State officials. A few days later, unsolicited, he was being strongly urged to become a candidate for Supreme Judge. The request was a surprise, but at last consenting, he was immediately chosen. His sole experience in law, as he put it, was four years' practice of "commerce in land." "I speculated, sold land, and bought two stores of dry-goods, amounting to $10,000." His first term of court was to him a "strange and novel business." This chanced to be held at Covington, Washington County, in the midst of many old acquaintances, some of whom had been comrades in the Rangers. These lads failed utterly to appreciate his present dignity. The sheriff, unmindful of the exaltation of his old companion in arms, made proclamation of the fact of his presence without rising from the rude bench which he occupied astride, saying in familiar tones, "Boys, the Court is now open; John is on the bench."

Even the religious gatherings of the frontier were often tinged with humor and afflicted by the practical joke. Camp-meetings were not infrequently resorted to by the younger people as a species of enjoyable picnic. An early historian tells of a happening, in which he may have been concerned, ludicrous enough to deserve mention. A party of fervent Methodists, under the preaching of their class leaders, were in the midst of a protracted meeting in one of the small cabins of the settlement. The subject under consideration was the presence of Satan in their midst. It was night, and with only a single candle to light them, they were grouped in the one room, the only window being open. Through this aperture some boys without suddenly flung a black calf, which, bleating furiously, overturned the candle, and scattered the assembled worshippers. These fled, firmly believing they had been visited in person by His Satanic Majesty.

In those days, little of ceremony was ever considered necessary. The courts were held in log houses, or in the bar-rooms of taverns, fitted up temporarily for the purpose. The decision of all questions, law as well as fact, was commonly left with the juries, and the law was oftentimes very rudely administered. Brown, to illustrate the size of St. Clair County, quotes a case occurring before a court at Cahokia to recover the value of a cow. Judgment was rendered for sixteen dollars, and the case was appealed. The adverse party, with his witnesses, resided at Prairie du Chien, in what is now Wisconsin, four hundred miles away. The sheriff, who chanced to be also an Indian trader, having received a summons for the party and subpœnas for the witnesses, fitted out a boat with a suitable stock of goods for the Indian trade, and started up the river. Having served his papers on the greater part of the inhabitants of Prairie du Chien, he made his return, charging mileage and service for each, as he had a legal right to do; his costs, and the costs of the suit, are said to have exceeded nine hundred dollars. Whether ever collected or not, history does not record, but it is safe to say the sheriff lost no money. Governor Reynolds relates a case occurring in the court of Prairie du Rocher, conducted against a negro who was charged with the "murder" of a hog. The case was really one of malicious mischief, for wantonly destroying a useful animal, but in the absence of a prosecuting attorney, the grand jury, groping about blindly in the law books furnished them, met with the precedent of an indictment for murder, and promptly applied it to the case in hand. It may be possible that righteous judgment was accorded the unfortunate colored brother under these circumstances, but he ran a risk not pleasant to contemplate.

Ford, in referring to the disinclination of judges unlearned in the law to instruct juries in their courts, mentions one who would always rub his head and the side of his face with his hand, as if perplexed, and say, "Why, gentlemen, the jury understand the case; they need no instructions; no doubt they will do justice between the parties." This same judge presided at a time when a fellow named Green was convicted of murder, and it became his unpleasant duty to pronounce sentence of death on the prisoner. He called the culprit before him, and said: "Mr. Green, the jury in their verdict say you are guilty of murder, and the law says you are to be hung. Now, I want you, and all your friends down on Indian Creek, to know that it is not I who condemns you, but it is the jury and the law. Mr. Green, the law allows you time for preparation, and so the Court wants to know what time you would like to be hung." To this kind request the prisoner replied, "May it please the Court, I am ready at any time; those who kill the body have no power to kill the soul; my preparation is made, and I am ready to suffer at any time the Court may appoint." The judge then said, "Mr. Green, you must know that it is a very serious matter to be hung; it can't happen to a man more than once in his life, and you had better take all the time you can get; the Court will give you until this day four weeks. Mr. Clerk, look at the almanac, and see whether this day four weeks comes on Sunday." The clerk looked as directed, and reported that that day four weeks came on Thursday. The judge then said, "Mr. Green, the Court gives you until this day four weeks, at which time you are to be hung."

The case was prosecuted by James Turney, then attorney-general of the State, who here interposed, and said: "May it please the Court, on solemn occasions like the present, when the life of a human being is to be sentenced away for crime, by an earthly tribunal, it is usual and proper for courts to pronounce a formal sentence, in which the leading features of the crime shall be brought to the recollection of the prisoner, a sense of his guilt impressed upon his conscience, and in which the prisoner should be duly exhorted to repentance, and warned against the judgment in a world to come." To this the judge replied: "O Mr. Turney, Mr. Green understands the whole matter as well as if I had preached to him a month. He knows he 's got to be hung this day four weeks. You understand it in that way, Mr. Green, don't you?" "Yes," returned the prisoner; upon which the judge ordered him to be remanded to jail, and the court was adjourned.

It is reported, however, that one, at least, of these judges of early days was very fond of instructing juries, and very prolix and positive in his mode of doing so. Being extremely ambitious to exhibit his learning, on one occasion he fairly outdid himself, but for some reason the jury failed to agree upon a verdict. Called back into the court-room, the judge indignantly questioned them as to the cause of their difficulty, whereupon the foreman answered with great simplicity and honesty, "Why, judge, this 'ere is the difficulty. The jury want to know whether that 'ar what you told us, whin we furst went out, was raly the law 'er whether it was only jist your notion." The judge, it is said, promptly and emphatically informed him that it "raly" was the law, and a verdict was found accordingly.

The militia was the cause of much humor throughout the early days of the Illinois country. Yet, as we read now of the requirements, it would seem to have been no laughing matter. All free white residents of the State, between eighteen and forty-five, were held as active members, and duly enrolled. They were compelled to provide themselves with musket and bayonet, canteen, two spare flints, cartridge-box to contain not less than twenty-four cartridges, with powder and ball suited to the bore of their gun. To be an officer was an expensive luxury, but as this was considered a stepping-stone to political preferment, the expense was probably not often wasted. Companies had to muster four times yearly, battalions once each year, and regiments as often. Uniformity in dress was not always insisted upon, and the ragged lines were often strangely and wonderfully attired. But the officers seldom failed to be generously arrayed, the contrast between their magnificent display of gilt braid and the tatterdemalion outfitting of their men being painfully apparent. The military titles of general, colonel, and major, which graced so many public men at this period and later, were usually of militia origin, and possessed little significance. Honors were easy however, and strutting general and dazzling colonel were jocularly hailed as "Joe" or "Sam," by the good-natured backwoodsmen whom they temporarily commanded. The training days were looked forward to as a time of frolic and relaxation, of gossip and political wire-pulling. Much horse-play was indulged in, and generally an abundance of liquor was in evidence. Yet these musters were no light affairs, when one considers the distance many were compelled to travel to attend, and the fines imposed upon absentees. For failure to be present, fines were assessed by court-martial — for privates, fifty cents to one dollar and fifty cents, and so on up the line to two hundred dollars for commanders of divisions. Fathers were held liable for fines imposed on minor sons, guardians for their wards, masters for their apprentices. Quakers, Dunkards, and other religious persons conscientiously scrupulous against bearing arms, were relieved by paying three dollars each.

In the early days the need of militia organization was so apparent, and the muster had so many features of enjoyment and sport connected with it, as to be almost popular, but in later years it became abhorred. Shafts of wit and ridicule finally drove the old system from the State; some of the means used to attain this end may be gleaned from a speech made by Abraham Lincoln, in review of those times. He said :

"A number of years ago the militia laws of this State required that the militia should train at stated intervals. These trainings became a great bore to the people, and every person nearly was for putting them down; but the law required them to train, and they could not get it repealed. So they tried another way, and that was to burlesque them. And hence they elected old Tim Langwell, the greatest drunkard and blackguard, for Colonel, over the best men in the country. But this did not succeed altogether. So they raised a company, and elected Gordon Abrams as Commander. He was dressed in peculiar style, one part of his pants was of one color and material, and the other different. He wore a pasteboard cap about six feet long, resembling an inverted ox-yoke. The shanks of his spurs were about eight inches long, with rowels about the circumference of common saucers. He carried a sword made of pine wood nine feet long. They also had rules and regulations, one of which was, 'That no officer should wear more than twenty pounds of codfish for epaulets, nor more than thirty pounds of Bologna sausage for a sash'; and on the banner were borne aloft these words: 'We 'll fight till we run, and run till we die.' This succeeded to a demonstration. They were the last company that trained in Springfield."

Along about 1836 Western humor turned to money-making, and as subsequently explained, the joke was plainly on the East. It culminated in the great town-lot craze, which spread like wildfire the full length and breadth of Illinois. Chicago started the boom, and so profited by the early experiment that in a year or two it changed from a village of a few houses to an ambitious city of several thousand inhabitants. The story of the sudden fortunes made there during this rise in land values excited at first

On returning, the same order of procession was followed. The feasting and dancing lasted for days, at the end of which the whole company were so exhausted as to be unfit for their ordinary duties.

CHAPTER XXVI

SOME NOTABLE BORDER CHARACTERS

ONE tendency of frontier life is to develop into more vivid contrast the strong and weak points of character. The restraints of civilization do not retard, nor greatly conceal, the exhibition of peculiarities, and rugged natures stand forth unpolished. Sham is despised, frankness admired, and no reason exists why anyone should appear other than he really is. The Illinois country was rich in this respect, and many a true man and noble woman bore portion in those rough years of development, stamping their own individualities forever on the character of the State, and sending the thread of their personal influence down to future generations. Only very few of these can find mention here, nor can such hasty sketches ever do slightest justice even to those few. All to be hoped is, that through such dim pictures the reader may discern real men and women, and realize that history in its better purpose is but a record of individual ideals and labor. These old-time Illinoisans lived and hoped, worked, loved, sorrowed, and passed away, separate and peculiar entities, even as we are now, and their lives were merged into the vaster life of the State we love.

In the earlier history the memory of three women, who were in few ways similar, arises into peculiar prominence, each occupying a niche entirely her own, but all alike worthy of reverence for true womanliness. These three were Mme. Le Comte, Mrs. John Edgar, and Mrs. Robert Morrison, residents of Kaskaskia. They left indelible impress on the period of their existence, and a brief record of their lives has been preserved in Davidson and Stuvé's History of the

State, gathered from the personal recollections of Governor Reynolds and others.

Mme. Le Comte was born of French parents at the old trading-station on the St. Joseph River, in Michigan, about the year 1734. Her maiden name has not been preserved, nor do we possess any details relating to her earlier life or education. Undoubtedly, the latter was very slight, probably no more than the merest rudiments picked up from the station priest, although she later moved in the highest society of Kaskaskia, and had every appearance of refinement and gentility. Her early home was in the midst of the Pottawattomie Indians, and from that date until the day of her death she remained both friend and adviser to the red tribes of Illinois. She became proficient in their languages, and gained a deep insight into their native character, exercising a remarkable influence over them. She was married at Mackinaw to a fur trader whose name was either St. Ange or Pelate, and moved to Chicago, later going down the Illinois and Mississippi Rivers to Cahokia. Here, her husband dying, she was married to M. Le Comte, a Canadian having some property. From this marriage sprang one of the largest and most influential French families in the early Illinois country. Much later in life, after the death of Le Comte, she contracted a third marriage, this time with that Thomas Brady known in border history for his unfortunate marauding expedition against Fort St. Joseph in 1778.

Mme. Le Comte, for so she was called throughout the Illinois country to the day of her death, was in many respects a typical French woman of the frontier, but of the highest grade. She was possessed of an iron constitution, a strong mind, and dauntless courage. In person she was remarkably attractive, her manner winning, possessing all the geniality of the French nature. She travelled much in frontier fashion, and underwent great exposure to inclemency of weather, yet scarcely knew what sickness meant.

Accustomed to it from childhood, she lived a hardy and frugal life. Among the Indians her influence was so remarkable as to be almost unique in border history. No official in French authority ever wielded such power for good or ill over the savages of the Illinois as did this rosy-cheeked, black-eyed Frenchwoman. And she used this power to good account for the benefit of the settlements. Clearly as this was proven previously, it became more and more evident after the conquest by Clark. That occurrence led to a breach between the Illinois French and their Indian neighbors, which was never healed — the former sided with the Americans, while the latter ranged themselves unreservedly upon the British side. The long peace of years was broken, and many a meditated attack on Cahokia did Mme. Le Comte frustrate by rare sagacity and friendly counsel. It is said, that so infatuated with her were the savages, they would invariably advise her of their intended attack on the village. It was at such times the intrepid heroism of the woman became evident. Alone, and in the night, she would go forth to meet the frenzied warriors, riding straight across country to their hostile camps at the Quintin Mound, or the foot of the bluffs, or wherever it might be. At times she remained with them for days together, pleading for the safety of her village, counselling peace, and appeasing the anger of the savages. Nor did she cease until her cause was won. Many a time did she return home followed by a long train of warriors changed from bloodthirsty enemies to quiet friends. Mme. Le Comte lived at Cahokia to the extreme age of a hundred and four, honored, respected, and loved by all who knew her, and to the last a power for good along the border.

The second of this trio of notable frontier women was Mrs. John Edgar, of Kaskaskia. Her sphere of influence was utterly different from that of Mme. Le Comte, as was her nationality, yet in some respects it was wider and more lasting. For many years this brilliant, accomplished woman, accustomed to all the refinements of polite society, reigned as the acknowledged queen of fashion in the remote Illinois country, and presided with dignified grace over her husband's magnificent mansion at Kaskaskia. This home was for nearly half a century the abode of hospitality and resort of the *élite*. It was within these spacious walls that soldiers and governors met in social gayety, and here the Marquis de La Fayette was entertained in 1825 with a banquet and ball. Nor do social honors alone crown Mrs. Edgar's memory; as an American patriot she deserves immortality. By birth, education, and environment she was an American, but at the outbreak of the Revolutionary War her husband was an officer in the British navy. Slowly she won him over to the patriot cause, and at the same time originated a wide plan for encouraging the desertion of British soldiers. In this she was extremely active and successful, furnishing the fugitives with arms and uniforms, and guiding them to the American camp. Some of these runaways being captured, Mrs. Edgar was exposed and her husband implicated, which led to his fleeing the service, and coming out openly upon the patriot side. He served a while in the American army, but, deeming it safer to seek greater seclusion, came finally to Kaskaskia. The greater part of his property was confiscated, but through the exertions of his wife, who remained in the East two years longer, about twelve thousand dollars was safely secured. In Kaskaskia Edgar prospered, and for many years they were the most wealthy family in Illinois.

Mrs. Robert Morrison came to Kaskaskia as a young lady, unmarried, finding her husband among the young merchants of that town. From the first she was a rare acquisition to the society life of the place, but especially did she uplift the ideals and intellectual refinement of that rough colony by her remarkable literary ability. This lady originally accompanied her brother, Colonel Donaldson, to St. Louis in 1805, but Kaskaskia soon became her permanent home. Well educated, full of the joy of life, and of great energy, her mind was gifted with originality and romance. Almost immediately she became the centre and inspiration for a higher intellectuality than these remote regions had previously known. Her charming home was soon a gathering spot for a constantly growing coterie of brilliant young minds, destined to make their marks on the nobler life of the new State. Her own intellectual gifts inclined her to cultivate the art of poetry, in which she became proficient, producing many pieces of high value; her prose contributions to Eastern publications were also greatly admired by good judges of literature. Her pen, always ready, discussed subjects of every conceivable nature, not even avoiding the political issues of the day, regarding which she exercised no inconsiderable influence. A feat of much ingenuity was her work of rendering the Psalms of David into verse. In later life this lady united with the Catholic Church, and so strong was her example, that many others, unsolicited, followed her. She became the mother of a large family, lived to an advanced age, and died at Belleville, in 1843.

Shadrach Bond, the first delegate to Congress, and the first Governor of the new State of Illinois, was also among the earlier Americans to settle permanently in this region, but must not be confused with his uncle, that Shadrach Bond who arrived in 1782. While not a great man in intellectual breadth, he was still a typical character, representing the highest class of the intelligent pioneers. Bond was born in Frederick County, Maryland, in 1773, and was raised a farmer on his father's plantation, enjoying few opportunities for education, yet early evincing a marked inclination for books. At twenty-one years of age, being one of a company of neighbors, he floated down the Ohio, helped to scull the heavy keel-boat up the Mississippi, and finally settled down to farming in the American Bottom, in Monroe County, near Eagle Creek. It was a totally undeveloped country, a wilderness on every side, and there necessarily followed years of hard struggle against both nature and savagery. But Bond stuck, and won his battle, gaining constantly a wider and firmer influence over the rough bordermen. For many years he was, unquestionably, the leading local character in the political life of the new commonwealth, and a conspicuous figure in its social affairs.

Bond, from Governor Ford's description, was a substantial, farmer-like man, possessed of plain, strong common sense, and a jovial, hearty manner. He was of a convivial, benevolent disposition, and naturally a shrewd judge of men, as well as of the trend of events. In person he was erect, six feet in height, and after middle life he became portly, weighing two hundred pounds. His features were strongly masculine, marked with character, and rugged, his eyes hazel, his hair jet. He was a great favorite with the ladies because of his genial ways and love of social gayeties. Among men he was what is now known as a "good mixer," his apparent frankness of manner, thorough honesty, and unostentatious intercourse with people of every degree rendering him one of the most widely known and popular leaders of the young settlements. After leaving the Governor's office, he was appointed register of the land-office at Kaskaskia, where he lived quietly until his death in 1830. The county of Bond perpetuates his memory.

The first two practising lawyers in the Illinois country are worthy of mention, not only because of their being pioneers in this profession, but also on account of their real worth and peculiar characteristics. For several years following 1790 the bar of Illinois consisted of but a single member, but he was a host in himself. This legal phenomenon was John Rice Jones, by nativity a Welshman, born in 1750. When he first came to the Far West is not clear, but he was certainly the earliest practitioner in this region, even antedating organized courts. He would have proved a remarkable man in any country, being an accomplished linguist, the possessor of a good classical education, and a thorough knowledge of legal theory and practice. His circuit in earliest days extended from Kaskaskia to Vincennes, including Clarksville (opposite what is now Louisville, Kentucky). The trip was made on horseback, over dim trails, and amid much hardship and exposure, but Jones was never idle, and seldom discouraged or disconcerted. As a speaker, he was the wonder and pride of the frontier, and in moments of excitement or anger his power for invective was scathing. His words stung, and his quick, nervous sentences sunk deep. His influence over a frontier jury, whose every characteristic he instinctively understood and played upon at will, was said to be irresistible. At Vincennes he was elected a member of the Territorial Legislature, and in 1807 rendered valuable services in revising the Indiana statute law.

Unfortunately for his highest reputation, Jones later became involved in what may justly be termed one of the border brawls of the period, which arose between the American settlers and their Spanish neighbors across the Mississippi. A body of men, organized without authority, but commanded by George Rogers Clark, commenced a series of depredations on numerous Spanish traders in the Illinois country, who were plundered of goods and merchandise, in retaliation for similar alleged offences by Spaniards of Natchez. In these outrages Jones took a prominent part, acting as commissary of the American forces, and selling all stolen goods that were found unsuitable to the uses of those men engaged. These acts came very near embroiling us in a serious struggle with Spain. Later, Jones removed to Missouri, became a member of the Constitutional Convention, and a candidate for United States Senator in opposition to Mr. Benton. He held office as Judge of the Missouri Supreme Court until his death in 1824. Wherever he went his undoubted ability and force won him immediate recognition.

Illinois' second lawyer was a man of entirely different character, yet of unquestioned mental capacity. This was Isaac Darnielle. He possessed a strong natural intellect, excellent education, and a fair knowledge of law. An easy, approachable manner, a portly, good-natured appearance, coupled with an off-hand generosity in money matters, made him extremely popular among the masses of the people. As a lawyer he met with good success, and was an agreeable speaker, but somehow lacked the facility for winning the confidence of men. It was said his early education was directed toward the ministry, and that he had even spoken from the pulpit before turning to the law as being more congenial. But his great forte, if posterity does him justice, must have been, in the language of another, "in the court of Venus, where he apparently practised with consummate art, and with more studious assiduity than his books ever received." His reputation in this respect became firmly established all over the infant Territory, and however he may have failed in winning the trust of men, he met with little difficulty in touching the hearts of women. He was never married, and yet seemingly was never without a wife, and this course of procedure brought its inevitable consequences. While youth and vigor remained, all went well, but with advancing age Darnielle was obliged to abandon his profession, and finally died in Western Kentucky, at the age of sixty, an impoverished and neglected school-teacher.

Ninian Edwards, governor of the Territory, and later of the State, and United States Senator from Illinois, was among the most prominent Illinoisans of those early days, and was a man of exceedingly fine talents. He was born in Monroe County, Maryland, in 1775, and was consequently thirty-four years old at his first arrival at Kaskaskia. His education was collegiate, and at the time of coming west to Kentucky, he had already commenced the study of law. Selecting lands in Nelson County on behalf of a brother and sister, who had sent him there for that purpose, he acquired some farming property of his own, and remained to care for it. Having ample means to gratify every inclination in such a new country, and not restrained by the influence of society, the young man drifted into dissipation and other indiscretions. At the end of two years of this wild life, young Edwards broke completely away from his dissolute companions, removed to Russellville, and at once devoted himself to laborious study. Nothing in his after life better illustrates the sterling manhood of the man than this firm refusal to be permanently ruined. Admitted to the bar, he at once attained eminence. By the time he was thirty-two, he had been Judge of the Court of Appeals, and Chief Justice of the State. Soon after, an associate justice of this same court, Boyle, received the appointment of Territorial Governor of Illinois, but did not desire the position. It was arranged between the two that Edwards should have the appointment, and Boyle become Chief Justice. He arrived at Kaskaskia in 1809, and was ever after, so long as he lived, connected intimately with Illinois, and a prominent figure in her political and military history. For the first nine years he was practically the entire source of authoritative power throughout the wide Illinois country, which he ruled with the aid of three judges of his own appointment.

"Edwards," says Governor Ford, "was a large, well-made man, with a noble, princely appearance, never condescending to the common low arts of electioneering. Whenever he went out among the people he arrayed himself in the style of a gentleman of the olden time, dressed in fine broadcloth, with short breeches, long stockings, and high, fur-topped boots; was drawn in a fine carriage driven by a negro; and for success he relied upon his speeches, which were delivered with great pomp, and in a style of diffuse and florid eloquence. When he was inaugurated in 1826, he appeared before the General Assembly wearing a golden-laced coat, and with great pomp he pronounced his first message to the houses of the legislature. His manners were always courtly, and he was extremely pleased at making a good social appearance, being ever a special favorite among the ladies. Even in preparation for an arduous Indian campaign, his camp at Edwardsville was transformed into a seeming picnic-ground by the vast numbers of the gentle sex thronging thither, and the gay parties given them by the Governor and his officers. He died of the cholera at Belleville in 1833."

One of Governor Edwards's opponents for that position of honor in the campaign of 1826 was Adolphus Frederick Hubbard, who certainly deserves mention here for his very oddity. His speeches indicate the mental calibre of the man. During this struggle he once delivered himself as follows; "Fellow-citizens, I offer myself as a candidate before you, for the office of Governor. I do not pretend to be a man of extraordinary talents; nor do I claim to be equal to Julius Cæsar, or Napoleon Bonaparte, nor yet to be as great a man as my opponent, Governor Edwards. Nevertheless I think I can govern you pretty well. I do not think that it will require a very extraordinary smart man to govern you; for, to tell you the truth, fellow-citizens, I do not think you will be very hard to govern, nohow." This individual had long before made himself famous for odd speeches, one of the most widely repeated being an address delivered in the legislature on a bill to pay a bounty on wolf-scalps. It ran thus:

"Mr. Speaker, I rise, before the question is put on this bill, to say a word for my constituents. Mr. Speaker, I have never seen a wolf. I cannot say that I am very well acquainted with the nature and habits of wolves. Mr. Speaker, I have said that I had never seen a wolf. But now I remember that once on a time, as Judge Brown and I were riding across the Bon Pas prairie, we looked over the prairie about three miles, and Judge Brown said, 'Hubbard, look! there goes a wolf!' And I looked, and I looked, and I looked, and I said, 'Judge, where?' And he said 'There'; and I looked again, and this time, in the edge of a hazel thicket, about three miles across the prairie, I think I saw the wolf's tail. Mr. Speaker, if I did not see a wolf this time, I think I never saw one. But I have heard much, and read more, about this animal. I have studied his natural history. By the by, history is divided into two parts; there is first the history of the fabulous, and secondly of the nonfabulous, or unknown ages. Mr. Speaker, from all these sources of information, I learn that the wolf is a very noxious thing to devour; that he rises up in the dead and secret hours of the night, when all nature reposes in silent oblivion, and then commits the most terrible devastations upon the rising generation of hogs and sheep. Mr. Speaker, I have done, and return my thanks to the House for their kind attention to my remarks."

John Reynolds, fourth Governor of Illinois, was likewise identified with the earlier days, and was a typical frontier character and politician. He stands forth peculiarly prominent in the annals of the time, from having written and published an interesting but disconnected account of his own life, and a contemporary State history. He was born in Pennsylvania, in the year 1788, of Irish parentage, and reached Illinois in 1800. In early manhood he travelled to Tennessee and attended school, receiving, he claimed, a "classical education"; but, as Ford remarks, "no one would ever have suspected it from either his writings or speeches." This, however, may have been merely an eccentricity of the man. Reared from his earliest years among a frontier people, where he imbibed their peculiarities of manner, customs, and speech, he disliked polish, despised fashion, and became addicted to inordinate profanity. He apparently never tried to rid himself of these early habits, seeming rather to be proud of them, as thus evidencing his closeness to the common people. Nevertheless, blunt, coarse, rude as he very often was, this Americanized Irishman possessed talent of no mean order, and a vast amount of shrewdness. His garrulity made him even more conspicuous, and, considering the high positions to which he attained, he may certainly be ranked among the public oddities of Illinois.

His imagination was fertile, his ideas poured forth regardless of logical sequence, and even of truth. In life, he was by turn farmer, lawyer, soldier, judge, legislator, congressman, and Governor, and in all these varied positions it is but just to say he achieved fair success. One knowing him says: "Passing his entire life on the frontier, he had acquired all the by-words, catchwords, odd sayings, and grotesque figures of speech ever invented by vulgar ingenuity; to these he added a copious supply of his own, compounding all into a language peculiar to himself, which he insisted on using in both public and private." With a kind heart, always ready to do a favor, never harboring resentment, it was small wonder he won and held votes, completely overwhelming the Baptist preacher who ventured to run against him for the highest office in the State. In appearance we are told that Governor Reynolds was "tall of stature, his face long, bony, and deeply furrowed, and under his high, narrow forehead rolled his eyes, large and liquid, expressive of volubility. His nose projected well downward to his ample mouth." Governor Reynolds always sympathized with slavery, and in his last days he clouded his record by open acts, almost amounting to treason, in his efforts to aid the seceding South. He died at Belleville, in May, 1865.

Beyond Ninian Edwards, already mentioned, we must content ourselves with brief mention of a few of the earliest United States Senators from Illinois, as being typical of the highest life of the people represented. Jesse B. Thomas was Edwards's colleague, and served from 1818 until 1829. He was at the time of first election a Federal judge, and had borne himself with great dignity on the bench, although reported to be far from a master at the law. By nature a politician, he possessed little talent as a speaker, but much skill as a manipulator. After retiring from the Senate he attained to no further honors, and died in Ohio about 1853.

John McLean, of Shawneetown, elected to the Senate in 1824, to succeed Edwards, was in many respects the most gifted man of his period in Illinois. Born in North Carolina in 1791, he came to Shawneetown as a young lawyer of twenty-three, and was soon prominent both at the bar and in political life. Three years later, he was elected to Congress after a campaign strangely marked by courtesy between himself and his opponent, Daniel P. Cook. Hitherto frontier politics had been fought with bitter personalities. He was also frequently a member of the legislature, and once Speaker of the House, but never forgot to remain a gentleman, even on the "stump." McLean was a born orator, a large man, finely proportioned, with light complexion, and frank, open face. Men instinctively felt confidence in him, while his eloquence swayed them at his will. His death, which occurred in the very prime of his manhood, at thirty-nine, was considered a great public loss, and the legislature, in memory of his signal services, named a county of the State in his honor.

Elias Kent Kane served in the Senate from 1824 until the time of his death in 1835. He was a native of New York, coming to Illinois as early as 1814, and was possessed of purity of character, honesty, and benevolent disposition. David Jewett Baker was a Senator from Illinois for a short time by appointment of the Governor, but failed of sanction from the legislature. While a studious, painstaking lawyer, he is especially remembered for his active battle, both by tongue and pen, against the introduction of slavery into the State. He thus gained many bitter enemies, and was once openly attacked on the streets of Kaskaskia. His death occurred at Alton in 1869.

The first native Illinoisan ever elevated to the United States Senate was Samuel McRoberts. He was born in what is now Monroe County, April 12, 1799, received a good English education from a private tutor, and studied law at Lexington, Kentucky. He was, in turn, Circuit Clerk, Circuit Judge, State Senator, United States District Attorney, Receiver of Public Moneys, and Solicitor of the General Land-office. In December, 1840, he was elected to the United States Senate, but died March 22, 1843, at Cincinnati, on his way home from Washington. McRoberts, in appearance, was a little above medium height, sparsely built, and of a nervous temperament. His head was well shapen, but he was swayed by a stubborn will, made more conspicuous by high ambition and great energy. As a lawyer, he was deeply read, and he won his way by power of will, rather than the usual arts of the politician.

Products of the frontier, representing many different trends of thought and degrees of education and ability, these few of the many who helped to uplift Illinois from savagery to civilization illustrate, each in his or her own way, something of the nature of the people behind them — rough, perhaps, but manly, coarse from necessary environment, yet ever moving steadily upward toward higher things, types of true Americans.

CHAPTER XXVII

THE OLD-TIME PREACHERS

IN the very earliest of the pioneer days, during the period of American occupancy, previous to which the Roman Catholic priesthood had held undisputed sway throughout the Illinois country, the preachers of the gospel sprang largely directly from the body of the people, without any previous training, except in religious exhortation and unguided study of the Scriptures. In primitive times it was not considered necessary that a teacher of religion should be a scholar. The appeal was made to the heart and not the head; he was to know the Scriptures literally, to appeal fervently, to paint hell and heaven so vividly as to awaken repentance in the sinners before him. The congregations gathering in the wilderness were composed largely of unlearned men and women, and they were most easily touched and persuaded by preachers who saw things from their own narrow standpoint, and who could move them by use of their own peculiar idioms of speech.

They were often rough in language, but always in earnest. Says one who knew them: "Sometimes their sermons would turn upon matters of controversy, arguing, with little learning but much fervor, on free grace, baptism, free-will, election, faith, good works, justification, sanctification, or the final perseverance of the saints. Vivid, indeed, were the startling word-pictures drawn of the hereafter, and imagination never failed them in describing the bliss of heaven, and the awful terrors of hell." To their faith these things were very real, and their earnestness of belief and description had tremendous effect on the untutored minds of those composing their backwoods audiences. Much which actually occurred in these primitive gospel meetings, within the shadow of groves or sheltered behind the walls of some lonely log cabin, when the itinerant preacher, travelling from settlement to settlement through the wilderness, gathered together a little group to hear his words, is to-day almost beyond belief.

The ruder of these *avant-courriers* of the Cross, being plucked directly from the mass of the people, and almost totally devoid of even common schooling, made up in loud declamation and violent gesticulation their manifest lack of informing matter. And it was equally astonishing to what length they could speak with nothing really to say. One or two poorly digested ideas, crude and illogical, would be spun out for an hour or even two, apparently to the great edification of their hearers. A sermon's merits were tested in three ways,— by its length, its flowery, ornate language, and by the vigor of action exhibited in its delivery. Oratory was largely a matter of sound and bluster, driven home by strange, forcible gesticulation. The congregation must be moved, plunged into tears, shaken by spiritual terrors, driven into some outward manifestation of remorse for sin, or else the preaching was held as an utter failure. The simple-hearted borderers, usually grave and quiet enough in their daily, plodding, home duties, responded quickly to professional play on their emotions; and he was hailed and welcomed as the strongest exponent of the Word who could create the greatest excitement in his meetings.

Nevertheless, much as we may find now to criticise in the methods then employed by Methodist circuit-rider, or itinerant Baptist or Presbyterian, these early preachers of Illinois performed an important and necessary work. Their earnestness, suffering, hardships, and unselfish ministry entitle them to the world's respect. They inculcated justice and morality, and in their own way, a sadly unpolished way, perhaps, yet the surest for their age, drove deep into the consciences of the people the story of the Nazarene, with reward for virtue and the certain punishment of sin. In charity, in humbleness of life, in abundance of toil, they practised all they preached. At this time, when the country was so poor that a paid and settled ministry was impossible, these men travelled and preached without charge, often laboring week-days to aid those in whose homes they stopped, and always ready to sacrifice for the sake of others who struggled. They were true evangelists, living literally day by day, year after year, the life of self renunciation laid down by Christ. They believed with positive certainty that they saw the souls of men rushing to perdition, and they desired no higher mission in life than to grasp and save. Their words and efforts did much to mould the character of the early population, and upon their self-devotion to duty rest the foundations of Protestantism in Illinois.

Of all the religious gatherings of the frontier, the camp-meeting was the culmination. Here the settlements for miles around gathered together in a vast spiritual and social feast, and the emotional nature was given complete sway. Preachers from far and near, often representing different denominations, gave utterance to their faith, and the scenes witnessed were as full of color as the strange wilderness in which they were enacted. Henry Howe has drawn the picture of such a gathering, worthy of reproduction.

"The notice has been circulated for several weeks or months, and all are eager to attend the long-expected occasion. The country, perhaps for fifty miles around, is excited with the cheerful anticipation of the approaching festival of religious feeling and social friendship. On the appointed day, coaches, chaises, wagons, carts, people on horseback and on foot, in multitudes, with provision wagons, tents, mattresses, household implements, and cooking utensils, are seen hurrying from every direction toward the central point. It is in the midst of a grove of beautiful, lofty, umbrageous trees, natural to the Western country, clothed in their deepest verdure, and near some sparkling stream or gushing fountain, which supplies the host with wholesome water for man and beast. The encampment spreads through the forest, over hundreds of acres, and soon the sylvan village springs up as if by magic; the line of tents and booths is pitched in a semicircle or in a four-sided parallelogram, enclosing an area of two acres or more, for the arrangement of seats and aisles around the rude pulpit and altar for the thronging multitude, all eager to hear the heavenly message.

"Toward night, the hour of solemn service approaches, when the vast sylvan bower of the deep umbrageous forest is illumined by numerous lamps suspended around the line of tents which encircles the public area, beside the frequent altars distributed over the same, which send forth a glare of light from their fagot fires upon the worshipping throng and the majestic forest with an imposing effect, which elevates the soul to fit converse with its Creator, God.

"The scenery of the most brilliant theatre in the world is only a painting for children compared to this. Meantime, the multitudes, with the highest excitement of social feeling, added to the general enthusiasm of expectation, pass from tent to tent, interchange apostolic greetings and embraces, and talk of the approaching solemnities. A few minutes suffice to finish the evening repast, when the moon (for they take thought to appoint the meeting at the proper time of the moon) begins to show its disc above the dark summits of the mountains, and a few stars are seen glimmering in the west, and the service begins. The whole constitutes a temple worthy of the grandeur of God. An old man in a dress of the quaintest simplicity ascends a platform, wipes the dust from his spectacles, and, in a voice of suppressed emotion, gives out the hymn, of which the whole assembled multitude can recite the words, to be sung with an air in which every voice can join. We should esteem meanly the heart that would not thrill as the song is heard, 'like a noise of many waters,' echoing among the hills and mountains. The service proceeds. The hoary orator talks of God, of eternity, of a judgment to come, and of all that is impressive beyond. He speaks of his experiences,— his toils and his travels, his persecutions and his welcomes, and how many he had seen in hope, in peace, and in triumph gathered to their fathers; and when he speaks of the short space that remains to him, his only regret is that he can no more proclaim, in the silence of death, the unsearchable riches and mercies of his crucified Redeemer.

"No wonder, as the speaker pauses to dash the gathering moisture from his own eye, that his audience is dissolved in tears, or uttering exclamations of penitence. Nor is it cause for admiration, that many who prided themselves on an estimation of a higher intellect and a nobler insensibility than the crowd, catch the infectious feeling, and become women and children in their turn, while others, 'who came to scoff, remain to pray.'"

A peculiarity of these intensely emotional meetings, which has never been clearly accounted for, was known as "the jerks." That such occurrences were common there can be no doubt, probably resulting from intense nervous strain. It took, however, many forms, influenced by the temperament of the victim. Most frequently the subject was instantaneously seized with spasms or convulsions in every muscle, nerve, and tendon. His head was thrown or jerked from side to side with such rapidity that it was impossible to distinguish his visage, and the most lively fears were awakened lest he should dislocate his neck or dash out his brains. His body partook of the same impulse, and was hurried on by like jerks over every obstacle, fallen trunks of trees, or in a church, over pews and benches, apparently to the most imminent danger of being bruised and mangled. It was useless to attempt to hold or restrain him, and the paroxysm was permitted to exhaust itself gradually. Oftentimes, under the spell of this strange mental phenomenon, the victims would fall to the floor unconscious, or in trances. The great Methodist-Presbyterian camp-meeting at Cane Ridge in 1801 was especially memorable for such results. An observer writes of this occasion:

"Few, if any, escaped without being affected. Such as tried to run from it were frequently struck on the way, or impelled by some alarming signal to return. No circumstances at this meeting appeared more striking than the great numbers that fell on the third night, and remained unconscious of external objects for hours together. To prevent their being trodden under foot by the multitude, they were collected together and laid out in order, on two squares of the meeting-house, until a considerable part of the floor was covered, where they remained in charge of their friends, until they should pass through the strange phenomena of their conversion. The number that fell at this meeting was reckoned at about three thousand, among whom were several Presbyterian ministers, who, according to their own confession, had hitherto possessed only a speculative knowledge of religion. There, the formal professor, and the deist, and the intemperate, met with one common lot, and confessed with equal candor that they were destitute of the true knowledge of God, and strangers to the religion of Jesus Christ."

The progress of early Protestant religious work in Illinois can be traced with very fair accuracy, although undoubtedly there were numerous obscure laborers in the field — licentiates and local preachers — whose names have not been remembered. The most careful epitome is Short's essay in the "Historical Transactions" for 1902. While a wandering Separate Baptist preacher, the Rev. James Smith, was in all probability the first to deliver a Protestant sermon within the present limits of the State, coming here, presumably on a visit to friends, as early as 1787, the earliest organized religious body performing definite labor in this region was the Methodist. Smith, as detailed elsewhere, was captured by the Indians, and finally redeemed by the contributions of the settlers.

During his brief period of service in Illinois, among his converts was numbered Captain Joseph Ogle, who later became the leading Methodist layman in the new settlements, a class-leader, and occasional local preacher. Ogle arrived in Illinois as early as 1785, and died in 1821, aged eighty years, a high type of the borderman. The earliest Methodist preacher to invade this section of western wilderness was Joseph Lillard, a local preacher from Kentucky, who gathered a small class in Monroe County, and installed Ogle as class-leader, in 1793. Lillard was a typical pioneer preacher, a sort of advance scout, never remaining any length of time in a district, but laying the foundation upon which others could follow and build. He was gifted with rude eloquence, and delighted in controversy. Some five years later, during which period Ogle had held his class together under much difficulty, another travelling preacher of this denomination, John Clark, visited the field, and by his efforts somewhat increased the membership and interest. He remained, however, only a brief time, and passed across the river into Missouri in 1798.

The same year which marked Clark's arrival, there came to the settlements their first resident minister. This was Hosea Riggs, and his subsequent work proved both important and permanent. He settled on the American Bottom, in St. Clair County, and was instrumental in organizing a number of Methodist societies throughout Madison County. He remained in Illinois until his death, which occurred at Belleville, in 1841. Mr. Riggs, while not an educated man, possessed pulpit ability of the kind best adapted to the region in which he labored. The Illinois mission was organized, under the care of the Kentucky Conference, in 1803, with Benjamin Young named as travelling pastor. A number of meeting-points were established, principally in the Wabash neighborhood, but little permanent work was accomplished. In 1806 Jesse Walker was assigned to this charge. His labor was enthusiastically undertaken, and proved successful. Settlement after settlement was reached by this indefatigable missionary, and the gospel was fearlessly preached where it had never before been heard. He, more than any other, was instrumental in spreading the doctrines of Methodism throughout Southern Illinois.

A PIONEER ILLINOIS PREACHER

In the year 1807, Mr. Walker conducted successfully the first camp-meeting ever held within the present limits of the State. It took place about three miles south of Edwardsville, in Madison County, and resulted in numerous conversions, and an awakening of religious interest throughout all the surrounding region. The first American male child born in Illinois — Enoch Moore — was converted at this time, under Walker's preaching, and afterwards became a local Methodist preacher of considerable note. The camp-meeting continued for several days, with many manifestations of power. Among other Methodist preachers who travelled in Illinois during the earlier days — all being circuit riders, with no fixed place of abode, or definite salary — the more prominent were: John Clingan, James Ward, William McKendree (afterwards Bishop), Samuel Parker, James Axley, John Scripps, Samuel Thompson, Jesse Haille, and Stephen Biggs. The constant sacrifices and perils of these humble messengers of the Cross are almost beyond belief. Their days were passed in the saddle; their nights in exhortation and prayer. No hardship of the wilderness was unknown, no toil too great; through storms of Winter and across the parched Summer prairies they rode to keep their appointments in the little settlements, their clothing often in rags, their bodies weak from lack of nourishment. The implied pecuniary reward for such unremitting service was eighty dollars a year, but fortunate indeed was that preacher who ever received the half of it.

In the year 1812, Peter Cartwright was named as elder of the Wabash district, within the limits of which he had toiled as an itinerant some years earlier. In 1824 he removed to what was then the uttermost frontier of Sangamon County, and became the most famous of the early missionaries of the church, his ministry covering all the northern and western portions of the State. He was a remarkable character, a preacher of exceptional power, possessing phenomenal energy.

His religious influence was widespread, and in his later years he prepared an autobiography, giving many a vivid picture of the hard life of circuit-riders, and the peculiar conditions under which they were compelled to labor. Another early preacher of great power and influence for good throughout the Illinois country, to which he devoted the best years of his life, was Peter Akers. Zadoc Casey was a well-known local Methodist preacher in Illinois for over forty years.

Some few of these earliest preachers were more distinguished by their eccentricities, than by their religious labors. Among these the most remarkable, perhaps, was William Stribling, whose extraordinary command of language became the laughing-stock of the border.

Baptist work within the State was nearly, if not quite, as early undertaken as that of the Methodist Church, but, from the nature of the church government, was not so immediately successful. The Baptist polity looks to the settled pastorate, as, indeed, do nearly all of the Protestant denominations; but in a new, sparsely settled, and poverty-ruled land, the itinerant system of Methodism gives great advantage. The first Baptist preachers to visit Illinois were not educated men, but were adapted, from their controversial gifts, as well as rough and ready speech, for successful labors among the pioneer settlements. We have little detailed record of their earliest labors, yet that these were widespread, and in a way sufficient, is evidenced by their proving such constant thorns in the flesh of their Methodist brethren. Continually in the reports of the latter do we meet with complaints of their interference and argumentative inclination. That they were successful in spreading their doctrines widely, and in winning converts, is evidenced by the fact that in 1834 they had within the State nineteen associations, with one hundred and ninety-five associated and five unassociated churches, one hundred and forty-six preachers, and 5,635 communicants. It is doubtful if any other religious body in Illinois was, at that date, as strong.

They, besides, enjoyed the honor of bringing to Illinois the first educated ministry. By 1820, several scholarly Baptist preachers had located within the State, the earliest and most widely known being the Rev. John M. Peck, who located at Rock Spring, St. Clair County. This gentleman possessed not only rare natural gifts, but was also highly educated, achieving considerable success as an author. The higher class of men who from this date began coming into the State and assuming charge of permanent congregations were either sent or encouraged to come by Northern and Eastern missionary societies, who helped to meet their expenses. For a long time they were looked upon with jealousy and distrust by many of the old, uneducated race of preachers and their loyal followers. Yet the time had come for a change; towns were springing up everywhere, and the people required a settled ministry. Slowly, as the lines of the frontier receded, the younger men, with new methods of work and broader culture, pressed their way to the front, and the emotional border religion became more and more a memory.

The Presbyterian ministry were early in this region, and performed excellent work even in the itinerant days. They apparently did not experience as great difficulty as the Baptists in coöperating with the Methodist preachers in religious exercises, probably because their details of belief were not so radically opposed. Quite frequently these two denominations united in camp-meeting services, Methodist and Presbyterian preaching from the same stump, and vying with each other as to which should win the greater popular approval for fervid speech and violent gesture. The first minister of this latter denomination to reach the Illinois country was John Evans Finley, who came to Kaskaskia in 1797. He was soon followed by two licentiates, J. F.

Schermerhorn, and Samuel J. Mills. These were still alone upon the field as late as 1812. The oldest Presbyterian church within the State is that at Sharon, in White County, which was organized by the Rev. James McCready in 1816. By 1830, however, this denomination numbered fifty churches and thirty-four ministers.

The other branches of Protestantism were considerably later in planting their banners on Illinois soil, although few, if any, of importance in the religious world were unrepresented by 1840. As early as 1834, the Episcopalians and Congregationalists had several churches organized and supplied with ministers. The latter, undoubtedly, had numerous ordained representatives in the Illinois field prior to this date, but they preferred working under the Presbyterian polity, the impression long prevailing in religious circles that the Congregational government was not adapted to the West. Probably the first to actually try the experiment were those pastors who accompanied colonies from the New England States, continuing in Illinois all the conditions of their former Eastern churches.

With this incoming of a more highly educated ministry, there was inspired a desire for better educational facilities. It is impossible here to trace the story of primitive school-teaching, but we know that, in Illinois history, it began with some faithful pioneer mother giving to her children some fragmentary knowledge from her own memory. The first school in this entire region, established since the American conquest of the Territory, was opened near Bellefontaine, by Samuel Seely, in 1783. John Doyle taught in the same neighborhood at about the same time, and his successor was Francis Clark, who was addicted to intemperance. He was followed by an inoffensive Irishman, named Halfpenny, who persevered in his vocation for several years. The branches taught were spelling, reading, writing, and arithmetic, and these in a very imperfect manner. Later still, an eccentric clergyman named John Clark gratuitously instructed the ambitious youth of the settlement.

In 1825 was enacted the first law providing for the incorporation of common schools, although, when the State was admitted to the Union in 1818, one thirty-sixth part of all the public lands was reserved for school purposes. Coincident with this starting of common schools, and the arrival of an educated ministry, was the demand for higher institutions of learning, in the securing of which the various church organizations were largely instrumental. Illinois College was founded at Jacksonville in 1829, and by 1850 had seven teachers, thirty-four students, and ninety-three alumni, with a library of four thousand volumes. It was made possible largely through the efforts of the "Yale Band of Seven," a ministerial organization. McKendree College was founded at Lebanon, St. Clair County, in 1835, by the Methodists, and by 1850 had four teachers and sixty students, its library containing eighteen hundred volumes. The Congregationalists and Baptists were represented as early as 1835 by Knox College at Galesburg, and Shurtleff College at Upper Alton, both successful institutions. Others rapidly arose throughout the State as population and wealth increased and the spirit of refinement took possession of the people.

CHAPTER XXVIII

BORDER OUTLAWRY

ALMOST every district of the United States in its earlier days of scant population has been the scene of open crime. Outlaws, fleeing in desperation from the restraints of civilization, where enforcement of law has become methodical, find in the wilderness a certain license for the carrying on of their nefarious trade. The settlements are small and widely scattered, with broad spaces of unknown forest and prairie lying between; neighbors scarcely know one another, and the usual machinery of government is either not yet fully organized, or very imperfectly enforced. It is easy, under these circumstances, to attain secrecy, while the very life of the border naturally breeds a class of rough and desperate men, capable, under efficient leadership, of the commission of almost any crime. Such has been the frontier story from the very beginning, and through just such an experience Illinois was compelled to battle her way into the ranks of the law-abiding.

Probably there is no county in the State without its local traditions of organized outlawry during the period of earlier occupancy; its tales, oftentimes weird and gruesome enough, of unpunished crimes, extending often over many years, until popular sentiment became too strong to continue to harbor the criminals. Localities are even to this day pointed out by the older residents as having been the headquarters of famous gangs of horse-thieves, negro-stealers, and counterfeiters, whose record of crime, indeed, probably covered every atrocity known to our modern statutes.

We have seen in our travels about the State, many

such localities, and have been regaled with local traditions of former "bad men" which would afford most interesting reading could fact and fiction only be satisfactorily divorced so that real history be born. In one county a mysterious murder-house yet stands deserted and feared even by modern neighbors; in another, names and details were furnished to form a thrilling romance. Along the rough land bordering the rivers these legends are most numerous, and not a few of the outlaw names mentioned have attained some notice in history; while the interior counties, even those originally settled by staid New England colonists, are not wholly without their records of early and reckless criminal life. In Munson Township of Henry County, such a gang, famous in its time for desperate deeds, held sway for many years, extending their operations almost up to the time of the Civil War, and in Knox County the delver after the curious in border life is told of a famous plum thicket, tangled and impenetrable save by means of a secret path, where hundreds of stolen horses were securely hidden away on their long journey southward.

Apparently, as guided by these various old-time tales of lawless adventure, and the few glimpses afforded by acknowledged history, we may conclude that the numerous outlaw gangs infesting Illinois Territory were usually organized for specific crimes, the nature of which was somewhat determined by the peculiarities of the country in which operations were being carried on. Along the rivers deeds of violence were more prevalent, acts of piracy being frequent, and oftentimes accompanied by murder. Emigrants were sometimes attacked in force, while the solitary traveller, whether by boat or on horseback, was held up remorselessly, being indeed fortunate to escape with his life. The rough hills of the southern section of the State contained many a rendezvous for such robber bands, but the most famous hiding place was at Cave-in-Rock, on the Ohio, a short distance below Shawneetown. Here, about 1800, flourished a famous robber band under command of a bloodthirsty desperado named Meason or Mason. He was a man of more than ordinary talents, of gigantic stature, and was both a land and water pirate, infesting the rivers and woods, and impartially despoiling all who fell in his way. Sometimes he plundered the descending boats, but generally preferred to wait, and take the owners with their money on their return. Finally, driven from his cave by encroaching settlements, Meason and his band moved farther south into Tennessee and infested the great route then known as the "Natchez and Nashville Trace." Here he became a terror to every traveller. Associated with him in every species of outlawry were his two sons, and a well-organized gang of miscreants, their operations extending from the Mississippi to the Pearl. A reward was offered for him, dead or alive, and he was finally killed by treachery, two of his own band, in hope of securing the reward, striking him from behind with a tomahawk, while he was engaged in counting some ill-gotten treasure. Both traitors were afterwards executed, and the entire gang either killed or scattered. Cave-in-Rock, where they hid so long, was peculiarly adapted for such a purpose, its partially concealed entrance commanding a wide view both up and down the river. Within, it is about one hundred feet long, eighty wide, and twenty-five in height. The floor is nearly level throughout the entire length of the centre, the sides rising in strong grades, like seats in the pit of a theatre. It is even now a great curiosity, being connected with another, still more gloomy but of less size, situated exactly above. These are united by a vertical passage of about fourteen feet, to ascend which is like passing up a chimney, while the top of the bluff is yet far above. Many a legend of suffering and torture, wild feasting, and desperate encounter, haunts this spot, which was later occupied by other desperate bands, and became the terror of the river.

Yet these were not alone in their work of crime along the Illinois waterways. From the Wabash to the Fever there were many bands operating, no less desperate, although never attaining to equal nefarious fame. The most notorious of these was a quite extensive organization of cut-throats, under command of two desperadoes who infested the Mississippi below St. Louis, and carried on a regular and extensive system of river piracy, principally in the neighborhood of Grand Tower. In 1787, a richly laden barge, owned by a Mr. Beausoliel, came up the river from New Orleans. At what has since been named Beausoliel's Island, some of these robbers boarded the vessel, overpowered the crew and the owner, and forced them below. Beausoliel's whole fortune was in the barge, and he was consequently in agony. But all was saved to him through the heroic daring of a negro, one of the crew. This negro, Cacasotte, was short and slender, but exceedingly strong and active, and the peculiar characteristics of the race had, in him, given place to features of exceeding grace and beauty. As soon as the robbers had taken possession, Cacasotte appeared overjoyed. He danced, sang, laughed, and soon induced them to bebelieve that his ebullitions of pleasure arose from their having liberated him from irksome slavery. His constant attention to their smallest wants won their confidence, and he alone was permitted to roam unmolested and unwatched through the vessel.

Having thus far effected his object, he seized the first opportunity to speak to Mr. Beausoliel and beg permission to rid him of the dangerous intruders. He laid his plan before his master, who, with a good deal of hesitation, acceded to it. Cacasotte was cook, and it was agreed between him and his fellow-conspirators, two negroes, that the signal for dinner should be the signal for action. When the hour arrived, the pirates assembled in considerable numbers on the deck, and stationed themselves on the bow and the stern and along the sides, to prevent any rising of the men. Cacasotte went among them with the most unconcerned look and demeanor imaginable. As soon as his comrades had taken their stations, he placed himself at the bow, near one of the robbers, a stout, herculean fellow, who was armed *cap-à-pie*. Cacasotte gave the preconcerted signal, and immediately the robber near him was struggling in the water. With the speed of lightning he ran from one to another, as they were sitting on the sides of the boat, and in a few seconds' time had thrown several overboard. Then seizing an oar he struck on the head those who had attempted to save themselves by grappling the running-boards; then he shot, with rifles that had been dropped on deck, those who swam away. In the mean time his comrades had done almost as much execution as their leader. The deck was soon cleared, and the robbers who remained below were too few to offer any resistance. But these did not comprise all the band; the remnant continued their depredations until the next year, when they were broken up, and all kinds of valuable merchandise, the fruits of their crimes, were found on the island.

At a later period, the celebrated counterfeiter, Studevant, fixed his residence in Illinois, on the Ohio, and for several years set the laws at defiance. Howe's description of him and his work follows:

"He was a man of talent and address, possessed mechanical genius, was an expert artist, skilled in some of the sciences, and excelled as an engraver. For several years he resided in a secluded spot, where all his immediate neighbors were his confederates, or persons whose friendship he had conciliated. At any time, by the blowing of a horn, he could summon from fifty to a hundred armed men to his defence, while the few quiet farmers around, who lived near enough to get their feelings interested, and who were really not at all implicated in his crimes, rejoiced in the impunity with which he practised his schemes. He was a grave, quiet, inoffensive-looking man, who commanded the obedience of his comrades and the respect of his neighbors. He had a very excellent farm; his house was one of the best in the country; his domestic arrangements were liberal and well ordered. Yet this man was the most notorious counterfeiter that ever infested our country, and carried on his nefarious art to an extent which no other person has ever attempted. His confederates were scattered over the whole Western country, receiving, through regular channels of intercourse, their regular supplies of counterfeit bank notes, for which they paid him a stipulated price — sixteen dollars in cash for one hundred in counterfeit bills.

"His security arose partly from his caution in not allowing his subordinates to pass a counterfeit bill or do any other unlawful act in the State in which he lived, and in his obliging them to be especially careful of their deportment in the county of his residence, — measures which effectually protected him from the civil authority; for, although all the counterfeit bank notes with which a vast region was inundated were made in his house, that fact never could be proved by legal evidence.

"But he became a great nuisance from the immense quantity of spurious paper which he threw into circulation; and although personally he never committed any acts of violence, and is not known to have sanctioned any, the unprincipled felons by whom he was surrounded were guilty of many acts of desperate atrocity; and Studevant, though he escaped the arm of the law, was at last, with all his confederates, driven from the country by the enraged people, who rose almost in mass, to rid themselves of one whose presence they had long considered an evil and a disgrace."

Many of these outlaws, widely scattered, and no longer possessing a talented leader in crime, became professional horse-thieves, and connected themselves with the numerous desperate gangs which, in that early day, operated extensively throughout every section of the State. "Nigger-stealing" was confined almost entirely to the more southern counties; but the stealing of horses became a much wider general industry, and few, indeed, were the counties without a well-organized gang engaged exclusively in this business. So extensive did this species of crime become, that regular routes of travel, with convenient hiding-places, such as that already mentioned in Knox County, were followed the entire length of the State, and for many years the legal authorities were utterly powerless to convict, owing to the wide influence exercised by the outlaws in those neighborhoods where they made their homes and freely spent their money. Pitched battles between these desperadoes and the officers of the law were frequent; murder was more than once resorted to, and court-houses were even burned to destroy evidence, the whole country being at times in a state of terror. The depredations continued almost unchecked until the people themselves rose in the form of "Regulators," hanging and driving out at the muzzles of rifles the worst offenders.

Regarding the work of these "Regulators," only the more important affairs can be dwelt upon, but they were probably more or less in evidence in every portion of the State. The fact that Nauvoo, during the Mormon occupancy, was a very hot-bed of crime, and especially a hiding-place for many dangerous counterfeiters, had much to do with those uprisings which finally drove the "Saints" beyond the Mississippi. As early as 1816 these uprisings of honest settlers began for the purpose of ridding the country of undesirable characters. We must confess that, much as mob rule is to be deprecated, these men were largely justified by the circumstances. The entire region was already overrun by counterfeiters and horse-thieves, while highway robbery and even murder was not unfrequent. No traveller was safe, no settler felt sure of retaining his stock overnight. Even the smaller towns were boldly invaded in search after plunder, and isolated merchants were held up at the point of the gun. In many counties the outlaws were so numerous and well organized as to set the laws impudently at defiance. Sheriffs, justices of the peace, and constables were of their number, and even some of the judges of the county courts; while numerous friends, some apparently of the highest respectability, shielded them from punishment. When arrested, they easily escaped from the poorly constructed jails, or packed the jury, or used lying witnesses to prove themselves innocent. Conviction, by the usual course of procedure, proved practically impossible.

It was under such intolerable conditions that the people finally took the law into their own hands. The Governor and judges of the Territory, realizing the necessity for such urgent action, winked at these proceedings, and for a time lynch law ruled the entire region, and purged it of a great deal of evil. These bodies of Regulators, as Governor Ford describes them, were in numbers about equal to a company of soldiers, and their officers were elected as in the militia. Their active operations were conducted almost entirely at night. When assembled for duty, they marched, armed and equipped as if for actual war, to the residence or lurking-place of some undoubted criminal, arrested, tried, and punished him on the spot. The usual punishment inflicted by these impromptu tribunals was a severe whipping and banishment from the Territory, although there were many instances where old offenders were promptly hanged on the nearest tree. In most of the districts thus patrolled this method proved sufficiently efficacious, yet for many years a large and desperate gang of ruffians held almost absolute control of Pope, Massac, and other counties bordering the Ohio River, resisting every effort to dislodge them. They even built a fort of considerable strength in Pope County, and for a time set the government at open defiance. It was not until 1831 that measures were taken which resulted in their overthrow. Then, all the honest settlers in that region rallied under arms, and attacked the outlaws' fort, even using a piece of artillery. The place was taken by a fierce assault, one Regulator and three of the robbers being killed. The remaining outlaws were taken prisoners and tried for their crimes. Even later than this occurred a somewhat similar clash in Edgar County, in which another gang was summarily dealt with, its members severely whipped and driven from the county. He who afterwards became Governor French was a prominent member of the Regulators engaged in this affair.

From here the outbreaks against lawlessness shifted to the more northern counties, where frontier conditions still invited to open outlawry. Well-organized bands were for many years operating unchecked north of the Illinois River, engaged in murder, robbery, horse-stealing, and the making and passing of counterfeit money. While few districts were entirely free from such criminals, the largest number of them rendezvoused in the counties of Ogle, Winnebago, Lee, and De Kalb. In Ogle they became so numerous and powerful that any conviction for crime was rendered impossible. Acquittal was certain to follow any attempt at indictment.

At the Spring term of 1841 seven well-known outlaws were confined in the Ogle County jail. The judge and lawyers interested in their cases had assembled at the little village of Oregon, preparatory to the holding of court in the new court-house just completed. The jail stood near by. During the night a gang of sympathizers stole out of the darkness and set fire to the new building, hoping, in the excitement which would follow, to rescue the prisoners. This scheme failed, but the court-house was entirely consumed. Before the wave of popular indignation consequent upon this lawless act had subsided, the court convened, and three of the prisoners were tried, convicted, and sentenced to the penitentiary. In the trial one of their confederates had managed to get on the jury, and refused to agree on a verdict until the eleven others threatened to lynch him in the jury-room. The four other prisoners obtained changes of venue and never came to trial, as they all broke out of jail, and made their escape.

OLD COURT-HOUSE AT PEORIA

RESIDENCE OF COLONEL DAVENPORT ON ROCK ISLAND, WHERE HE WAS MURDERED

This affair thoroughly aroused the law-abiding residents of that region, and they resolved to take the law into their own hands. They were determined that delays, insecure jails, changes of venue, hung juries, and perjured evidence should no longer protect open criminals from just punishment. All over Ogle and Winnebago Counties they organized into companies of Regulators, and proceeded to work, whipping the more notorious rascals and ordering others to leave the country. Among those who were sentenced to banishment was a family named Driscoll, consisting of the old man and several sons. The father and some of the boys had been in the Ohio penitentiary, and were well-known thieves. The old man was a stoutly built, hardened, desperate man, while the boys had been brought up in the atmosphere of crime. This family determined not to be driven away, and, joining with others of a like determination, resolved to terrorize the Regulators by threatening death to the leading members of that organization. To prove such threats were not idle, they decided to begin by assassinating the Captain.

For this purpose, one Sunday evening about dark, just after the family had returned from church, some of the Driscolls went to Captain Campbell's house. Pretending to be strangers inquiring their way, they called their victim out into his dooryard, and then deliberately shot him dead before the eyes of his wife and children. Before daybreak the news had spread over the whole surrounding country. From all quarters the people came pouring in toward the home of the murdered man, which was in White Rock Grove. Here they were still more influenced by viewing their dead leader and witnessing the sorrow of his wife and children, and the avengers spread out over the country in search after the murderers.

The actual committers of the atrocious crime had made their escape, but there was no doubt that Driscoll and his sons were connected with it, and they were made prisoners and taken to Washington Grove for trial. Here the old man and one boy were convicted, the other acquitted. This trial occupied nearly an entire day, and was conducted in an orderly manner, in the presence of the whole assemblage of Regulators, some three hundred men, including magistrates and ministers of the gospel. Those condemned were sentenced to be shot within an hour. Given every opportunity for repentance, and with the consolations of religion administered to them, they were brought out for execution. Placed in a kneeling position, their eyes bandaged, the whole company present fired upon them, so that none could be legal witnesses of the deed. Death was instantaneous, and from that hour the ascendency of criminals ceased in the northern counties.

Nowhere in the State did a similar condition of affairs continue to exist, except in Massac County, which for years was not only overrun but actually controlled by vicious lawlessness. Courts, and nearly all the county and township officials, were at one time actual participants in outlawry, and the entire region was apparently a den of thieves. In 1846 this carnival of crime was at its height, the condition such as to be now almost unbelievable. During the Summer of that year a number of these desperadoes made a raid into Pope County, and entering the house of an aged resident, robbed him of about two thousand five hundred dollars in gold. While committing this crime, one of the participants left behind a knife, which, having been made by a neighboring blacksmith, identified him with the act. Being arrested and tortured by the aroused neighbors, he confessed his crime, and gave the name of his associates. These also, being apprehended, were in turn tortured, and from them was learned a long list of confederates, scattered through various counties. To drive these out, Regulators were organized, but before they could act, the election for county officers occurred in August, 1846.

Every criminal influence united in this election, and, as a result, men were elected who were popularly believed to be favorable to the disturbing element. Whether true or not, the two defeated candidates for sheriff and county clerk took advantage of this general feeling of distrust to rally about them all the different bands of Regulators in Pope and Massac Counties for an organized attack on all suspected of crime. Assisted by numerous recruits from Kentucky, these men proceeded to drive out and punish all persons suspected, and by torture force them to betray their companions. In this way long lists of names were obtained. The usual mode of torture was to take their victim down to the Ohio and hold him under water until ready to confess. A few of these victims swore out warrants against their persecutors, but when the sheriff attempted arrests, he and the county clerk were both ordered to leave the country, under threats of severe punishment.

By September, 1846, the whole county was practically in the hands of these Regulators, the officials being powerless. Having started out to achieve law and order, under unscrupulous leaders this organization was becoming a lawless terror, threatening every one, whether rogue or honest man, who dared to protest against their proceedings. A reign of terror followed, which has scarcely a precedent in border history. The sheriff, county clerk, and several representatives in the legislature were driven out by force, and every corner of the region witnessed almost daily scenes of violence and outrage. About this time the circuit court was held for Massac, with Judge Scates on the bench. Several of the Regulators were indicted, and some were arrested by the sheriff and committed to jail. But the Regulators, assisted by large numbers from Kentucky, rose in open revolt against the law, and the sheriff was unable to raise a sufficient posse to carry on the duty of his office. The moderate men in the county, who probably outnumbered the others three to one, were so thoroughly terrorized as to refuse to take part, and the sheriff was compelled to use a set of fellows of ill repute.

The Regulators took every advantage of his predicament, and in their full strength marched down to Metropolis City, the county seat. Here the sheriff and his party were compelled to surrender, the jail was opened, and those imprisoned set free. The sheriff and many of his friends were driven out of the country, and several of his posse were murdered by being drowned in the Ohio. The entire region became divided into two warring factions, known as "Regulators" and "Flatheads"; all law was set at defiance, while violence was resorted to on every side. No man's life or property was safe in Massac or Pope County, the State government attempting little in the way of enforcing law.

An illustration of the atrocious deeds committed is found in the case of one Mathis. He was an old man, and with the avowed purpose of compelling him to give certain evidence required against his neighbors, some twenty Regulators visited his house at night. He and his wife resisted, and the old woman, being strong and active, knocked down one or two of the party. In return she was shot through the thigh, besides being struck several blows on the head with a gun-barrel. Mathis was carried away, and probably murdered, as he was never again heard of. Warrants were sworn out for the arrest of these ruffians, and ten of them were taken. These were carried to Metropolis City, and placed under guard at the old Metropolis House, and at once a large force of Regulators gathered and marched down to the county seat for the purpose of liberating the prisoners. Some trouble and shooting occurred, one man was fatally stabbed, the "Flatheads" were overpowered, and a number of them, including the sheriff, turned over as prisoners to the Kentuckians.

These were immediately taken away, all securely tied together, in the direction of Paducah. As they were never again heard of, it is presumed they were drowned in the waters of the Ohio. This state of terror reigned undisturbed until it died out naturally. The legislature took some action, but nothing sufficiently drastic to accomplish results. No one was ever legally punished for any of the outrages committed, but the disturbances slowly died away, and law gradually resumed sway throughout all this region.

For fifty years the upper Mississippi was haunted by bands of desperadoes, who found safe hiding-places on the seldom-visited islands or in well-hidden haunts along the shore. Travellers were attacked on both land and water, in the earlier days particular attention being paid to the Galena ore-boats, which were oftentimes compelled to run the gauntlet to St. Louis. Many of these bands coöperated with the Indians, who assisted them in their raids and hid them later in their villages. Nauvoo, both during and after the Mormon occupancy, contained many bad men, besides its nest of counterfeiters, who operated extensively in piracy along the upper river, and not infrequently added murder to their lesser crimes. Those desperadoes who murdered Colonel George Davenport in his lonely home on Rock Island were from Nauvoo, and the story of their desperate crime is stranger than any romance. They were convicted and hanged, their fate having much to do with the subsequent clearing away of these rascals from the river. This, however, was not so much accomplished by the strong hand of the law, as by thicker settlement, and a better popular sentiment, which rendered crime unsafe.

CHAPTER XXIX

THE EARLY STEAMBOAT DAYS

THE Western water-ways have witnessed many strange forms of transportation since the advent of the white man. The first explorers found the narrow Indian canoe, usually of Algonquin manufacture, sufficient for all purposes, but as time rolled on and new necessities arose, these primitive contrivances gave way to others scarcely less unique. Succeeding the canoe came in due season, at the demand of trade, the flat-boat, the pirogue, the Mackinaw-boat, the keel-boat, the barge, the horse-boat, and last, but not least, the "broad-horn," or produce-boat, which for many years was extensively used in floating heavy loads to the market of far-away New Orleans.

This huge, ungainly craft worked very well so long as it could float downward with the current, but to ascend with it was almost an impossibility. Yet, occasionally, even this miracle was accomplished. Labor was cheap, a broad sail could often be used to advantage, and otherwise sweeps, poles, and tow-ropes were always at hand. Yet, as a rule, keel-boats and barges were found more generally available for the up-stream voyage, and even with such carriers it commonly required four months of most disheartening toil between New Orleans and the falls of the Ohio. In the fur trade the pirogue and the Mackinaw-boat were mostly used. These were constructed roughly at the far-off forts, loaded with peltries, manned by *voyageurs*, and sent down the river on the Spring floods. Few of them were ever taken back again, but disposed of in any way possible, or left to rot along the banks.

The entire commerce of the Mississippi, until the coming of the steamboat, was confined to the shipment of lead ore, and the bringing in of the small amount of provisions required by the miners. This was largely done by means of keel-boats of about one hundred tons capacity. Barges were also used for the down-stream trip. The first steamboat to penetrate into these upper waters, or above the Des Moines Rapids, is believed to have been the "Virginia," which arrived at Galena in 1823, and the same year reached Fort Snelling; but the keel-boats and barges continued the more popular for many years later. The old-time barge was a cumbersome, slow, and dangerous contrivance. These boats were from twenty-five to one hundred feet long, with a breadth of beam of from fifteen to twenty feet, and a carrying capacity of from six to one hundred tons. The receptacle for the freight was a large covered coffer, called a "cargo-box," which occupied a considerable portion of the bulk. Near the stern was a small apartment, six or eight feet long, where the captain or owner was quartered at night. On the elevated roof of this cabin the steersman stood to guide the unwieldy craft. It usually boasted of two masts, the main reliance being a large square sail set well forward, capable of relieving the men greatly when the wind was right. About fifty men were usually necessary as a crew, and their labors on a long voyage were varied — sometimes they pulled at the heavy oars, or towed the boat from the shore. Occasionally they were obliged to "warp" their slow way along, and then again to take a spell at "poling"; in fact, it was pole and warp, and tow and row for months at a time to fetch a cargo from the Gulf to St. Louis.

We are reliably informed that, previous to the coming of the steamboats to these waters, say in 1817, the entire commerce from New Orleans to the upper country was carried in about twenty such barges, averaging one hundred tons each, and making but a single trip each year. The first appearance of the keel-boat, and possibly also of the barge, on the Mississippi, above the Ohio, of which there is any official record, was in 1751, when a fleet of such boats, under command of Bossu, a captain of French marines, ascended as far as Fort Chartres. One of these was left helpless on a sand-bar, another struck a snag and sank, while the general hardship of the voyage was indignantly commented upon. Manuel White, in describing a trip he made on such a boat from Louisville to New Orleans in 1801, which required sixty days, says: "There was not to be seen on the banks of the Ohio, from the foot of the falls to the mouth, but a small settlement called Red Banks, another called Yellow Banks, Fort Massac, and a cabin below Cave-in-Rock."

The first steamboat to navigate the Western waters and along the Illinois shore was named the "New Orleans." She left Pittsburg in September, 1811, on her venturesome voyage. This vessel was one hundred and sixteen feet in length, twenty feet beam, and four hundred tons burden. The engine possessed a thirty-four-inch cylinder, with boiler in proportion, and the total cost approximated thirty-eight thousand dollars. There were two cabins, one aft for ladies and a larger one forward for men. The ladies' cabin contained four berths, and on this initial trip was occupied by the owner, Mr. Roosevelt, and his wife, who were the only passengers. The crew consisted of the captain, an engineer named Baker, Andrew Sack the pilot, six hands, two female servants, a man waiter, a cook, and a dog named "Tiger." The people of Pittsburg turned out *en masse* to bid them good-bye, and they received similar ovations at Cincinnati and Louisville. In many ways it proved an adventurous voyage; the passage of the falls of the Ohio was made with difficulty and some peril; the great comet of that year blazed in the sky overhead, and they felt the effect of the earthquake which wrought such damage at New Madrid, and barely escaped being caught in its grasp. The terrors of fire also threatened them on one occasion, and great difficulty was experienced from shoals, snags, and sawyers. To add romance to the other adventures of the trip, the captain fell in love with Mrs. Roosevelt's maid, and prosecuted his suit so successfully that a marriage was duly celebrated at Natchez.

It is interesting to note the checkered careers of those first frail steamboats — all more or less experiments — that navigated the waters of the Ohio and the Mississippi. The second boat built was the "Comet," of twenty-five tons. She made a voyage to Louisville in 1813, and reached New Orleans the following Spring. After two trips she was sold, and her engines utilized to drive a cotton-gin. The "Vesuvius" was the third boat, and registered three hundred and forty tons. Under command of Frank Ogden, she started for New Orleans in June, 1814, but grounded on a bar just below the mouth of the Ohio, where she rested until December, when the river rose and floated her off. A very similar experience occurred to her at New Orleans. Finally taking fire, she burned to the water's edge. The "Enterprise" was the fourth boat, of forty-five tons burden. Henry M. Sheve was her commander, and she was used chiefly in transporting troops and munitions of war. She was considered unusually fast for those days, having a record of six hundred and twenty-four miles in six and a half days, which in these later times awakens a smile. She was wrecked at Shippingport in 1815. The "Ætna" was the fifth boat, and under command of Captain Robinson de Hart, made six trips between Louisville and New Orleans. Her end is unknown.

The sixth boat, the "Zebulon M. Pike," has a history of greater interest, as she was the first to ascend the Mississippi above the mouth of the Ohio, and to reach St. Louis. The "Pike" was built at Henderson, Kentucky, in 1815, and performed a maiden trip to Louisville, two hundred and fifty miles, in sixty-seven hours, averaging three and one-fourth miles per hour against the current. "The hull," says a writer of the day, "was built on the model of a barge, and the cabin built on the lower deck inside of the running-boards." The vessel was propelled by a low-pressure engine with a walking-beam, there being but one smoke-stack, and no houses over the wheels. In a rapid current, the crew were compelled to aid progress by the use of main strength. They diligently operated poles and running-boards the same as if they were on a barge. Captain Jacob Read took the "Pike" to St. Louis, running his boat only during daylight, and thus consumed six weeks in making the trip between Louisville and St. Louis. He tied up at the foot of Market Street, August 2, 1817. The scattered inhabitants along the Illinois shore gazed in wonder as this strange apparition went chugging noisily past their little settlements. At St. Louis all the citizens gathered on the bank to welcome their novel visitor. Among them, tradition says, was a group of Indians. As the boat approached, the glare from the furnace and the volume of murky smoke filled the untutored savages with sudden dismay. They fled to the high ground in the rear of the village, and no assurances of safety could induce them to approach the snorting monster again. The "Pike" made several trips over this strip of river, but was finally snagged in March, 1818, in the Red River.

The "Dispatch," the "Buffalo," and the "James Monroe" followed, but it remained for the tenth boat to demonstrate beyond further question that steamboating was destined to be a success on Western water-ways. This was the "Washington," four hundred tons, and a two-decker, the first to carry her boilers on the upper deck. Under command of Captain Shreve, she left Shippingport, and made the round trip to New Orleans in the unprecedented time of forty-five days. The thirty-fifth boat built was the "General Pike," and her title to fame rests in the fact that she was the first used in the West exclusively for passengers. Her cabin was forty feet in length and twenty-five in breadth. At one end were six staterooms, and at the other end eight. Between was a saloon capable of accommodating one hundred passengers.

The time required in travelling by these early boats seems something extremely tedious to those of us living in the present age of rapid transit, but in that day it was considered remarkable, and many thought it would never be surpassed. In 1815, it required twenty-five days, two hours, and forty minutes, by the fastest steamers, to make the trip from New Orleans to Louisville, a distance of 1,486 miles. Very gradually this was improved upon. In 1828, the "Tecumseh" cut it down to eight days, four hours, and finally in 1853, the "Eclipse" established her record as the swiftest boat afloat, by covering the distance in four days, nine hours, and thirty minutes. In 1823 there were public rejoicings at Louisville over a steamer arriving there in fifteen days and six hours from New Orleans, and the captain, answering a toast, gravely announced that he really believed the voyage might be made in six hours less. This same reduction in time is noticeable on all the rivers. From New Orleans to Cairo, the "J. M. White," doing ordinary business along the way, made the 1,024 miles in three days, six hours, and forty-four minutes. From Louisville to St. Louis the run was made in 1855 by the "Southerner" in forty-three hours, a notable improvement over the six weeks required in 1817. On the upper river, as early as 1859, the "Louisiana" ran from St. Louis to Keokuk in sixteen hours and twenty minutes; ten years later, the "Hawkeye State" is said to have reached St. Paul in two days and twenty hours, and the "Cataract" attained La Salle, on the Illinois River, from St. Louis in twenty-three hours, forty-five minutes.

These early records of increased steamboat efficiency

and speed were attained in the course of regular business done at the various landings. At one time, however, rivalry between the different lines became very fierce, and resulted in numerous hard-fought races for supremacy. In such cases, boats were often stripped for the contest, and pressed to the utmost by enthusiastic crews, coaled from barges while going at full speed, and few if any stops made until the goal was reached. The most famous races in waterways bordering Illinois were those between the "Baltic" and the "Diana" in 1854; and that tremendous struggle of 1,218 miles between the "Natchez" and the "Robert E. Lee" in 1870. This last was probably the greatest steamboat race ever run in the world. The "Baltic" and the "Diana," between whose crews considerable rivalry existed, chanced to leave New Orleans on the same day, bound for Louisville, the "Baltic" being slightly in the lead. Neither boat had ever exhibited any great speed, and while the result was what might be termed a slow race, it was an extraordinarily long one, hotly contested to the end, and became intensely exciting to the participants. During all of the 1,486 miles covered, there was not an hour of the time when the two boats were out of sight or hearing of each other. An artist chanced to be on board the "Baltic" at the time, and he immortalized the event by transferring to canvas, in oil, a night scene, in which were graphically depicted the two imposing steamers in the foreground. The "Baltic" won the race, but the time does not seem to have been recorded.

The "Natchez-Lee" race attracted international attention, and immense sums of money were wagered on the result. There had long been great rivalry between the boats and their commanders, T. P. Leathers of the "Natchez" and John W. Cannon of the "Lee." In June, 1870, the former made the fastest time on record between New Orleans to St. Louis, three days, twenty-one hours, and fifty-eight minutes. When Captain Cannon heard this, he determined to beat it if possible. He stripped the "Lee" for the race, removing all parts of her upper works likely to catch the wind, took down all the rigging that could be dispensed with, and engaged another steamer to proceed up the river, one hundred miles in advance, to supply her with coal in midstream. All business was refused for way-landings, and no passengers were received. Meanwhile the "Natchez" received a few tons of freight, accepted some passengers, and advertised to leave for St. Louis on June 30. During the afternoon of that day the "Lee" backed out from the levee, and five minutes later the "Natchez" followed her. The whole country was interested in the race, it having been widely advertised by the press, and the details of its progress being reported by telegraph. Crowds gathered at the various cities along the way, and even at out-of-the-way points people stood straining their eyes to catch sight of the flying racers. Everything possible to increase speed was resorted to, and thus night and day the two contestants sped up the river in a struggle for mastery. But at Cairo the race was virtually ended, although the "Lee" continued to St. Louis at top speed, arriving there in three days, eighteen hours, and fourteen minutes from the time of her leaving New Orleans, thus beating by thirty-three minutes the previous record of the "Natchez." The latter steamer became enveloped in a fog above Cairo, and was delayed for six hours. The conclusion of the race resulted in much controversy, but it was generally conceded that the "Lee" had won fairly.

From the very beginning of steamboat navigation on the Western rivers, accidents have been numerous and often fatal. Comparatively few, however, of those which may be ranked among great disasters have occurred in Illinois waters. The earliest of these was the loss of the steamer "Mechanic" in 1825, while on the way from Nashville to

Marietta, Ohio, having on board, at the time, General La Fayette, General Carroll and staff, Governor Coles of Illinois, and several others of prominence. About midnight, May 6, while ascending the Ohio, one hundred and twenty-five miles below Louisville, and close to the mouth of Deer Creek, the boat struck a snag in midstream, and immediately began to settle. The night was very dark, and much confusion ensued, but General La Fayette was hurried on deck, and assisted over the rail, where a yawl waited to convey him ashore. In the excitement he fell overboard, and being then far advanced in years, narrowly escaped drowning before help arrived. He lost eight thousand dollars in money, besides much personal property. Captain Hall, devoting all his attention to his distinguished guests, forgot his own interests, and lost a desk containing nearly two thousand dollars.

A most distressing accident, by which sixteen persons were instantly killed and several others badly scalded, took place on the Mississippi, while the boat " Dubuque " was on her voyage from St. Louis to Galena. The locality of the disaster was off Muscatine Bar, eight miles below Burlington. The "Dubuque" was running under a moderate pressure of steam at the time, when the flue of the larboard boiler, probably on account of some defect in the material or workmanship, collapsed, throwing a torrent of scalding water over the deck. The pilot immediately steered for the shore and effected a landing.

When the consternation and dismay occasioned by the explosion had in some measure subsided, Captain Smoker, the commander of the " Dubuque," and such of his crew as were not disabled by the accident, made their way with considerable difficulty through the ruins to the after part of the boiler-deck, when it was found that the whole of the freight and every other article which had been there deposited were cleared off and blown far away into the water.

The unfortunate deck passengers, together with the cooks and several of the crew, were severely scalded either by the hot water or the escaping steam. Many of the injured, in their agony, fled to the shore. It was several hours before any of them died; nor could medical relief be obtained until a boat, which had been despatched from Bloomington, returned with several physicians who resided at that place. At ten o'clock that night, eight hours after the explosion, the steamboat "Adventure," Captain Van Houten, came up with the wreck and took it in tow as far as Bloomington.

On the third of January, 1844, the entire city of St. Louis was thrown into consternation by the news that the steamboat "Shepherdess" had been wrecked in Cahokia Bend, only three miles from the centre of the city, and many lives lost. The following is Captain Gould's account of this disaster:

"The 'Shepherdess,' while ascending the Mississippi River on her way from Cincinnati to St. Louis, and at eleven o'clock in a dark and stormy night, struck a snag just above the mouth of Cahokia Creek. The concussion was very severe, and it is believed that several planks must have been torn from the bottom of the boat. According to the report of the officers, most of those who were in the gentlemen's cabin had retired to their berths; four or five gentlemen, however, were sitting up by the stove, as it was cold Winter weather. The ladies were generally undressed for the night.

"In less than two minutes after the boat struck, the water rose to the lower deck, where most of the passengers in that part of the boat were asleep. The captain, who was on duty, ran to the cabin occupied by the ladies, and assured them that there was no danger; he then returned to the forecastle, and is supposed to have been washed overboard, as nothing was ever seen or heard of him afterwards. As soon as the shock was felt on board, one of the pilots attempted to descend into the hold for the purpose of examining the leak, but he had scarcely entered when the rush of water drove him back.

"About this time shrieks and exclamations of affright and distress arose from the deck below, and several ladies, who hastened to the stern railing, reported that they saw a number of persons struggling in the river. Certain it is that the water rushed in with tremendous rapidity, and before three minutes had elapsed it had risen to the floor of the upper cabin. Some of those persons who were on deck saved themselves by getting into the yawl, which was cut loose and rowed to the shore with a broom. The water rose so rapidly that it soon became necessary for all to seek safety on the hurricane-deck. This position was not attained without great difficulty, for the bow had sunk so deep in the water that the only access was via the stern. However, it is believed that all the people from the cabin succeeded in reaching the hurricane roof. In the meanwhile the boat was drifting down the stream, and a few hundred yards below, she struck another snag which rose above the surface. This threw the steamer nearly on her beam ends on the larboard side. Drifting from this snag, she again lurched to starboard. At each lurch several persons were washed off; some of them reached the shore, but many were drowned. A short distance below, just above the first shot-tower, the hull struck a bluff bank, which again careened the boat nearly on her side. Here the hull and cabin parted; the former sunk and lodged on a bar above Carondelet, while the cabin floated down to the point of the bar below that place, where it lodged and became stationary.

"The steamer 'Henry Bry' was lying at the shot-tower above Carondelet, and as the cabin passed, the captain of that vessel, being aroused by the cries of the passengers, took his yawl to their rescue. This little boat could only take off a few at a time, but by the strenuous exertions of the captain of the 'Bry,' many were saved. This humane gentleman almost sacrificed himself in the work of benevolence, and did not desist until he was covered with a mass of ice, and benumbed to that degree that further effort was impossible. About three o'clock the ferry-boat 'Icelander' came down, and took off all who remained in the detached cabin."

In 1849, at a time when cholera was raging in St. Louis, thousands being struck down by the dread scourge, there occurred a fire on the river, which added vastly to the prevailing horror. The following description is from Scharf's "Sketch Book":

"While the disease was raging at its fiercest, the city was doomed to another horror — the city was burnt — fifteen squares were laid in ashes. The fire commenced on the steamer 'White Cloud,' lying between Washington and Cherry Streets. The wind was blowing fiercely on shore, which fact contributed materially to the extent of the marine disaster, and although the lines of all the boats were cut and hauled in, and they shoved out into the current, the burning boat seemed to outstrip them all, with the speed with which she floated down the river; and in perhaps thirty minutes after the fire broke out, twenty-three steamboats had been abandoned to the prey of the flames, and a half a million dollars' worth of property had been destroyed. So devastating a fire had never before been known in the United States.

"Fifteen blocks of houses were burned or seriously damaged, causing the loss of ten million dollars. The fire was finally extinguished by blowing up several houses with powder, but in doing that, several lives were lost, although great care was taken to give timely warning. The list of sufferers made eight or ten columns in 'The Missouri Republican.'"

The story of the upper river navigation can be given only briefly, as it has had few historians, and left little detail on record. Here, during a large portion of the year, navigation is difficult and uncertain, being obstructed by rapids and low water; nor did the earlier erected bridges detract from the danger. The first bridge across the Mississippi was at Rock Island. Gould says:

"It was a drawbridge, and built without any legal authority, simply by a charter from the State of Illinois. It was commenced in 1853, and was the most dangerous obstruction to navigation ever constructed, on account of its being located over a chain of rocks, producing boils and cross currents which were difficult to keep a boat in. Many lives were lost in passing through the draw, and under the bridge, and many rafts were broken up. One fine steamboat, the 'Effa Afton,' was sunk and a large number of lives lost. An effort was made by the river interests to have the bridge removed as an illegal structure and dangerous to navigation. But such was the persistency of the proprietors, they defeated every effort in the several courts to which it was carried, and after fighting the bridge for more than ten years with the money and influence of the Merchants Exchange, of St. Louis, as well as that of many citizens along the river, and the best legal talent that could be employed, the bridge remained until removed by Act of Congress in 1872, when by a sort of compromise the Government built another bridge higher up the river, at the head of the Island, and removed the old one."

The steamboat lines operating north of St. Louis have been numerous, but few have proven successful financially. The "Di Vernon" was the first boat of the St. Louis and Keokuk Packet Company, and made her initial trip in 1842. A few years later, an opposition line put into commission three boats, the "Swallow," the "Anthony Wayne," and the "Edward Bates." The intense competition resulting proved the ruin of both. Others followed rapidly, covering the waters of the entire system from St. Louis to St. Paul; but perhaps the more interesting history of river navigation was previous to this organization of companies, those earlier days when steamboating was purely an adventure. A well-known river writer has said:

"All early settlers, as well as the old boatmen, will remember the 'Rosalie,' Captain Mike Littleton; the 'Quincy,' Captain Cameron; the 'Boreas,' Captain Fitheon; the 'Knickbocker,' Captain Gould, and many others long since forgotten.

"There were also many boats running above the rapids from St. Louis, among which will be remembered the 'Warrior,' Captain Throckmorton; the 'Winnebago,' Captain Atchison; the 'Joe Daviess,' Captain Scribe Harris; the 'Pizarro,' Captain Smith Harris; the 'Rolla,' Captain Reynolds; the 'Gypsy,' Captain Gray; the 'St. Croix,' Captain Bersie; the 'Illinois,' Captain McCalister; the 'Rapids,' Captain Cole; the 'Fulton,'

Captain Orrin Smith; the 'Brazil,' the 'Irene,' the 'Ione,' the 'Time and Tide,' the 'Falcon,' the 'St. Peter,' the 'Montauk,' and many others."

Steamboat navigation on the Illinois River was somewhat late in opening, no regular line being in operation previous to 1835. Among boats there previous to this date may be mentioned the "Criterion" in 1828; the "Orion" and the "Express" in 1832; the "Miner" in 1833; the "Lady Jackson," the "Wisconsin," the "Cold Water," the "Utility," the "American," the "Springfield," the "Champion," in 1834; the "Banner," the "Winnebago," the "Adventure," the "Illinois," in 1835.

In Scharf's "History of St. Louis" is this account of early Illinois River steamboats:

"The steamboat 'Ottawa' was the first boat built on the Illinois. She was constructed in part at Ottawa, added to at Peru, and finished at St. Louis. She was of the very lightest draught, seventeen inches, and had a powerful engine; the design being to take two keels in tow in low water, the steamer herself being light, so that whenever there was seventeen inches of water on the bars she would be able to reach St. Louis with one hundred tons of freight weekly. Her length was one hundred feet, breadth twenty feet, and the cabin laid off entirely in staterooms. The owners resided in Ottawa. There is no date by which to determine the appearance of this specimen of marine architecture. It must, however, have been pretty early, as none of the present generation of 'old boatmen' know anything of the 'towboat' 'Ottawa.'"

"As early as 1844," says Gould, "Captain Samuel Rider, one of the most mechanical and inventive boatmen ever on the Illinois River, built at Griggsville landing, a sort of nondescript boat he called 'Olitippa,' which was propelled by horses upon an endless chain. The boat had no cabin or cargo-box, and the hold was too shallow to stow freight in. She was designed expressly to carry freight in low water, which, of course, had to be stowed on the main deck, as she had no other; and the cook, the officers, and the men occupied the same location. The clerk's office was carried in the captain's hat, and as there were but few ladies travelling on the Illinois at that early day, a chambermaid was dispensed with. Later on, when accidents on the rivers were more frequent from fires and bursting of boilers, the 'Olitippa' would doubtless have become very popular, as but little apprehension could have been felt from either cause on her. She proved to be what she was designed for, a light-draught boat (only ten inches) for the Illinois River. But when she drifted out of her home element into the strong currents of the Mississippi, she was at sea without a rudder, or without power to avoid snags or ice-shores."

It is impossible to dismiss this subject without some reference to the river floods which from time to time have swept the Mississippi Valley. The first authentic account of the American Bottom being submerged is that of the flood in 1724. A document is to be seen in the archives of Kaskaskia, which consists of a petition to the crown of France in 1725, for a grant of land in which the damage sustained the year before is mentioned. The villagers were driven to the bluffs on the opposite side of the Kaskaskia River. Their gardens and crops were destroyed, and their buildings and property much injured. We have no evidence of its exact height, but the whole American Bottom was submerged. This was probably in June.

In 1772, Fort Chartres was destroyed by a sudden rise of waters, but from 1785 to 1811 there were no destructive floods, although an occasional overflow proved sufficient to fill the lake and low grounds on the American Bottom. This was in the year preceding the great "shakes," as the earthquakes were called. The river began rising at St. St. Louis early in May, and by the fifteenth it had spread over a large portion of the American Bottom, but by the first of June it was out of its banks only in low places. On the sixth it again began to rise, and continued to increase in volume until the fourteenth, when it came to a stand; the greater part of the bottom, Kaskaskia, Cahokia, Prairie du Pont, Cautine, and nearly all the settlements along the low lands were under water, and the inhabitants had fled to the high bluffs. The " common fields" at St. Genevieve were entirely submerged ; the corn was nearly covered.

A story is still told by the old inhabitants of the village, that the panic-stricken people appealed to Father Maxwell, the village priest, to " pray away the water." It is said he gave no encouragement at first, until the water came to a stand. Then he proposed to the people to drive off the water by saying masses. This they did, and as the water fell rapidly, the ground was soon dry, and a fine crop of corn was raised, which was divided with the priest in conformity to the agreement for saying the masses.

In 1826, and at irregular times since, the water has risen very high and wrought much danger, not only to settlers along the Illinois shore, but to steamboats navigating the rivers.

CHAPTER XXX

THE COMING OF THE RAILROAD

THE line of special demarcation between the days of the frontier and modern conditions is very easily traceable in Illinois history. The old and the new stand distinct and apart, divided by that wizard, steam, whose long lines of gleaming rails now gridiron the State. While various other causes undoubtedly contributed toward this same result, and every influence of growth and prosperity tended toward permanent advancement, yet it was the coming of the railway which immediately achieved this purpose. Under the magic of its extension, barter became commerce, and petty trade between neighbors grew into a world-wide exchange of commodities; population came in fast-increasing throngs, no longer deterred by the hardships of wilderness travel. These brought with them wealth, refinement, the enterprise of financial exploitation; isolated settlements grew into pleasant towns, while many of these, favored by situation or the consolidation of wealth, pressed swiftly forward into great and important cities. On all sides, land long lying vacant found occupants, venturesome souls pressing out into the wide prairie stretches, encouraged to believe that within a few years, at most, the favoring railway would extend its iron bands as a reward for their patient toil. The East became linked to the West, and an impetus was thus given to every form of commercial life which made of Illinois one of the great States of the Union; her struggling childhood had passed away forever, her years of fair womanhood begun.

It is not difficult to trace the winding path leading up

to this consummation of all that the hardy pioneers dreamed of, but it is sometimes hard to conceive the reasons why certain steps were taken along the devious course of legislation leading thereto,— the mistakes, the failures, the wild visionary schemes fluttering on every side, the fierce opposition offered to what we now know to have been wise, the party strife that retarded, the jealousy of cities and of political leaders continually blocking the way. We can only remember that these walked in darkness, whereas we stand in light, and remain charitable alike to the mistakes made and the ill judgment shown. The end was inevitable, and in spite of opposition won slowly to the final betterment of the State.

We will not attempt here to trace this movement in great detail, but content ourselves with making its more salient and picturesque steps reasonably clear, and in this will follow largely the facts as stated by Davidson and Stuvé. In 1826 the first railroad in the United States, connecting Albany and Schenectady in New York, was built. Its successful operation instantly fired the imagination of the ambitious men of that period. It promised to work a sudden revolution in all commercial affairs, and there early began an era of road-building which is even yet far from having reached its limit. Far-seeing men in Illinois at once perceived its value for the development of the resources of the State, and took steps toward this attainment. The State, at the time, was peculiarly isolated, and necessarily provincial, her only communication with the East being by means of river or lake, or through a long, wearisome journey by wagon overland. The scattered settlements within her borders, some few already budding into small but ambitious cities, were connected by rudely constructed earth roads, over which rolled the occasional stage-coach, or the heavily laden wagon. Travelling was mostly on horseback. Under these conditions, trade must remain extremely limited, commerce in its wider meaning unknown, and development of resources extremely slow. The railroad promised immediate relief for all these existing evils, and even dull minds felt the call for united action.

As early as 1836, the matter was brought formally before the legislature for consideration, during the administration of Governor Duncan. As is apt to be the case in times of popular enthusiasm, so much was undertaken, considering the then impoverished condition of the treasury and the sparseness of population, and consequent meagreness of revenue, that the entire project naturally died from lack of nourishment. It is interesting to read the numerous theories advanced at that period, as to the probable cost of railway construction, and the wonderful benefits which would immediately accrue to the people and to the State treasury. Each legislator had apparently discovered an Aladdin's lamp with which he proposed to illumine the surrounding regions. The railroads laid out at this time — and for the construction of which money was actually voted in the form of bonds, with commissioners appointed to borrow on the credit of the State — were known as the Central Railroad, outlined to extend from Cairo to the Illinois and Michigan Canal; railroads from Alton to Mount Carmel (called Southern Cross Road), and Alton to Shawneetown; the Northern Cross Road from Quincy to the Indiana State line (the modern Toledo, Wabash, and Western Railroad), together with various branches to nearly every important town in the State; while two hundred thousand dollars was graciously voted as an olive branch to those few counties whose claims to recognition in railroad-building might have been overlooked. Altogether, the then magnificent sum of $5,850,000 was thus appropriated for railroad-building, while an equally generous amount was set aside for river and other improvements, made necessary by such railway construction. But even this amount was soon discovered to be not half large enough to carry out the work as pro-

TWO FAMILIAR SCENES OF PIONEER DAYS

THE MAIL-COACH AND THE PRAIRIE-SCHOONER

posed. Illinois then had a census population of 271,727; the taxable wealth of the State three years later was only $58,889,525, and yet her legislators deliberately assumed, on her behalf, an expenditure of $20,000,000 !

However, this "grand system" fell by its own weight, and, with the exception of a part of the Northern Cross Railroad, the work, which was begun simultaneously in various portions of the State, came to no more than a few excavations and embankments, some of which still remain as curiosities in their neighborhoods. The portion of the Northern Cross Road, leading from Meredosia to Springfield, was actually completed at a cost to the State of one million dollars; but its income proved insufficient to keep it in repair, and it was subsequently sold for one hundred thousand dollars in State indebtedness. Of this road, some eight miles of track was laid in 1838, running from Meredosia east, the first rail being laid May 9. The first locomotive that ever turned a wheel in the great valley of the Mississippi, marking the dawn of a new era, was operated over this track, November 8, 1838. George W. Plant, later a successful merchant of St. Louis, officiated as engineer. The locomotive ran the distance of eight miles and back, carrying, as passengers, Governor Duncan, Murray McConnel, one of the public commissioners, two of the contractors, and the Chief Engineer of the road, George P. Plant. This occurred only twelve years later than the first railroad in the United States was operated; but now there followed a necessary pause. For the next twelve years nothing was accomplished, and for the best of reasons,— money was lacking, and even the State herself trembled on the brink of repudiation. Everything seemed to fall upon her at once, the collapse of the internal improvement system, the suspension of banks, and a depreciated currency, until the total State debt attained to the vast amount of $14,666,562.42. But in 1850 the Chicago and Galena road was completed by private capital as far as Elgin, and from that date there distinctly dawned upon the State the great railroad era which has since covered Illinois with a complicated network of these iron arteries of commerce, affording rapid and easy communication with almost every county.

During this period the impoverished condition of the State treasury and the sparseness of population, and consequent lack of taxable property, were not altogether responsible for the slowness of railroad development and exploitation. It resulted rather from what has since been known as "State policy," arising from the narrow dullness of certain politicians, and originating in the commercial rivalry of several ambitious Illinois towns, of which Alton was the most conspicuous. Outside capital and enterprise were eager enough to invade the Illinois field, yet, almost without exception, the plans of such projected railroads led directly across the State, with their eastern termini in Indiana, at either Vincennes or Terre Haute, and reaching westward to St. Louis, in Missouri. This did not look right to the average Illinoisan of that region, as such a condition must inevitably result in the building up of important cities just beyond the State limits, to the deterioration of local points. Moreover, a wider argument was urged, that by this scheme Illinois' commerce would be largely diverted to defray the expenses of foreign governments, to her own manifest detriment. Practically every town in central and southern Illinois united in the determination to defeat such charters. Vast mass-meetings were held, especially at Salem and Hillsboro, in the Summer and Fall of 1849, to discuss the situation. At the latter, it is said, twelve thousand people were present; the principles of "State policy" were enthusiastically endorsed, and every possible precaution taken to prevent foreign railroad companies from invading the sacred soil of the State — unless they would agree to make a terminus on Illinois territory.

This short-sighted, and indeed blind, policy no doubt considerably retarded the development of Illinois, and certainly called down upon her legislators the most sarcastic comments of other States, whose newspapers characterized such a course as selfish, narrow, and contemptible, a re-enacting of the fable of the dog in the manger. But the Alton influence continued to control the politicians and a majority of the people until the administration of Governor French, when the more healthy condition of the State treasury put a somewhat different aspect on internal affairs. At the commencement of Governor Ford's administration in 1842, it was officially announced that there was not money enough in the State treasury to pay postage on a letter. Everything was almost at a standstill in point of revenue; there were whole counties containing scarcely more than a log cabin within their boundaries, and only six small cities (really no more than towns) in the State,—Chicago, Alton, Springfield, Quincy, Galena, and Nauvoo. The State had borrowed itself out of all credit, and there was not good money enough in the hands of all the people to pay the interest of the debt for a single year. But Illinois proved an infant Hercules slumbering in the cradle, and under the fostering care of Governors Ford and French, began to exhibit its true strength.

During this period a new loan was floated, amounting to $1,600,000, that was used to complete the Illinois and Michigan Canal, which now began to yield an annual revenue in tolls; canal lands worth half a million dollars were sold far above the appraisement; three-fifths of the one-and-a-half-mill tax authorized in 1845 now paid twelve dollars out of every sixty dollars of annually accruing interest; and if the two-mill tax, authorized by the new constitution, could have been diverted in that way, the whole annual interest on the internal improvement debt proper could have been paid. Auditor's warrants were worth ninety-five cents on the dollar, such was the improved condition brought about by rigid economy, and a thorough system of retrenchment under the new constitution. The infant Hercules began to sit up and look around. The Legislature of 1851 again took hold of railroad measures, and in a better spirit than had characterized its predecessors. But the benumbing incubus of "State policy" was not, even yet, entirely shaken off, and nothing definite was accomplished except the granting of a charter to the Ohio and Mississippi Company. This, however, was a good beginning, and much of the credit must be given Senator Douglas, whose frank letter on the subject exercised wide influence throughout the State. In this he said that if he were a legislator he would certainly grant a charter for the proposed road from Illinoistown to Terre Haute, and also to Vincennes, and to other lines across the State when any considerable portion of the people desired it. He would give a preference to the towns and cities of Illinois where it could be done without injury or injustice to others, but he would never sacrifice the great agricultural interests for the benefit of a much smaller interest in the towns. The country was not made for the towns, but the towns for the convenience of the country. This sensible advice not only exercised an immediate influence, but also contributed largely to further future action.

Toward the conclusion of this controversy, which continued until the special Legislature of 1853, the efforts of those interested in "State policy" centred entirely upon the defeat of the proposed charter for the Atlantic and Mississippi Railroad, known as the "Brough Road," projected from Terre Haute via Vandalia to St. Louis. This was fought with exceeding bitterness. But these efforts failed, and "State policy" disappeared forever from Illinois politics. To show to what extremes its advocates were willing to go, Joseph Gillespie, the special champion of the Alton interests, introduced a bill into the Senate in 1853, by which all existing chartered railroad corporations were to be protected for ten years against the building of any competing roads within twenty-five miles, unless existing corporations first consented thereto. To quote Davidson and Stuvé:

> "This amazing proposition was a fit climax to all the monstrous, absurd, and pernicious schemes of the 'State Policy' party. While many of the other States of the Union, animated by a noble spirit of enterprise, were removing legal obstructions, and instead adopting broad and liberal railroad incorporation laws, throwing wide open their borders, and inviting capital from abroad to build railroads and create competition wherever it inclined, it was coolly proposed in the great State of Illinois, which needed development very badly, to draw a cordon of exclusiveness around her borders, and within to combine with soulless corporations in the monopoly of all improvements, and hand over to them, bound by the strong cords of the law, the people of the State to be fleeced without stint."

The bill failed to become a law.

But the one happening which, occurring at exactly the proper moment, turned the current of popular approval in the right direction was the magnificent donation of some three million acres of land by Act of Congress to the State as security for the building of the Illinois Central Railroad. This was in September, 1850. The final passage of the measure, after two previous defeats, was hailed with demonstrations of great joy by the people and the press. Almost immediately Illinois Internal Improvement bonds made an advance of ten per cent in the New York market. The total railroad mileage in the State at that time was insignificant, consisting merely of a small section of the Northern Cross Road, from Meredosia and Naples, on the Illinois River, to Springfield; the Chicago and Galena, from the former city as far as Elgin; and a six-mile coal track across the American Bottom from opposite St. Louis to the mines in the bluffs. The first ten miles of the Chicago and Galena (which since

1865 has been consolidated with the Chicago and North Western Railway) was finished from Chicago to Harlem, December 30, 1848, and completed to the Mississippi River, at Fulton, in December, 1855. It was the first railroad turning a locomotive wheel in the city of Chicago, and the first to connect the commerce of the Mississippi with that of the Lakes — the dream of a generation at last fulfilled.

The act by which the general Government thus made possible the immediate building of the Illinois Central, granted a right of way for the railroad through the public lands the width of two hundred feet, from the southern terminus of the Illinois and Michigan Canal at La Salle, to a point at or near the junction of the Ohio and Mississippi Rivers, and for branches to Chicago and Galena. But the main grant to the State, which enabled this gigantic work to be undertaken without delay, was the alternate sections of land, designated by even numbers for six sections deep, on each side of its trunk or branches. The road was to be begun simultaneously at its northern and southern termini, and completed within ten years. The minimum price of the odd-numbered sections, which remained in Government ownership, was raised from $1.25 to $2.50 per acre. The entire body of land was taken out of market for two years, and when restored in the Fall of 1852, it, in fact, brought an average of $5.00 per acre. So, while the public lands were thus by the prospect of the building of the road rendered more salable, and at a much higher price, and the Government not only lost nothing in dollars and cents but in both time and cash gained largely, the gift was, nevertheless, a splendid one, and resulted in almost measureless benefit to the State.

The point of departure of the Chicago branch from the main line was not fixed in the act,— an omission which resulted in much contention. Many worthy and ambitious towns came at once into bitter competition. La Salle was

A FAMOUS HOSTELRY—THE METAMORA HOUSE

WHERE MANY PROMINENT ILLINOIS MEN MET IN THE EARLY DAYS

eager for it; Bloomington, already figuring on a continuation of the old Alton and Sangamon (now the Chicago and Alton), wished this Chicago connection badly; while Shelbyville, which was a point on the old original central survey, and never dreamed of being left off the main line, entered the contest for the branch also, and lost both. But the company, in their location of a route, took little consideration of anything except to run their line wherever there was the largest amount of vacant land which could be brought within the limits of the Government grant. This proved the controlling influence, both regarding the main trunk and the branches. The Legislature spent much time in dealing with the various questions naturally arising under so important a grant, especially as to the projected route, and the place for beginning the branch to Chicago. Nothing very definite was reached, and the point of divergence was finally left with the company to be situated anywhere "north of the parallel of thirty-nine degrees, thirty minutes, of north latitude." The point selected is the site of the present city of Clinton. Regarding the main stem, the decision was but little less definite, the only point fixed being the northeast corner of Township 21 North, Range 2 East, third Principal Meridian, from which the road should not vary in its general course more than five miles. This made it reasonably certain that the main line would pass through the towns of Clinton, Decatur, and Bloomington. Without taking time to dwell upon the numerous schemes with which speculators, eager to gain by this tremendous transaction, flooded the Legislature; the many bills introduced, a few valuable, the most bad; or the rather tiresome details of legislative action over matters of minor importance,— it is sufficient to say that, all legal obstacles having been finally overcome, in March, 1852, the contracts for construction were let, and the work went rapidly forward, without further serious interruption. Dunleith was reached June 12, 1855, and Chicago, September 26, 1856.

But alas, for the best interests of the State, the Legislature had voted all this valuable concession out of public control and ownership into the hands of a syndicate of capitalists! It gave them the use of the donated land for the purpose of raising the necessary funds for carrying out the project, and accepted in return their pledge of an annual payment of interest from the gross earnings of the road. The men to whom this great concession was made, and who later formed the company that built the road, were Robert Schuyler, George Griswold, Gouverneur Morris, Jonathan Sturgis, George W. Ludlow, and John F. A. Sanford, of the city of New York; and David A. Neal, Franklin Haven, and Robert Rantoul, Jr., of Boston. To quote again the pertinent language of Davidson and Stuvé:

"This work was one of the most stupendous and ingenious speculations of modern times. By means of it a few sagacious capitalists became the owners of a first-class railroad, more than seven hundred miles long, in full running order, complete in rolling-stock and every equipage, and millions of acres of land, worth in the aggregate perhaps $40,000,000, without the actual outlay of a cent of their own money. This project was among the first to illustrate the immense field there was opening up in this country for bold and gigantic railroad operations by capitalists; and as contrasted with the State Internal Improvement scheme of 1836–37, it was furthermore an example of the superiority of private enterprise over State or governmental undertakings. The State at that time, with a population of about 350,000, mostly small farmers, authorized a loan exceeding $10,000,000, to construct public works. One of these was the Central Railroad, upon which a considerable sum was expended. Hard times and a general collapse followed in rapid order. Now, with this grant of land from the general Government (not far short of 3,000,000 acres within a belt of fifteen miles along the route of the road) to aid its construction, these gentlemen, backed by credit and capital, step forward, propose to take the lands and build the road, which is to belong to them when built. The State accepts the offer, incorporates the gentlemen's scheme by perpetual charter, and endows them with this munificent domain and all the property and remains of the old Central road. After the road is put in operation, the company pays the State annually seven per centum of its gross earnings in lieu of all taxes for ever. Having acquired a vested right, the State has no other than police control over the company, and as it is a foreign corporation, disputes between them must be settled in foreign, i.e., United States courts. The minimum valuation of lands acquired, so soon as the road should be completed, was $20,000,000, exceeding by $6,000,000 the cost of the road, estimated at $20,000 per mile; which, in Illinois, was liberal, because she presented the most uniform and favorable surface for the construction of railroads of any other State in the Union. Two-thirds of the land was stipulated as security for the principal of the construction bonds, 250,000 acres to secure the interest fund, and the remainder as a contingent fund. The construction bonds found ready sale at par, and built the road. The land sales yielded interest to set off in part the accruing interest on the bonds. The redemption of the bonds completed, the road and all its appurtenances remain the property of the fortunate gentlemen who had the sagacity to see how it could be built without costing them a cent.

"But they did not reap all the developed benefits of this grand enterprise. The alternate sections of land reserved by the Federal Government within fifteen miles of the route of the road, numbered as many acres as the grant to the State; it had been for twenty-odd years in market at $1.25 per acre without sale, but now when again put in the market in the Fall of 1852, it was eagerly taken up and readily brought from three to seven dollars per acre, and more, had not settlers and speculators combined not to bid against each other. As it was, the sales averaged five dollars per acre. The Government thus realized a profit of some $9,000,000 by its munificent policy of giving away half its land in this locality. This was indeed casting bread upon the water, which after many days, returned several fold.

"But, besides the general Government, the State, too, was at the same time benefited by having its unsettled interior opened up to tides of thronging immigrants, its rich soil brought into cultivation, population increased, and its resources and taxable wealth augmented by many millions of dollars. The products of the newly developed region found a ready avenue to the markets of the world. Chicago, too, was thus furnished with another iron tentaculum to reach far into the interior of the State for commercial food to give increase to her marvellous life. But the greatest immediate benefit resulting from the building of the road and branches accrued to the lands within due and proper marketing distance of the lines, estimated at the enormous amount of ten million acres in private hands."

CHAPTER XXXI

HISTORIC SPOTS AS THEY APPEAR TO-DAY

TO one seeking those spots throughout Illinois hallowed by historical associations, there must come more often disappointment than pleasure. Many will be found impossible to locate, even with the most diligent research and the aid of a vivid imagination; others are uncertain, so obscured by the haze of years and less important occurrences as to divide local investigators into hostile camps; while, nearly without exception, the almost criminal neglect of a great State regarding the proper preservation of these memorials of important historic happenings brings a tinge of sadness to all who reverence the great names and deeds of the past. Illinois history has been crowded with events well worthy of perpetual remembrance, events stirring and heroic, tinged by romance; events having vital bearing not only upon the State, but the nation, of far too great importance to be lost in the haze of the careless years.

From 1813, for a period of at least twenty-five years, Shawneetown situated on the Ohio River but a few miles below the mouth of the Wabash, ranked as the most important city of the Territory and State, the chosen home of wealth and refinement, the social and political centre, and the residence of men who carved their names deeply upon the rock of Western history. In an out-of-the-way corner, not easily accessible to the ordinary traveller of to-day, few realize the abiding interest which yet invests this old town, and yields to it a peculiar atmosphere of the earlier days. Generations have come and gone since Eddy, Marshall, McLean, and hundreds of others scarcely less famous or worthy, walked these shaded streets in the long ago, but the town which knew them then has not so greatly changed with the speeding years. Long without a railroad, it yet remains quaint and old, a village quietly brooding over its past glories, and containing many an ancient relic of those stirring times when history was being fresh chiselled from the stone. The famous old tavern in which La Fayette was entertained with such formal ceremony, and where every distinguished Illinoisan of that age was at some time a guest, was but lately destroyed by fire, and much yet lingers to bear the awakened memory back even to territorial days, when nearly all of this Illinois country was an almost trackless wilderness, and brave souls fought for life along this far frontier.

The Henry Eddy house, where the great editor lived and worked, stands almost as he left it, fronting the main business street; while still looking calmly forth upon the peaceful Ohio, the first brick building erected in the town, the old Marshall house, historic as the original home of Illinois' first State bank, established in 1813, and the centre of all early financial operations, remains almost without a change in outward appearance. Everywhere about the ancient town one is constantly happening on such reminders of the past, the old-fashioned homes peeping forth from amid those great trees guarding them, constantly wooing the memory back to days and events long vanished, and, by the many, long forgotten. A strange history of light and shadow hovers about this quaint old place.

Shawanoe Town it was in that far-off past when the fierce tribes of the Shawnees swept the valley of the Ohio, and held this as their western stronghold. But far away, beyond even that era of tradition, the great mounds on which the town is built, and which even yet yield up their treasures of dead, bespeak an antiquity greater than history can measure. Here, undoubtedly, was once the metropolis of an utterly vanished race, and their voiceless memorials, in

LAST RELIC OF FORT CHARTRES

THE POWDER-MAGAZINE

PRESENT ASPECT OF THE SITE OF FORT MASSAC

mounds and graves innumerable, dot all that ancient trail leading from New Haven to the Negro Salt Wells. The one locally referred to as Dutton's is the most famous. Here, in 1800, drifted the first white settler, named Michael Sprinkle. He erected his lonely cabin of logs on the summit of one of these old Indian graves, and there he remained for fourteen years, while there slowly gathered about him the nucleus of the growing town. By 1806, the inhabitants had a mail route connecting them with the far-off East; by 1810 their lands had been surveyed; in 1811, with wondering eyes they looked out upon the first steamboat that ever ploughed the waters of *La Belle Rivière;* and in 1812 the Government honored them by the establishment in their midst of a land-office. It was the salt trade of the Illinois Salines, situated close at hand, which gave such early importance to Shawnee, but the class of men developed here by the exigencies of frontier life would have yielded distinction to any community. This was the home of the first State bank, the centre of the first wild land speculation, the scene of the greatest money panic in the early history of the State. Here was published the second paper in Illinois, "The Illinois Emigrant," and here, in houses yet standing, Robert G. Ingersoll studied law and John A. Logan was married. Here, in later times, dwelt, and worked his miracles of finance, that Colonel Sellers whom Mark Twain has immortalized. Time and time again has Shawnee been buried beneath the rising waters of the Ohio, in spite of protecting dykes. Sixty-six feet above low-water mark that stream has swept, rising to eight feet two inches in the stores nestling behind the shelter of the levee. Steamboats have navigated her streets; yet, old and quaint, prosperous and beautiful, Shawanoe Town yet smiles out above the wide, defeated river, proud of her glorious past and hopeful of her future, rich in historic memories and names that can never die.

Just below this site, but exactly where as yet undetermined, only "at the first landing after leaving Shawanoe Town," Croghan, the English Ambassador to Pontiac, met his disastrous defeat at the hands of a band of Kickapoos and Mascoutins ; while twenty miles farther down the stream is that famous Cave-in-Rock which for many a year sheltered within its black heart those terrible gangs of outlaws under command of Mason, Murrell, and Ford. It is a shallow and gloomy hole even yet, the walls written over with names of peaceful visitors, its portal gaudily decorated with patent medicine advertisements; while the upper cave, as in the past, can be attained only by means of a most laborious climb up a rude tree-trunk ladder. This gruesome spot, which in those old border days witnessed many a scene of revelry and bloodshed, is to-day no more than a curiosity, its past victims, white and black, forgotten. Just below it, where, in 1801, there stood one lone cabin, there is to-day a thrifty village ; but in all of Hardin County there exists, even now, not a mile of railroad to link its population with the civilization all about them. Here one sees the old river towns just as they existed in other generations.

All of this Illinois shore is historic, and has witnessed many a strange flotilla sweep by, both in peace and in war. Along every nook and bend have been the camping-spots of wearied emigrants, of war-worn soldiers, of adventurous hunters and preying outlaws. Here the great family arks have drifted down the current, the men toiling awkwardly at the long oars, the women and children gazing in wonderment on the new land ; here have been seen the uniforms of French grenadiers, British Highlanders, and the buff and blue of the Continental troops. Along here came Clark's backwoodsmen in moccasins and fringed hunting-shirts, and many an adventurer of high and low degree, not a few of whom have left their mark upon the Old World's story. The towns one sees nestling along the bank are old, their names associated with early State history, their houses telling of that interesting past in which they bore part bravely and well — Elizabethtown, Golconda, Metropolis, America, Post Wilkins,— all a part of the great story of colonization and development, of early privation and achievement.

Old Massac, on the site of a yet more ancient fortification, and close beside Mermet's old log chapel of the Assumption, is passed just before the steamer rounds in to the Metropolis wharf-boat. Crowning a prominent bluff which commands a wide view up the river, it is still exceedingly imposing from below, and well worthy, from the standpoint of beauty as well as history, of being restored and preserved by the Daughters of the American Revolution. Above, along the old redoubt, now largely levelled by time and the warring elements, one can dream long of the stirring deeds enacted here, and of those gallant soldiers who have looked forth upon this surrounding scene of river and forest. This is, indeed, historic ground, and no words can do justice to its memories. The old ramparts, now almost shapeless, may yet be traced into something of their former condition, the position of the bastions defined, and even the dim outlines of the ancient building within their shelter outlined with some degree of accuracy, while the old-time well which once supplied the thirsty garrison has left its deep imprint in the soil. It is easy, indeed, to stand in the centre of this old redoubt, on the very spot where St. Ange, Aubry, Macarty, Wilkinson, St. Clair, and Burr have stood, and reconstruct the demolished earthworks, crowning them with the log palisade, and filling the parade-ground with gallant, brilliant figures; easy to lean out above crumbling bastion, and look far away to the mouth of that little creek where Clark's frontiersmen made daring landing on the Illinois shore, and mark that strange new flag with its stars and stripes gleaming brightly against the blue of the sky. Fort Massac! What wealth of romance, forgotten and lost forever, lies hidden beneath your green-clad ruins! What brave hopes have been buried here! What great deeds have here found birth! Careless, indeed, is that child of Illinois who will fail to give you honor.

Rounding the point below Cairo where these two great rivers of the West unite, and pushing up against the swift current of the Mississippi, the way is not long until we come into that region first settled by the white explorers of the Illinois. Of the earliest American settlements, those at New Design and Bellefontaine, almost no memory remains. It is extremely difficult, even if possible, to exactly locate their sites, and the names have long since vanished from off the maps. Burksville Station, on the railroad, near the centre of Monroe County, is probably about where New Design once stood. Burksville, two miles west of the station, is itself a very old town, and contains houses ancient enough in appearance and architectural design to make one believe its history might extend even to this early period. Unfortunately, throughout much of this neighborhood little interest in local history has been developed, and the residents are of small assistance to an investigator. Certain it is, however, that nothing remains which can be definitely associated with the earliest settlement of American pioneers.

In the region occupied by the first French settlements the result is more satisfactory, although here ruin and decay mark much which a little care would have easily preserved. Renault is still an isolated village, containing an old French house or two; St. Philippe and New Chartres have utterly vanished, save as one finds here and there on the old sites a few wild garden plants, or occasionally the remnants of a well. The site of the former is covered by a farm, although even to this day a portion of its long line of field is known locally as "The King's High-

RUINS OF RILEY'S MILL, NEAR KASKASKIA

way," perhaps a dim memory of that excellent road along which the negroes of Renault toiled on his service.

Prairie du Rocher, situated at the edge of the American Bottom, with the great rock sentinels of the bluff towering high above its little houses, has fared better then any of these other towns of the old French *régime*. Yet, in the long years that have fled, and especially since the late coming of the prosaic railroad to her borders, she has lost much of those characteristics connecting her with the picturesque past. Here and there an old French residence rewards the traveller, and the narrow, shaded streets bespeak plainly the earlier days. A few descendants of Renault's negro slaves are to be met with, while French names, many of them famous in the long ago, are common among the residents. But Prairie du Rocher is no longer a French village; the sunny, sleepy contentment of the fathers has departed, and the new generation, intensely American in spirit, retains little interest in that dim and fading past in which their town bore so prominent a part. To one who seeks historical material, the quaint old cemetery, containing the body of many a French pioneer and soldier, or friar of the black or the gray robe, offers the greatest reward.

Four miles away, along an ordinary country road leading across the level bottom-land, lie the remnants of Fort Chartres. A farmhouse occupies the site, and the occupants draw their water from out the old well that once supplied the fort. It is a lonely, desolate spot, the ancient stone walls levelled even with the surface, yet plainly traceable along three sides. The fourth side, which was undermined by the river, has entirely disappeared. The wagon entrance to the present farmyard occupies the exact position where the great gates formerly swung, and it is even possible to determine something of the ground-form of those various buildings of stone which once stood within. The outline of the ditch, which we are told was never completed, may be dimly seen, while the cellars, supposed to have belonged to the commandant's house and the barracks, now nearly filled level to the surface with *débris*, are visible. All that remains unchanged by time is the old powder magazine. It stands, massive and picturesque, within the area of what was once the southeastern bastion, its walls four feet thick sloping upward about twelve feet from the ground, and rounded at the top. The interior, nearly thirty feet square, remains entirely uninjured, although the guarding doors are of course absent.

Standing beside this venerable relic of the past, and looking forth through the ancient gateway where so many have stood and gazed during the vanished years, or marched forth to battle, one can do no better than reëcho the words of Edward G. Mason, written on this very spot:

"Here one may well invoke the shades of Macarty, and De Villiers, and St. Ange, and easily bring back the past. For, as it is to-day, it has seen them all as they went to and fro before it or examined its store of shot and shell; it has heard the word of command as the grenadiers drilled on the parade-ground hard by; it has watched the tawny chieftains and their followers trooping in single file through the adjacent gateway; and past its moss-grown walls the bridal processions of Madelaine Loisel and Elizabeth Montcharveaux and the other fair ladies from the fort have gone to the little church of St. Anne. And gazing at it in such a mood, until all about was peopled with 'the airy shapes of long ago,' and one beheld again the gallant company which laid the foundations of this fortress with such high hope and purpose,—the hurrying scouts passing through its portals with tidings of Indian foray or Spanish march, the valiant leaders setting forth from its walls on distant expeditions against savage or civilized foe, the colonists flocking to its storehouse or council-chamber, the dusky warriors thronging its enclosure with Chicago or Pontiac at their head, the gathering there of those who founded a great city, the happy village at its gates, and the scenes of its momentous surrender, which

RESIDENCE OF PIERRE MENARD, NEAR FORT GAGE

FROM PRESENT-DAY PHOTOGRAPH

sealed the loss of an empire to France, — it seemed not unreasonable to wish that the State of Illinois might, while yet there is time, take measures to permanently preserve, for the sake of the memories, the romance, and the history interwoven in its fabric, what still remains of Old Fort Chartres."

It is seventeen miles to Fort Gage, over the level bottom land, and along the edge of the frowning bluffs, including ferriage across the Kaskaskia River. A hard, toilsome climb up the steep rock-strewn side of a high hill is necessary before you attain the earthworks crowning the summit, but once there, the view spread out across the wide valley is well worthy the struggle. Almost at the foot of this bluff, preserved with care, and remaining outwardly just as when it was one of the famous homes about old Kaskaskia, honored by having La Fayette as guest, and many others whose names have become part of history, stands the former residence of bluff old Pierre Menard, the first Lieutenant-Governor of Illinois. What rare scenes of gayety and sorrow, revelry and despair, its walls have witnessed! What memories of departed glories must ever haunt its shadows, as, with that silent fort far above, it still faces those cruel waters which have engulfed all its old companions!

The ruins of the fort are well preserved, the walls of earth from which the palisades have long ago disappeared being considerably higher than at Massac, and more easily traceable in their entirety. Yet it is imposssible to determine where the gate originally swung, nor is there any trace remaining of that roadway which must at one time have wound upward to the summit. Beyond the fort lies an old French cemetery, overgrown with grass, with many of the monuments lying overturned and broken on the ground. Here, from the summit of the ancient redoubt, can be obtained the best possible view of all that remains of Old Kaskaskia, and of where the main town once stood in its pride, now covered by the rolling waters of that remorseless river which caused its slow destruction. And little enough there is that is left — a mere shack or two, tottering helplessly on the verge of the stream, which is only biding its time to drag them down also; the old court-house, sad relic of those proud days of power when Kaskaskia was the chief city of Randolph County and of the State as well; the trembling, dismantled remains of the priests' house, said to have been the first building ever erected of brick west of the Alleghanies. Under that rushing yellow flood the lost years of history, of romance, of tender memory, lie but half recorded. Few, indeed, are the spots about which cluster such recollections of great events and honored names. The French, the English, the American Kaskaskia, about it hovers every memory of those stern old days of struggle and endeavor; and the desolate spot where it once stood in its simple beauty is glorified still by the deeds of two hundred years of history. Of its old-time neighbor and rival, Cahokia, there is little remnant, if any, the site being now utilized for switching purposes by a railroad.

Farther up the Mississippi, twenty miles beyond Warsaw (near which place Forts Edwards and Johnson were built and garrisoned in 1814), is the most interesting town remaining in Illinois — Nauvoo, the famed city of the Mormons and the Icarians. Situated partly on the flat, and partly upon the high bluff beyond, beautiful at a distance because of the diversity of its peculiar architecture and the picturesque grouping of its ancient homes, it is no less attractive when one wanders along its narrow, rock-strewn streets, and amid the old-fashioned houses, each with its story of the past. The marvellous Old Temple has gone, the space it once occupied remaining still a vacant spot on the high bluff summit. Nor are there many relics of the Icarian struggle, save an almost shapeless ruin here and there; but the old Masonic Temple, the building where "The Expositor" was published just once, the old Mansion

PORTRAIT OF JOHN MARSHALL

FROM PAINTING BY MIFLIN, 1834; NOW IN POSSESSION OF COLONEL MARSHALL'S DESCENDANTS

House with its secret closet, the old Post-office building, and the former homes of Joseph and Hyrum Smith, Elder Heber C. Kimball, Brigham and Joseph Young, and numerous others, bring vividly before the mind the stirring events of Mormon occupancy and the struggle waged here for supremacy. Twenty miles away, at Carthage, stands the old stone jail where the Smiths were killed. Nauvoo, still a typical river town, untouched by any invading railway, remains, like a leaf torn from out an old book, possessing a charm peculiarly its own.

Many a point of historic interest in the State must be passed over lightly. Black Hawk's Tower looks out over the beautiful valley of the Rock, where once lay the famed village of the Sauks. The spot has been degraded into a cheap amusement park, and a like unfortunate fate has befallen that superb rock where the Fox nation died in heroic starvation, and where Fort St. Louis lifted its palisades in guardianship over the Algonquins in the heart of this Illinois country, when La Salle and Tonty ruled the wilderness. Below it stretch the broad Utica meadows, fair as in the old days when Marquette preached there to the wondering Illinois. Campbell's Island, the scene of Rector's magnificent fight in the War of 1812, is also a resort for Summer pleasure, but the exact spot of that gallant struggle, which, from discoveries in the sandy beach, has been identified beyond question, is soon to be marked by an appropriate monument.

Few spots in Illinois are more interesting historically than those immediately surrounding the Peoria Lake, the "Pimiteoui Lake" of La Salle. From the earliest days of French exploration down to the expiring of the fur trade, this region teemed with events. It had ever been an Indian trading and council ground, and great villages from time immemorial stood along the *détroit* or strait connecting the two lakes. Little is known of French history on this spot between 1700 and 1765, except that traders were almost constantly there. In the early days of French permanent settlement, that is, from 1765, an exceedingly large trading town, said at one time to have exceeded four thousand souls, sprang up in the same neighborhood, long known as Le Pé; but later, for some cause unknown, the population, or what remained of it, shifted to the present site of Peoria, the old French claims skirting the shore for some distance below the modern Rock Island Railroad depot. This latter building is believed to occupy almost exactly the position where Fort Clark formerly stood, when General Howard left it, reporting it to the officials in the East as the strongest post of its kind in the West.

Along the bluffs on either side of the lake and river, as well as beside the straits, numerous remains of ancient fortifications have been discovered, many of them, no doubt, having been thrown up by French and American fur traders in protection against Indian treachery, or else relics of the English invasions of the Revolution, or the American advance of 1812. Unfortunately, these old-time forts, grass-grown and apparently most ancient, have sadly divided local historians in their eager search after the more probable site of La Salle's Fort Crèvecœur. In truth, so vague are the existing descriptions of the exact spot chosen by these earliest explorers for their first fort-building in the Illinois country, that unless other material be discovered in the French archives, or the buttes of the old palisades (possibly yet preserved in the earth) be accidentally uncovered, this is a point which must likely remain unsolved. No one dare proclaim beyond a doubt whether La Salle's choice lay along the strait, or upon the river below the lower lake; yet the present writer has little hesitation in saying that both spots now designated by local historians as their choice for Fort Crèvecœur must be considered erroneous, even from the vague description left us.

RESIDENCE OF JOHN MARSHALL, SHAWNEETOWN, IN WHICH FIRST BANK IN STATE WAS ESTABLISHED, 1813

SMALL VIEW TAKEN BEFORE LEVEE WAS BUILT

The very purpose of building this fort, which was temporary, and to secure, without interruption from the Indians, the construction of a vessel with which to navigate the Mississippi, would seem to preclude at once the possibility that it was ever located upon a high and almost inaccessible bluff far away from the river shore, and consequently seriously removed from the work to be accomplished. The small number of La Salle's followers would also be against such a probability. This natural argument, strong as it is, can only add its weight to the direct evidence of those taking part in its construction. Mason is extremely cautious in his use of the descriptive language employed, and his translation may be safely relied upon, although our conclusions differ widely. Briefly, it is this. The spot chosen for fort-building was on the left bank of the Illinois River, about two miles and a half below its exit from Pimiteoui Lake. A great thaw (the nature of which every Peorian will easily understand) had cleared the river of ice from the lake to the place selected, and the builders went there in canoes the evening of January 15, 1680. The spot decided on was a low hill (Hennepin, in one passage, says a small eminence), a little more than a mile from the Indian village, two hundred paces distant from the bank of the river, which spread to its foot in the time of heavy rains. This description would seem to do away with any possibility that it could have crowned the high, steep bluff, or even occupied so inaccessible a position as the ledge where the Daughters of the Revolution have erected their memorial. Yet, there is a spot just below, and seemingly strangely overlooked, which almost exactly, taking into account the probable shoreward trend of the stream during the intervening centuries, meets the requirements. Here can be traced still the low hill, the small eminence, undoubtedly now far less marked in bold outlines than when Hennepin first surveyed it, with the two ravines, one on either side, but greatly choked by accumulated *débris*, and of less importance than formerly. Many things have combined to change the configuration of the ground, and it is marvellous that even so much remains to recall the mind to the friar's simple description. A long-used wagon-road, and the grading of a railway, have caused the trench connecting the two ravines to vanish totally, but otherwise the position is not only possible, it is far more probable than any of the others, and had it been left untouched by man, might possibly be identified beyond a doubt. Wesley City is the site of a very old French village, the encroaching river already making inroads on the ancient and almost forgotten burial-ground, and uncovering the foundation-posts of buildings long since vanished in decay. As early as 1819 the American Fur Company had a factory here, very likely throwing up at that time those earthworks on the face of the bluff, even if that work had not been previously accomplished by the earlier French inhabitants. It was known for years as the Trading Post, yet even the buildings then used have almost totally disappeared. On the spot which may have been occupied by Fort Crèvecœur an old distillery once stood. It likewise has vanished, while the house of Joseph M. Wilson, now upon the site, in its turn begins to look picturesque and ancient. Impossible as it must be to say definitely that here stood La Salle's first fortification in the Illinois country, the fourth in his great scheme of conquest, yet, to the mind of the present writer, it remains by far the most probable spot.

Much more remains to be told, much more remains to be seen,— the place of battle on the willow-islands at the mouth of the Rock River, the old homes of Bishop Hill and Albion, the lead-fields about Galena with their scarcely written story, the site of Apple River Fort and its heroic defence, the old centre of Indian trade at Danville, the place where Clark and his men conquered the swollen

Wabash, and that spot of mysterious tradition in Kendall County we know as Maramech, — all alike invite to deep research and careful study; for few indeed are the happenings along those early years without their influence on a wider history than that of the mere State in which they chanced to be enacted.

"Not without thy wondrous story,
Illinois, Illinois,
Can be writ the Nation's glory,
Illinois, Illinois."

THE END

INDEX

INDEX

McC

MUR